I0092743

INDIE AUTHOR CONFIDENTIAL

SECRETS NO ONE WILL TELL YOU ABOUT WRITING, VOL. 4-7

M.L. RONN

"Indie Author Confidential: Vol 4", "Indie Author Confidential: Vol 5", "Indie Author Confidential: Vol 6", and "Indie Author Confidential: Vol 7": Copyright 2021 © M.L. Ronn. All rights reserved.

Published by Author Level Up LLC.

Version 1.0

Cover Design by Pixelstudio.
Cover Art for Volumes 4-5 © pevunova / Depositphotos.
Covert Art for Volumes 6-7 by jasoshulwathon.
Editing by BZ Hercules.

Time Period Covered in This Omnibus: 2021

Special thank you to the following people on Patreon who supported this book: Jon Howard, Megan Mong, and Lynda Washington.

Some links in this book contain affiliate links. If you purchase books and services through these links, I receive a small commission at no cost to you. You are under no obligation to use these links, but thank you if you do!

For more helpful writing tips and advice, subscribe to the Author Level Up YouTube channel: www.youtube.com/authorlevelup.

INDIE AUTHOR CONFIDENTIAL

Secrets No One Will Tell You About Being a Writer

VOL. 4

M.L. RONN

VOLUME 4

INTRODUCTION

This volume covers the first quarter of 2021, a new year and hopefully much better than 2020!

It's refreshing to start a new year and put my new strategy into action.

The last volume was decidedly marketing-focused. I concluded both my "Beast Mode" and "Amnesia Mode" challenges, racking up a record amount of books and book sales.

Now I'm returning to form and writing fiction. This volume is more production and editing-focused, as that was where I spent my time. I also believe this is a great way to start a new year that (at the time of this writing) still seems just as uncertain as 2020.

Sometimes the best thing to do is the only thing you can do: write.

My Core Strategic Priorities

As a refresher, my mission is to create content that entertains and/or educates my audience, preferably both, and to remain nimble in an ever-changing industry. I do this by focusing on five strategic priorities:

- Become a world-class content creator
- Become a world-class marketer
- Become a technology-driven writer

- Become a data-driven writer
- Become the writer of the future

I believe these five priorities are most important for me to have a long-term, sustainable career.

What's in This Volume

In this volume, I discuss a new challenge where I dictated while riding an exercise bike, and the incredible insights that came from it, including some weight loss!

In the World-Class Marketer section, I talk about some lessons I learned with advertising a poetry collection, Amazon keywords, and a big mistake I made with a book cover design this quarter that I hope won't hurt me too much.

I also talk about my return to dictation after several years, and new styles of dictating that have made me insanely more productive.

There is also a large section in this book about an editing data and analytics project. I've described my ideas for this project in previous volumes under the title of a "personal editing rules engine." This quarter, I finally deployed it, and the results are mind-blowing. I've cleared the way to producing squeaky-clean manuscripts free of grammar errors and typos. A good deal of the technology and data sections are dedicated to the editing project because it's a huge leap forward in my production process.

I also spend some time talking about new thoughts around my editing process, and how I've developed a more nuanced approach to research, self-editing, and working with my editors.

Additionally, I also give an update on items that I mentioned in the last volume, such as applying for a TED Talk and my 2021+ author strategy.

And, as always, I offer some fun ideas you can steal in your writing business. No volume of *Indie Author Confidential* would be complete without some bold ideas!

Enjoy, and happy 2021.

M.L. Ronn
Des Moines, Iowa
February 3, 2021

BECOME A WORLD-CLASS
CONTENT CREATOR

BE A GLACIER

You're either shrinking or expanding, so they say.

I was watching a video interview with Arnold Schwarzenegger, and the Governator was talking about his workout routine. Interestingly, it made me think of my *writing routine*.

What's the typical workout routine? Legs day, arms day, cardio day, rest.

What if your writing routine was "writing day," "self-improvement day," rinse and repeat? Or something else like "writing day," "marketing day," "business day," and so on?

You can get obnoxious with this, of course, but it's a great concept. I've always struggled with finding a balance between writing and marketing, and this is the simplest way I can think to fix it.

Write every day, but on the days when writing is not primary, meet your quota and then focus on something else.

I've been doing that the past few days as I write this chapter. Day A is a writing day. Day B is a self-improvement day. Self-improvement happens to include marketing.

When I'm writing, I'm shrinking. I'm pouring what I know onto the page, and my brain is smaller afterward.

When I'm learning, I'm expanding.

It's like a glacier.

Fun thought exercise.

LESSONS LEARNED FROM AN UNPRODUCTIVE WEEK

The second week of January 2021 was the most unproductive week I had in a long time. My entire writing business came to a screeching halt, even the manuscript I was working on.

A family member had some health issues that I needed to deal with.

My boss at work tendered her resignation. She'd hired me two months prior and my future was uncertain.

I had an urgent deadline I needed to hit for *Writer's Digest*, and I was contractually obligated to do so.

Rioters stormed the United States Capitol building, causing damage and threatening the fabric of American democracy.

I was already dealing with a rough spot in *Dead Rat Walking*. The events of the week stopped.

I had to walk away from everything and handle the issues in my personal life. I stopped writing, and the only writing-related items I did were continuing my podcast episodes and daily blogs. Aside from that, I did nothing.

That's unusual for me. I am tirelessly productive, even on bad days. I'm always looking for ways to move my writing efforts forward, and generally, I do. I don't take vacations from writing, and any time off is usually because of personal circumstances.

Unproductive weeks happen to the best of us, even prolific writers.

I dealt with it by walking away for a short amount of time until it was safe and productive to return to the desk.

It means that I had to push my finish date of *Dead Rat Walking* back by one week. It also meant that I put more stress on myself to hit my deadline. But overall, I'm glad I took the week off to recalibrate, focus my thoughts, and take care of myself and my family.

If I had continued writing during that period, I would have been so distracted that the words and progress I made in the business wouldn't have been worth it. In fact, I might have made *mistakes* that could have been costly and time-consuming to fix later.

In times like this, I remember the law of averages: if you (try to) write every day for 365 days, you're going to have an amazing word count at the end of the year, even if you miss a couple of weeks here and there. That's the case for me. The fact that I lost one week in January isn't going to stop me from publishing a lot of books this year.

This experience retaught me how important it is to stop and reflect every once in a while. I have a high-octane personality and am always thinking about what's next. Sometimes you just have to think about "what's now." The next always takes care of itself.

NAVIGATING A BUSY SEASON

My final semester of law school began this quarter. I'll be done in May 2021.

The start of the spring semester is always busy. It's when I hit my peak season and everything feels like it's on the verge of breaking apart if I'm not careful. What's on my plate:

1. Writing books
2. Marketing my books
3. Working a full-time job
4. Studying for classes
5. Raising a family
6. Working part-time for the Alliance of Independent Authors
7. Teaching insurance classes
8. Managing my emails
9. Producing content for my YouTube channel, daily blog, and three podcasts

Things get crazy around mid-terms. Somehow I always survive. I'm looking forward to eliminating law school from the equation forever, as I found that it added almost enough pressure to break everything.

But I persist. And this semester got me thinking about the processes I've followed to stay sane and on top of everything.

- I batch content ahead of time for my YouTube channel and podcasts. I try to preschedule as much content as I can, giving me as much breathing room as possible.
- I halt any major appointments or business decisions around mid-terms and finals.
- I rely greatly on the automation I've set up in all areas of my business. It pays off dividends, especially during a busy season like this.
- I let my audience know when things will get busy so they know if I am not as present, there is a reason. Communicating with my audience is key.
- I clear my inbox to zero at the beginning of the semester. It doesn't last me long, but it lasts me enough to get through the first two weeks or so.
- I work ahead in my class. I typically finish reading the textbook about a month before finishing the class. It's a painful investment, but I find that once I've finished reading the textbook, the amount of time I spend on the class drops dramatically, sometimes by 50 percent.
- I hire people more. I've hired part-time assistants to help me with one-off tasks that I don't have the time or energy to do. That helped me a lot, especially with video editing.

Anyway, life is hectic for me, but my goals are to keep momentum, to keep moving forward, and to be as consistent as possible. In just a few months, I'll have a lot more time per year, so I'll be able to breathe.

But I've found that learning how to anticipate and manage busy seasons is one of the secrets to my productivity. Where others would quit writing altogether, I maintain my writing and have benefited from it in a big way.

A LETTER TO MY 2014 WRITER SELF

I talk to writers all the time. Being a new writer isn't easy. It's a unique experience that I believe becomes harder to relate to the further away from you are from it.

There's so much to learn and the journey is an emotional rollercoaster. It's hard to think clearly, and even harder to make sound decisions because learning how to be a self-published writer is like drinking through a firehose. Every decision you make will have long-term consequences that you can't comprehend…and you can't think long-term because you're so focused on the *now* of creating the book. And on top of all that, there's the stress of money, time spent away from your family, and the nagging thought in the back of your head about whether all this time, money, and energy you're spending on a *dream* is going to work out.

Yet new writers are endlessly optimistic. It's a beautifully complicated, emotional, and optimistic time to be alive.

This got me thinking about what advice I would give to my 2014 self. If I could travel back in time to give writing advice to myself, what would I say?

Dear Michael,

Greetings from 2021! Though we are separated by seven years, I understand you very well because I am you.

Congratulations on writing your first book, How to Be Bad. It was an amazing feat to pull off, but you did it.

I regret to inform you that it won't sell very well, despite your optimism. In fact, you'll rebrand the book in a few years and it still won't sell.

But I have good news: as I write this letter, I've just started production on my fifty-fourth book, and it will probably sell pretty well!

It won't be until 2020 that you see the type of success you expect, and even then, you won't be making a living. But you'll be proud.

If I may, I'd like to give you some advice.

1. *Now that you've written your first book, you know the territory of a writer. It will never get easier to write a book, but you'll improve your confidence.*
2. *Keep reading voraciously and never stop. It will be difficult to balance writing, reading, business, and marketing, but it will be vital to find harmony between them.*
3. *You'll win (almost) every time you follow your instinct.*
4. *The more you write, the more you will succeed.*
5. *Learn how to use Amazon and Facebook ads without ignoring them at first, for God's sake!*

Keep doing what you're doing. There will be many nights where you'll question whether this will work out. There will be times when you feel like it won't work out, especially when you publish book after book and don't see the financial numbers you'd like to see.

But your experience is valuable and people all over the world will be watching you every day to see how you are doing and what you think about things related to the writing life.

Keep documenting your journey and keep finding ways to connect with your readers.

Sincerely,
Future Michael

I don't think that letter scratches the surface of deep advice, and that brings me what I truly learned in this exercise: you can't skip past being new. No advice can truly help you. You're going to do what you're going to do, and if you're lucky, one day you'll wake up, realize that you've made enough mistakes, and start truly seeking advice that will be meaningful. You'll be frustrated at that point, but you'll find the advice that works best for you. This didn't happen for me until early 2015.

The key is that hopefully you haven't made career-ending mistakes, such as signing a bad contract, falling prey to a scam, or getting your publishing accounts canceled because you used bad judgment with a marketing technique. If you didn't do any of those things, you're golden. If you did, you may not have a career.

So if you're reading this and are a new author, just focus on surviving and try to avoid dumb mistakes that will end your career. Do that and you'll move to the next phase of your career, which is a lot calmer, less emotional, and (God willing) more productive and financially rewarding.

ALL THINGS IN LIFE ARE CYCLICAL

This is a long story, but I promise there is something good at the end (a couple of things, actually).

Growing up, I was a strange kid. I had an unusual taste in music. Even at a very young age, I was a jazz aficionado. My gateway to jazz (like a lot of people) was Steely Dan. Back when I was a kid, there were two types of people: those who had intense emotional experiences when they heard the music of Steely Dan for the first time, and those who thought Steely Dan was a joke. (Actually, that's still true today. If you're a Steely Dan fan, you understand me 100 percent. They still don't get the love they deserve.)

Since around the age of five or so, I was attracted to stuff in music that I couldn't explain, but I knew it when I heard it—mainly chords, harmony, composition, emotion. Other people just cared about lyrics, the groove, and whether they could relate to what the singer was singing about.

I wanted to be a musician for a long time. One day in high school (2002ish), I happened to share some of my music with my uncle, who was a band manager for a very popular local band in St. Louis that achieved international acclaim. He listened to my songs and brought up a crate of CDs that he had picked up while on tour. He thought I should check them out. To this day, I have no idea how my uncle compiled a crate of Japanese pop and funk CDs.

On the very top of the crate was the *Natsuko* album by Carlos

Toshiki & Omega Tribe. I had never heard of them before, but I was used to listening to music in Japanese because I collected video game music. Plus, as someone who listened to jazz, I was used to international artists.

I inspected the album, and to my surprise, on the back cover was a black man sitting on a couch with some Japanese guys. I was intrigued...a black man, a member of a Japanese band???

To say the album blew me away was an understatement. The Omega Tribe to this day remains one of my favorite bands of all time. I own all their work. Their music helped me get through a rough freshman year in high school.

I was fascinated by the fact that a black man sang with them, wrote songs, and performed as a full member of the band, and not merely a backup singer.

I didn't know this at the time, but the band was part of a gigantic musical movement in Japan called "city pop," which, in a nutshell, is 80s pop infused with jazz chords, with very high composition and production value. I won't get into city pop here—look it up sometime.

Anyway, I was hooked on city pop in 2002 before ANYONE in the states (that I know of personally) knew what it was. Everyone I knew thought I was crazy importing records from Japan. They didn't see the point of listening to music you couldn't understand. But for me, it was about more than that.

I always respected Joey McCoy for his story and his contribution to the musical genre, even though I didn't know much about him. I credit him and the Omega Tribe with my gateway into a genre that I have become a lifelong fan of.

In 2017, I wrote a novel called *Honor's Reserve* and even named the lead character of the series after McCoy (Grayson McCoy). I shared a similar story of how I discovered him in an author's note at the back of the book.

(I named every lead character in my *Galaxy Mavericks* series after my favorite musicians. It was fun, but until today, I didn't think anything would come of it).

Fast forward to 2021, and some very interesting things have happened.

First, city pop is mainstream now. Awareness of the genre started in the early 2010s with the Vaporwave movement. Vaporwave is an underground music movement where artists take old recordings from the 80s and 90s, slow them down, chop them up, and add effects such as distortion to create a completely new experience. While the genre itself is controversial because of copyright infringement issues, it made the 80s and 90s cool again because it made millennials like myself reminisce about our childhoods. It's also a way to discover new music because listeners like to seek out the original tracks that inspired the Vaporwave versions. Vaporwave is the millennial reincarnation of crate diving at a record store. When artists started using city pop songs as the basis for Vaporwave tracks, many people discovered the genre. That's one way that city pop became mainstream.

There were also viral videos. The song that pretty much blew the Internet open was "Plastic Love" by Mariya Takeuchi. It has 48 million views and counting at the time of this writing. I knew this song before it was cool.

Suddenly, English speakers discovered what I had fallen in love with almost 20 years ago. Now, city pop is cool, but trust me, it wasn't like that in 2002 or even 2008. The only way you could get it (if you even knew about it) was to import records or find it in other clandestine ways. One of those ways was buying digital iTunes Japan gift cards, switching over to the Japanese version of the iTunes Store, and then searching for your favorite artists in kanji, but only then you got 30-second samples, so it was hard to find good songs. But you could buy stuff there before Apple locked down their international stores. I told you I was serious about this stuff...

Anyway, city pop is having a moment. (Somewhat) Mainstream artists like Thundercat and Benny Sings have paid tribute to it. This past year, Apple Music and Spotify onboarded a CRAPTON of city pop music—something that you would have never been able to find just a year or two ago. It's still very weird to play city pop on Apple Music.

All those artists who found success in Japan but almost nowhere else are now having their moment, with a generation of young people who were either barely alive or nonexistent when the music was recorded. Record companies are finally figuring it out and cashing in on it (in a good way).

When I found a bunch of city pop albums on Apple Music, I was surprised to see that there was some more information on the bands available in English on the Internet. On a random whim, I discovered that someone had created a Wikipedia page for Joey McCoy, which was neat to see.

And to my shock, I saw MY NAME on the Wikipedia page. Someone referenced my author's note in the back of *Honor's Reserve* and posted on the page that I had named one of my characters after him.

Ironically, Google Books indexed *Honor's Reserve* and just happened to include the page from my author's note where I talked about Joey McCoy. That was how the person discovered the reference. How random is that?

It turns out that Joey McCoy even recorded an album of his own that long-time Omega Tribe fans are just now discovering and buzzing about on Reddit and other places.

(I'm fairly certain that I sold a few copies of *Honor's Reserve* from that Wikipedia page—it rarely sells any copies these days, but I've noticed sales starting up again—nothing substantial, but noticeable. I don't actively advertise it.

There are a lot of people right now giving Joey his props. It seems he's moved on from his music career, but how amazing is it that he's still alive to see people from all corners of the world appreciating his musical skills. Not every artist gets that honor. It's too bad that he's probably not getting compensated that much for the recognition.

All right, so what does this have to do with you?

Everything is cyclical.

So what you published a book that gets zero sales? What if something happens in the cultural zeitgeist 30 years from now that makes younger generations interested in your work?

Sure, it's a long time, but you never know, right?

And, what if, instead of quitting, that you were still writing 30 years from now (if you're still alive), and you have a crapton of books that new generations can discover?

That, my friends, is what this post is about.

Everything has its time. If an obscure 80s genre from Japan can catch on fire worldwide, then maybe one of your books can too.

That's why you shouldn't give up. This isn't the 80s, where it was hard to maintain a career if the planets didn't align. Now you can have a career forever and continue to get paid for your work. You just have to have the courage to write, publish, and keep your book for sale. And it can earn money for you long after you publish it.

This is the greatest time in the history of the world to be a writer.

WRITING AN ARTICLE FOR WRITER'S DIGEST

I received an opportunity to write for *Writer's Digest* magazine, which was an amazing honor. The opportunity came because the editor happened to watch a video I produced back in 2014.

Ironically, I almost didn't record this *exact video*. I had to change the lighting in my basement because I filmed my old videos down there. The lighting, which was pretty good in my early videos, was never the same. I hated it.

This particular video was one of the first videos I recorded in the new lighting, and as much as I hated it, I published it anyway because I didn't want to miss a week of producing content. The video garners few views, and I never thought twice about it.

Fast forward to 2021 when my video setup is much better, more sophisticated, and the content is better…and the video that prompted her to reach out was the 2014 one. If that's not evidence that you should create content even though it's not your best, I don't know what is.

Anyway, we discussed writing an article about writer's block.

I read several back issues of the magazine and got a feel for what current contributors were writing. I also searched what people were saying about the magazine. I got a sense of what to write and how to say it. The magazine's target audience is newer writers, so I needed to speak to them at a higher level but still deliver deep value, and in a way they've never heard before. Then,

I had to tie that to the magazine's vision and aesthetics, *and* meet their word count quota.

Somehow the balancing act worked, and I wrote an article called: *Drift: The Curiously Effective Way to Beat Procrastination.* It will debut in the May/June 2021 edition of the magazine.

THE WRITING WHILE MOVING CHALLENGE

In the last volume of this series, I discussed a wild and wacky idea for a project that involved an exercise bike, a novel, and a lot of ingenuity. I called it "the writing while moving challenge."

I have an exercise bike that is getting lonely. I need to write new fiction. I am also fat and need to lose weight. Why not address all three problems at the same time?

I also need to write more books under my M.L. McKnight urban fantasy pen name.

Here's the idea: I will exercise for at least 60 minutes every day. While exercising, I will dictate a new novel. I can only write via dictation, I can only dictate while I am on the bike, and I cannot use my hands, except to correct outrageous errors by my dictation software, Dragon. I speak an average of 150 to 160 words per minute. That is approximately 9,000 words per day and 63,000 words per week. Theoretically, that would net me 270,000 words per year, which is approximately 5.4 novels at 50,000 words each.

But it gets better. Dictation is quite infamous for its accuracy issues. Even a top-of-the-line program like Dragon can make a lot of mistakes while you dictate. In many ways, you must learn to speak and think differently as you are telling your story. Many find this method of writing difficult; I find it intriguing.

In 2016, I dictated my *The Last Dragon Lord* series in Dragon. I also wrote that series into the dark, which means that I did not outline the story; I just wrote whatever came into my head, and then fixed it as I went. I also wrote the series in one draft. This is extraordinarily difficult to do with dictation, but I managed it.

It's such an interesting concept. What if, on this exercise bike, I wrote an entire series via dictation into the dark AND in one draft? That's a little crazy... But I'm willing to do it because I need to write new fiction, and I am full of new ideas that I want to get on to paper.

So I started the challenge around the middle of December 2020, not knowing where it would go. In fact, I practiced for the challenge by dictating this very chapter that you're reading! This chapter was my first official test to see how it went.

My first challenge at the time of this writing is to figure out which story I want to write, do the basic research, figure out what the first scene is, and then write it.

I also want to know how much a novel is worth in pounds and miles. Generally, it takes me approximately 40 hours to write and prepare one of my novels for publication. What would that look like in pounds and miles? I am fascinated to know the answer.

2021 is a new year and I want to get healthier as a writer. I believe that this is the ultimate test of writing skill and complexity.

Anyway, it's time for me to get off the bike now, so I'm going to stop. I look forward to dictating more chapters and letting you know how this goes!

My Setup

Here's what the dictation setup looks like. I attached a microphone boom arm to the desk and put my Blue Yeti Microphone on it. Then I used an old text book to prop up my computer.

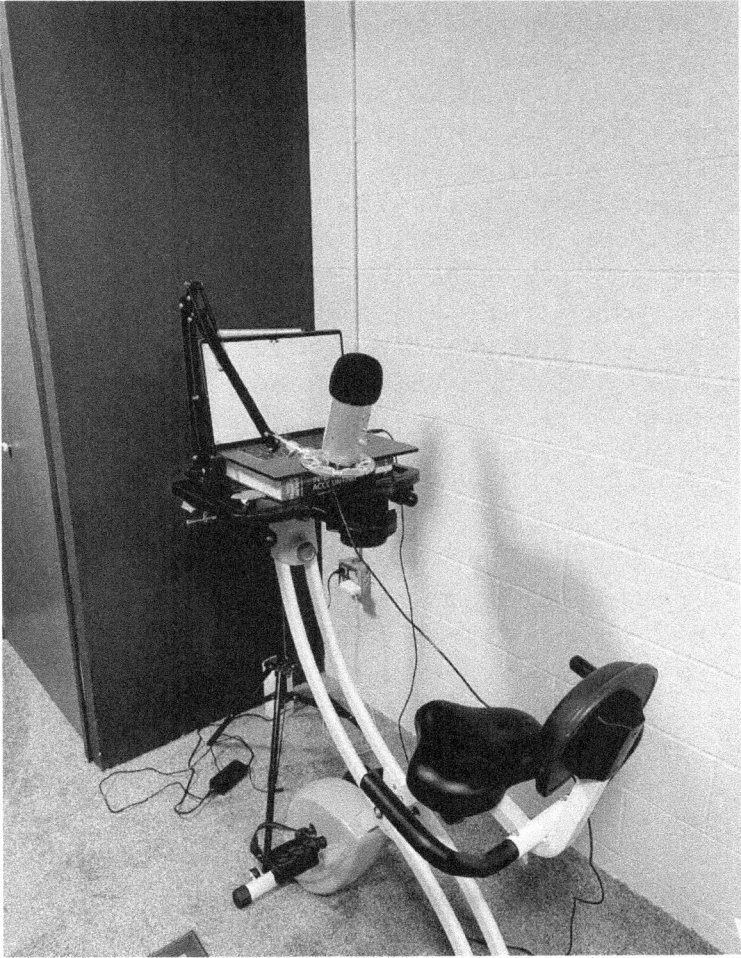

How It Went

Okay, I'm not dictating this section. But this project was a success.

I started off only dictating on the bike, but my first few days were so high word-count wise that I decided to incorporate other ways of writing into the project, such as writing on my laptop and writing on my phone.

The results: I wrote 60,000 words in 30 days. I had a bad week where I didn't write any words at all, so if you take that out, I technically wrote the novel in 21 days.

I used the bike 50 percent of the days that I wrote and burned 1,050 calories and traveled 31.5 miles in approximately 630 minutes (10.5 hours). The challenge also netted me around five pounds lost!

The entire project probably took around 30 hours, so I spent at least a third of that moving, which is great.

Speed-wise, this is not my fastest novel. My fastest record is seven days. My longest is 18 months. But this novel does rank near the top.

Lessons I learned:

- It's easy to tell your story while moving; it just requires a mindset shift.
- Writing into the dark and in one draft is indeed possible on an exercise bike.
- Whenever I didn't know what to write next, hopping on the bike helped me with the writer's block. I thought being on the bike would have the opposite effect.
- The sections I wrote on the bike were nearly indistinguishable from the sections I wrote by hand or on my phone (to me, at least).
- I noticed considerably better sleep and general well-being throughout the project and afterward.
- My highest word count day was well over 5,000 words of clean fiction with no cleanup required. For me, a usual fiction writing day (typing) is somewhere between 1,000 and 2,000 words.

- There were some days where I wouldn't have been able to write at all, but a 30-minute dictation session at night netted me a word count that looked as if I didn't struggle at all that day.
- Because this book required a fair amount of research on subject matter that I wasn't familiar with, I had to stop frequently to research.
- When I wasn't writing at my computer, I wrote the book on my phone and also dictated on my phone while doing tasks such as laundry and dishes.
- I also dictated the novel while walking around my office, untethered to my keyboard and computer.

Overall, this novel was many different writing styles all converging into the final product. I have some more thoughts on this in the Writer of the Future section, but the willingness to experiment with a new way of writing paid off, and it made me more flexible with my storytelling in the future.

IMPROVING MY RESEARCH PROCESS WITH FACT-CHECKERS

I recently finished my 30th novel. It's crazy to think that I have written so many novels since 2013, but this was a great opportunity for me to reevaluate how I produce my books, and how I can produce them more efficiently in the future.

I believe that every few dozen novels or so, it's a good idea to test your processes and your assumptions to see where your weaknesses are. I have written enough novels at this point to have production down to a science, but I still feel that there are areas where I could do better.

One of those areas is in research. Research is a major time suck for a writer. The hardest part is knowing what to research, where to find it, and what to use. I know a lot of writers who spend hours if not months researching elements for their novel, only to not use most of it. That is woefully inefficient.

I wrote a book called *How to Write Your First Novel*, and it is one of my better-selling books for writers. In it, I talk about breaking up research into two categories: foundational research and just-in-time research.

Foundational research is research that you need to do to start writing. Nothing more, nothing less. For example, if your book takes place in the city of Chicago, and you don't live in Chicago, you need to do a lot of research to portray the Chicago parts properly on the page. In this way, foundational research helps you create the foundation for your story.

All research *after* you start writing is just-in-time research. You research what you need when you need it. Instead of spending hours or months researching a topic, simply write the story. Then, when you come to a section that you're not sure about, stop writing and go research. In my opinion, this is far more efficient than frontloading your research because you are only researching what you need. Everything you find with just-in-time research ends up in the novel. Unless you write in a genre that requires in-depth research such as regency romance or historical fiction, this is a far better way to tackle the problem of research.

I have used foundational research and just-in-time research for years, and this technique has helped make my novels more realistic and accurate. However, how good is my research? In other words, how do I know if the details that I am researching are accurate?

I have been experimenting with fact-checking my research in recent novels. It's one thing to research subject matter in your book, but another thing entirely to verify that your research is accurate.

I find that every novel I write has about two or three subject matter areas that I need help in. My most recent novel took place in the city that I don't live in, featured an animal that I was not familiar with, and featured a sibling relationship, which was new territory for me. I did as much research as I could, but I had this nagging feeling that I needed to have someone look at the novel to verify if what I wrote made sense.

This is where the concept of fact-checking comes in. You recruit several people to evaluate what you have written to verify if you executed properly on your research. You can research a topic until you know it inside out, but there's a difference between knowing something well and writing it accurately. Fact-checkers test your skill as a writer.

With my newest novel, I recruited three different groups of fact-checkers: one group who live or had lived in the city of

Chicago for a very long time and were familiar with it; another group who were familiar with rodent biology, and who had degrees in biology or bioengineering; and a final group who were female fantasy readers who had younger brothers and who had given them relationship advice (something that happens in the novel with my main character and his sister).

I explained to the fact-checkers what I was looking for, and I gave them basic instructions. Then I sent them excerpts from the novel that contained items that needed to be fact-checked. For example, I sent my Chicago fact-checkers only the sections about Chicago, my biology fact-checkers only the sections about biology, and my female readers only the chapters from the point of view of the hero's sister (who featured prominently in the story). It was a little awkward sending them only parts of the novel, but I believe this was more respectful of their time. It also allowed them to get through comments much faster. Most of the fact-checkers took less than a week to provide their feedback.

The result? We'll see. I believe that, ultimately, readers decide the merits of the story, but I want to do all I can to make sure that they have an enjoyable reading experience and that little technical details don't pull them out of the story. In fact, if I can get these technical details right, it will enhance readers' enjoyment of the story.

This technique was inspired by mega-bestseller Arthur Hailey, who was a household name in the 1960s and 1970s. Many of his novels topped the *New York Times* bestseller list.

I am a big fan of Arthur Hailey and consider him to be one of my all-time favorites. I was pleasantly surprised when I discovered that his wife, Sheila, wrote a biography of how she met him and their marriage. The biography talked about Arthur's writing process and how he researched his novels. His novels take place in a single setting such as an airport, hotel, bank, or auto factory, and it features thriller plots from the perspective of the employees who work there. When you read his novels, you get the sense that he has meticulously researched every element of the places where he sets his novels. Fortunately, Sheila talked about his process in the book. She mentioned how he took copious notes, read as many books as he could about the topics he needed to research, and even conducted field interviews with industry experts (I imagine that being a *New York Times* bestseller will open a lot of doors with industry executives). For his book *Wheels,* he worked on an assembly line for a few hours to understand line workers. He would take pages and pages of notes, organize them using a notecard system, and then incorporate his research into his novels as he wrote.

Reading about his thought process got me thinking about my research process. I write science fiction and fantasy, so the level of research I need is not as substantial as Arthur Hailey's, but good research is a bedrock of good fiction.

The feedback my fact-checkers gave me was amazing. Not only did they answer the questions that I posed to them with good detail, but they also described how they think about certain issues, which was more helpful than the actual feedback they provided. I found that learning how someone thinks about something and why they think the way they do is an underrated window into writing more engaging characters. For example, my Chicago fact-checkers had very strong opinions about certain things in the city, such as gentrification.

When you can get inside people's heads, you can exercise mind control on the page because you can go deeper into an issue or explore different perspectives of an issue that readers haven't considered, lending more authenticity to the novel. That's gold for a fiction writer.

To find my fact-checkers, I used my network and asked for help on my podcasts and daily blog. Several of my readers reached out offering help, which was humbling. I also found fact-checkers on Upwork.com. I posted a job with a description of what I needed with a small budget and a one-week turnaround, and I screened applicants based on their experience and responses to interview questions in the job description. My Chicago fact-checking job attracted almost 70 people who lived in the city or were very familiar with the city. In short, it's not hard to find people who have the experience you need. You just need to ask for it.

Another area where you can weave fact-checking into your book is through beta reading. I believe the beta readers are an underrated resource that writers don't tap in to. For example, beta readers are not just readers; they are parents, professionals in an industry, members of their community, and so on. They have hobbies other than reading and unique perspectives on life that they are willing to share if you ask them. When you lead by asking for these types of experiences, you can attract higher quality people to help you with your story. Let's say that you have a fantasy novel that has religious overtones based on Judaism. Why not look for a fantasy reader who is a devout follower of the Jewish religion and deeply involved in their synagogue and the Jewish community as one of your *beta readers*? Most people don't think about that; they just want to find anyone and everyone willing to beta read for them, missing out on their life experiences.

In my opinion, it is better to have beta readers with the experience you're looking for than generic beta readers who will read anything. I no longer recruit beta readers who don't exclusively read in the genre I write in, for example. A reader who is well-versed in the genre always gives better feedback than someone who "just likes to read everything."

I enjoyed the fact-checking process so much that I have decided to make it a part of all of my novels moving forward. I believe it made a measurable difference in the quality of the novel.

SOME THOUGHTS ON EDITORS

Few lessons I have learned are more important than those I have learned while working with an editor.

Editing is subjective. You don't know whether you hired a good editor until after you publish your book. This is because readers are the ultimate arbiters of quality, not the writer or editor.

Your book can be squeaky clean and free of typos, but readers still might not buy it if there are issues with the story.

Just because YOU feel good about your story, that doesn't mean your readers will like it. You can hire a developmental editor, copy editor, proofreader, and even utilize beta readers and sensitivity readers, but readers may still dislike your story. Yet the common wisdom is to hire as many editors as you can afford and hope that it makes a difference.

In recent years, I have taken a more nuanced approach to editing.

Most people think of editing in three phases: developmental, copyediting, proofreading. I don't personally believe in developmental editing, but it is a valid method. Copyediting, however, has two distinct phases. Understanding these two phases will help you write better stories. The first phase of copyediting is what I call continuity editing. This is not developmental editing; rather, it is about the continuity and cohesion of your story. A developmental editor will look at your story and recommend structural changes if the editor feels it is needed. My vision of a continuity editor does not recommend structural changes; in fact, those are out of the question unless there is a serious plot hole.

Instead, they focus on making sure that the content *within* your existing structure is cohesive, typically at the sentence and chapter level. All line edits they recommend are a direct consequence of inconsistencies they find. So this type of editor *needs* to be a skilled copyeditor.

Here are some examples of "continuity editing."

First example: your character's eyes are blue on page 2, but green on page 10. This is a classic continuity issue that an editor can help you with.

Second example: your character's actions don't make logical sense to the reader. For example, if your character is carrying four grocery bags to their car, and they just open the car door and get in, a reader might say "Wait a minute...If the character is caring that many bags, shouldn't they put one of the bags down and open the door?" Then, the reader might put your book down. A good continuity editor can help you avoid this problem.

The third example: plot holes. Let's say that your character has a sword that gets destroyed in chapter 30, but then the sword magically reappears in chapter 40 with no explanation. This is also a continuity problem.

These are precisely the type of errors you want to eliminate story because they pull readers out of the story. A continuity editor looks at your story in both the macro and micro to help you root out these issues.

However, many authors don't often think about their story in terms of internal continuity. They just send it to a copyeditor and hope that the editor will catch both continuity *and* grammatical errors.

In my experience of writing over 30 novels, very few editors I've worked with specialize in catching both continuity and grammar errors consistently. While they *will* certainly catch both, they're usually good at catching one or the other. I've worked with over a dozen editors, and when you work with that many people, you notice things.

I discovered this nuance by accident. I was interviewing for copyeditors and requested sample edits of the first chapter from the two top candidates. What happened next completely changed how I see copyediting.

The first editor was an ace at catching continuity issues—this person caught things in the first chapter alone that most editors would have missed. Just thinking about their edits even now, I shake my head at the little micro-detail she found, combined throughout the novel. There was no way I *couldn't* hire this person. However, they missed a LOT of line editing issues, more than I was comfortable with. That said, they gave me a great edit. There's value in having someone with their type of mind.

The second editor gave me a solid line edit that was as good as any I've ever received, but they missed many of the continuity issues that the first editor caught. There was no way I couldn't hire this person, either.

If I hired one editor, I would have grammar issues, and if I hired the other, I would have continuity issues. When you put both editors' work products together, you got a full, comprehensive edit.

That got me thinking about my prior editors. I reviewed their work and discovered that while they were good in both categories, each editor demonstrated an above-average skill level one category over the other. It was uncanny.

That experience taught me to start screening editors in terms of their strengths, and that while there are editors who excel in both categories, it's more realistic to hire two people to help you with continuity, spelling, and grammar. It also provides you with diversity of thought, which is never a bad thing.

THE BOOK COVER DESIGN PARADOX AND THE LOOMING DESIGNER SHORTAGE

I needed a cover designer recently, and I discovered that the market changed substantially since the last time I ordered a fiction cover design in 2019.

I visited the websites of all the designers that I'd used in the past. All of them had either raised their rates between 20-50 percent or were no longer accepting commissions. That was a bummer.

Then I researched new cover designers and had a hard time finding a designer whose aesthetic jibed with my tastes. Those I *did* find had waiting lists of six months or more!

(Waiting periods have always been a problem with designers. As they take on more clients, the waiting period goes up and you have to be strategic about getting on their calendar. But still...)

I'm not indicting designers. They're just running their businesses. But I'm running a business too...

As someone who produces novels quickly, I can't tolerate a six-month or more waiting period.

Don't we always talk about writing and publishing fast in our community? Isn't the common advice to publish often? How can you do that with six-month or more waiting periods? It makes planning a lot more difficult. I find that to be an interesting contradiction.

So what's a writer to do?

I did more research, and found that the cost of cover design in general had gone up substantially in just two years.

Earlier than 2019, you could find a pre-made cover for less than $75. At the time of this writing, you would be lucky if you could find a decent premade cover for under $200.

Earlier than 2019, you could find a decent cover designer for between $300 and $500. Now you would be lucky if you found a decent cover designer for under $400. The most expensive designers used to be around $600-$700; now I see high-end cover designers charging well over $700 – *and* with a six-month or more waiting period!

This sounded alarm bells for me.

The costs of cover design are increasing, but you're not getting any more for your money than you got two years ago. I attribute this to the fact that designers have to pay their bills, and they're getting pickier about their clients. I also blame the pandemic.

If this trend continues, we're headed for a cover designer shortage. There won't be enough people to fill the demand. Therefore, the prices and waiting periods for good designers will keep going up.

For someone as prolific as me who publishes around 7 to 10 books per year, most of them based on my whims, that's a problem because I can't plan ahead! It's hard to have publishing flexibility when you have to wait longer than two or three months. Ideally, you want as few waiting periods as possible.

Also, it's worth pointing out that if we're seeing the costs increase today, what will they be two years from now? Ten years? You're going to pay more, wait longer, have to switch designers frequently, and you'll get nothing more for your money.

This is most disastrous for new writers. If the trends continue, there could be a day when a new writer has to pay $1,000 or more just to get an average cover.

A full-time writer and bestseller is less likely to care about this problem because they can afford the extra few hundred dollars. They may make well over that (in profits) in a single day. So while they may not like it, they'll chalk it up to the cost of doing business.

The ones who get squeezed are the authors in the beginning and middle of their journeys…authors who are working full-time jobs, with families, who don't have unlimited money, and who are (rightly so) worried about the financial prospects of "making it" as a writer. What about them?

This problem does not exist with editors. Editors raise their rates and leave the industry all the time, but you can always find someone else.

You can always find an editor to suit your budget. If I wanted, I could attract an editor in twenty-four hours and have them working on my book by the end of the week. Prices are going up somewhat, probably tracking with the costs of living, but they're far more manageable on the editing side. This problem is unique to cover design.

I haven't heard anyone else talking about this problem, so for now, I'm talking to myself, but there are three solutions to this problem that I can think of.

The first is to learn how to design your own book covers. If you can do that, you'll save money and avoid waiting periods. In fact, it's the greatest cost-saving and production efficiency I can think of as a writer. You would cut your production costs by *at least* half, making it far more affordable to publish flexibly, and rapidly.

You can learn to create a decent book cover with enough time, energy, and money. There are online courses you can take. If you read prior volumes of *Indie Author Confidential*, you'll know that I have written that there is a demand for more detailed instruction of this kind. An influencer designer who wanted to build a big following could do so by teaching authors how to create their own book covers step-by-step, in a professional way that gets results.

However, most writers I know of don't have an appetite for creating their own covers, nor do they have the skill level to do it. Also, anything you create as a writer is likely to be inferior to what a professional cover designer can create for you, no matter how much time, money, and effort you put into learning how to do it yourself. There are downsides. But in the future, if you want a cover quickly, you may not have another choice.

For my novel, I was lucky enough to find someone with only a two-month waiting period with only a slightly increased cost. I might not be so lucky next time, so I'm planning for that now.

I hope I'm wrong, but if I'm not, a crisis awaits. In the coming years, I don't foresee that the number of new (good) designers entering the market will outpace the existing (good) ones who have higher costs, longer wait times, or a full client list.

It makes good sense to start learning how to do your own covers now. Hire a designer to create a cover template that features your name prominently. Then just use that template as the basis for the covers you create yourself.

The second solution to this problem is technology. Perhaps in the future, there will be artificial intelligence that uses computer vision to help you design covers that are more high-quality than what you can do on your own. But even if it were possible, technology always has limitations and trade-offs and it won't save us completely.

The third solution is to hire your own cover designer to keep in-house or to enter into a contract with a designer that guarantees a certain amount of books for them each year in exchange for a fast turnaround time so you can "skip the line." Some designers may start offering this. For example, pay X amount and you'll get the cover in nine months. Or, pay Y amount and you'll get the cover in one month with more responsive service. Or, pay me Z amount and you'll get a discount and a better waiting period in exchange for a guaranteed amount of books. I don't like any of those options, frankly, because it creates more division between haves and have-nots, and it locks down designers from the general public. But if enough people complain about a shortage and waiting periods, I don't see how this doesn't become a reality.

In the future (read: today), the best-selling authors will lock down the talented cover designers, and it will be next to impossible to work with them. That's why we lowly writers have to start planning for an even worse iteration of this future. And that planning begins now.

If you have a good cover designer currently, write like hell and do everything in your power to keep them. Otherwise, when you find yourself in need of a new designer—and you will eventually, because it's only a matter of time before situations change—be prepared to pay more for the same product.

This is also an opportunity for alternative cover designer business models to arise, such as a business that operates with a team of designers instead of a solo operation. The companies that will win in the future with mid-list and new authors will be those who can create a cover in two months or less, rain or shine. Reliability of delivery is the future with cover designers. We don't have that now.

ROYAL ORDER OF EDITING

I've been thinking about something that I call "the royal order of editing." If one were to follow this, they would cover all of their bases.

Phase 1: Self-editing.

Phase 2: Alpha reader. An alpha reader is a first reader who reads the story and gives you feedback on whether it works.

Phase 3: Developmental editor.

Phase 4: Fact-checkers.

Phase 5: Continuity editing.

Phase 6: Beta readers.

Phase 7: Copyeditor.

Phase 8: Proofreader.

Phase 9: Advanced spelling and grammar checkers like Grammarly or ProWritingAid.

Is this "order" overkill? Probably. But it's helpful to think about with every project because some books need more editing than others.

TRYING TO GET MY MESSAGING RIGHT

When I was working on my sales database project, I struggled with how to explain it. At first, I was way too technical. Then I went in the opposite direction and was too high-level. Ultimately, it took two to three months for me to settle on the right message.

Later in this book, I'm going to discuss an editing data and analytics project I'm working on, and it poses the same risk:

- it will help authors be more efficient and productive with their self-editing;
- it's a highly technical project in nature, but the result is not; and
- it uses tools most authors have never heard of, or aren't familiar with.

This book is me documenting my journey, so I give myself permission to be a bit more detailed than normal. That's one of the main selling points of the *Indie Author Confidential* series. However, when I'm explaining the project on my podcast or YouTube channel, or in passing to another influencer, I have to tell the right story, or people won't get it.

So that's where I am with this project right now. As you read the editing data and analytics chapters in the Data-Driven Writer section, I hope that I will explain the issue in language that helps you understand the project and the value it provides. If not, I'll keep trying.

BECOME A WORLD-CLASS MARKETER

NO HASSLE, NO BS MARKETING

I participated in a marketing promotion that included a bundle of writing books, courses, and more. One of my books was included. The bundle was a great product.

When customers bought the bundle, they could download my book by clicking a Book Funnel link.

A reader reached out after buying the bundle to thank me for not making it overly difficult to access my book. According to the reader, every other content creator in the bundle required customers to set up logins or give their email address to receive the creator's content.

I appreciated the note. I believe in making it easy to grab a product once you've purchased it. Sure, I could have used the opportunity to build an email list, but I chose not to.

I prefer that people download the book as easily and quickly as possible, and then if they like it, they can engage with me further.

This is the opposite of what most marketers would do. It's not a "marketing best practice" and I lose out on email subscribers in the short term, but I win in the long term because the people who *do* engage are more likely to consume my content and buy my books…mainly because I didn't spam them to death or chase after their engagement.

It's like dating. Go out with someone and see where it goes. Would *you* appreciate it if the person you're dating wants to get into your pants on the first date? Exactly.

Marketing is like that too.

BOOK SIRENS

A fellow writer sent me an email recommending that I check out a service called Book Sirens.

I did some research on the company, and I was pleasantly surprised. Book Sirens is a service that helps you secure book reviews from avid readers. It solves a (not so) age-old problem that self-published writers have had since the beginning of self-publishing as we know it: getting reviews.

When you publish your first book, you don't have an audience. So it's hard to go find people who would be willing to read your book in exchange for a review. A lot of people use Goodreads, reader forums, and other ways to reach prospective readers, but this comes with a risk. Book Sirens aims to eliminate this risk.

Here's how it works: the website is a community of avid readers who sign up for accounts in exchange for communications from the website. Authors upload their books to the site, and Book Sirens notifies readers that your book is available. Readers can then choose whether to download your book or not based on your cover and your description. You only pay when readers download your book. Of course, they don't have to leave a review, and some of them will not. However, Book Sirens states that many of their readers DO leave reviews. The great thing about this is that it doesn't violate Amazon's terms of service and it is an easy way to get your book into the hands of strangers.

Book Sirens isn't just for new writers, though. Even writers like me can take advantage of the service, leveraging it for new releases.

I've seen a lot of services come and go in the self-publishing community, but I've never seen anything quite like this. The website has amassed a very large community of eager readers, I've heard nothing but good things about it, AND it plays nice with the Amazon terms of service! I can't tell you how many times I have seen service providers in this community who violate Amazon's terms of service for one reason or another. I remember (not so fondly) a particular service that I used back in 2014 that promised to get you at least 50 to 100 reviews on your book by paying the service a finder's fee. Amazon decided one day that it didn't like this and they made it a personal mission to remove all reviews from its site from this service. The service did NOT violate Amazon's terms, but Amazon felt it was bad for customer trust.

I even remember a service that scraped Amazon's publicly available reviewer information for email addresses based on comparable books to yours, and then they provided you with a list of those reviewers' email addresses. That was pretty cool because you could email people with a cold pitch and get a pretty good response rate. But again, when Amazon found out about this service, they simply stopped making reviewer data discoverable to scraping software. There went yet another method of obtaining reviews. After that, I didn't think that there would be a legitimate way to procure reviews. And then I found Book Sirens. I can't for the life of me find any way that their service violates any terms.

Also, the Alliance of Independent Authors has rated Book Sirens as "Recommended," which means that they give it a seal of approval, which is a pretty big deal given that the Alliance of Independent Authors is a watchdog organization that gives brutally honest reviews of self-publishing service providers.

I signed up for an account immediately. I haven't been able to use it because I don't have a new book to launch yet, but I plan to incorporate Book Sirens into my marketing strategy.

TO BOX SET OR NOT TO BOX SET?

In December 2020, I published volume 3 of my *Indie Author Confidential* series. I also used this opportunity to create an anthology collection that compiled volumes 1 through 3. I priced this at $9.99, which is a discount compared to buying all three volumes individually.

I've always struggled with this particular arrangement. Which book do you advertise? Do you send people to volume 1, or do you send people to the anthology?

Readers fall into both camps. Some people don't like to buy box sets for one reason or another; others prefer to have all books in one place if possible to keep their library cleaner.

This also becomes more complicated when you introduce Amazon Ads into the mix.

In the past, I haven't done a very good job of letting people know that an anthology exists. This time, I wanted to change that.

On the individual volumes 1 through 3, I updated the first line of the book description to let readers know that an anthology exists, and I included a link to where they can buy it. I only advertised the anthology. I figured that advertising volume 1 individually would confuse things.

While it is too soon to determine whether this method worked, I am fine with it because it is the right thing to do for my readers. I also think it's fairer. No one likes to buy an individual book only to find out that they could have saved a few dollars by buying the anthology. Book retailers haven't exactly made it easy to discover anthologies either. In a perfect world, authors would be able to select a box that tells book retailers that a book exists in an anthology, and after the reader clicks the buy button, they would get a pop-up notifying them that the book they wish to buy also exists in a collection. If they wanted, they could click through to the collection or buy the book as they originally intended. In my opinion, that's the only way to solve this problem, and no retailer that I know of has this functionality.

Sure, I'll miss out on a couple of bucks from those people who choose to buy the anthology over the individual volumes, but the people who purchase individual volumes can also continue to do so if they please. Depending on how this goes, I may go back to some of my earlier box sets with fiction and try the same strategy.

IMPROVING THE AD CONVERSION RATE OF A POETRY COLLECTION

I have been scaling up my Amazon Ads. Until now, I only ran ads on my more popular books.

I expanded my ad campaigns to titles that historically haven't sold well, including my poetry collections, *Android Poems* and *Muse Poems*.

To my surprise, I was able to sell a handful of copies per month of each. My ad campaigns in general were more effective on my poetry collections than some of my fiction series!

Some of the techniques I used:

- I waited for 100 clicks before taking any action. This gives me enough of a sample size to decide on. When I ran the initial campaigns, there was very little interest in the collections. I receive clicks, but no sales. My conversion rate was around 1:35, which means that I only received a sale for every 35 clicks. For your ads to be profitable, you need around a 1:10 conversion rate. I lost a lot of money in the first 100 clicks.

- After 100 clicks, I rewrote the book description to make it read like newer, bestselling poetry collections that were similar to mine. The biggest change was to include a sample poem in the description. 100 clicks later, I improved my conversion ratio for *Android Poems* to 1:24 and I lost half as much money as I lost during the first

100 clicks. Major improvement, but not good enough. I made additional adjustments to the book description that brought me down to around 1:12, which is very profitable because most of the sales are for the paperback edition.

- *Muse Poems*, however, went in the opposite direction all the way down to 1:86. I believe it was because the sample poem wasn't resonating with readers. I switched it and brought my conversion rate back to around 1:24, which is where it is currently. I lose money on this collection every month, but I'm still selling copies and reaching readers, so that's worth the investment.

I'm blown away that I was able to get restore sales for my poetry collections. It just doesn't seem real. But *Android Poems* now turns me a tidy little profit every month and hopefully will long into the future.

CLUBHOUSE

One of my YouTube subscribers invited me to join Clubhouse, which is an invite-only social media network that is the "new kid on the block" at the time of this writing.

Clubhouse is an audio app that uses "rooms" where people gather to talk about topics that interest them. You can find rooms for writing, music, entrepreneurship, and much more (even rooms where people have contests to see who has the most sexual moans…not kidding).

Anyway, I tried Clubhouse and it was interesting, to say the least. It reminds me a lot of Anchor.FM. Most people know Anchor as a podcasting service, but it wasn't always that way. It was an audio app where people had their own "stations" and spoke whatever was on their mind in the form of short audiograms. You could reply to people's audiograms and start conversations, and listen in on other people's conversations. I liked the old version of Anchor a lot, though the user interface was difficult to manage.

Clubhouse is trying to tap in to the same audience that Anchor had, which, ironically, was predominantly people of color.

I joined a few conversations, but I wasn't crazy about the etiquette rules there. While you can join conversations to listen in, it's frowned upon if you offer your two cents unless solicited. As such, I didn't speak in any conversations unless I was asked to join a room.

Clubhouse will be much, much bigger in the future. Is it for me? I'm not sure. I don't have the time to explore a new platform right now, but I'm not ruling it out.

AUTOMATICALLY ADD TO CART WITH AN AMAZON LINK

An author in a Facebook group shared a tip on how to send readers a link that automatically adds your book to the shopping cart on Amazon. You can do this by creating a special link and appending it with your book's ASIN and a syntax command. I won't share what it is because these things always change, but you can search for how to do it on the Internet.

At the time of this writing, it works quite well and you can add a series to it so that readers can buy an entire series in one link. An excellent marketing tool for your email list!

However, this link doesn't allow for link localization, so you have to build it manually for each Amazon store.

A few volumes ago, I talked about Genius Link, a link localization service that I use and recommend. Genius Link has a feature called Advanced Targeting, where you can route people to different links based on parameters such as their country, device, operating system, and so on. Add to Cart links were a perfect use case for this feature.

I loaded all the country-specific links into Advanced Targeting and created a dynamic link where customers were routed to the proper Amazon store. This way, you only have to give out one link, and you can make it a clean, short link using your domain.

This is a very useful technique to sell more books. You can use such a link on your website, social media, podcast, and email list.

READER SIGNALS

When I wrote my book *Shadow Deal*, I developed a way to test my idea against the market to see how it would perform.

When I looked at comparable books, I noticed that each book gave off certain signals to the reader. When I looked at the most successful books and put all those signals together, I could often get a clear picture of why a book was successful.

I called these signals "reader signals."

Some examples of reader signals include:

- Book title
- Series title
- Number of books in series
- Foreground of the cover, or main character
- Background of the cover
- Font of the book title and author name
- Reputation of the cover designer
- Price (ebook, paperback, audio)
- Formats available
- Headline of the book description
- Body of the book description
- Call to action in the book description
- About the Author section on the product page
- Number of reviews and review average

And so on. Overall, I found around 80 reader signals that I

could clearly distinguish, mostly *the product page alone*.

As an exercise, I looked at my book and defined the reader signals for my new book, *Dead Rat Walking*. How many signals could I match from comparable books?

First, I used the Urban Fantasy Book Database tool that I created that catalogues many different urban fantasy series (over several hundred). Unfortunately, I didn't find any comparable books. Uh-oh, right?

Then I did some Internet searches and also looked for books with a shifter main character similar to mine. I only found one. Another uh-oh. However, I did find books that had minor characters similar to mine. I used some of those as comparables and then broadened my search to find books with similar storylines.

Overall, my search for comparables wasn't a fruitful one. I've been here before, and I know how this movie ends…This series may not do well. But you never know until you publish it.

My early search is a decent indicator that I'm either before my time or I have an idea that is slightly off-market. However, I'm okay with that, and I've adjusted my expectations accordingly.

But I digress. Despite the grim prospects, I was able to still match many of the common reader signals in the urban fantasy genre:

- Title: *Dead Rat Walking* (a play on the shifter trope)
- Series Title: *The Chicago Rat Shifter* (indicates the name of the city in the series, and the type of supernatural character, and the genre)
- Number of books in series: between 3-5 (which is how many urban fantasy readers will want to see before they invest in a series)
- Cover foreground: A human character sitting in a sewer, surrounded by rats (the rats are prominent too)

- Cover background: a graffiti-ridden sewer (Graffiti is a common signal for urban fantasy, especially on famous traditionally-published book covers. A sewer is also very urban.)
- Price: $2.99 for ebook, TBD for paperback, but nothing out of line with what other authors charge

You get the picture. I did this with all 80 signals, tweaking and adjusting wherever the book fell out of line with the market. Note that I did not change the book itself—just the packaging. And despite what I change, the packaging still is an accurate description of what the reader will receive when they read the story.

I'm still early in my experiments with reader signals, but I believe the exercise is helpful if only to get you thinking about how your book aligns with the market.

If you're interested, I did an in-depth analysis in fine-tuning the reader signals for my book *Shadow Deal* as part of my *Writing to Market* course, which you can find at www.authorlevelup.com/writetomarket

KEYWORD COURSE BY DAVE CHESSON

I learned that Dave Chesson published a course on his Kindlepreneur website on how to select keywords and categories for your books. I was technically still in "Amnesia Mode," so I downloaded the course but didn't get to it before I transitioned away from marketing for a while.

This quarter, I watched the course and took extensive notes. Dave is an SEO master, and learning how he approaches metadata selection is helpful if only to understand how he thinks about it.

While I highly recommend that you take his course (it's only $50 at the time of this writing), here were some of my major takeaways:

- thinking about keywords in groups can be a helpful exercise. When you make a list of possible keywords, group them based on similarity. Then run them through Publisher Rocket to figure out which ones have the best earnings potential. I have always done this the other way around.
- BISAC categories and Amazon categories are not the same. I always knew this, it's more helpful to think about how to map BISAC categories and Amazon categories so that I know where my book will end up. Today, I've just been picking categories and hoping for the best, not really understanding how to change them.

- Amazon SEO is all about continuing to return to basics. It's always changing. The techniques I have been using were out of date.

I won't share any more because I believe you should buy the course. I plan on using the detailed lessons I learned with *Dead Rat Walking* so I can give the book the best possible chance to succeed.

NEGLECTING MARKETING

Last quarter, I was hyper-focused on marketing. I discussed my "Amnesia Mode" project, and how I learned many new marketing tips and strategies. I also discussed how I grew my sales with Amazon Ads. Overall, those efforts were successful.

This quarter, I haven't been marketing at all. At least not for my backlist. I have been more focused on book production, setting my strategy for the coming year, and a new editing data and analytics project that I will discuss later in this book. I've also been focused on my final semester of law school.

I've neglected my marketing. That said, my sales are still doing pretty well, and they are slightly up.

I've learned over the past few years that you don't have to market your work every day, or even every week. Sometimes you can get by with less than that, but you'll only get by. Eventually, the numbers do drop off.

I've been trying to find ways to be more consistent with my writing and marketing. I find that I "seesaw" between them. When I write, I write with all my force. When I market, I market with all my force. I do both in short bursts. So far, it has worked well, but my system is flawed. It breaks down after a few months when I realize how long I have *not* been doing the other thing.

I don't know the answer to the problem, so I'm just articulating it here. Perhaps a step in the right direction is to hire people, but I'm not convinced that a marketing assistant will materially improve your sales. I believe that an ad manager could, but for reasons I'll discuss later in this book, that's not technically possible right now.

This got me thinking about ways to automate and outsource your marketing so that even though you're not doing it every day or every week, it feels like you are.

My mind went first to social media, which is what most people do—hire a social media manager. Frankly, I've never had much of a presence on social media outside of YouTube, and I don't intend to change that.

My mind went second to ad management, and third to... nowhere.

Neglecting your marketing is normal when writing isn't your full-time job. That's where I settled this matter for now.

ILLUSTRATED COVERS: THE PANACEA FOR ALL PROBLEMS?

I discussed the looming cover designer shortage in the World-Class Content Creator section.

Another problem with cover designers is finding the right designer for your needs, especially if your character is a person of color. It's difficult to find models of color on stock photography sites. Sometimes you can find good models, but there aren't enough images of that person to sustain a series. As a result, many cover designers who work exclusively with stock images can't help authors in this situation.

The answer? Get an illustrated cover. It's more expensive, but you won't have to worry about the stock photo issue. You also won't have to worry about character poses or backgrounds.

Illustrated covers are trending in fantasy in particular and have been for the last few years. I decided to give it a shot. I'll share how it works out and if creating one had an impact on my sales.

In the next chapter, I'll share a unique problem with illustrated covers that you'll want to consider if you decide to purchase one.

BOOK COVER ADVENTURES

Sometimes you get that feeling in the bottom of your stomach that you screwed up, like you made a misstep that will cause you trouble in the future.

That was how I felt when I got the cover design back for my newest novel, *Dead Rat Walking*. The designer did a good job illustrating the image—no concerns there. But I couldn't help but feel déjà vu.

Upon seeing the cover, I was taken back to the book cover for my book *Eaten: Season 1,* which was probably the worst cover I've ever designed. I'll share more about that cover later in the book, but the gist of that cover was that I confused the designer and wasn't clear in what I wanted. It was my fault, not his.

This time around, I did *not* confuse the designer. We were both aligned around the concept. I also did not overwhelm her with information—I was thoughtful in how I presented the concept, giving her enough direction while letting her do her thing. She did exactly that.

Yet, I still kept feeling like something was wrong when I saw the final cover for the first time. I couldn't pinpoint it. I spent the better part of the day thinking about it.

For starters, when I put the cover on a Pinterest board next to other top-selling urban fantasy covers, it didn't measure up. The scale of the character was too small, especially at the thumbnail level. He didn't stand out.

The typography didn't work either. It screamed post-apocalyptic, not urban fantasy.

The color scheme was too dark. The cover wasn't bright enough.

All signals were pointing toward trouble, and none of it was the designer's fault. I kept thinking that I should have done a better job thinking of a concept that would sell the cover more, although I spent a fair amount of time doing market research and thinking about the cover and how to make it fit within the market.

So I did what I always do when the cover isn't working: I worked with the designer to fix it. I voiced my concerns and gave her specific bullet point feedback on what I wanted to change, using the market as the North Star.

I juxtaposed the cover on the Pinterest board in several different positions and took screenshots so she could see how it stuck out.

There were only two possibilities:

- We'd make the design work.
- We wouldn't make the design work.

Again, this wasn't on the designer. This was on me. If the second scenario came to pass, I considered an unfavorable but possible option: I could hire a separate person to do the typography once we fixed some of the layout and composition issues on the illustration itself. This would add an extra expense to the project (and the series), and I didn't like that option. But that's always a risk you take with illustrated covers. Sometimes the illustrator nails the image but bombs the typography.

Anyway, we got the cover to a good spot. It's still not 100 percent where I wanted it to be, but it gives off the right signals.

I don't trust my emotions, though, because sometimes the cover is just fine and there are other issues that sink a book.

If I ultimately fail, the lesson I learned the hard way with this project was the importance of character scale. That will be one of the first requirements I discuss with the designer next time. If you screw up the character scale, you screw up the entire cover. Scale is everything on urban fantasy covers. If anything, it should be bigger than normal. You live and you learn.

Additionally, for the next cover, I'm giving the designer an action scene to illustrate. And that scene will be in a bright setting so that the cover stands out. That will make sure I don't end up here again.

Time will tell how well I steered the designer on this project. She was fantastic and I will be working with her again, but I've published too many books to make these kinds of mistakes. I'll do better next time.

WHAT BEING REJECTED FOR A TED TALK TAUGHT ME

In the last volume, I discussed how an opportunity to apply for a TED talk came up suddenly, and how I rushed to apply for it.

I was rejected.

Around the beginning of the year, I received a form rejection. I wasn't selected for the role, or even to be an alternate for the role.

It was a tough blow. I've wanted to give a TED talk since the first time I saw one, and I thought I had put good preparation into the application and my demo video.

But these things happen. I thought about it for a day and permitted myself to be a little down. Then, the next day, I moved on.

Why did they turn me down? I have no idea, but it was probably because my pitch just wasn't the right fit for what they were looking for.

I always have to remind myself about a story that happened to me early in my career.

I once applied for a job that I wanted. I wanted it so bad that I was envisioning myself in the role already because it was such a perfect fit for me. My interview went amazingly well, and I thought for sure I'd get the job.

I didn't.

I was crushed. Devastated.

I found out later that the hiring manager was a narcissistic jerk. The person that got the job instead of me ended up leaving the company in disgrace because the manager was impossible to please.

If I had gotten that job, I would have been miserable and it would have dead-ended my career.

I got another job several months later that wasn't nearly as glamorous but opened the door for me to double my salary in just a few years.

Yeah, fate.

Ever since then, I learned to be grateful for the jobs I got, and especially grateful for the jobs I didn't get.

The same is true with rejection.

Be grateful for the times you are accepted, but be especially grateful when someone turns down an opportunity to work with you. Even though it's painful, it's probably for the best.

Rejection still stings nonetheless, but I always remind myself of that story any time I face a hard rejection.

What did I learn from the TED experience?

1. I can pitch like my life depends on it, and it may even help.
2. I can prepare a pretty good pitch in 24 hours if I need to.
3. Sharing about the application publicly was a little embarrassing since I didn't get the role, but maybe someone learned something.

When one door closes, another one opens. Right around the time I received the TED rejection, I received an acceptance to write an article for *Writer's Digest* magazine. The magazine's acceptance and the TED rejection were within days of each other. It's funny how that works.

That's why I try not to let rejection bother me too much. It's just a numbers game.

I've accumulated thousands of rejections for opportunities that have come up in my writing career. The TED talk rejection is just another badge of honor on my writer's journey.

BECOME A
TECHNOLOGY-DRIVEN WRITER

AI, BLOCKCHAIN, AND VIRTUAL WORLDS

Joanna Penn published a book titled *Artificial Intelligence, Blockchain, and Virtual Worlds: The Impact of Converging Technologies On Authors and the Publishing Industry*. I always buy Joanna's books on launch day, and this one didn't disappoint.

Joanna has been a pioneer in the emerging tech space for authors for years, building her business on the back of emerging technology. Not only was this book different than what she normally writes (in a good way), but it was a masterclass in building thought leadership in a space that she already dominates. I highly recommend that you pick up the book; it is quite short at around 60 pages, but it gives you a lot to think about for the future of your author career.

I've said for a long time that self-published writers will need to adapt to the times. The techniques that made us successful today are not going to be the same techniques that make writers successful in 2030. This is because of emerging technology, the rapidly changing publishing industry, and reader tastes. Joanna keenly understands this and has done great work in shepherding writers into the future. This is one of the reasons I admire her so much.

Here are my takeaways from the book:

- The future is here now. It is not something that is coming. Many of the technologies that Joanna talks about in the book are nascent, but they do already exist.

- The future belongs to writers who understand copyright. There will be amazing opportunities for writers who understand licensing and contracts. For example, licensing your voice into a voice double can be a lucrative endeavor if you understand how to negotiate the terms.
- AI as co-author is an interesting future. Imagine writing a book with the assistance of an AI that knows everything you have ever written, your book sales, what your readers want, and how to write just like you. What kinds of amazing work could you create?
- Blockchain isn't quite there yet, but it has the potential to completely disrupt and disintermediate the ways that authors are paid. Out of all the technologies in the book, this one seems the least far along, but when it reaches a watershed moment, it will be a big deal.

I won't share any more of Joanna's tips because you should read the book.

LESSONS LEARNED AFTER BUYING A STANDING DESK

I finally bought a standing desk. I've been saving up for the last few years. I didn't want to settle for an easy solution—I wanted to buy a real standing desk with all of the benefits.

I bought a desk from Uplift.com, which I highly recommend. It took about two hours to put together by myself, and the instructions were simple to understand. The desk also came with a smattering of accessories that improve its functionality, such as cable management clips, zip ties, a tray for hiding your cables, a magnetic sleeve for routing your cables, and even tabletop grommets with outlets in them.

When I was done setting up, I had the best workstation I've ever had in my entire career.

People have been asking about my setup, so here it is:

- Uplift desk with two grommets: one with two power plugs and another for wire management.
- A 36-inch monitor to use as my main screen, and a laptop stand to prop up my laptop.
- A Mac docking station that has ports for USB, Ethernet, HDMI, and SD cards to save ports on my laptop.
- A surge protector underneath the desk in a wire tray that powers my monitor and desk.
- Lots of clips, zip ties, and hooks that route my cables around the desk and keep everything off the floor.

- A magnetic surge protector that clips to the side of the desk that powers additional items that I may need to unplug from time to time, such as my laptop and lamp.
- Velcro straps with adhesive strips that secure my external hard drives and podcasting audio interface underneath the desk, out of view. I can simply attach and reattach the equipment as needed.
- A wireless charger for my smartphone plugged in under the desk.
- A boom arm for my microphone that swings out of the way when I don't need it.
- A studio light that clams behind my monitor, giving me flattering lighting.
- A headphone hook that clamps to the desk that stores my headphones so I can grab them conveniently when needed and keep them out of the way otherwise.

This is an all-season setup. In seconds, I can raise or lower the desk to a preset height.

If I need to write, I can do so in whatever position I like.

If I need to record a podcast episode, I simply turn on my audio interface, swing the microphone over, open my recording app, and start talking.

If I need to do a podcast or YouTube interview, I swing the microphone over, turn on my webcam and studio light, and switch on my ethernet connection.

All this, with almost nothing on my desk.

That's why investing in a *real* standing desk was worth it. I couldn't do any of this stuff with my old desk without moving things around and disrupting my office.

Now I don't have to worry about that, and I have a healthier, camera-ready, and more productive writing setup that will be tax-deductible.

DIFFERENT WAYS TO WRITE

A few years ago, I tried Dragon Anywhere for dictation and didn't like it. I felt that the usability and accuracy weren't to my liking compared to the desktop version. I had written it off and didn't think twice about it.

Recently, a reader reached out and asked my thoughts on Dragon Anywhere. Because it had been so long since I used it, I decided to try it again.

I found that the app had improved significantly since the last time I used it. In fact, I liked it so much that I purchased a subscription immediately. Dragon Anywhere has helped me dictate my books while on the go; for example, I am dictating this chapter right now while washing my dishes. Being able to dictate on your phone is practical and a way for many Mac users to access the power of dictation, even though Dragon for Mac has been discontinued.

That got me thinking about all the different ways in which you can write a novel in today's environment.

You can write a novel on your desktop or laptop using a writing app. This is the traditional way of writing.

You can also write by hand. There's nothing wrong with that either.

You can also, as I do, write on your phone using a mobile writing app.

You can dictate your book using software like Dragon, but this does require investment in software and certain hardware.

You can also dictate on the go using Dragon Anywhere.

You can dictate into a digital voice recorder or voice recorder app on your phone and upload the audio to Dragon to be transcribed, or you can hire a transcriptionist to turn your speech into text.

In other words, there is no excuse not to find a way to write and be more productive in today's new world of publishing. The question is how you want to accomplish it.

Instead of saying "I can only write on my computer," think instead: "I will write based on my circumstance at the time." For example, if you are at home on a Saturday night sitting in front of your desk, then writing on your desktop or laptop makes sense.

If you have carpal tunnel or repetitive stress injuries, then it makes a great deal of sense to adopt dictation when you are experiencing pain. If you are at the doctor's office, or in the park, or somewhere where it doesn't make sense to have your computer in front of you, then writing on your phone is a suitable option.

Think about the mode of writing as merely a tool to help you get the writing done.

With the most recent novel that I wrote, I wrote part of it on my phone, part of it on my laptop, part of it while dictating on an exercise bike, and parts of it while standing up and walking around speaking the story.

This is why I believe that this is the greatest time in the history of the world to be a writer. Never before have writers had such unparalleled flexibility in how they choose to tell stories for which readers are willing to pay them.

As I say all the time, your writing app and writing style are the most important early decisions in your career. Your goal should be to find the writing app that fits you like a glove. When you do that, you'll automatically become more productive because you won't waste time arguing with your writing app. Instead, you'll spend your time focused on the nuances of your story.

BACK ON MY DRAGON

Around Christmas, I hurt my back. I was walking my dog and tripped over an uneven part of my driveway. I woke up the next morning looking like the Hunchback of Notre Dame. It didn't help that it was the first week of winter and extremely cold, which is never good for people who have arthritis and back pain.

This happens to me a few times a year. This time was really painful, so much that I had to limit my computer time because it aggravated the pain. Writing on my phone was a godsend that helped me maintain high word counts even in the jaws of pain.

During this period, my wife sustained an eye injury. Thank goodness it was just superficial, but she couldn't use screens for a week. It got me thinking about dictation again and how it's such a valuable skill to have. In fact, I argue that it's one of the most underrated moneymaking skills in today's self-publishing economy.

The average person types around 40 words per minute, but they speak 150 to 160 words per minute. Prose doesn't fly out of their mouth at that rate, but heck, even if you spoke 80 words per minute, that would double your word count.

I wrote about my exercise bike challenge previously in this book, but before that, I remembered my fantasy series *The Last Dragon Lord* fondly. It's my most popular fiction series to date, and it's the first one where I learned Dean Wesley Smith's Writing into the Dark method, and how I learned to write novels in one draft. I also wrote it with Dragon, the famous dictation software.

I remember being so frustrated with Dragon for Mac! It would misunderstand even the most simple words. I had to RELEARN how to speak for it to understand me; ironically, it improved my diction. Dragon also misunderstood proper nouns, which was an exercise in frustration with fantasy. But I worked through that, patiently teaching it how to pronounce almost all the proper nouns in the story.

I hate cleaning up errors unless I have to, so I *forced* myself to use Dragon without ever touching the keyboard. It took several weeks, but I learned how to dictate super smooth and clean prose. It was such a valuable skill that it helped me rack up record word counts.

Unfortunately, a lot has changed since 2016, and I had to revamp my dictation workflow. For starters, Dragon for Mac was discontinued, so I had to buy the Windows version. My investment in running Windows on a virtual machine using Parallels continues to pay off. In just a few minutes, I had Dragon up and running.

And WOW is the Windows version superior in every way. It doesn't suffer from the accuracy issues that the Mac version had. It's also smoother with fewer bugs. I can't tell you how many times I lost chunks of my story in the Mac version because it would quit unexpectedly. That hasn't happened with the Windows version once, and I doubt it will.

So I'm back on my Dragon. It's good to flex my dictation muscle again. The first day I dictated, I racked up around 1,500 words in about 30 minutes, which is quite slow at 50 words per minute. But I'm rusty and still relearning how to use Dragon. I do not doubt that I can improve my speed to around 80 words per minute once I am more comfortable.

During my exercise bike challenge, my goal was to dictate for at least one hour per day for one month. At 80 words per minute, that's 4,800 words per day *just on the exercise bike.* It doesn't count my time at the keyboard or on my phone, where I consistently write anywhere from 2,000 to 5,000 words per day. I'll let that sink in.

What would happen if you could write between 6,800 and 14,800 words of *clean prose* every single day for the rest of your author career? Good god…That's a novel every week, or at best, every few days. On the low end, that's 2.84 million words every year! That would put you solidly into pulp writer territory, possibly into the top one percent of all writers who have ever lived.

This is how dictation can help you become a technology-driven writer. Dictation serves as a cybernetic of sorts, helping you write faster and become a better version of yourself. And it's powered by artificial intelligence.

Also, remember that other forms of artificial intelligence will disrupt how we write novels. The future belongs to writers who can create amazing stories the fastest, and who have the biggest catalogues. The writers with the most books win. If you have a lot of books *before* the disruption, it'll be easier for you to survive because you'll have access to more opportunities that emerging tech can provide.

What if you could harness the power of dictation and future artificial intelligence to help you write stories even faster? Imagine have a dictation session, going to bed, and letting an AI take over, matching your word count for the day. Then, when you pick up the next morning, the AI reads the story to you, and then you pick up where it left off. Very interesting. We'll see if it's plausible.

THE FUTURE OF WRITING APPS IS ABOUT CONNECTIVITY

I've noticed an increase in emails from developers wanting my advice around creating new writing apps for writers.

I put out a call in 2019 that I'd help any developer who wanted me to review their software and offer feedback. That offer still stands, and in 2020 alone, I spoke to over a dozen developers. Each one surprised me in amazing ways. There are a lot of people working on apps with interesting feature ideas.

One developer asked me what I believed the "pie in the sky" future of writing apps *should* be.

The answer is simple: the future of writing apps should be about connectivity.

Today, you create your book and have to transport it between closed ecosystems. For example, you write your novel in a writing app, send it to Microsoft Word or Google Drive for your editor, reimport it back into your writing app, then export it to software for publication. That's three different ecosystems that aren't connected. And frankly, those ecosystems aren't interested in working together either, which is why they're going to be disrupted and completely irrelevant in the near term.

In Volume 2 of this series, I wrote about the idea of "one command center" that a writer can use to write, edit, and format their novel. The idea was around a single app that is multi-platform and access based so that you invite editors and formatters to work on your book within the app itself. In short, it would function much like the Adobe Creative Cloud does today; you can import and edit Adobe files in different Adobe programs with incredible ease and convenience. For example, I can import a Photoshop file into a Premiere video file and even manipulate the layers of an image while editing a video. That's the type of connectivity and synergy we need in the writing space.

Whoever figures this out is going to disrupt the market. As long as the app continues to evolve, the writing experience is akin to the leaders on the market today and it is available multi-platform with feature parity, writers won't think twice about switching. I even suspect that they'd be willing to pay a subscription.

Imagine an app with the smoothness of Scrivener, the tracked changes ability of Microsoft Word, and the formatting precision of Vellum. All with the ability to invite your freelancers into the book file itself to help you improve it. It's a no-brainer. Hell, freelancers such as editors and formatters might start working exclusively with an app like this.

The good news is that I'm aware of an app that is taking this exact approach and will be launching soon (at the time of this writing). I have no idea if my ideas influenced the developer (probably not), but I'll cover it in a future volume *Indie Author Confidential* when it launches, and if it's as good as I think it will be, I will consider putting my full support behind it. I predict it's going to do very well, and if that happens, the entire writing app market will look entirely different in the next few years.

CATCHING MISSING DETERMINERS

I'll be talking in the next chapter about an editing project I'm working on to help me improve the quality of my manuscript edits.

Part of that project involved reviewing my last five novels and looking for trends in changes that my editor recommended.

One of the trends was missing determiners and prepositions. It's easy to leave "and," "a," "an," "the", "to" and "of" out of sentences. Since determiners are only two characters, they're easy to miss during self-editing, and my editors don't always catch them either. I find that when I'm dictating, I miss determiners at an even higher rate. For some reason, Dragon doesn't pick them up well.

I investigated if there was a way to solve this with a standalone application using Natural Language Processing. After speaking to a few data scientists, we determined that it was too expensive and too involved. We also found that Grammarly handles this issue in particular well enough after some testing. ProWritingAid catches them as well—and it catches different ones too.

While I can't say that I agree with everything Grammarly and ProWritingAid recommend, the fact that they can catch missing determiners is worth using them for that reason alone.

Missing determiners keep me up at night. Despite *me* not being able to see the error, a reader sure can.

If this a problem you have in your writing, use ProWritingAid (paid) and Grammarly (free). Together, they'll help to minimize the determiner problem.

STITCHING TOGETHER BOOK REPORT AND AMAZON AD REPORTS

If you run Amazon Ads, you need to understand how your ads are performing.

I watch my ads closely, paying attention to the profit and conversion rate to determine if a set of ads is working.

Your profit is determined by the amount of money you make on a book minus the ad spend.

Your conversion rate is determined by the number of clicks your ads receive divided by the net units sold. This gives you a number that is best expressed as a ratio, such as 1:10 or 1:20. The lower the number, the better. My experience has been that anything less than 1:10 is usually profitable.

How do you calculate all of this? Amazon Marketing Services provides one report for your ads, and KDP provides another report for your sales.

I used Book Report instead for my sales. I selected the option to view my sales for the month:

I simply copied the table with my sales and units sold into Microsoft Excel:

Then, I went to the Amazon Ad dashboard, selected portfolio view, and clicked "Export." This works best if you use portfolios and name them based on the book title.

In Excel, I converted the sales data into a table and added a couple of extra columns to the end:

Then, I copied the Amazon Ad data into the spreadsheet just

to the right of the table and converted it into a proper Excel table.

Next, I used a VLOOKUP formula to "stitch" the two tables together like so:

And, of course, I did some basic formula work:

When I was done, I had all of my sales and ad data on one table. This took me about five minutes.

In five minutes, I can see how my ads are performing without having to do any data entry. I do this at the end of the month to determine how my ads performed.

AUTOMATING MY BOOKKEEPING

I don't know about you, but I don't exactly enjoy doing my taxes. I also don't enjoy spending several hours each month cataloging all of my receipts for my accountant to review at the end of the year. My time is best spent writing, not focused on my nation. Yet I do have to run a business. And running a business means keeping good records and staying on top of your paperwork. I find that most of my receipts come to me via email and I find that I do the same things with those emails every month.

So I had an idea: what if I could automate my receipts so that when an email receipt arrives in my inbox, a system could take that receipt, rename it, catalog it, and even fill out a spreadsheet with all the information about the purchase so that I no longer had to do it? (I explored this topic in earlier volumes under the topic of "email parsing.")

It turns out that this is very doable. I purchased a subscription to the service Zapier, which allows you to connect your web services.

I ran a pilot. Since many of the transactions I made are from PayPal, I created a workflow where any PayPal I received that came to my inbox was automatically cataloged and entered into a spreadsheet without me having to lift a finger, based on certain requirements.

Here were the rules and steps:

- If the email was from PayPal,
- mark the email as read,

- move it to my folder titled "Expenses",
- parse the following fields: "date," "amount," and "description", and
- pass the parsed data to a spreadsheet with corresponding columns

The pilot wasn't perfect, but it was a success. All of my December PayPal receipts were entered successfully onto the spreadsheet. I could easily send that spreadsheet to my accountant and he wouldn't bat an eyelash. He wouldn't even know that it was automatically generated. That, my friends, is the definition of efficiency. It will take me a while, but I plan on implementing this with most of my receipts. This will allow me to automate the majority of my bookkeeping, saving me several hours each month, especially at tax time.

LIVESTREAMING WITH OBS

Last year, I started experimenting with live streaming. Every month, I did a "Writing Power Hour" where I invited my community to join me as I dedicated 90 minutes to writing. We wrote together as a community in 20-minute increments, five-minute breaks, and a question-and-answer session at the end for anyone who wanted to ask me writing-related questions.

The power hours were such a success that I will continue doing them for the foreseeable future. However, my screening setup is quite basic.

Several YouTubers in the writing space are quite savvy at streaming; I spoke to a few of them to ask them questions about their setup and how they stream. All of them pointed me to OBS, which is a free broadcasting software that is easy to use, but difficult to master.

I have the hardware I need; the software is free, but live streaming professionally requires some thought. First, I need an overlay. An overlay is a graphic that has your name, social media icons, a space for your webcam, and a space for any other items you want to share on your screen. In my case, I thought it would be nice to include a timer on the screen for people so that they know where we are in the writing sprint. I also thought it would be nice from time to time to have a space for sharing my screen in case I want to show my audience something.

It sounds like a relatively simple affair, but to do an overlay correctly, you need to have solid branding. Until now, I have not engaged in any branding for "Author Level Up." I have avoided commissioning a logo because I'm not prepared to go down that route yet. I should already have a logo, but it's not needed. If I were to do an overlay correctly, I would have a logo and branding already set. That's why I was a little hesitant to do this. However, I do need to improve my professionalism. I decided to commission an overlay anyway, with the understanding that I am going to have to do this again down the road once I get my branding affairs in order.

Why am I waiting on branding? First, I am in sore need of a new website. I plan on commissioning a logo in getting branding designed when I'm ready to build my new website. That might be at least one or two years from now.

Anyway, I spun my wheels a lot while thinking about improving my live streaming game. Probably too much. But there are always things you have to consider down the road. I should have my overlay situation resolved next quarter, and I look forward to sharing my audience feedback on how my new streaming setup looks.

SMALL JOB PROGRAMMERS

Programming costs are cheaper than you think. You can hire a programmer to solve quick problems for you on a site like Fiverr or Upwork.

Gig sites get a bad reputation, but I've been able to automate many areas of my business and obtain custom solutions to common author problems, all under $100.

I paid an Excel macro VBA programmer to create some difficult macros that I couldn't do myself. It cost me around $280 for a few different jobs. I also paid a developer to write a custom PowerShell script that I also needed for my sales database. That was $85. The result was that I was able to automate my entire sales calculation process, saving me at least four to five hours per month. The $368 I paid is pennies on the dollar compared to the time, money, and energy I got back. Plus, each job only took the programmer a couple of hours, if that.

Another time, I hired a small job programmer was to improve the performance of my website to meet Google standards.

For my editing analytics project that I'll discuss in the next chapter, I hired a programmer to create a custom Microsoft Word macro that helped me catch repeated words in all of their various tenses because this is a common issue I have when writing.

If you know when to engage them, programmers can help you with a lot of tasks. The key is understanding how the tools on your computer work.

Are you using your computer and your applications' full horsepower? The answer is probably not. But if you can unlock even just a few extra features, it's amazing what you can do.

ZOTERO FOR RESEARCH

My research process is clunky and I need a better tool to improve my productivity.

I realized this when I was researching *Dead Rat Walking*. I was using Evernote, whose Web Clipper is fantastic, but I found that organizing research leaves a lot to be desired.

I did some research and found a free app called Zotero, which is a Windows application that is designed for academics. It allows you to save content from the Internet, organize it, and prepare citations accordingly.

I played around with it and liked it. I'm not sure if it's "the" app for me, though.

It seems asinine to suggest that writers need an app for this. It's just not a priority, and the features of many writing apps such as Scrivener are just fine for most people. But I couldn't help but think there is probably a better way—at least for *me* to internally organize my material so that an app can help me store it.

Another thing about research is that you want to make sure you save your findings forever. You may never need them, but if you write a sequel ten years from now, you'll be glad you did. I'm not convinced Evernote will be around forever—it seems to be struggling financially these days and its app usability has declined in recent years. So I know that Evernote is not the answer.

I'll keep looking. But Zotero is worth checking out.

CUSTOMIZING MY NEWS FEED WITH AI

In the Ideas You Can Steal section, I write about an idea for a content curation service for writers using artificial intelligence.

Just for fun, I did some Internet research one evening to see if this type of product existed on the market and whether the technology existed for a layperson to curate content of their choosing.

The answer was not yet, but I did find an interesting way to use artificial intelligence to create a custom blog news feed.

It involved downloading an open-source AI kit, using Pocket (the feed reader service), and a willingness to train the AI by clicking on headlines that you wanted to read. If you did this enough, you would have a custom feed of your favorite blogs, based on articles you clicked on those blogs in the past. It was a crude proof of concept, but a decent one.

I can imagine a future where this type of curation is available for all entertainment mediums, driven entirely by the user. On the Internet, we *already* live in bubbles of our own choosing based on our preferences. It's only going to get worse, but there's a benefit to this too.

With all the noise out there, it can be hard to know what content to consume. For example, I listen to at least a dozen podcasts. I *want* to listen to every single episode and give it my full attention, but that's simply impossible. I would love a service that DJs the episodes for me, serves me segments it thinks I will like, and then I can choose what I listen to in full, if I listen to anything at all.

I imagine this with books too, beyond what Goodreads offers. However, the tech has to be easy for the end-user.

As I will discuss later in this book, the company that can solve the discoverability problem will win pretty much everything.

BECOME A DATA-DRIVEN WRITER

MORE EXCEL DATA TRICKS

The more I use Excel, the more I realize it has a marketing problem. It is hands-down the most powerful app ever created. I believe that Excel can help anyone live a better life by helping them make data-driven decisions, but Microsoft bungles this.

Let me give you an example. I've talked at length about how I created a sales database that gives me a nice and clean pivot table I can use to answer any question about my sales.

I track my yearly expenses in a separate spreadsheet (with a pivot table), and I've always thought it would be nice to (easily) track whether a book is profitable or not. In other words, did the book make more than I spent to produce it? This is difficult to do without data entry, and you know how much I hate data entry.

I discovered that Excel has a feature that allows you to tie the data in two or more different pivot tables together so that you can create one master pivot table that contains ALL of the data.

To keep this simple, this means that I can tie the data from both my sales reports and my expense reports into a single pivot table so I can answer the question "how profitable are my books?"

Pretty cool, right? You'd think this would be called "multi-pivot tables" or something easier to understand. Instead, Microsoft calls it a "data model." I can't think of a term that is more frightening to a non-data person like your average writer.

Anyway, I recognize that this chapter may not resonate with you. But know that Excel can do almost anything with data that your heart desires if you know how to speak its language.

AMAZON ALEXA FLASH BRIEFINGS: COLOSSAL FAILURE ON AMAZON'S PART

Amazon Echo devices have become increasingly pervasive in the United States and around the world.

I have several Amazon Alexa devices in my home. A couple of years ago, I thought that they would become all the rage. They have.

I also thought that a new feature that Amazon Alexa devices offered called flash briefings would also become popular. Flash briefings are like micro podcasts that your Amazon Echo device reads to you. My "Writing Tip of the Day" podcast was originally designed for Amazon flash briefings. Only at the last minute that I decide to syndicate the show to traditional podcast channels.

"Writing Tip of the Day" is almost 2 years old at the time of this writing, and it barely gets 100 listens across Amazon Alexa devices per month, despite flash briefings being a major selling point for Amazon Alexa app developers. By contrast, "Writing Tip of the Day" receives anywhere between 3,000 to 5,000 listens per month on traditional podcast channels. It's not even a contest.

Amazon doesn't promote its flash briefings. They don't give you any tools to advertise them. They aren't discoverable on the Amazon website unless you specifically search the flash briefing store. And most importantly, they don't give flash breathing listeners a good way to rate, review, or share shows that they like. In my opinion, this is a colossal failure on Amazon's part.

Will I stop doing flash briefings? No, because it doesn't take any extra effort. It's just an additional checkbox I select when I upload my audio, so it's not a big deal.

My "Writing Tip of the Day" podcast is the most rated and highly rated podcast on the Amazon flash briefing store in the United States with a whopping six reviews at the time of this writing. Globally, I probably have around 10 reviews. Every other show in my niche has less than that.

I hope that Amazon does something to revise its flash briefing format because it is an untapped opportunity.

URBAN FANTASY MEGA SURVEY

My friend and fellow urban fantasy author John P. Logsdon facilitated a mega urban fantasy reader survey where he and a team of urban fantasy authors asked many questions about reading habits.

(John, Ben Zackheim, and I created the Urban Fantasy and Paranormal Romance Book Database, which is also the best-kept secret in the urban fantasy genre. Just sayin'.)

The amount of data was staggering. Over 800 avid urban fantasy readers responded to the survey.

While I can't share the raw results publicly, I can share some of my key takeaways as it relates to a new urban fantasy series I'm writing.

Eight-hundred readers is still a small sample size in my opinion, and because these readers are primarily followers of self-published authors, there's a strong support of self-publishing that I don't believe would play out the same way if you had a full swath of the general urban fantasy readership. So while there are biases in the data, it's still helpful.

- Seventy-five percent of readers said that the gender of the main character did not impact their reading decision. That seems to suggest, despite female characters being most prominent in urban fantasy, that readers *will* read male-driven novels, and there's a market opportunity that hasn't borne itself out yet. (My new series follows a male hero.)

- Fifty percent preferred the first-person point of view, 34 percent preferred third-person, and 41 percent didn't care. (My series is written in the third-person, which puts it in the minority.)
- Ninety percent of applicants preferred stories with snarky humor. (My story is about a hero and his sister who have a snarky relationship.)
- Seventy percent of readers preferred romantic tension. (My Book 1 doesn't have a romance, but the main character has just endured a bad breakup and is dwelling on it.)
- Seventy-five percent said that they're always willing to try new authors. (My pen name is a new pen name.)
- Eighty-eight percent didn't care if a book was self-published. Two percent only preferred traditionally-published authors. Again, this data is highly biased in my opinion.
- The top three areas where readers find new authors were recommendations from another author, Freebooksy/Bargain Books, and Amazon Ads.
- Fifty-eight percent use Kindle Unlimited.
- Sixty-seven percent said that they'd only start a series if there are five or more books available in it.
- The majority of respondents indicated that the book description was the most important marketing material they reviewed first to evaluate a book, followed by the type of supernatural character, then the cover, then the book sample.
- Sixty-one percent do NOT listen to audiobooks.

While I admit to cherry-picking the data to use in this article, there wasn't anything in the survey results that put my current series off-market. In fact, my series should fit right in with reader expectations.

The data tells me that Kindle Unlimited is the right choice and that $2.99 is the right price point. It also tells me that audio isn't necessary until or unless the book starts selling well. Then audio is a smart move as more readers get used to the medium in the coming years.

The data also tells me to spend at least 80 percent of my packaging decisions on my book description, followed by the book cover. The book description is *that* important. That's also helpful data for Amazon Ads, because if an ad campaign isn't working, it will probably be because my book description isn't strong enough.

It's not always easy to glean data from readers, but I'll take all the data I can get.

BALANCING WORDS AND NUMBERS

I was in a meeting at work with an individual who bombed me with slide after slide full of numbers that had no context. I had to keep asking, "What does this mean?"

I was in another meeting shortly after that where another individual was presenting a business case for a project. I had to ask "What data do you have to support this case?" because the presentation was based on feelings and emotions, not actual market data.

Most writers are word people. The very thought of working with data numbers freaks them out. I know this because I use to be one of those people.

Some writers are numbers people. They can look at numbers all day. When it comes to logical arguments and craft, they're more comfortable retreating to their land of numbers.

The proper place to be is in the middle. Word-focused writers shouldn't be scared of data, but they shouldn't feel the need to be data experts either. Numbers-focused writers shouldn't be scared of the "wordy" parts of writing, but they shouldn't be compelled to be craft wizards.

Just rely on your strengths and seek a little bit of the ground that you're not familiar with.

SMARTPHONE APP DATA: AN UNTAPPED GOLD MINE?

I had a chat with a developer who was talking to me about his process for creating smartphone applications for iOS and Android. He is a developer by trade and has developed some successful apps, one that has over one million downloads.

He showed me what he was working on, which was a great app that helped writers in the writing process.

We started talking about the possibility of creating an app for my community, though nothing serious. Personally, it's not on my to-do list any time soon, but the developer was telling me how the data and analytics of apps are an untapped gold mine.

Essentially, he told me that I could monitor people's habits while using the app. For example, if I embedded my YouTube videos on the app, I could monitor how long they watched my videos, their demographics, and other quirky habits. That's potentially valuable information, though not for me right now.

That got me thinking about the merits of a smartphone app in general. Is it really to create value for your audience, or is it really for the data?

One of my objections against creating a smartphone app is that it's inconvenient. If I wanted to create an app that collected all of my podcasts, YouTube videos, and blogs, it's a lot to ask someone to download that app and use that exclusively. More than likely, they're going to want to listen to me on a podcast app where they do all of their other consumption. Same with YouTube. I worry about that with app development, especially when it comes to selling books directly.

So while that option is not for me right now, it's undeniable that there's a treasure trove of data there if I ever wanted to pursue it.

API ADVENTURES

I believe that application programming interfaces (APIs) are the future. I've discussed APIs in prior volumes of this series, but I'll give another refresher.

In my quest to understand APIs, I took a course on API basics. The instructor gave one of the best examples I've heard to explain an API in simple terms.

You're hungry. You have two options. You can make a delicious meal from scratch or you can go to a restaurant.

If you go to a restaurant, you simply order off the menu, and in a few minutes, a server brings your food.

APIs are like going to a restaurant. Like a restaurant, data that you obtain from an API is easier to obtain, made-to-order, and more convenient than if you created the data yourself.

The second analogy I've heard is that an API is like a plug and socket. The application is the plug, and the data is the socket. When they connect, you get electricity. I like the restaurant analogy better.

An API is how a developer plugs in to existing data.

For example, if you've ever used a social media app and found yourself wanting to use a GIF, you can click a button and access the entire library of a site like Giphy. You can even search for just the right GIF to use without leaving the social media site! That's an API at work. The social media site calls the GIF website, and you can navigate the GIFs (data) accordingly.

To give another example, I use a WordPress plugin that

connects to the YouTube API and lets me display all of my YouTube videos on my site. This updates automatically. Users can watch my videos without leaving my website, and I still get credit for it on YouTube. This is a nice convenience perk to make it easy for viewers of my website to engage with my content for the first time. That's another typical use of an API.

APIs allow for increased interactivity and functionality among applications.

They hold so much promise in many areas of the writing life. The biggest areas I have my eyes on in the publishing space are as follows.

Sales data. It doesn't make sense that authors have to download their sales data from a dashboard every month. Most authors are not Excel-savvy anyway and struggle to analyze their sales data in a meaningful way. If retailers offered APIs, a developer could create an app that pulled the authors' sales data into the application, manipulate and analyze it, and prepare nice charts so that it lifts the burden from the author.

Publishing and publishing updates. Why upload a book to a dashboard when you can just use an API? I foresee the writing apps of the future connecting directly with retailers so that you can write, collaborate with an editor, format, and publish, and maintain your books from the same interface. This will become increasingly more important the more "prolific" authors rise to prominence—authors with dozens if not hundreds of books. They won't have the time or the patience to manage books on a dashboard. They'll want to manage their intellectual property from one place.

Book monitoring. In addition to publishing and updating your books, an API relationship can also help you spot when something is wrong. Maybe you just finished a promotion and forgot to raise your price. Or maybe the HTML in your book description is broken. Or maybe you've published the wrong book! With retailer API access that monitors your metadata on an hourly or daily basis, a developer could create a solution that warns you anytime something is wrong. It could even warn you when your book is selling more than you expected!

App connectivity. APIs can also connect apps so that they can run synchronously. Imagine Vellum interfacing with Scrivener, for example. Or, if you wanted to integrate a special Internet dictionary with your writing app, the writing app could connect with the dictionary. Writing apps don't offer this kind of interfacing currently, but I believe they will.

Author-created APIs. Imagine that George R.R. Martin woke up one day and decided that he wanted to let people write fan fiction in the *Game of Thrones* universe. It's difficult to remember all the characters, history, spellings, and events that happened in the series, so he could create an API that interfaces with your writing app to give you editing assistance *in the moment* while you're writing instead of having to look it up in a wiki. Click an icon of the *Game of Thrones* logo on your writing app menu, search what you're looking for in a pop-up window, obtain the information you need, and keep writing. The interface could even offer spell-checking and basic fact-checking, scanning your manuscript for any misspellings or possible incorrect references to the *Game of Thrones* canon.

There are more creative uses too.

MORE LOVE FOR MICROSOFT WORD MACROS

In the last volume, I discussed a unique way to use Microsoft Word macros for my editing rules engine project. I described Microsoft Word macros as a sleepy, boring topic. More accurately, I said: "No one (except me) wakes up in the morning and says, 'I bet Microsoft Word macros can help me solve problems!' Nope. The very idea of Microsoft Word macros puts most writers to sleep. It's boring, too technical, and they can't see the benefit."

But I found another excellent way to use Microsoft Word macros to improve the accuracy of my dictation.

A major problem with Dragon is that it misunderstands proper nouns. You can teach it some words, but it still struggles if you don't say the word the same way every time.

Another issue with Dragon is that to get the best accuracy, you have to use it with Windows Notepad, which eliminates the ability to do any formatting.

Macros can help.

Every time I wrote during my initial warm-up sessions, I paid close attention to how Dragon printed the word. If the misprint was consistent, I added the word or phrase to a list. I then put that list into a find and replace macro in Microsoft Word. Once I was done dictating, I copied the text into Microsoft Word, where I would run the macro to fix any of the prior issues. Then I copied it into Scrivener, knowing that the text was as clean as I could make it.

I also used the macro to change the formatting of the text to play nicely upon pasting it into Scrivener.

Combine this macro with a rules engine and a good copyeditor and proofreader, and you have a recipe for insane daily word counts and a higher quality story with fewer errors.

IN PRAISE OF PAUL BEVERLEY

I wanted to use this chapter to make more people aware of Paul Beverley, who is, in my opinion, the pre-eminent world expert in Microsoft Word macros.

Paul is an editor in the United Kingdom who has created over 800 macros to assist editors in editing their clients' work.

I don't know any editors who use Word macros because, frankly, it's an acquired taste. However, Paul published a free book and dozens of videos on his website to help people understand why they are important. He also does training sessions. His macros are free.

While Paul's target audience is editors, there's no reason *writers* can't use his macros.

When I first discovered Paul's work a few years ago, I will admit that I couldn't "see" how macros could help me. I didn't even know what a macro was at the time.

It took a few years for things to "click," and now that they have, I believe that Paul is an underrated gift to the writing community.

Here are a few of his macros:

1. ProperNounAlyse produces a list of all the proper nouns in your story so you can tell if anything is accidentally misspelled.
2. HyphenAlyse scans your story for any words that should be hyphenated.

3. Duplicate Words highlights every instance of a duplicated word, such as "said said" or "she she."

4. Comments Exporter exports all of your editor's comments to a table so you can review them all together.

And more.

But perhaps the most powerful tool Paul created is a macro called FREdit.

FREdit is a scripted find and replace. Let's illustrate its usefulness with a common problem that Scrivener users have.

For some reason, Scrivener doesn't handle curly quotes consistently. Sometimes it puts the quotes facing the wrong way—especially if you use them after an em dash. It's maddening.

If you wanted to eliminate this problem manually, you could search for an em dash followed by an open quote, replace all with an em dash followed by a close quote.

Or you could load these characters into FREdit and it will catch them every time, along with any other error you want to catch.

Maybe your next book won't have the weird em dash issue. Then FREdit will simply skip it as if it didn't exist, and move on to the next issue.

So FREdit basically acts as a storage engine for your errors and flags them any time they show up in your writing.

I hope you can see now why this is so powerful, and why it is now an indispensable part of my workflow moving forward.

We have Paul Beverley to thank for his macro brilliance.

Check out his website at http://www.archivepub.co.uk/book.html.

THE RISE OF EDITING ANALYTICS

Sometimes I venture down rabbit holes that seem odd. If you made it this far reading this series, then you probably know what I am talking about.

The topic I'm going to explain next may seem like one of those rabbit holes, as the next several chapters explore different aspects of it. However, I want to reiterate my mission as a writer: to entertain my readers in the niches I write in, and to remain nimble in an ever-changing industry.

Everything I do daily is about adding value for my readers and removing roadblocks. The most obvious example of that is writing books and marketing, but that's not the only example. Improving your productivity means more books for your readers to enjoy. Managing your business expenses and streamlining them means more money in your pocket at the end of the year that you can reinvest back into your business, which helps readers. Unlocking data and analytics in your writing business means you can find ways to deliver better value to your readers and delight them more. Adopting emerging technology means that you can be there when readers' habits and preferences change, which they almost certainly will.

So everything I do as a writer, marketer, and business person, is about adding value for my readers.

I can think of no better way to add value for your readers than to learn how to tell better and cleaner stories. Readers love a book with minimal typos, but they also love a book that doesn't have plot holes or obvious craft errors. These are invisible expectations that they don't explicitly ask for, but if you don't deliver, they'll let you know all about it. Therefore, every writer has a vested interest in learning how to produce cleaner manuscripts consistently.

In the writing community, we're addicted to writing productivity. Everyone wants to know how to write faster. At the time of this writing, "word sprints" are popular—where people try to write as many words in a single session as possible while worrying about editing later. National Novel Writing Month (NaNoWriMo) is a challenge where writers all over the globe try to write a 50,000-word novel in November. Writers are adopting dictation at a rapid rate to speak their stories at higher word counts. The common advice is to release a new book every few months so readers don't forget about you. In short, everyone wants to know how to write like a machine and reap the benefits.

This isn't new. In the good old days, pulp writers made a living writing fast. There were pulp writers who wrote more in one month than some writers wrote in their lifetime. So the inner desire to write fast isn't a new phenomenon.

But what about writing fast *and* cleanly? In other words, just because you write 5,000 words per day, how clean is your manuscript when you send it to your editor?

In my opinion, editing quality is the other side of the equation. As a practical tip, I'm not a fan of writing fast and sloppy. I believe it's better to do it right the first time.

When you send your book to your editor, that's the ultimate test. It tests both your writing and self-editing skills.

If you write 5,000 words every day, that's great, but how many errors is your editor finding? If it's a lot, you might want to do something about that because it's probably costing you.

I'm not telling people to slow down. In fact, I think you should write as fast as your brain and fingers allow. Rather, I'm suggesting that it's worth it to take some time to think about how you can improve your self-editing so that you can send squeaky clean manuscripts to your editor.

The writers who write fast *and* ship clean manuscripts win. It's the pinnacle of efficiency. How good are you at both sides of the equation?

This has been on my mind a lot lately. I write quickly but find that my editor often corrects the same type of mistakes in my manuscripts. I do my best to avoid repeats, but I can't remember every single edit she recommends.

I want to avoid making repeat mistakes, as that would save my editor time, reduce my editing costs over time, and result in a better product for my readers.

In previous volumes in this series, I wrote about the concept of an "editing rules engine" and natural language processing artificial intelligence for writers, and how I believe these are viable solutions to easing the burden of self-editing while still producing a cleaner manuscript.

I believe that writers can use the power of data and analytics to help them write better stories. Your story is nothing more than a series of data points, and so are the edits your editor recommends. I believe that this data tells a story (but not of the fiction variety), and I believe there is a logical way to analyze it to gain insights into how you can become a better writer. I also believe you can approach this problem with technology and automation so that you don't have to do it manually (which would be too time-consuming).

I call this concept "editing analytics"—using data and analytics during the editorial process to help you improve your story.

Most people think of editing analytics in terms of statistics: your story has X adverbs, is X words long, and so on. I've never found that helpful because statistics don't help you tell better stories. Just because you have 100 adverbs in your manuscript doesn't mean readers will care. They probably won't. Same with your sentence length, or silly things like ending a sentence with a preposition. Fixing your book based on these types of "analytics" will hurt your story, not improve it.

Artificial intelligence programs such as Grammarly compare your work against the writing of millions of other users and make recommendations based on edits of other users' work. This is also not helpful. (Grammarly is a helpful service, but it can only help you find last-minute typos, not help you become a better storyteller.)

Editing analytics is about using analytics from YOUR work (and YOUR work only) to gain insights into how to become a better writer. It's about discovering errors that you shouldn't be making so you can prevent them in the future. It means looking back on the editing data of a few of your novels so that you can be more proactive.

(Developmental editing is out of scope here. We're talking strictly about copyediting and proofreading.)

As I said before, your book is full of data points that are untapped and underrated. To develop an editing analytics mindset, you need to think about your story as a series of data points, not a story. This seems counterintuitive, but it's similar to thinking about your book as a product. When you transition your thinking, you'll see opportunities where others see chunks of written words.

This quarter, I finally made significant progress toward creating a prototype for my editing rules engine. My 30th novel seemed like a good place to start; it's the first book in a brand new series and it's the first novel I wrote with mixed writing methods. I wrote it on my laptop, Scrivener iOS on my phone, via dictation while sitting down, standing up, on an exercise bike, and while doing chores. I also wrote the book quickly—in about 21 days. I amassed 61,000 words from a diverse array of methods, and I wanted to know how clean the manuscript was for my editor.

For example, dictation tends to be a sloppier writing method because programs like Dragon frequently misunderstand you. Might it be true that dictated sections in my novel trigger more edits from my editor? Would those edits be spelling and grammar-related, or story-related? Maybe it's true that dictation leads to more continuity-type errors. I don't know, but I can find out using editing analytics. It could also be true that dictating a chapter has no impact on the number of edits I receive.

Let's not forget that our books go through self-editing, and that muddies the data somewhat, but the question stands: how good is your writing and your self-editing, and can you improve them?

The key is to focus on *what* triggers edits. Maybe there's something you're doing unconsciously that your editor has to keep correcting. Maybe there are trends you can find in your manuscript by looking at your edits differently. You won't know until you dig deeper.

That's why I believe that editing analytics is an incredible opportunity because it can help you be a better version of yourself.

MORE PROGRESS TOWARD MY EDITING RULES ENGINE

I built a prototype of an editing engine to help me deliver cleaner manuscripts to my editor.

Here was my process before the pilot:

1. Write the book
2. Send the book to the editor
3. Receive edits back
4. Learn a few "takeaways"
5. Write the next book and hope that I didn't make the same errors

The result was I continued to make repeat mistakes, and I missed many of the lessons my editor caught in earlier books.

With the editing engine pilot, I added additional steps to the process:

1. Write the book
2. Send the book to the editor
3. Receive edits back
4. "Score" the manuscript to see how many edits I received and how many edits could have been prevented
5. Teach selected edits to the editing engine so that it can recognize them
6. Write the next book

7. Run the manuscript through the editing engine so it can identify similar mistakes that would have been "repeat" mistakes

8. Send a cleaner manuscript to my editor

The result is fewer repeat mistakes. It also saves my editor time and allows them to focus on other more important issues in the manuscript—issues that only an editor can find.

The first step in building the engine was to create a chapter-scoring engine.

When I look at an editor's edits, I want to know a few things:

- How many edits did they recommend (as tracked changes)?
- How many comments did the editor make on the manuscript?
- What is the breakdown of those edits (spelling and grammar versus continuity and story)?
- How many edits did I receive per chapter?

That's a basic picture that you can glean from your edited manuscript with the right tools. You can accomplish this in seconds with automation in Microsoft Word.

The real insights are at the chapter level.

I created a tool that I called a "chapter-scoring model." It sounds fancy, but it's simple: it looks at several data elements present in each chapter and then gives each chapter a score based on how well it underwent my editor's scrutiny.

The model is based on both objective and subjective factors. The data elements for the chapter scoring are:

The total number of spelling and grammar errors. These usually take the form of tracked changes on a Word document. These are the most important edits in the editing engine because you can teach the editing engine to spot them using code.

The total number of continuity and story-related edits. These usually take the form of comments in your Word document. Editors are usually hesitant to change a story issue, but they will point it out. Some comments, however, are spelling and grammar-related, so I filter out comments that don't meet these criteria. Also, I can't teach continuity edits to the editing engine. These are uniquely in the editor's territory.

The total number of spelling and grammar-related edits and continuity and story edits. This is perhaps the most telling number. A chapter with a higher number of total edits means it required more of the editor's attention, which is a bad sign. It's not all bad, though—you get good data and can learn a great deal!

The number of writing sessions per chapter. A chapter with a higher number of writing sessions may indicate more errors, especially if those sessions are spread out over several days. On the other hand, a chapter written in one session may not necessarily be better either.

Duration of chapter creation. If you start writing a chapter in January, suffer writer's block, and don't resume writing until March, that may indicate that more errors are present, especially of the continuity type, since it may take some time to remember the story.

Writing method. Some forms of writing are cleaner than others. Trust me, I would know. I find that text written by hand on my computer tends to be the cleanest, followed by text dictated while seated at my desk, followed by words written on my phone, and so on. Words I dictate using Dragon Anywhere always require the most corrections in self-editing.

Mood while writing the chapter. I believe mood is underrated. My theory is that if you feel good when you're writing, you'll produce fewer errors, but it could also be true in certain instances that being in a state of "flow" produces more errors because you're not thinking about spelling and grammar when you're getting the words down.

These components work together within the model. For the prototype, I gave them all equal weights.

The next step was to determine a baseline. Sure, I want to track the number of total edits, but what is "normal" for me?

Fortunately, I save all of my edited manuscripts and leave the edits untouched so I can refer to them later. I've done this with all 50+ books I've written because I knew they would come in handy one day.

Using a Microsoft Word add-in, I took my last five novels and counted the number of total edits and edits per chapter. This took about five minutes. My results were surprisingly consistent from book to book, even with different editors: between 275 and 400 total edits, with about 7 to 11 edits per chapter on average. I have no idea how that stacks up against other writers, but I can at least tell you that readers rarely complain about errors in my books.

Using my averages for each objective category, I used that to create a scoring system based on a five-point scale with the average in the middle.

For example, my average number of edits per chapter is nine. If I receive less than nine edits per chapter, that component scores more favorably. If I receive more, it scores worse. I performed a similar exercise with the other components so that every component has a score associated with it.

Then I simply created a spreadsheet to capture the data for each chapter with the scoring working behind the scenes.

The lower the score, the better. With a simple sort, I filtered the chapter scores to see how they ranked. I started with the chapters with the worst scores to see what the drivers were.

With one test chapter, I noticed that the number of edits was well over the average. In examining the chapter, I found that it was a fast-paced chapter. The editor made a lot of comments around continuity and paragraphing. I had a healthy amount of grammar errors too. While this is only one chapter, it could be an indicator that other fast-paced scenes may score similarly. If that's true, then I can start looking to the future by spending more time on these chapters when I self-edit my next novel to see if I can bring that number down. I might also want to bring this to my editor's attention. Therefore, the existence of a fast-paced scene becomes an indicator that I can also track at the chapter level. Not only do I have backward-looking data that tells me they're a problem, but I also have forward-looking insights that I can use to reduce my errors.

I also discovered that one particular error was showing up again and again in my chapters—repeated words within a small radius. For example, I used the word scream four times on one page, which was painfully obvious to my editor. I'll discuss how I tackled this problem in the next chapter.

But the scoring engine showed me a tremendous amount of insights, even with a limited demo that didn't utilize the entire engine. When it's time to send my 30th novel to my editor, I predict that it will teach me a lot. It will also test some assumptions I have, such as:

- Sections written while in a good mood generate fewer errors in editing.
- Writing on my phone doesn't produce any more noticeable errors in editing than writing on my laptop.
- There is a relationship between the number of spelling and grammar edits and the number of continuity edits in a chapter (I just don't know what they are).

Once I receive the manuscript back from my editor, I will score it using the methods I just described. Then I will review the spelling and grammar errors in each chapter to determine which ones could have been prevented if I could have taught them to the editing engine.

For example, I can solve the repeated word problem. That accounted for 12 errors in the first five chapters *alone*. That's an entire chapter's worth of edits! Imagine what your editor would say if they reviewed an entire chapter and found no errors...

Another example of an error that the engine can catch is a misused word. One time, I used the word "cadence" incorrectly when I should have used "interval" instead. I can teach the engine to search future manuscripts for every instance of "cadence," and if I use the word, generate a comment with a warning to check the usage of the word. The comment can even include the sentence I got wrong in a prior novel, just to show me how I screwed up in the past. Microsoft Word's Editor, Grammarly, or ProWritingAid can't catch these types of errors. I can do this with a Word macro (Word macros aren't so sleepy after all!) that can be written in just a few minutes. The macro code is identical for virtually any word I use incorrectly. I can also do this with hyphenated words, or words that should be hyphenated, and if the edit is black-and-white, I can have Word just find and replace the offending item. Any changes will show up as a tracked change!

Another common example that I mess up frequently is numbers. Any number under ten should be spelled, and any number over ten should be expressed as a numeral. Also, my editor recommends spelling out percent instead of using a symbol. I can program the macro to catch these types of errors.

These errors seem obvious, but you'd be surprised how easy it is to miss them. Programming them ensures that you will always catch them and that they never are a problem for you ever again. The more edits you teach the engine, the more comprehensive it gets.

Once I teach the editing engine a slew of edits from the editor's recommendations, I can count those edits, subtract them from the overall scoring, and then see how the chapters score. I can then express the difference as a percentage, and say with confidence that, for example, "If I had run the manuscript through my editing engine knowing what I know now, it would have resulted in a manuscript that had 16 percent fewer errors." That's powerful.

Then, with your next book, you can run the manuscript through a slightly modified version of the scoring engine, and, using indicators (like fast pacing) you can potentially *predict* which chapters will pose the most problems for your editor. If you wanted, you could flag those chapters for your editor as a heads-up.

In a sense, the scoring engine can become a predictive model, especially if you pair it with natural language processing. Using something like this with artificial intelligence would be like pouring gasoline on your analytics. My prototype only utilizes Word macros, but there's an entirely different universe of edits that would open up if I integrated this with natural language processing, namely the ability to catch more sophisticated errors that a macro can't catch, such as dropped articles, which are the bugbear of authors and editors everywhere.

There's so much to explore here.

In an earlier volume of this series, I wrote about a fictional app called Shapeshifter that will be the writing app of the future. Providing editing analytics in addition to writing analytics is one way that such an app can help writers become a better version of themselves.

ELIMINATING REPETITIVE WORDS FROM MY FICTION

My editor has to constantly correct a particularly pesky problem in my manuscripts: I repeat words too much within a short radius. For example, I used the word scream four times on one page and didn't realize it. My editor found other similar instances throughout the novel. Thank goodness she caught that!

That got me thinking about how I can prevent this problem in the future. For starters, no writing app or advanced spell-checking app I know of can catch this problem. Yet it feels like something that can be addressed programmatically. Your writing app can search for a word...why not create some additional logic around it?

I reviewed every instance in the manuscript where my editor pointed out repeating words, and I noticed that the repeated words always happened within a 100-word radius, usually between 5 and 25 words. The most extreme case was 81 words.

My gut told me that I was onto something, so I posted a job and had around a dozen or so developers look at a sample of my work, examining the problem.

Turns out that Microsoft Word macros can help me (again!)

I spoke with a developer who said that he could write a macro that would take the following steps:

- Analyze all words within a 100-word radius.
- Highlight every instance of any repeat words within the radius.

- Proceed to the next 100 words, and repeat.

The macro would sweep through the entire manuscript. The developer also promised to build me a filtering tool where I could add words I wanted to exclude, such as common words like prepositions, pronouns, dialogue tags, proper nouns, and so on. The only thing he couldn't help me with was perfect tenses of words, like break/broken. It would have been too difficult for him to program every word. I considered that to be a fair compromise.

A week later, the developer sent me a Microsoft Word user form macro that worked quite well.

The developer created a Word userform that allows me to add words to an exclusion list that I DON'T want to check for, as well as change the increment of the repeats. It also has a separate tab where it will show me a list of all the repeated words so I can easily determine if I need to add new words to the exclusion list.

When I run the macro, it highlights every instance of repeated words, using colors to help me identify frequency.

I can look at a page and tell instantly by color where the repeats are. I'll admit that it took some getting used to, but I adjusted to it quickly.

In reviewing Dead Rat Walking, I found at least 100 instances of often-repeated words that needed to be fixed. Leaving them would have presented poorly. I'll let that number sink in…

For example, I used the word "water" seven times on one page. Not only would ebook and print readers have noticed, but it also would have sounded terrible in the audiobook edition! I found a way to cut my usage of "water" down to around three times.

I also discovered words that I repeat regularly. So many of my repeats were "face", "ground", "up", "down", "dark", and so on. I would say that around 80% of the issues I caught involved the same words. That's insightful because I can now create a separate macro that looks for overused words and highlights them separately so I can view them in isolation. That would allow me to add them to the exclusion list on the repeated word macro so I can focus on the uncommon repeats. Over time, I'll keep refining this so that it becomes stronger.

It took me around six hours to sweep my manuscript for repeated word issues, and I caught a lot of them. But I probably missed some, and that's okay.

It's also worth noting that sometimes repeating a word makes sense and it's the only option. I didn't replace every single repeat—that would have been silly. I merely looked for ways to say the same thing a little differently so that it wouldn't trigger the reader to say "he just repeated that word five times in a sentence." The edits were minor, and even subliminal at best.

Anyway, this was a huge success, and one of the more effective parts of my new editing workflow.

APPLYING EDITING ANALYTICS TO MY NOVEL

Since I've spent a lot of time in this volume covering the editing analytics project, I figured it would be a good idea to share some early results.

I'd like to share the results from all the chapters above.

TRACKING MY EDITS

I keep all of my editing documents, so I reviewed my last five novels and categorized the edits. I used macros to count how many edits I received, which gave me:

- The average number of total edits (spelling+story). My average is 290 edits per novel.
- The approximate number of total edits per chapter. My average is 8.5 edits per chapter (based on 50K).
- This is approximately one edit per 177 words for an average of novels that are 50,000 words. Ideally, you want this number to be as high as possible.

And yes, I'm sharing these numbers out of transparency. No idea how I stack up to other writers, but you can certainly compare your numbers to mine.

Anyway, these numbers became my baseline.

Then I went through each novel, looking for anything I could teach to my macro set. This took me about two hours, and I found approximately 150 items that I could train the engine to catch reliably.

I ran the manuscript for *Dead Rat Walking* through the workflow to test everything.

THE NUMBERS

In two minutes...

The workflow caught 178 errors.

I accepted 166 of those errors. Sometimes the engine isn't always right. Still, 166/178 is a 93 percent success rate.

(The errors that I accepted were all, without exception, items that my editor would have corrected. This isn't theory. It's practical.)

Since Word counts double when counting many tracked changes (due to insertions and deletions), I divided this number by half to get the closest approximate number of "actual" edits, which was 83.

The engine also caught seven additional duplicate words that did not show up as tracked changes.

The engine also caught seven errors that Word likely would have captured if I had spell-checked the document prior. I did not, mainly because I was curious how much Word's spell-checker would contribute to the errors caught.

I also caught two errors by eye as I was glancing through the manuscript.

That brings the total number of errors to 99.

99 errors / 38 chapters = approximately 2.36 errors per chapter

Word caught 7 out of 99 errors, which is seven percent of the overall total. So if you ever wanted to quantify how much Word contributes to a book's manuscript quality, that's how you do it.

A seven-percent error capture makes Word spell-checker essential in my opinion.

PRETEND WITH ME FOR A MOMENT

If my editor usually catches an average of 290 total edits per novel, and I captured 99 of those edits before I sent my novel to her, that means the engine (probably) reduced my total edits by 34 percent.

If my editor usually catches an average of 8.5 edits per chapter, and the engine catches an average of 2.36 (spelling and grammar) edits per chapter, I reduced the number of edits per chapter by 25 percent.

The reduction numbers get even better when you consider that the numbers I tracked include both spelling and story errors. If you look at just the spelling/grammar edits by themselves (which I didn't do due to time), it's an even more drastic reduction.

Also, the repeated word part of the workflow isn't turned on yet, so that will account for more errors caught next time.

And Grammarly and ProWritingAid both would each catch somewhere between 6-12 errors if I had used them. So I could have been looking at 120-130 actual errors caught, and that's on the conservative side.

The more errors I take off my editor's plate, the more she can focus on other things that may be hiding in plain sight. In other words, the more errors I find ahead of time, the more errors she can find after the fact because they'll "stick out" more.

As you can see, this starts adding up in a very big way. All with free tools, just a little bit of programming costs (my choice), and an understanding how to use the full horsepower of the technology that's already on your computer.

BECOME THE WRITER OF
THE FUTURE

PICK TWO SKILLS TO MASTER

My first real job was as a proposal development specialist at a web development company. This was in 2007 when businesses finally realized that they needed websites. I'd accompany the CEO to meetings with local businesses, listen to small business owners describe their business needs, and then I'd prepare a proposal that included a timeline and a price.

As we prepared for a meeting one day, the CEO said something once that was groundbreaking to me at the time: "The client can choose between speed, quality, and price, but they can only pick two."

Of course, this is a mantra in business, but I had never heard it before.

Speed.

Quality.

Price.

Clients could buy a cheap website that we developed quickly, but the quality would be lacking.

Or they could buy a high-quality website that we'd develop quickly, but it would cost them.

What does this have to do with writing? Nothing at all. But it has everything to do with being a writer.

In the first *Kingdom Hearts* video game, the main character, Sora, has to pick two skills that he will master in battle throughout the game. He has three choices: strength, magic, and defense.

He can master strength and magic, but he'll have bad defense, leaving him open to higher damage from enemies.

He can master magic and defense, but his strength will be lacking.

Or he can master strength and defense, but he'll never be good at magic.

This is a similar metaphor to the speed, price, and quality choice. I believe it applies to being a writer.

Writing.

Marketing.

Business.

Pick two. Or rather—figure out which two you're inherently good at.

Whichever two you pick, you'll always trail behind with the one you don't choose.

For me, I'm a decent writer and I understand business. But marketing has always been my Achilles' heel.

Some writers are great at marketing and business, but their writing needs help. Others are great at writing and marketing, but they have no business skills and do things like sign terrible contracts or burn through their money.

It's up to you to figure out what your top two skills are. You may never master the third, but you can improve your proficiency in it over time.

FACING SELF-DOUBT: THE ONLY BATTLE THAT MATTERS

I receive emails from writers weekly who battle with self-doubt.

They are afraid of starting their books, or they can't seem to finish.

Many of them are quite successful people. Executives, entrepreneurs, or people who have a lot of experience in an industry.

Yet when it comes to writing a novel, they freeze up.

In their personal or professional lives, they would have no problem conquering an issue. They wouldn't hesitate to make a decision. If something needs to be done, they do it.

But in the world of a writer...

It's a big problem. I've dealt with self-doubt too. The only way I escaped it for good was having a near-death experience (which I don't recommend).

The answer to the problem is so simple yet so hard for most people: keep going. Self-doubt tries to fool you into thinking that you can't finish your book, or that you're a terrible writer. The thing about self-doubt is that while its *words* are sharp, it can't take any *action* against you. Its power comes from its words, but when you decide that its words have no power over you, it can do nothing. Then it gets *really* scared and says even more horrible things to you. It'll dig deep into your childhood and fling insults at your like you've never heard before. That's because it's scared. When you turn it into a cornered animal, it will lash out.

And then, in that moment, when you stand firm in your

decision that its words have no power over you, you win. Self-doubt will evolve to challenge you again, but the matter of you becoming a writer is settled. If you can get that far, things become easier. Not "easy street" by any means, but easier.

If you want to become the writer of the future, you have to become a writer. Winning the war against self-doubt is what separates long-time professionals from amateurs.

WHY CHASING NOTORIETY LEADS TO DESTRUCTION

I read a depressing article on Slate about women and the notability problem on Wikipedia. I didn't know that a supermajority of articles on Wikipedia is about men. The Wikipedia community has strict guidelines on who receives coverage on the website, requiring sources that imply "notability," like newspaper articles, magazine articles, and prestigious awards. Because women don't get their fair share of coverage and recognition in these places, they don't receive nearly as many articles on Wikipedia, even though they are just as deserving if not more than many of their male counterparts.

What was particularly depressing about this article is that Wikipedia doesn't seem interested in making any changes to their guidelines. How many times a week does the average person use Wikipedia and not even know about the website's blatant bias against women? People of color? Other minorities?

This got me thinking about how authors chase notoriety and how it's a futile effort.

So many authors want prestigious awards, coverage on television, newspaper mentions, and other traditional media outlet spotlights. They believe that this coverage is critical, and it becomes a barometer for how successful they are.

Who doesn't dream of having their own Wikipedia page? There used to be a seedy group of individuals on a social media group who conspired to get each other Wikipedia coverage.

Sometimes it worked, and sometimes it backfired. But getting a Wikipedia page was so important to these people that they were willing to bend ethical rules to get it. I always thought it was pointless.

Self-published writers are the opposite of "notable" in the mainstream sense of the word. Traditional publishers scoff at our existence. The newspapers that do cover us generally aren't friendly. Don't even think about television or cable news coverage. The authors who infiltrate these media outlets are usually disappointed. Yet despite this, legions of authors still think that traditional media is required to legitimize their careers.

If you can't get a Wikipedia page, how the heck are you going to get coverage in traditional media?

This is why I say that chasing notoriety (or, rather, notability) is a fool's errand. Be careful what you wish for because you just might get it.

The article reinforced one of my core beliefs, which is to focus on myself and what I can accomplish. If that happens to attract traditional media, so be it. But you can live a great life and have a wonderful writing career without ever being featured in a newspaper. And you can sell a lot of books without some big-name critic gushing about your book.

AMAZON AND RETAILERS ARE NOT EVOLVING

Self-published authors are becoming more sophisticated every day. Many have transitioned into publishers and packagers of content, publishing the works of other authors. Other authors have become so successful that they are running full-time businesses with employees.

Amazon and other retailers are still treating authors like they did in 2010, with the assumption that an individual account is sufficient for most authors' needs.

I've struggled to understand why retailers don't allow authors to delegate access to their dashboards. Retailers should allow only authors to access their account and financial information, but designate access to other individuals who can assist them in managing their books, with the ability to review and approve actions and even revoke access immediately if needed.

Long-term, I'd like the ability for an assistant to review my books to make sure nothing is amiss, and I'd even like to grant them access to sales data *without* granting them access to my bank data, for example.

For an author who runs a full-time business where an assistant helps them with day-to-day operations, this would be a godsend. It would also be a godsend for a place like Amazon Ads, where an author could grant access to a marketer who can manage ad campaigns. Yet none of this is possible today, and it doesn't seem to be on the horizon any time soon.

If more than one person signs in to an author's account, it will flag security algorithms, so even if you can manage it, it's a dangerous proposition that can get your account canceled.

As we move into a future where authors are becoming more sophisticated and successful, I'd like to see retailers evolve too. I would be fine with paying for these features if that's what it took.

THE POWER OF PICKING THE RIGHT PEOPLE

So much in life boils down to picking the right people.

In the writing life, this means hiring the right editor and cover designer. "Right" is subjective, but for me, the right person does what they say they are going to do when they say they are going to do it, gives you a quality product that indicates they treated your work with care, and they offer a drama-free experience. I have zero patience for drama.

For my latest novel, I hired fact-checkers to assist me in validating the research for my book. I needed to fill six positions and posted them on Upwork. Within hours, I had dozens of proposals, far more people than I could hire!

As a former hiring manager at work who was responsible for hiring and firing people, with a pretty good track record of hiring good talent, I am methodical and ruthless in my hiring process. I weed out candidates quickly.

I had three jobs:

- two fact-checkers to review the Chicago scenes in my story
- two fact-checkers to review the rodent biology in the story (the novel features rats prominently)
- two female readers to read chapters with the hero's sister to verify how well the female readers will respond to her

Here are my criteria for any job:

1. Does the person have the skills to do the job?
2. Does the person have the will to do the job? In other words, what signals show me that they want it?
3. Are there any red flags?

For the Chicago fact-checkers, I had two requirements:

*   The person needs to either live in Chicago or have lived there for a long time, preferably with knowledge of the Logan Square neighborhood.
*   They had to describe their Chicago background.

Without exception, almost all of the applicants were Chicagoans or people who lived there for at least five years or more.

As I reviewed their proposals about their qualifications and why they wanted the job, I paid careful attention to:

*   Red flags in their responses. I looked for anything that seemed odd. With a platform like Upwork, sometimes people will say anything to get a job. Sometimes they even post stock language to every proposal. Those people always receive hard no's from me. Once you weed those people out, you usually have a lot of good people left.
*   Their enthusiasm. A lot of freelancers found the job intriguing and unusual compared to their usual gigs. One freelancer even offered to visit locations in-person and take photos and videos of the areas so that I could make the writing even more realistic. I like to reward genuine enthusiasm.

- Their track records on the platform. Anyone with a history of bad performance received additional scrutiny. Is the bad performance something they did or did they catch a bad break with a crazy client? There are lots of crazy clients out there—I know that first-hand, so I have some sympathy. First-time freelancers were acceptable.

Ultimately, I selected a Chicago native who lived on the south side his entire life and a northwest-sider who lived in Logan Square for a long time. Both met the deadline, offered detailed feedback, and gave me exactly what I needed. No hassles and no drama.

My rodent biology job was tougher. I needed someone who had a biology degree or who had extensive experience working with rats.

I received proposals from people on the platform who were qualified—a fair number of doctors and seasoned biologists. One candidate worked in pest control. However, the struggle was finding someone who I thought could convey biological details to me in a format I could understand, and who would give me information that I could use in the story. There was also a language barrier with some candidates. I only hired one person who met my criteria, and he was one of the more unusual candidates who, on paper, didn't meet my criteria. He didn't have a biology degree; however, he went to school for biology and worked with rats for a long time but decided he wanted to do something different with his career. He did editing on the side. He ended up being the perfect candidate because he gave me scientific details but in a format I could use.

I found the other fact checker elsewhere. I prefer not to settle when hiring people. Settling always leads to trouble.

The female beta readers also went smoothly. I was looking for:

- a female who had a younger brother
- who could give me feedback on whether the female character in my story was believable or not.

I ultimately selected two candidates who told me stories about their relationship with their brother that were most like the relationship in my novel. One delivered me good, detailed feedback. The other ghosted me after I hired her, so that was a pain. I hired my third choice, who delivered good feedback in a couple of days.

Sometimes you hire bad fits. Sometimes you should have seen the red flags earlier; other times, there's no way you could have known the person would be a bad fit. That's what happens when you engage with so many random people. Sometimes you pick 'em wrong. That's just how it goes.

But when you pick the right people for projects, it makes the projects go smoother. You also do a service to your readers because you make their experience more enjoyable, especially in the case of editing.

LESSONS LEARNED AFTER 50 BOOKS

I recently celebrated publishing my 50th book and 30th novel. That got me thinking about lessons I've learned since I wrote my first book back in 2013.

I thought it would be fun to share 50 lessons, one learned from each of my first 50 books.

Lesson #1: *How to Be Bad/Magic Souls.* Success didn't come as early as I thought it would. It still hasn't come. I thought I was going to be a bestseller by the end of my first year. Thank God I didn't because I would have made egghead mistakes.

Lesson #2: *Reconciled People.* Some books just can't be improved upon. This short story collection is routinely at the bottom of my book sales each year. I've revived sales somewhat with Amazon Ads, but the book is what it is, and for what it is— a literary short story collection—it's a good testament to my storytelling skill at the time I wrote it. Sometimes books are your own personal monuments.

Lesson #3: *Theo and the Festival of Shadows.* This novel taught me how to be more strategic with my spending. After hearing a podcast interview with a successful self-published author, I thought it would be a good idea to purchase several hundred dollars' worth of book promotion ads to improve my book sales. Never mind the fact that the book was selling maybe one copy per week. I lost all of that money. I sold around 85 copies of the book at 99 cents, resulting in a whopping $29.75. I only received a small number of reviews from the campaign too. It was one of my biggest early failures, and hard to justify losing that kind of money with a baby on the way.

Lesson #4: *Callback from the Muse/Muse Poems*. My first poetry collection. These poems are my earliest published writing, written between 2009 and 2010; I wrote this collection for my senior project to complete my English degree. I received an A on the project and graduated with honors. That said, self-publishing a poetry collection was unusual in 2014 and ahead of its time. However, publishing this collection was a lesson in repurposing content. Since I had already written the poems, it cost me nothing to compile them because they were already edited. I bought a premade cover for $40, and it was an easy way to add another title to my name. Even to this day, I'm always thinking about how I can repackage content to add value to my readers.

Lesson #5: *Eaten: Season 1/Food City*. This is probably the novel that defined my early career. It was about a group of terrorist vegetables attempting to take down an empire of processed foods. That sentence alone turns heads and raises eyebrows, but the book cover was godawful. I don't blame the designer; it was entirely my fault because I confused him. I didn't understand what genre the book was in, and I didn't understand what made a good book cover. I micromanaged the design too. The result was a confusing mess that became a black eye on my author brand for a long time. The unfortunate part is that the story itself was well-received. But the idea was so unusual that readers didn't take a chance on it. This book taught me what it feels like when you utterly and completely fail at your marketing.

Lesson #6: *The Indie Author State of the Union (2014 edition)*. This was my first nonfiction book and a spiritual precursor to the *Indie Author Confidential* series. Every week, I saved the top news articles from the self-publishing community, summarized them, and offered my opinions on them. I compiled those opinions in this book. It was my way of learning about the industry because it forced me to pay attention to publishing industry news. The book sold almost no copies, but it helped me learn rapidly.

Lesson #7: *Eaten: Season 2/Salad Days*. Because of the cover conundrum with Book 1, I tried to salvage the situation by designing my own cover. Ironically, my poorly designed cover was light-years better than the professional one I paid for, but the series still sold no copies. The book taught me that I have no business designing my own covers, but that one day I might have to.

Lesson #8: *Nutrizeen*. This was a novella in the *Eaten/Moderation Online* universe, told from the perspective of one of the main characters, a milkshake scientist named Geoffrey Foster who is the architect of the processed foods' empire and cruelty toward vegetables. He has an awakening and flees with his children to become a good guy and start a new life. The story is told as an autobiography. While I enjoyed writing it, *Nutrizeen* helped me uncover all sorts of world-building problems with *Eaten/Moderation Online* that I had to go back and fix. I unpublished the book because it raised more questions than it answered. This is only one of two books I've ever unpublished. I swore that I would never make such egregious world-building mistakes again, a lesson I carried into my next series, *The Last Dragon Lord*.

Lesson #9: *Indie Poet Rock Star*. This was my first "thought leadership" book. After self-publishing my own poetry collection, I wondered why more poets didn't do the same. I looked across the industry and predicted that within five to seven years, they would. I wrote a manifesto on why poets should consider self-publishing, how to do it, and how to build websites and market their work. Seven years later, many of the predictions I made in *Indie Poet Rock Star* came true. Self-published poetry is mainstream now, with traditional publishers trying to imitate the self-published look. *Indie Poet Rock Star* also landed me on the radar of Orna Ross, founder of The Alliance of Independent

Authors (ALLi), which was an important connection for me.

Lesson #10: *Android Paradox*. This was my first taste of success. I managed to tell a fun, fast-paced science fiction story about an android and his human engineer. *Android Paradox* sold a decent amount of copies in the first year, and the audiobook version was also well-received—my first fiction audiobook. The book taught me the value of tapping in to your readers to figure out what they want.

Lesson #11: *Android Deception*. This was the first sequel I ever wrote, and my first taste of what writing a series felt like.

Lesson #12: *Android Winter*. This was the first Book 3 I ever wrote, and the conclusion to my first series. Much like *Android Deception*, I learned how to write a series with this book.

Lesson #13: *Indie Poet Formatting*. This book is a companion to *Indie Poet Rock Star*, and it teaches poets how to format poetry collections for ebook and print using Scrivener. To write this book, I had to become a book-formatting expert. I credit this book with teaching me many advanced formatting lessons that I would carry with me throughout my career.

Lesson #14: *Interactive Fiction*. This book teaches writers how to write interactive novels in my unique style. I wrote it primarily to catalog my thoughts and preserve my process. I also credit this with being the only book to date that lost me a writer friend. A fellow writer took something I said in the book personally, even though I wasn't writing about them. I learned that the words I write have power—and sometimes your words can alienate people, even though that's not your intention.

Lesson #15: *The Indie Author State of the Union (2015 edition)*. The second book in the series. It taught me how to prepare for releasing a book at the same time every year. I launched both books in this series in December.

Lesson #16: *Old Dark (The Last Dragon Lord, Book 1)*. *Old Dark* was a unique idea—the story of a bloodthirsty dragon lord who survives an assassination attempt and wakes up 1,000 years later in a future ruled by his enemies. It was also the first book that I learned to write without an outline, using Dean Wesley Smith's writing into the dark method. It was also the first novel I wrote almost exclusively using dictation and writing on my phone. I relearned how to write while writing this novel, and it paid off in a big way. It taught me that no matter *how* you write a story, readers will buy it if it's engaging. Once I wrote "The End" on this novel, I was never the same—my writer's brain was completely broken and I was hooked on dictation and writing on my phone. *Old Dark* was also the first novel where I hired a cover designer to create unified branding for all my novels moving forward, which was a big step in the right direction for my author brand.

Lesson #17: *Old Evil (The Last Dragon Lord, Book 2).* After I wrote this novel, I broke the news to my editor at the time that I used dictation and writing on my phone. She didn't believe me at first because the story was just as clean as what I usually sent her when I typed by hand. That taught me that it doesn't matter how you get the words down—if you self-edit and hire the right editors, readers won't know the difference.

Lesson #18: *Old Wicked (The Last Dragon Lord, Book 3).* Finishing this series validated that I learned my lesson from *Nutrizeen* by creating a successful fantasy world that felt real. I used many techniques from *Nutrizeen* in the entire Last Dragon Lord series, culminating in *Old Wicked.*

Lesson #19: *Death Marked (Modern Necromancy, Book 1).* This was the first book in a series I co-wrote with my friend Justin Sloan. Just co-writing a novel in and of itself successfully is an important lesson in coordination, communication, copyright, and contracts.

Lesson #20: *Death Bound.* The first time I wrote a love interest in a story, including a kiss. Actually, Justin wrote most of it—but I learned a crash course in writing a little romance!

Lesson #21: *Death Crowned.* The lesson we learned in this book was that if your cover designer uses stock photography, to make sure that they have enough images of the model to sustain your series. My designer gave us a great cover for Book 1 and 2, but when we got to Book 3, she had to use a different model for the hero. It's very noticeable. That experience taught me to be more involved when the designer is scouting models ahead of time.

Lesson #22: *Android Poems.* My second poetry collection. I submitted all the poems to literary magazines, and one of them was published, netting me a modest payment. That process taught me how to submit my work to literary magazines like a pro.

Lesson #23: *Honor's Reserve (Galaxy Mavericks, Book 1).* Oh boy, where do start? The *Galaxy Mavericks* series is a multicultural space opera, with the first seven books following a new main character. This book was the first book in the series, about a member of a force called The Galactic Guard. The hero rescues people who are stranded in space. I had never written space opera before. While I had a basic understanding of astrophysics, I had a lot to learn. I did extensive research in this book: astrophysics in particular. I also researched the United States Coast Guard because they inspired the armed forces in the book. I hired a fact-checker who was a career Coast Guard member, and the Coast Guard-inspired sections passed muster. However, my astrophysics did not. Readers ripped the book apart for this reason. While *Honor's Reserve* was as good a story as I had written up until that point, the science was so bad that readers put it down. I was always a little embarrassed by the book until I finally worked up the courage to hire an astrophysicist, who read the book and validated my worst fears. It wasn't all bad, though: I realized that if I had hired him (as a fact-checker) before I published the book, *Honor's Reserve* probably would have done pretty well. It's something I plan to do for the entire *Galaxy Mavericks* series. I always felt like

I never gave it a fair shot. *Honor's Reserve* taught me the importance of fact-checkers, a lesson that I was finally able to master with *Dead Rat Walking*, which I have discussed extensively in this book.

Lesson #24: *Phantom Planet (Galaxy Mavericks, Book 2)*. This is the second book in the series, but I wrote it first. *Galaxy Mavericks* is the first series that I wrote out of order. Out of nine books, this is the order I wrote it: 2,1,4,3,5,6,7,8,9.

Lesson #25: *Zero Magnitude (Galaxy Mavericks, Book 3)*. Once in a dozen novels or so, you stumble across a book that flows off your fingers so well, it seems like it came from heaven. In a surprising bout of inspiration, I wrote *Zero Magnitude* in seven days. It holds the record for the fastest novel I've ever written.

Lesson #26: *Garbage Star (Galaxy Mavericks, Book 4)*. Another book with an interesting concept, but bad science. It's unfortunate because this novel explores new territory that I hadn't written to date—the dynamics of a multi-generational family.

Lesson #27: *Solar Storm (Galaxy Mavericks, Book 5)*. I wrote this book backward just to see if I could do it. The book begins in the present, but each chapter steps back in time so you see the making of and unraveling of the hero, who is a cyborg antihero. The reader experiences the story backward, even though they are reading the book forward, if that makes sense. I wrote this book front to back too, so I had no idea what would happen as I went back in time. An all-around fun novel that ends in a way I didn't expect. It taught me the importance of having fun with your writing. *Solar Storm* was also my 20th novel.

Lesson #28: *Rogue Colony (Galaxy Mavericks, Book 6)*. A novel with a sympathetic heroine who could have benefited from having her book be earlier in the series. That's one of the downsides to writing into the dark with a series this big that follows multiple characters. I have since learned how to manage this better.

Lesson #29: *Orbital Decay (Galaxy Mavericks, Book 7)*. A main storyline told through the perspective of the series villain. The novel taught me a lot about writing villains.

Lesson #30: *Planet Eaters (Galaxy Mavericks, Book 9)*. This is the book where the six heroes finally band together to fight the series villain. The book was a masterclass in joining seven storylines together without continuity issues. I aimed high with *Planet Eaters*, and whether I succeeded or not, I learned how to deal with little issues that make a big difference in the story, such as switching point of views, when to use certain point of views, and how to keep all the main characters top-of-mind. The book was a juggling act, and in some respects, one of the most difficult novels I've written.

Lesson #31: *Horizon Down (Galaxy Mavericks, Book 9)*. The final book in the *Galaxy Mavericks* series, and the final nail in the coffin of a series that was doomed from the start. I wrote nine books in the series, only to ever sell a few dozen of the first three books. I believed in the series idea, and I don't regret writing it, but I made so many tactical errors. It taught me that I had so much more to learn and experience as a self-published writer. I frequently call *Galaxy Mavericks* the nadir of my fiction career. Nothing I ever wrote has been worse in execution. However, the lessons I learned from this series are a multitude that is hard to articulate. I wrote this series in nine months, which took the better part of a year, but by most accounts, that's incredibly fast. I also managed to secure cover designs for all the books in that period, which was also a major feat given how long it takes to get on a designer's calendar. The entire series was a masterclass in learning how to be efficient as an author. This was also the first series I formatted in Vellum, making my paperbacks more professional. After experiencing so much success with *The Last Dragon Lord*, this series taught me how nothing is guaranteed, and that every novel you write is a clean slate, for better or worse. Also, this series bumped me into the 30+ book club. The covers benefited from the unified branding that I established with *The Last Dragon Lord* series, and for the first time, my books finally had cohesion and my portfolio started to look good visually. The designer who did the covers for this series redesigned many of my earlier covers as well. Overall, the several thousand dollars' worth of "tuition" I paid to publish this series helped me mature as a self-published writer.

Lesson #32: *Be a Writing Machine.* The book that changed my career in so many ways, which was such a stark contrast after *Galaxy Mavericks.* This book is my process of writing fast and being efficient as an author. I learned that people love hearing about writers' processes and their personal experience. I never thought in a million years that people would buy the book, but it became a sleeper hit.

Lesson #33: *Dream Born (Magic Trackers, Book 1).* My first foray into urban fantasy, and a more down-to-earth, traditional series that followed one point of view. This series made a big statement by putting a black woman on the cover—something I had not seen on fantasy book covers until then. Now it's a lot more common. Story-wise, *Dream Born* is what you'd expect from an urban fantasy, and it taught me a lot about the urban fantasy genre, which I came to like a lot, so much that I decided to keep writing in it moving forward. However, there was a lot about the genre that I missed—if I had set the novel in a real city, it might have done better. Instead, the city was loosely inspired by Chicago. I learned that urban fantasy readers prefer real cities.

Lesson #33: *Nightmare Stalkers (Magic Trackers, Book 2).* Another "once in a dozen" novel. I wrote this book in eight days, and it was the most fun I've ever had writing a novel.

Lesson #34: *Evil Waking (Magic Trackers, Book 3).* This is the only book I've written that addresses racism. I don't think I did it justice, but it was the first time I wrestled with it directly on the page. I learned that it's not easy.

Lesson #35: *How to Write Your First Novel.* I did extensive market research for this book to figure out how to position it. I read a lot of comparable books and dissected what I thought made them successful, and what they might have been able to do better. This reverse-engineering process worked quite well, and it served as the basis for how I decide to write my writing self-help books.

Lesson #36: *Shadow Deal (The Good Necromancer, Book 1).* My attempt at "writing to market" but in my own way. I wrote this book in public, sharing my progress every day in a free course. I also shared my process of research, writing, self-editing, hiring alpha readers, editors, cover designers, and even marketing. This is also the only book where I completely wrote "what I knew." It takes place in my hometown of St. Louis, Missouri, in a neighborhood I spent a lot of time in, and with characters inspired by family members and friends. *Shadow Deal* is a different kind of story in that regard, but I built on several lessons I learned while writing the *Magic Trackers* series, namely how to give my hero a distinct voice and how to portray black characters on the page.

Lesson #37: *Mental Models for Writers.* Another flex in thought leadership. I used the market research techniques I used with *How to Write Your First Novel,* adapting the "mental model" theme for writers. This book landed me on "The Creative Penn" podcast with Joanna Penn a second time. I explore *a lot* of ideas in this book.

Lesson #38: *The Indie Writer's Encyclopedia.* I learned that you can write an encyclopedia/dictionary hybrid and it will sell. I'm still shocked when someone buys a copy. It aims to teach writers all the terms they need to know to be a successful writer. This book is uniquely suited to my personality, which is why it worked. It taught me the value of doubling down on your personality.

Lesson #39: *The Writer's Craft Playbook, Volume 1.* Another thought-leadership book, and my first successful lead magnet for my writing books, after many attempts. This book taught me how to write a good lead magnet and dramatically increased my email list.

Lesson #40: *150 Self-Publishing Questions Answered.* I wrote this book with The Alliance of Independent Authors (ALLi), using the immense amount of data they have about self-publishing. I've talked about this book in prior volumes of this series, but it was a masterclass in using data and analytics to drive your content. All the chapters were pulled directly from the most common questions on the ALLi blog and podcast. I also narrated the audiobook for *150 Self-Publishing Questions Answered,* which taught me how to produce clean, ACX-approved audio.

Lesson #41: *Indie Author Confidential, Vol. 1.* The inaugural book in this series taught me the value of documenting your experience. The topics are items that I discuss on my "Writer's Journey" podcast every week. I believe that if I become a successful writer, the value of this series will increase tenfold, especially the more books I publish in it. I also wrote this book during the beginning of the pandemic, and I'll always be grateful to it for giving me something productive to focus my anxiety on during those difficult first months in 2020.

Lesson #42: *Indie Author Confidential, Vol. 2.* This book focused a lot on my sales database adventures, which taught me how to distill a difficult concept and make it relatable. It was very hard to discuss my sales database project with people without their eyes glazing over. This book helped me collect and organize my thoughts.

Lesson #43: *The Reader's Bill of Rights.* This book helped me reconnect with my readers, and why I'm a writer in the first place, which is important to remember the longer your career becomes.

Lesson #44: *The Author Income Problem.* I outlined my manifesto around a sales database in this book. In many ways, this is an indirect descendant of *Indie Poet Formatting* and *Interactive Fiction.* It takes a difficult concept and tries to walk authors through how to solve it.

Lesson #45: *250+ Writing Tips, Volume 1*. I turned an entire year's worth of my podcast, "Writing Tip of the Day" into a book to make it more useful to my audience. Another lesson in repackaging content.

Lesson #46: *The Indie Author Bestiary*. My first attempt at blending fiction and nonfiction. The book takes the biggest struggles of the writing life and transforms them into mythical creatures, which is an unusual concept. The story is told in the second person present tense, which is surprisingly difficult to do when writing a self-help book when you're telling a narrative. I aimed big with this book and I felt like it did what I needed it to do.

Lesson #47: *The Indie Author Atlas*. I hired an illustrator to create maps for my book. This is the first time I worked with an illustrator.

Lesson #48: *Beach Poems*. This is a poetry collection I wrote in 2016 but haven't published yet, mostly due to forgetting about it. This book is a constant reminder to not sit on your work!

Lesson #49: *Reaper's Way (The Good Necromancer, Book 1)*. The first novella I ever published. That is a unique honor in and of itself.

Lesson #50: *Dead Rat Walking (The Chicago Rat Shifter, Book 1)*. This book is a testament that every book you publish teaches you something. While I don't know how *Dead Rat Walking* will perform, if it does well, it will be a validation that you CAN be successful if you keep learning and evolving. If it doesn't do well, I'll learn more lessons from it just the same.

There you go. Those are 50 lessons I learned after 50 books. I look forward to the next 50!

WE LEARNED RESILIENCE

I was talking to my sister and we were discussing virtual learning and how difficult it has been for our kids to learn during the pandemic. She made a good point: sure, they didn't learn as much math and science as the state wanted them to, but they learned how to deal with all the craziness of 2020. They learned resilience. That's underrated. Meanwhile, a lot of adults lost their minds.

We all learned something in 2020. Even writers.

If you are still writing after all the insanity that has transpired, congratulations—that's a badge of honor. If you didn't write during this pandemic, but you believe in your writing dreams so much that you're reading this book, you get the same badge of honor—it's no less remarkable a feat that you're still here.

Anyway, we all need reminders sometimes of how difficult a time like this is. The whole world is in a pressure cooker.

Ways to stay productive and focused during this time:

- Acknowledge that it's okay not to be okay right now. Then take care of your mental health.
- Keep writing, if you can. Even if you can't afford to publish right now, the act of writing will keep you grounded. The act of writing itself costs nothing, and if you're in hard times due to all the stuff going on right now, you can always publish later. Or publish and get it edited later.

- Find ways to channel your emotions into productive habits. This is why I am doing crazy challenges throughout the pandemic (beast mode, amnesia mode, exercise bike challenge, etc.). It keeps me focused on the writing and off the news.
- Keep finding ways to be grateful and have fun with your writing. You'll do better in all areas of your life if you can find a way to stay centered emotionally, though we will all struggle from time to time.

If anyone needs the kick in the pants to start writing again, maybe this will be it for you. Scary to think about all the writers out there who will never pick up the pen again because of this pandemic. Not just because of loss of inspiration, but also because of health and death.

The rest of us will still be here, still writing and going after our dreams long after this is over, and it will be because we all learned something during this difficult time—how to keep going even in the face of impossible odds.

Keep writing and, as Dean Wesley Smith would say, keep having fun.

THOUGHT LEADERSHIP IS LIKE SENDING A MESSAGE IN A BOTTLE

I've learned over the years to publish my thoughts publicly. Sometimes you never know what will happen.

Let me give you two examples.

First, in 2014, I published a video called "Drift." It was about how I use writer's block as a way to become a better writer. The video maybe got a few hundred views at most. Fast forward to 2021, and the Editor-in-Chief at *Writer's Digest* watched it and it prompted her to reach out to discuss a collaboration. Out of the 300 videos I've published, one of my worst-performing videos led to an opportunity. Wow.

Second, in 2015, I published a book called *Indie Poet Rock Star*, which was a book that taught poets how to take advantage of the self-publishing boom, something that was barely on poets' radar at the time. That book caught the attention of Orna Ross, who is the founder of The Alliance of Independent Authors, and an avid poet herself. That led to a mutually beneficial professional relationship, and helped me meet movers and shakers in the industry. All because I wrote a book that people would have advised me *not* to write at the time because there wasn't a market for it.

That got me thinking about what type of opportunities await for content that I'm creating today.

Writing is like sending a message in a bottle. Some bottles take a very long time to wash up on shore, but when they do, you never know what can happen.

LEVELS OF AWARENESS AS A WRITER

When I talk to people about my 2021 strategy, I always wonder if it makes sense.

Last year, when I was discussing my sales database project publicly, I received several comments from people in my community who (rightly so) said that they weren't making any money from their books, so there was no reason for them to care about automating their sales.

I tend to do things backward in life. Many of the things I focus on as a writer (particularly data, technology, and the future) are what people start thinking about after they become successful. So I admit that I am a little weird in that regard.

I believe that there are different levels to writing awareness:

- Craft
- Marketing
- Business
- Everything Else

In that order.

When you start your writing journey, you're hyper-focused on writing craft and productivity. The only thing that matters is starting and finishing your book.

Then your awareness bubble moves outward a little, and you focus on marketing. Once you start making some money, the bubble moves out a little more, and you think about business.

Once you've got that under control, then the bubble just keeps moving outward.

Sure, it's not common wisdom, but what would happen if you started instead in reverse? What if you started your awareness as a writer with a keen understanding of where the industry was going, and then narrowed your bubble based on that?

So your awareness bubble would start big and then shrink:

- Everything else (data, technology, and so on)
- Business
- Marketing
- Writing Craft

My personal experience has been that you can get stuck in the writing and marketing awareness bubbles for a long time. Sometimes your ability to have success in those bubbles depends on your awareness of business and everything else.

I also believe that getting stuck in the writing and marketing bubbles will be deadly for writers moving forward, especially in an industry that is ripe for disruption with emerging technology.

THE IDEAL WRITER OF THE FUTURE

I was thinking lately about what the perfect life would look like for a writer. If we could zoom five to ten years into the future and eliminate every problem that a writer faces, what would the ideal writing life look like for the writer of the future?

The ideal writer of the future would never suffer from writer's block. The moment they conceive an idea, they will be able to shepherd it from thought to finished product in record time.

They will be masters of their writing app, unlocking potential that others miss. This will make them more productive and more prolific.

They will be masters of the writing craft.

They will be writing machines, writing book after book with no burnout.

They will be editing machines, using a mix of experience, intuition, technology, and data and analytics to edit their works strategically and in record time.

They will work collaboratively with the right professionals to make their books a reality.

They will publish and manage their books effortlessly, preferably through seamless integration with their computers and book retailers.

They will use technology to find the right markets for their books so they can sell more books.

They will capitalize on emerging technology to increase their reach, improve their influence, and create a legacy. Artificial intelligence will become a writer's best friend, helping them become a better version of themselves. They will also use these technologies to grow their businesses in their sleep.

That's how I see the ideal writer of the future, and if you think about it, that reality already exists. It's not as ideal in some situations, but writers can do almost everything I described.

That's why this is the greatest time in the history of the world to be a writer. You can start living the future today. All you have to do is know where to look, how to transition your thinking, and how to make strategic gambles. If you can do that, you can step into the future today.

2021 STRATEGY PROGRESS

Last year, I shared my 2021 author strategy, which will guide me for the next several years. I've shared a detailed mind map about this at www.authorlevelup.com/2021strategy

My mission is to educate and entertain my audience in the genres I write, and to remain nimble in an ever-changing industry.

I will achieve my mission through five strategic priorities:

1. Become a world-class content creator
2. Become a world-class marketer
3. Become a technology-driven writer
4. Become a data-driven writer
5. Become the writer of the future

I wanted to give an update on how my progress is going in the first quarter of 2021, and some of the different projects within each of my strategic priorities.

WORLD-CLASS CONTENT CREATOR
Goal: 64 books published by 12/31/2021. I'm currently at 54 books written (including this one). That means I need to write 10 more books this year.

Develop a way to ensure consistency across my platform. This is just a fancy way of saying that I need to ensure that my work is consistent and that readers are receiving a consistent experience. The editing engine pilot is part of this project—

catching routine errors consistently will go a long way toward ensuring a better reader experience, but I'm also thinking about ways to do this across all areas of my platform, such as with my book formatting and my website.

WORLD-CLASS MARKETER

Grow my Amazon Ad imprint. So far, my sales are up by using Amazon Ads.

Improve my copywriting skills. The sales copy builder I discussed in Volume 3 of this series will help me improve my copywriting skills for the books I publish this year.

Reduce my tax liability. I've hired an accountant and we put together a strategy for 2021 to help minimize my taxes this year. I've also grown up and hired a financial advisor, something I was too afraid to do in the past.

BECOME A TECHNOLOGY-DRIVEN WRITER

Develop an automated way to enforce consistency. The editing engine pilot is a good example of this. Using automation, I reduced the number of errors in a manuscript by 34 percent before sending it to an editor. The errors that the editing engine caught will always be caught—it's a permanent, programmatic improvement.

Redesign my Book Wizard tool on Michael La Ronn.com and "Author Level Up".com. My goal when people are browsing my website is to get the right books to the right readers at the right time. How can I accomplish that strategically with a blend of automation and technology? I will work on this project later this year.

Implement a flexible book database that houses all the metadata for my books. The goal here is to be able to create an ONIX data feed so that I can publish my books at all retailers with the click of a button in the future when retailers enable this technology for self-published writers. I may not have time for this project.

Automate my bookkeeping. I've talked enough about this topic in this book that I don't need to cover it anymore here.

BECOME A DATA-DRIVEN WRITER

Make minor enhancements to my sales database. I need to continue improving and refining this, and I'll need some programming help.

Invest in learning the basics of Python, Webhooks, and Application Programming Interfaces (APIs). This is good knowledge to understand for the future.

BECOME THE WRITER OF THE FUTURE

Read 50 books. I'm way behind in this area, but I have time to catch up.

Implement direct print and audiobook sales onto my website. No progress here yet, but I do have an audiobook distributor lined up.

Complete my law degree. My last classes end in Q2, so I'm looking forward to being done so I can free up more time to accomplish my other goals in 2021. The legal knowledge I'm gaining will help me in the future.

Complete 12 WMG workshops to improve my writing craft. WMG Workshops are taught by Dean Wesley Smith and Kristine Kathryn Rusch. I haven't taken any yet this year but plan to start in the second quarter. The WMG workshops are writing craft tip extravaganzas.

BRINGING IT ALL TOGETHER

All of the items in this chapter gel together to help me stay nimble.

The fact-checkers and improved research methods I'm experimenting with will make big improvements in the quality of my story.

The content improvements I'm making with my editing engine will make a big difference in the quality of my editing.

The progress I'm making in Amazon Ads and copywriting will help me sell more of my books I write this year.

My adventures with automation, Excel and Word macros, and Natural Language Processing are starting to pay off. I built and deployed up my editing engine pilot in a weekend, whereas this would have taken me weeks if I did it last year because my knowledge base wasn't as strong.

I'm continuing to unlock insights on the data that are hiding in plain sight around me.

And most importantly, I'm keeping my eye on the future.

I'll share more progress on my strategy in the next volume so I can keep myself accountable, but you can view the details of my 2021+ strategy by visiting www.authorlevelup.com/2021strategy.

IDEAS YOU CAN STEAL

WRITE A PILOT SERIES

In 2014, when I started publishing, I ran an experiment with the small audience I had at the time.

I had four great story ideas, but I couldn't decide which one to write.

The ideas were:

- An urban fantasy with an angel hero
- A post-apocalyptic series about a multigenerational, multicultural family
- A spy technothriller
- A time-travel adventure

Keep in mind my audience was very small, around 25 people. But they voted for the urban fantasy and spy techno-thriller.

Then I wrote a pilot introduction chapter for both ideas. I shared the pilot chapters with my audience and asked them, "Which one would you want to keep reading?"

The spy series won. That eventually became my *Android X* series. That series went on to do surprisingly well, one of the early bright spots in my early publishing career. It recouped all the costs of editing and cover design in about a year. That was my definition of success back then (and honestly, still is now).

All these years later, I'm thinking about doing it again, but with a twist.

When I did my Amazon Ad experiments late last year, I

noticed a trend: the books that performed the best with my ads were books that you could clearly slot into an existing Amazon category.

Some examples of books that did well:

- *The Last Dragon Lord* series (dragons)
- Poetry Collections (Poetry)
- Short Story Collection (Short Story Anthologies)

Some examples of books that did not perform well (initially):

- My urban fantasy about a dream mage
- My urban fantasy about a necromancer

It's not that dream mages or necromancers are bad ideas. This isn't an indictment on the books. However, Amazon struggled to serve them to similar books without a lot of work from me. It's not used to looking for necromancer books because that character type is off-market right now.

So I had an idea that you can steal: what if I wrote two pilot chapters for two completely different series, asked my existing fiction audience to read and vote for which one they'd like to keep reading, and then:

- pay for professional covers for both stories as if they were novels
- have both chapters professionally edited
- publish both introductory chapters on Amazon for free or $0.99, and put them in Kindle Unlimited
- pretend that each title is a real book and support it with the proper keywords, a strong book description, and so on.

- optimize the book description by explaining that this is an exploratory pilot and that the book that wins will become a full series.
- End the book with a call to action to click if they like the book, as well as a link to the other book and a request to join my mailing list.

Then (and here's what makes this an interesting idea) I would run Amazon Ads to both pilots to see what happens.

When the experiment was over, I would have solid data points.

- Which pilot did my existing audience like the best, and why?
- Which pilot had the best ad performance? Did the Amazon Sponsored Product Automatic ads turn on? If yes, that's an indicator that Amazon could find comparable titles. If no, it's an indicator that there's something off-market about the book.
- What are the comparable titles for the book as revealed by the ad search term reports?
- How does the ad data compare to my existing audience's preferences? Do they want the same thing?

As you can see, this is like the exercise I did in 2014, but it's supported by data.

There are caveats, though. First, Amazon is not the whole world. It's one retailer out of many, and the ads would primarily be run in the United States. US readers are not a barometer of other countries, so that's a downside. However, I could run ads in the United Kingdom, Canada, and Australia too, but that doesn't completely solve the problem.

Second, trends change over time. The ad data is just a snapshot in time. The "loser" pilot shouldn't be viewed as a loser at all.

Third, this depends entirely on my execution. Both pilots would need to be alpha-read, beta-read, and professionally edited and proofread. I'd also need to invest in professional covers for both pilots, covers that would be *final*. So that would be an investment. But is it worth it to spend a few hundred dollars for the chance to net three to four figures each month for the foreseeable future? At this stage in my career, I can afford the risk, though it would sting if I failed.

But hey, that's why ideas exist—for us to prove whether they work or not!

INDIE AUTHOR AI CO-AUTHOR COLLECTIVE

As I think about artificial intelligence, I'm constantly reminded of how much data you need to get meaningful results.

This will probably be true with using AI to write books. Until AI engines can do more with less data, you would need a LOT of books for an AI to write in your author's voice.

Traditional publishers could easily build a corpus of data by adding their entire backlog into an AI system. Self-published writers will lack that ability.

However, a group of self-published writers in the same genre could band together, feed all of their books into an AI engine, and then use that as the corpus for new artificially-generated books. The books would be derivative works based on the authors' books. The authors could then publish under a pseudonym that suggests AI, such as "James Urban.AI" for urban fantasy. Then the authors could publish the book, co-market it, and split the royalties.

Imagine if 100 prolific indie authors did this in a genre. It would be a smart way to fight back in the AI battle that is almost certain to come: traditional publishers of the future, who will use artificial intelligence and data and analytics as the basis for their insights and publishing decisions, versus self-publishers, who have almost no data and analytics other than their own.

HIRING AN AUDIOBOOK PROOFER

I read a great guest blog post on "The Creative Penn" written by Max Cantrell, who is an audiobook proof listener. Just as you'd hire an editor to check your work for errors, Max is the guy you'd hire to listen to your audiobook to listen for errors such as misspellings, mispronunciations, or noise artifacts in your narrator's recording.

A unique problem with audiobook creation is comparing the narration with the text to make sure they match. You'd be surprised how many times a narrator will accidentally skip a word or pronounce a word incorrectly, almost always unconsciously. I once had a narrator say a person's last name correctly in one sentence and mispronounce it in the very next sentence. Even the best narrators might sometimes bump the table they're recording at, or their chair might squeak, or a background noise might show up in the recording. Narrators usually catch most of these artifacts, but not even the best can catch them all.

To produce a quality audiobook, it needs to be free of mispronunciations, missing words and phrases, and artifacts. The text needs to match the audio exactly.

Yet when I listen to my audiobook proofs, I don't like to sit in front of my computer and compare it to the text. It's mind-numbing, time-consuming work. If you have a 10-hour audiobook, it'll take you *at least* 10 hours to perform this task, likely more because you'll have to start and stop a lot to make notes. If you want to do this right, you have to do it twice—once to give the narrator a list of errors, and then again to make sure the narrator didn't make any additional mistakes while fixing the original errors.

I prefer to be multi-tasking when I listen to proof audio, because that's how most listeners are going to be consuming the book. I'm mostly listening for flow and quality. I prefer to do the text and audio comparison second.

It's a pretty smart idea to hire someone who can handle the comparison for you and give you a list of errors with timestamps that you can pass to your narrator. It serves as an additional layer of protection to ensure that you're creating a quality product.

While I recommend that you check out Max's services, I predict he has a lot of clients at this point. This is a job you can easily hire a freelancer to do on a site like Upwork or Fiverr. Simply pay them per finished hour of your audiobook, which might (at the time of this writing) be anywhere from $20 to $30 per finished hour. A 10-hour audiobook would cost you $200, which is what you would pay a *good* narrator *per finished hour.* This is a perfect job for a freelancer just starting who wants to build a portfolio.

I intend to use an audio proofer moving forward. It's a cost-effective way to improve the presentation of your content. Once you publish an audiobook, it's fairly permanent, so it pays to get it right the first time.

CLEVER DICTATION HACK

I stumbled upon a clever dictation hack that I'd like to pass along to anyone who is disheartened by the fact that Dragon for Mac has been discontinued.

Recently, I did a Writing Power Hour Livestream and wanted to dictate live so that my audience could see how I did it. I needed a way to share my screen.

I had two problems. The first problem was that I use Dragon on my Windows virtual machine, which I cannot share if I am screen sharing on my Mac. The virtual machine consumes too many resources and would jeopardize my stream quality. It's a big no-no.

The second problem was that I needed to share my dictation on-screen.

I decided to use Dragon Anywhere on my phone. Could I somehow get my phone's display onto my desktop monitor? Why, yes, I could, using the iPhone's "screen mirroring" feature. I downloaded a $17 app called Reflector that accepted the screen mirroring stream and displayed it on my Mac. Then I shared my screen, and voila! I could dictate with my phone on my desk but see the results on my computer screen.

(Android phones support screen mirroring too, and you can use Reflector with them.)

So if you have a Mac and want to use Dragon, purchase a Dragon Anywhere subscription and take the steps I just described. It's not perfect, and you don't receive all the benefits of the

Windows desktop version of Dragon, but you can dictate like everyone else and achieve very good results. In my opinion, Dragon Anywhere is almost as accurate as Dragon for Desktop, and you don't need special hardware.

METADATA CONSULTANT

There are many author services for self-published authors, including people who help with marketing.

However, I have (personally) not seen anyone specifically hold themselves out as a metadata consultant, especially for Amazon.

Picking the right keywords and categories on Amazon is critical. It's an ever-changing battle.

Someone who reviewed your book and helped you pick the right keywords and categories is an underrated service idea in my opinion. Especially if that person did this service all day every day. I've attended webinars with SEO consultants who talk about their process for picking the right metadata for a book. I would love to pay someone with that kind of mind to look at my books and offer advice I hadn't considered. It's easy to pick bad keywords, and you don't always know how to fix it.

A metadata consultant could also add value by reviewing your sales data and Amazon Ad performance to help you determine whether your keywords need adjusting. You can pay them an hourly fee for their help, or purchase a "maintenance package," in which they check in with you a couple of times a year to see if trends have changed.

The key is that this person must specialize in Amazon SEO. Anyone can claim to do this, but Amazon SEO knowledge is a special skill set.

GENRE CONSULTANT

Some readers are masters of their genre. These readers have read every single book in a subgenre, and they buy new releases on day one. They've read it all.

What would it be like to tap in to these readers' knowledge and experience? Book 30 minutes with "Dan the Space Man," who has an encyclopedic knowledge of space opera. Let him read the first three or four chapters of your book and tell you what it reminds him of.

"This is like that one novel in the 1970s by X author," Dan might say. Or, "It's like that, but it reads like X author."

If Dan says, "I've never seen anything like this before," that's probably a red flag. You shouldn't be able to stump him.

A thirty-minute conversation with Dan would give you a list of comparable books, an understanding of where the major tropes of your story compare to other books in the genre, and an understanding of some potential pitfalls. He could also tell you what to put on the cover to appeal to readers like him. This is, of course, one person's opinion, but my experience with readers has been that if one person says something, there are many more who believe it.

"Dan the Space Man" is a super reader, but also what you could call a genre consultant. Many successful writers have a good understanding of the genres they write in, but they don't have the time to read everything. Writers who write to market could use Dan's expertise too.

You can hire editors who have expertise in a genre, and while that is helpful, there's nothing like getting opinions from readers.

BOOK COVER HUNTER

What do you want on your book cover? I don't know about you, but I often struggle with coming up with a concept of what should be on the cover. The designer usually needs a basic idea to start from.

What if there was a way for you to feed images of book covers into an engine (maybe artificial intelligence-driven), and the engine would find similar book covers and return them to you?

You can (sort of) do this with Google Images reverse search feature. You can upload an image and Google will return visually similar images, mostly based on the color palette.

I envision something more powerful and targeted that can identify whether an image is a book cover and whether the cover is potentially in your genre. It could also "hunt" for similar images, crawling Amazon, Pinterest, and Google at the same time to give you a more comprehensive search. It would be an exceptional market research tool.

Combine this with the genre consultant I mentioned earlier and you'll have a recipe for a book that hits the market with both content and packaging.

STUDYING READER HABITS

I heard an interview with an influencer in the self-publishing space who talked about hiring a firm to do a marketing study where they tracked how readers browse for books on Amazon. They tracked the users' screens and paid careful attention to how they navigated Amazon and where they spent the most time on a product page. The insights were intriguing.

How interesting would it be if the authors of a subgenre got together and commissioned a similar study, but for other things? Show readers a bunch of book covers in rapid succession and see what draws their attention first, then ask them why they clicked. Or, show them different varieties of back matter and track how they engage with it to see if there's a particular style of a call to action that works best. Or, simply track users' screens to see how they search for urban fantasy novels, for example, to see if there are genre-specific quirks that authors need to know about.

I have no idea what a service like this would cost, but there is so much data out there waiting to be discovered.

MARKETING WORKBENCH

There are so many marketing tools for writers that it might be helpful to bring them under one umbrella. For example, I've mentioned several different tools in the *Indie Author Confidential* series that could exist in one place. Imagine an app or a website with the following tools:

BOOK COVERS

- A "book cover hunter," which hunts down book covers similar to yours
- A font dissector that can analyze a book cover and tell you what the fonts are
- A font list with the most common fonts broken down by genre, with trending data
- A report driven by AI that informs authors what's happening with book covers in the genre

BOOK DESCRIPTIONS

- A book description builder that helps you build a solid book description every time
- A copywriting swipe file

MARKETING

- Integration with a link localization service to help you build marketing links
- Integration with a social media scheduler
- A brand monitoring tool

These tools are mostly unrelated to each other, but it would be nice to access them in one place, or at least be able to link to them so that authors could go to one place to find the tools they need.

GENRE-BASED MUSIC

I discovered some new music by an artist I like on Apple Music. Several of the songs had a similar theme: supernatural love. The lyrics were mystical, mysterious, and fun. That got me thinking about what an interesting partnership a bestselling author could strike with a bestselling musician.

Here's an example of the idea: urban fantasy rock. A band records an album that is essentially urban fantasy short stories put to music: what it's like to be a werewolf, a man falling in love with a ghost woman, a treasure hunter fighting off ghouls in a temple in Peru, and so on. Pair *au courant*, top-notch musicality that fans of the (music) genre love with content that fans of a (book) genre love. You can tell a fascinating story and cover a lot of ground in just three verses and a chorus.

And if you'd like an example of what this could sound like, listen to a 1984 classic by Dave Grusin and Randy Goodrum called "Haunting Me."

Imagine yacht-rock romance, LitRPG electronica, literary jazz, epic fantasy songs sung in made-up languages, and so on. There are a lot of pairings you can explore when you explore demographics too.

There would be lucrative partnership opportunities between authors and artists working in the same genre, even cross-promotion and licensing opportunities. For example, the band could license a character to do an album from the character's perspective, or the author could make the band characters in one of their novels.

INFLUENCER DIRECT PLATFORM

I discussed in a previous chapter how I chatted with a developer about creating a dedicated app on which people could consume my content. I loved the idea but ultimately didn't pursue it.

If you think about this and apply next-order thinking, it becomes difficult for end-users to manage. Imagine if every influencer in the world had a dedicated app that served their content. If you follow 10 influencers, that's 10 apps you'd have to install on your phone, all with different features and functionality. That will never work.

Here's what could: a white-label app that allows influencers to upload their content in the same structure and format. Users merely "search" for influencers to follow in the app, and once they click follow, the influencer's content appears in the app's feed, and the user can also follow the influencer directly. It would be similar to a social media app, but it would allow direct engagement with the influencer as well as a community. It would be a more intimate way for influencers to serve their content. So in a sense, you're downloading one app and then choosing which influencers to follow within that app. Influencers would pay premium prices to get in, and the app would offer features that would be almost identical to a custom app solution, but for a more affordable price. The app would have a name like "Chasr: The App That Lets You Keep Up with the Influencers Who Matter Most." Something like that. Unlike social media apps, Chasr wouldn't encourage native content. It would instead serve content that exists on the channels, such as YouTube, a podcast, or a blog. All an influencer would need to do is *syndicate* their existing content to it. I can't stress this enough. Otherwise, the app becomes just like every social media app out there.

It seems to me that users want to interact with their favorite influencers more intimately, but they don't necessarily want to download an app for that one person unless they are fanatic about that influencer. Even then, it's doubtful that they would use *one person's app every single day* because of convenience.

PUBLISHING CONTENT CURATION SERVICE

For years, enemies of self-publishing decried the "tsunami of crap" that self-published books ushered onto the market. You don't hear that term very much anymore, but God, it was everywhere in 2010-2014. I don't miss that term. I never liked it.

But since we're talking about tsunamis, why don't we instead talk about the tsunami of information that exists about self-publishing? Ever since 2010ish, authors have had to navigate a never-ending amount of information on how to be a better author, marketer, and businessperson. There are services such as "The Hot Sheet" by Jane Friedman and *The Writer's Knowledge Base* by Elizabeth Spann Craig that curate self-publishing knowledge and each of these services is great in their own way. But there is no single service that I know of that can capture *everything*.

Eight years ago, I would have recommended that someone do this manually, but even a full-time curator would be embarking on a fool's errand. These days, I believe artificial intelligence can solve the problem. An AI can consume blog posts, books, podcasts, YouTube videos, and even comments on social media and contextualize them.

So many news articles these days are written and created by artificial intelligence, so AI already has the capability to consume content and create context. If it can do that, then it can also organize and recommend content based on what you are looking for, and aim to recommend the "right content to the right user at the right time."

Imagine wanting to know the hottest marketing trends. The service could spin a narrative about what people are doing right now based on recent content. It could even spin you a narrative based on how a certain marketing technique has evolved, such as Amazon Ads. As such, it might be able to warn you about certain practices that are either out of favor or no longer effective.

Simply ask your Amazon Alexa device "What's the self-publishing news?" And you'd get a daily 10-minute report broken into different industry segments such as traditional publishing, self-publishing, marketing, Facebook advertising, and so on. You might even get a highlights reel from the most popular self-publishing podcasts, with snippets that you might want to hear.

This could work on any device, not just Amazon Echos.

The curation service can help you navigate the tsunami and find knowledge too.

Imagine wanting to learn how to format a book. An AI would recommend to you the most up-to-date information based on context clues such as screenshots of the apps used and social engagement (users aren't complaining about the posts being out of date, for example), among other things. If you're using Scrivener for Windows to format a book, you'll receive Scrivener for Windows content. The engine might even flag certain articles if it thinks portions of them are out of date. The genius of an engine like this is that while it's likely to recommend popular content, the primary goal would be to recommend the *right* content based on what the user is searching for, which means that it could pull up obscure blog posts from lesser-known locales if they're the right thing for the user.

The future belongs to those who can crack the discoverability problem.

CONTENT CREATED WHILE WRITING THIS BOOK

Author Level Up YouTube Channel - Highlights

Watch at youtube.com/authorlevelup.

The Ultimate Guide to Book Editing (series): Watch the concepts that Michael talks about in this book in action.

How to Beat Self-Doubt as a Writer: Learn how to conquer self-doubt forever.

Interviews & Appearances

Be a Writing Machine (Writer's Digest Conference 2020): Discover Michael's secrets for being insanely productive, and how he wrote over 50 books while working a full-time job, raising a family, and attending law school classes in the evenings. This talk is based on Michael's top selling book, *Be a Writing Machine*.

How to Create Engaging Characters (GDEX 2020 Conference): In this presentation, Michael talks about his process for creating engaging characters that readers will love.

Mental Models for Writers (Escape from the Plot Forest Summit

2020): In this talk, Michael explains the power of mental models and how writers can use them to level up in every area of their life—especially writing their stories!

INDIE AUTHOR CONFIDENTIAL

Secrets No One Will Tell
You About Being a Writer

VOL. 5

M.L. RONN

VOLUME 5

INTRODUCTION

The second quarter of 2021 brought huge changes in my personal and writing life.

First, I completed my law degree. What a relief! Now I don't have to worry about reading gigantic books that take away from my writing time.

Second, I encountered a book called *The Conquest of Happiness* by Bertrand Russell. This book transformed the way I see my life. I made profound changes in my life in response to reading it. I'll share more later in the book, but the result was that I stopped producing "The Writer's Journey" and "Writing Tip of the Day" podcasts.

I've been stretching myself thin over the past few years, and I recognized that with law school behind me, it was time to start shrinking the responsibilities in my life. Working a full-time job, raising a family, running three podcasts and a YouTube channel, writing five to ten books per year, doing at least ten podcast interviews per year, speaking at five to ten engagements per year, and teaching six to ten insurance classes per year is just not sustainable. But, boy, was I doing it all and doing it at a crazy successful level.

So, I chose to leave many of those activities on a high note. In Q2 alone, I completed my final law class, taught my final insurance class, and released the final episodes of my podcasts. That's a seismic shift that I haven't been able to fully appreciate yet.

Bertrand Russell's book gave me a deep self-awareness about myself. While I was winding my activities down, I sensed that something new was coming—a new chapter in my life that I needed to prepare for. I didn't know what, but I listened to my spirit and spent a few weeks cleaning up my personal life.

Sure enough, shortly after all of this, a headhunter contacted me about a new job and made me an offer I couldn't refuse: an executive position at a global insurance company.

I wasn't looking for a job; it just happened, and the experience was surreal. In retrospect, this was the event my spirit was preparing me for.

I left a company for whom I had worked for 11 years, leaving behind friends and colleagues I knew well. I had a comfortable lifestyle and a good work-life balance that allowed me to build my writing career.

And it wasn't about the money, honestly. I knew that the new job was the right decision when, at the beginning of the fifth and final interview, the senior vice president of the company opened the interview with, "I noticed you like to write and read fantasy novels. Tell me your favorite series." When I told him that it was the Dresden Files, we spent the entire interview talking about Harry Dresden. We didn't discuss insurance at all. Not only did I land a rare executive position, but I also landed among colleagues who respected the writing side of my personality. That is incredibly rare in the corporate world.

I've said for years that my writing life and my work life feed off each other. I inserted a sentence about reading and writing in my LinkedIn profile—an act of courage in a very competitive world where showing an interest in the arts is often perceived as a professional weakness. That sentence helped me land a job. As an executive. At 33 years old.

If anyone needs proof that you shouldn't hide your creative interests from the rest of the world, let that be it. If your current employer uses it against you, find a new employer.

The new role came with enormous responsibilities. The first few months were intense. I worked 12-hour days, and I even worked on weekends to establish myself. Fortunately, the company I chose values work-life balance. I never receive emails over the weekend, and working long hours is always my choice, never mandated. Of course, because of my role, the work has to be done, and I know how to perform at a high level at work and in my writing.

The choice to scale back many activities made a tremendous difference in my ability to expand into this executive role without disrupting the other areas of my life too much.

That's precisely why I've spent the past decade investing in technology to help me be a part-time writer with full-time results. My preoccupation has been creating a writing business that runs itself. The new job put a big dent in my writing life for a few months, but now I'm (mostly) back to normal, writing the same way I used to.

During the time I was away, my Amazon Ads still ran. My books still sold on all retailers. I landed paid speaking engagements without having to lift a finger. I even generated an additional stream of income that will generate royalties for the rest of my life—again, without lifting a finger—licensing content that I created a few years ago. People still signed up for my email list, and my autoresponders fired like clockwork, selling books, and introducing my platform to new readers. My YouTube videos clocked record views and subscribers. That's how solid writing businesses operate in the 21st century—run by a founder who works a nine-to-five job.

And when I do need to be involved, I benefit from streamlined processes, advanced automation, and a team of assistants to help me accomplish tasks faster and more efficiently. I spend my time where it adds the most value—writing, marketing, and connecting with my audience.

Even though my personal life has changed drastically, my writing life has remained mostly the same.

I share this to show people what's possible if you work a day job. You can still build a writing business that you're proud of and be a world-class content creator.

Because of my job transition, this volume has slightly fewer topics than previous volumes, but you'll find it just as entertaining.

There are also three new changes:

- Moving forward, I'll be combining the Technology and Data sections. While both are important strategic priorities, they will not be a big focus for me in the last half of 2021 and 2022.
- This will be the last volume that contains Ideas You Can Steal. I will still capture ideas in this series, but I'll incorporate them into the other sections as I come up with them.

In 2022, I'll shift this series from quarterly to annually. I want to clear up more time to write fiction, so I'm reducing the scope of this series and the size of the volumes slightly to help me achieve that goal.

But for now (and always), you'll find a lot of interesting topics on these pages.

My Core Strategic Priorities

As a refresher, my mission is to create content that entertains and/or educates my audience, preferably both, and to remain nimble in an ever-changing industry. I do this by focusing on five strategic priorities:

- Become a world-class content creator
- Become a world-class marketer
- Become a technology-driven writer
- Become a data-driven writer
- Become the writer of the future

I believe these five priorities are most important for me to have a long-term, sustainable career.

What's in This Volume

In the World-Class Content Creation section, I discuss upgrading my YouTube studio and ending my podcast presence.

In the World-Class Marketer section, I discuss a lot of ideas related to cover design.

In the Technology and Data sections, I discuss my biggest achievement of the quarter: an automated editing engine. It's a victory on the level of my sales database in 2020.

In the Writer of the Future section, I muse on author job descriptions, thinking like an editor, and lessons learned from law school.

And, as always, I offer some fun ideas you can steal in your writing business. No volume of Indie Author Confidential would be complete without some bold ideas!

Enjoy.

M.L. Ronn
Des Moines, Iowa
June 8, 2021

BECOME A WORLD-CLASS
CONTENT CREATOR

COMMA USAGE: A REFRESHER (FOR MYSELF)

While I was working on my automated editing engine last quarter, I discovered that I have a problem with commas. I understand their usage, and you'll rarely see comma splices in my work (actually, I hope you never see those). My problem is with consistency.

Take the word "too." Do you put a comma before it?

One of my editors believed I should. My current editor believes I should not. Is there a wrong answer? No, but I better be consistent in my usage so that every time I use the word "too" at the end of a sentence, I'm punctuating it consistently. This applies internally for every book I write, but also to my entire portfolio. This little rule is something that readers will never notice, but it's a quality issue that improves the overall presentation and consistency of my entire body of work.

That got me thinking about the "rules" of commas and how many of them can be addressed by automation.

Can I make my comma usage more consistent using automation instead of having to memorize rules? The less I have to memorize, the better.

I grabbed the following rules from the Purdue University Online Writing Lab (OWL) website, a well-respected website used my many schools as a reference for English rules.

Rule: Use commas to separate independent clauses when they are joined by any of these seven coordinating conjunctions: and, but, for, or, nor, so, yet.

Example: I tried to stop crying, but I couldn't shake my emotions.

This rule is not programmable. My first question in researching automation and natural language processing (NLP) was simple: can computer software identify independent and dependent clauses?

In previous volumes of this series, I discussed NLP and how it can do part of speech (POS) tagging, which diagrams a sentence into nouns, verbs, adverbs, and so on. I assumed that it could also determine independent clauses.

I was wrong. Unfortunately, no open-source NLP programs that I know of can do this. That makes any grammar rule that relies on understanding the clause all but impossible. That said, programs like Grammarly and ProWritingAid can do this to some degree, but their methods are proprietary and not always accurate.

I spoke with a data scientist who specializes in NLP and he told me that English is a difficult language to perform NLP on because its grammar structure varies wildly.

Oh well. One day, when NLP can understand clauses, that will be a game-changer.

Use commas after introductory a) clauses, b) phrases, or c) words that come before the main clause.

Example: Because I was a student, I didn't have access to the company computer lab.

It might be better to phrase the sentence differently, like "I didn't have access to the company computer lab because I was a student," but the example is still a valid usage, and it explains why English can be so difficult.

This example also depends on determining the clause, so it can't be automated either.

Use a pair of commas in the middle of a sentence to set off clauses, phrases, and words that are not essential to the meaning of the sentence. Use one comma before to indicate the beginning of the pause and one at the end to indicate the end of the pause.

Example: I would love, if you have the time, to talk to you about my cousin Sarah.

Again, this rule can't be automated.

Do not use commas to set off essential elements of the sentence, such as clauses beginning with that (relative clauses). That clauses after nouns are always essential. That clauses following a verb expressing mental action are always essential.

Example: It's important that, you go to the barbershop today.

That example uses the comma incorrectly. This rule is contemplated by most grammar checker apps today, and they should catch these types of errors.

Use commas to separate three or more words, phrases, or clauses written in a series.

Example: Lily, Ellen, and Dominique went to the store.

This rule is also already contemplated by most grammar checkers today.

Use commas to separate two or more coordinate adjectives that describe the same noun. Be sure never to add an extra comma between the final adjective and the noun itself or to use commas with non-coordinate adjectives.

Example: I bought a shiny, expensive car.

This is a tough rule because what constitutes a "coordinate" adjective is subjective. If I exchanged the word "shiny" with "red," then a comma wouldn't be required ("I bought a shiny red car.") If I exchanged the word "red" with "head-turning," then I would need a comma again ("I bought a shiny, head-turning car.") I'm not sure how you teach an AI to recognize nuances like these. Given that this rule applies to any noun and any series of adjectives, the combinations are limitless.

I've seen grammar checking apps attempt to police this rule, but not with any real accuracy.

Use a comma near the end of a sentence to separate contrasted coordinate elements or to indicate a distinct pause or shift.

Example: The door at the end of the hallway was red, like a beacon in the dark.

I can see some situations where this rule can either be grammatical or stylistic. In fiction, for example, an author may choose to use a comma for a dramatic pause. In a self-help book, though, you might easily be able to remove the comma without a reader even noticing.

Use commas to set off phrases at the end of the sentence that refer back to the beginning or middle of the sentence. Such phrases are free modifiers that can be placed anywhere in the sentence without causing confusion.

Example: Let's say that I rented a condo on the beach, shall we?

I don't believe this rule can be automated.

Use commas to set off all geographical names, items in dates (except the month and day), addresses (except the street number and name), and titles in names.

No examples are needed. This is perhaps the easiest comma rule that can be automated.

Use a comma to shift between the main discourse and a quotation.

Example: "Let's go to the store," he said.

This is also easily automated. Some grammar checkers already do this.

Use commas wherever necessary to prevent possible confusion or misreading.

This isn't something that can be automated, but it's an important guiding principle. When in doubt, ask if the reader will be confused. If the answer is yes, punctuate it so that they won't be.

There are other comma rules, but this was a fun thought exercise to show just how difficult commas are to tame with automation.

A decent amount of the suggested edits in my editing engine pilot came from commas, which makes this even more problematic.

I decided that the best way to address the problem (for now) was to refresh my understanding of comma usage, which is part of the reason I wrote this chapter.

SEMI-COLONS

Earlier this year, I subscribed to the American Copyediting Society (ACES) as part of my automated editing engine project to help me better understand how editors see the world.

One week, they sent out a newsletter and included some book recommendations. One of those books was *Semi-Colon: The Past, Present, and Future of a Misunderstood Mark* by Cecilia Watson. It's a fantastic book that explores the history of the semi-colon, why it fell out of vogue, and why it deserves to still have a place in the English language.

Watson explores feuds between grammarians about semi-colon usage. She even discusses how a semi-colon sparked a massive court case in the United States.

The main takeaway from the book is that punctuation exists as a tool for authors to use. The field of grammar began as a way to standardize the writing of the English language because there were no punctuation (or even spelling) standards. Grammarians began with a lofty and noble goal of trying to make it easier for people to communicate with each other. However, the recommendations were often prescriptive.

Over the centuries, English rules have moved away from prescriptive to suggested, and the *author* now makes the grammatical choices that are best for the work, not a grammarian. You could argue that it's always been this way, but it's hard to imagine a world where readers and critics expressed frustration at an author because of how they use semi-colons. Yet that was what happened to Mark Twain. In some respects, many authors in the past have fought hard battles so that we can use semi-colons as much or as little as we want today.

As for me, I like semi-colons; I believe that an author should use them whenever they feel it necessary.

THE 5-5-50,000 CHALLENGE

I devised a new challenge to keep myself occupied while stuck at home. I called it the 5-5-50,000 challenge.

The idea: wake up at 5 AM for 5 days, write 5,000 words per day to arrive at a 50,000-word novel in one working week.

I wanted to do this project because I wanted to finish book two of my *Chicago Rat Shifter* series before my final law class began. I reasoned that if I woke up an extra 30 to 45 minutes earlier and focused on writing every day, looking for "cracks" to write in, that my word counts would add up in a big way. My goal was to dictate and write on my phone whenever possible.

It didn't happen.

I had some family issues that distracted me from the challenge. The first day, I hit around 3,600 words, which was respectable, but it was too far away from my ultimate goal. It was impossible to catch up, especially when I missed the goal on the second day.

But that's the nature of challenges. Sometimes you don't succeed. Perhaps one day I'll seek a rematch, but for now, it's on to the next challenge.

WRITING IS MIND CONTROL

The best writing craft advice I ever received was "writing is mind control."

Readers see what you want them to see. You control the images that stream across their mind as they read your story. When you understand this, you can level up your writing because you can ask: "How can I control the story as the reader reads it?"

Through mere words that you type into a word processor in a certain order, you control what readers see, and to a certain extent, how they see it. You can even influence how they feel.

You can think of it as good or bad, but it simply is. Even an email or a blog post that you write has the same power. You can impart good or bad qualities to it, but it's neutral. The values you place on it are your own.

But it's important to understand that, as a writer, the words you use have power. Only when you understand that power can you learn how to wield it. As for you and me, we use our powers for good, and responsibly.

When you think about writing as mind control, you make different decisions. Instead of focusing on typos, you instead focus on how to maximize your story's impact, how to intensify the images the reader sees, and how your message is being received. You don't get bogged down by technical details.

A lot of writers can't see past spelling and grammar errors, or plot. The moment you step away from those things (and can execute them competently), you have an infinite number of tools at your disposal to improve your writing. You start going deeper into the craft, and what you discover is weird, beautiful, and even crazy at times. That's the life of a writer.

Mega-bestselling authors exercise mind control. They know what you'll be thinking before you think it. As such, they give you exactly what you need when you need it to keep motivating you to turn the page.

What would it take to exercise this power in your writing?

I can't answer this question for you specifically, but I wrote a book called *The Writing Craft Playbook* that attempts to answer this question generally.

I explained this concept on my daily blog, and I used the words "writing is the act of getting inside people's heads and controlling their thoughts." One subscriber cautioned me and said that this line of reasoning scared them. They perceived it as me saying that writers should manipulate their readers.

That's not at all what I'm suggesting, though I acknowledge that this advice, in the wrong hands, could lead to that.

My logic is simple: I want as many readers as possible to keep turning the page and finish my books. I want to accomplish this as masterfully as possible.

How can I give readers what they want? What will make them bail from my story? Is there information I can give to help them see, feel, hear, taste, and smell the events in my story more vividly? I believe that asking these questions can lead to useful insights.

Ask those questions, and one day, you'll gain the power of mind control too.

WHY I LOVE THE 3RD-PERSON POV

For my new urban fantasy series, *The Chicago Rat Shifter*, I swam against the current trend in the urban fantasy genre of using the first-person point of view. I enjoy writing in the first-person because of the intimate relationship between the viewpoint character and the reader, but it has significant drawbacks.

First, you can only describe what your main character is feeling and thinking. It's quite rare to see an urban fantasy series with multiple first-person points of view. The challenge with that is making each character's voice distinct, which is why I suspect most authors stay away from multiple POVs.

Second, your narrative is restricted to that one character. You can't jump into the heads of supporting characters or even villains. This makes the first-person point of view rather flat and limited from a storytelling perspective.

Authors who write in the third-person have more tools at their disposal to exercise the mind control that I referenced in the previous chapter. One of those tools is the ability to tell the story from the perspective of different characters. I missed that.

With *The Chicago Rat Shifter*, I wanted to tell an engaging story in the third-person so that I could explore different characters. Most of the chapters in the series are told from the perspective of my hero, Cyrus Grant. In the first novel, I split the remaining chapters between Cyrus's sister, Becca, and the villain of the story. Alternating between these characters allowed me to do a few things:

- I could switch the point of view to escalate tension and pacing;
- I could switch the point of view to give the reader information before the hero learns it, which is an underrated technique; and
- I could explore the background of the villain to make him more sympathetic, something that you don't often see in urban fantasy.

Did I succeed? I don't know, because I haven't published the series yet. But I was missing the third-person and wanted to hone my craft. When I committed to urban fantasy a few years ago, one of my fears was that I would forget how to do the third-person skillfully. As I think about future series, I will alternate between the first-person and third-person to keep building my skill in both storytelling styles.

HEADER ILLUSTRATIONS IN MY NOVEL

I had an idea to take my book formatting to the next level: use header images for my chapters.

For my novel, *Dead Rat Walking*, I thought it would be cool to use images of rats intertwined with the chapter numbers. I've seen many traditional and self-publishers use header images in this manner. It adds flair and professionalism if done correctly. When done poorly, it looks tacky.

To accomplish this, I had to find an illustrator whose work matched my vision for the book. The illustrator would need to provide me with images for each chapter that I could load into Vellum, my book formatting software. Since the novel had 40-ish chapters, I needed at least 50 to 60 chapter illustrations based on the same pattern—one for each chapter number; I also had to account for the possibility that future novels in the series might have more chapters than the first novel. Once we settled on the illustration, it would have been a simple job to change the pattern for each number.

I shopped around for quotes, but I didn't find a freelancer that got me excited about their work. I started with Fiverr.com. I received hundreds of quotes, but most of the illustrators there specialize in children's books. Their designs were either too whimsical or not appropriate for an urban fantasy novel.

Next, I tried Upwork, and I found the freelancers there to be uninspiring for this project. It was probably bad timing.

Finally, I asked around for freelancers in my network who might be able to do this for me, but I didn't get any recommendations.

I decided not to proceed with chapter illustrations because I didn't want to settle for something that didn't match my vision.

I'm certain that one day in the future, I'm going to stumble across someone who will be able to do this for me, and I'll wonder why it was so difficult in the first place. But for now, I made my choice and moved on.

PRODUCING HARDCOVERS

What would it take to produce hardcover editions of my books?

The idea has been on my mind for the last seven years, but I keep delaying taking action because I don't like the answers:

- I need to buy ISBNs. Due to the size of my catalog and my fast production speeds, I'll have to pay at least $1,600 for a block of 1,000 ISBNs. For something that doesn't generate a value-add, that kind of investment is against my religion.
- I need to redesign my book covers. Fortunately, around 2016, most of the cover designers I worked with automatically sized my book covers to be hardcover-ready, so this was smart thinking on their part.
- I need to redesign my interiors. Depending on the trim size I need, I may have to create a separate output from Vellum. That's easy, but it does require a few steps.
- I need to maintain two separate editions for my print books. From a data archiving perspective, that requires some thought, but it's not difficult.

If I'm honest, I just don't want to pay the $1,600 ...I can think of many things I can buy for that and get way more in return. For example:

- a new computer
- software upgrades

- new camera gear
- hiring an assistant for one-off tasks
- a course that will teach me a new skill that I can use to make money
- investing in more automation
- better bookkeeping services
- hiring a developer to create a better, more functional website to help me sell more books
- stocks, bonds, cryptocurrencies
- contributing to my retirement accounts
- keeping that money in savings for a rainy day
- hiring a marketing consultant to upgrade my branding
- hiring a designer to create a new logo for the Michael La Ronn and "Author Level Up" brands

I came up with that list in just a few minutes. After all, I'm running a business.

There are only four reasons to buy ISBNs:

1. To produce hardcover editions of my book. At the time of this writing, IngramSpark is the only place I would use to create a hardcover (but Amazon may offer this in the future, which will be a game-changer).
2. So that my book sales will be tracked by data aggregation companies such as Nielsen, which helps reduce the "shadow industry" problem that self-published books have.
3. So that bookstores and libraries will take me seriously and stock my books on their shelves if readers ask.
4. So that, in the near future, I can bulk upload my books to retailers and make changes to my existing books without having to use retailer dashboards. StreetLib and PublishDrive both offer this feature, but you must have

ISBNs to access it. The writer of the future will treat book uploads as a data concern, not a manual entry concern where you have to log in to multiple dashboards to publish a book.

Do I want hardcovers? Yes, they're a worthy investment long-term.

Do I care about contributing to the self-publishing data landscape? Sure, but not enough to break my piggy bank to do it. There are advantages to not having an ISBN—namely, industry-savvy people can't look up your book sales. But that's a topic for another *Indie Author Confidential*.

Do I care about bookstore or library sales? Not really. I'm not sure they'd want to stock my books anyway due to the bias against self-publishers, though that seems to be changing. If I become famous and readers want my books, then bookstores will stock them anyway.

Do I care about automated uploading? Absolutely. I've discussed this at length in previous volumes of this series. But I'm well ahead of my time and I only know of one other indie author who even dared to mention this on her blog (and almost no one cared). Authors aren't thinking about this yet, and they won't until enough big-name six-figure authors start demanding it. Then everyone will want it. But we're still a few years away from that, so I can bide my time.

So, I decided to put this on hold again. The worst part is that the longer I wait, the more painful it will be when I do make the migration to official ISBNs (not the free ones that retailers give). I'll deal with that when the time comes.

A NEW WAY OF TEACHING

I bought a Wacom Tablet. I've always wanted one because I believe it's an instructor's dream.

There have been many times when I have wanted to draw something for my audience to help them understand a concept better. Writing is such an abstract field; if someone tells you that you need to "hook" readers, how the hell do you show that? We talk about showing and not telling all the time, don't we? So why don't we take that same approach when giving writing advice?

A question that I've always tried to answer is "how can I visualize the craft of writing?" I believe that if you can visualize the craft, you can teach it better. This is why my free book, *The Writing Craft Playbook,* has been a successful lead magnet for growing my email list. The book is a series of pictures that show how mega bestsellers hook readers. The pictures, which show illustrations of prose on a page with circles and X's, look like football playbooks.

I am surprised at how successful *The Writing Craft Playbook* has been. Ever since, I have wanted to level up the concept.

I downloaded a program called Open Board, which is open-source whiteboarding software that teachers use. And wow—it's fantastic.

Combined with screen capture software, I can use Open Board to create Khan Academy-style videos that let me draw on the screen, bring in videos, links, images, and many other things. I can draw wireframes, mind maps, playbooks, and so much more. I can even do this on livestreams. To my knowledge, this is unexplored territory.

In short, I like Open Board a lot. I also like the Wacom Tablet. I landed a speaking engagement with *Writer's Digest,* where I will be discussing the concepts in *The Writing Craft Playbook.* I'm using that event as a test run for the "look and feel" that I want to achieve with this teaching style. I will report on how that goes, but if it works, I will have created a new style of writing craft instruction for writers, one that hopefully helps break down abstract concepts in new ways to improve their writing craft.

ENDING TWO PILLARS OF MY WRITING PLATFORM

This quarter, I decided to end two pillars of my platform that have been transformational for me.

The first was my podcast, "The Writer's Journey," which I started in 2018 to document my writing process and the behind-the-scenes musings of a part-time writer. At first, the show existed to give my true fans more content to serve them better. The show started in a highly scripted format, where I shared aspects behind the scenes of my books. I enjoyed the scripted format, but it was difficult to maintain.

I never thought that anyone would listen to the show, but it was surprisingly successful. After the first six months, I noticed that my book sales and my email subscriptions increased.

Over time, I expanded the show into an improvisational format. Instead of scripting episodes, I turned on the microphone and talked about what was on my mind. I opined on current events in the publishing industry, interesting thoughts I had about becoming the writer of the future, and other random thoughts that my audience found engaging.

I received emails from listeners all over the world: Europe, Australia, New Zealand, the United States, Canada, China, Japan, and more. It made me smile to learn how people listen to my show; one listener tuned in during her lunch breaks; another listened while walking her dog; another listened while taking long walks on the beach. All my listeners had one thing in common:

they liked listening to what I had to say every week and they never knew what they were going to get.

As I reflect on the show, the most popular episodes were those where I became vulnerable and shared things I was struggling with, like my decision to seek therapy for the abandonment issues I suffered from my biological father. I openly shared my experiences with therapy, and many people wrote to me privately to express gratitude because it helped them. I didn't expect that.

I didn't realize it at the time, but "The Writer's Journey" was talk therapy for me. Even though I wasn't talking about personal issues every week, the act of talking about my problems was therapeutic. I held myself accountable to talk about my successes, failures, and everything in between.

I mentioned earlier in this volume that I encountered Bertrand Russell's amazing book, *The Conquest of Happiness*. After reading that book, which is a treatise on how to be happy in your life no matter what your circumstances, I discovered that I didn't need to record "The Writer's Journey" anymore.

Podcasting was my way of dealing with inward issues. I talked them out. Russell's book served as a mentor, and it showed me just how effective podcasting had been in my life up until that point. It also taught me that I no longer needed to do it because I had healed the part of myself that made me feel that I needed to do it.

The Conquest of Happiness also played another part. Russell was a British aristocrat who was a suicidal youth, but he learned to enjoy his life through focusing externally on others and special interests and diminishing preoccupation with himself. That's one of the big pieces of advice in the book: diminish preoccupation with yourself.

Writers are, by definition, preoccupied with themselves. They have to be. I believe that writing, at its root cause, comes from pain. We just can't see that because the writing makes us feel good.

Am I saying that writers are conceited? No.

But we have to learn to diminish that preoccupation. I am no exception to this rule. The *Indie Author Confidential* series is about my writing life. It's 100 percent my opinions and anecdotes from my life. The crazy thing is that people enjoy reading about it.

On the one hand, I internalized Russell's advice and it felt natural to me, but on the other hand, here I was with a massive platform that is all about me. I felt that I needed to reconcile the inconsistencies.

The podcast served its purpose, and when I saw it for what it was, it was merely a preoccupation with myself. It just happened to be content that my audience enjoyed because I shared advice and talked openly about the behind the scenes life of a writer. Again, it was a very odd feeling to see an action you've been taking for so long in a different light, especially, when you built an audience around it.

I realized that if I wanted to continue doing what I wanted to do, which is help, entertain, and educate people through the written word, I couldn't keep doing it by producing a show that was only about me. I needed to focus my efforts on others. Russell helped me see that it was time to for me to evolve and move onto the next level of service.

That's why I ended "The Writer's Journey." I didn't like ending a show that had built up so many weekly listeners, but once I had this revelation, I woke up one morning with no topics to discuss for the show, which had *never* happened before. It was time to end it, even though it meant that my sales would diminish. And they did.

The second part of my platform that I ended was my "Writing Tip of the Day" podcast. I started it in 2019 as an early adoption of Amazon Echo flash briefings, but I also syndicated it as a regular podcast. Every Monday through Friday, I offered a short writing tip. The show eclipsed "The Writer's Journey" in 2020 and was, after YouTube, my second biggest audience.

Whereas my reasons for ending "The Writer's Journey" were personal, I ended "Writing Tip of the Day" because I wanted to end the show on a high note, and I was starting to run out of ideas for episodes.

I batched the episodes, recording months in advance. That worked well, but looking at the future, I had to either change the format of the show or end it. I wasn't prepared to change the format—part of the show's charm was that it offered exactly what listeners wanted—a crisp writing tip.

I don't believe in creating subpar content that I'm not passionate about. That's not good for listeners or my brand. So I ended the show.

These decisions are never easy. Many listeners had grown accustomed to listening to "Writing Tip of the Day" during their morning routine. I had looked forward to having the show be there for them as they emerged from COVID-19 lockdown and started going to work again. But hey, you've got to be true to yourself, and sometimes that means ending things that bring people joy.

However, I'm sensitive to the fact that no one likes to have their favorite show canceled, so I tried to account for this in a few ways:

- I ended the show on a high note, without sacrificing the quality of content leading up to the final episode;
- I explained to my audience why I was ending the show;
- I explained where my listeners can continue engaging with me, even though I'm no longer podcasting;
- I left up the backlist episodes for future listeners to discover, and I'll pull them down once people stop listening for good;

- I ended the show with a final episode that serves as an "end cap," telling people that I'm still alive and where they can find me.

It's not perfect, but I did the best I could. I hope people understood and respected the decision.

As a content creator, I don't want the "golden handcuff" dilemma. I don't want to be tied to the content I create to the point where walking away means ending my career or completely choking off my income. I've seen too many writers and YouTubers fall into that trap, and it's ugly. There are no good solutions. I've always said that I'll make content that I'm passionate about, and the moment I stop being passionate about it, I'll stop creating it.

At the same time, I don't want to come across as fickle. I don't want people to think "I don't want to follow Michael La Ronn because every time he starts something, it ends." For this reason, I typically commit to any initiative for at least two years. I don't start anything unless I'm prepared to continue it for at least two years. In today's digital landscape, two years is an eternity. 2020 was drastically different from 2018 , and 2018 was drastically different from 2016. What matters is staying relevant and true to yourself, and just like society, I too am a work-in-progress.

NEW YOUTUBE STUDIO

Now that I've finished law school and ended my podcast footprint, I decided it was time to spend more time on my YouTube presence. I've been wanting to grow my YouTube channel but haven't been able to dedicate resources to it.

I recommitted to the future of my channel by rebranding it, doing data analysis into future videos that would bring new subscribers, and upgrading my equipment.

After upgrading my camera, lens, and lights, I rearranged my studio and created a new style for the channel.

As a person of color, I have always been sensitive about my camera appearance. I just couldn't seem to get it right. I started with a white background that mimicked classic Apple commercials, but the light was too bright and my skin was overexposed. Next, I experimented with shooting in my home office, but it was too dark, and the LED lights I bought were too harsh. Then, in my new house, I designed a set and bought equipment that was gentler on my skin, but it still wasn't good enough.

Now, finally, after seven years, I have a shooting style that is natural and flattering for my skin tone.

Here is the equipment that I bought:

- Canon M50 Mark II
- Sigma 16mm lens
- Elgato Key Light

- A camera reflector panel to fill in light on the side of my face
- Neewer LED Bi-Dimmable Lights (as background lights and a hair light)

If you're interested, you can check out affiliate links to my equipment by visiting www.authorlevelup.com/gear.

I have a small space, so I need an economical setup. The wide-angle lens lets me position the camera approximately one to two feet from my face without being an extreme close-up. And I still get a blurry background. The lens also does well in low-light, which means I can turn off all the lights in my basement and rely solely on my studio lights, something I couldn't do in the past.

Visit my channel if you'd like to check out recent videos with the new style.

THE WONDERS OF LIVESTREAMING

I started livestreaming on my YouTube channel in 2020. Once a month, I hosted a "Writing Power Hour," a 90-minute stream where I invited my community to join and write toward their work-in-progress with me live. We wrote in 20-minute increments, with 5-minute breaks where I answered questions and had a lively conversation.

My power hours were a huge hit. This surprised me because I didn't think anyone would be interested.

In the last chapter, I discussed my YouTube studio upgrade. I also upgraded my livestreaming capabilities. Originally, I used StreamYard, which was free and easy to use.

For software, I upgraded to eCamm Live, which is dedicated streaming software for the Mac OS. eCamm has an amazing feature where it lets you use your DSLR or mirrorless camera as a webcam on Zoom, Microsoft Teams, Skype calls, and more. In other words, I can achieve the same look on livestreams as I can on my YouTube videos, which is attractive to me because:

- it instantly improves the quality of my livestreams
- it creates consistency with my regular, non-streamed YouTube videos
- it improves my camera quality in future video interviews
- it increases my professionalism for online speaking engagements to a level that *no one* in the self-publishing

space is executing on, which makes me stand out,
leading to more speaking event invitations in the future

This is why I invest in technology and future capabilities. Incremental improvements over time lead to massive advantages in the future. I'm already executing at an above-average level; the next levels promise even more amazing capabilities, and I'm the only one experimenting with this style right now. That's cool.

Admittedly, I was fashionably late to the livestreaming game. Many YouTubers have been doing it for years. But I'm doing it in my way.

MAKING EYE CONTACT ON CONFERENCE CALLS

My new YouTube setup forced me to deal with a problem that I've always wondered about but never quite solved. It seems that I'm one of three people in the world who care about it.

The problem? Making eye contact on conference calls.

If I look at the person on the screen, my eyes are looking down. If I look at the camera, I can't see the person! It drives me crazy because I believe that even if you're on a conference call with someone, eye contact is still important. With my ALLi work as an Outreach Manager, I consider the ability to make eye contact especially important as I build relationships with key people in the publishing industry. Plus, being able to see someone properly means you can read their body language and respond accordingly.

Yet I am alone in my beliefs (again). In an era of working from home and "Zoom fatigue," people prefer to not even turn on their cameras.

However, I was working from home before working from home was a thing. The same problems with people turning on cameras then also exist now.

Here are a few reasons I think people don't like to turn their cameras on, and some of them are valid:

- People's homes are a mess.
- Their kids may be in the background.

- They may not feel comfortable putting their background on camera.
- They may be self-conscious about how they look on camera. (I once wore a shirt that did not play well on camera at all, so I turned my camera off for fear of making others sick.)
- They may be self-conscious about the lighting in their room. (I worked with a guy whose face was covered in shadows, making him look like a supervillain...on a work conference call.)
- They're not camera-ready; they might be wearing pajamas, or they haven't taken a shower yet.
- They keep the camera off to preserve Internet bandwidth.
- They're multitasking and don't want people to know. Hell, they might even be driving or shopping at the grocery store.
- They secretly don't like the person or people they're meeting with; they reserve camera time for people they like.
- They prefer to keep their cameras off to avoid accountability. It's a sign of disrespect, and the equivalent of hiding.

These reasons explain the reticence to turn on cameras when people are working from home.

However, if you put many of those reticent people in a different environment, with friends and people they like, talking about topics they're interested in—I guarantee they'll turn on their cameras.

In my writing and personal life, I make Internet calls all the time. Sometimes the calls are business-related; other times they're purely for pleasure and social interaction. No one has ever had their camera off. Not a single person.

But, I digress.

I just want to see people on conference calls and have them see me, and emulate in-person contact as much as possible. If you can look someone in the eye, then you're winning, in my opinion.

I researched solutions to this problem for weeks and found nothing that worked for my situation.

A few of the issues I faced:

- I have a small office space.
- My webcam sits on top of my computer screen, which means I have to look up to "look the camera in the eye."
- I need a simple solution because my job and writing life are fast-paced.
- I need a solution that works the same for work conference calls and podcast interviews.

I found a few videos online that recommended using a teleprompter to solve the problem. You position your webcam behind the teleprompter glass and use an iPad or camera monitor to reflect your conference call app onto the teleprompter. This way, you look directly into the camera, but the other person can't tell you're using a teleprompter.

I happened to have a teleprompter that I bought a few years ago, and this technique worked well, but teleprompters are bulky and complicated. It made my small desk feel even smaller.

I also found solutions where people used special devices that clipped onto your computer screen that served the same purpose as a teleprompter, but I didn't like those because they take up usable monitor space.

So I found my solution:

I bought a seven-inch camera monitor. Photographers usually attach these to the tops of cameras so the person being filmed can see what the camera sees.

- I bought a desk light stand. It clamps on my desk. Most people use these to hold ring lights. Because the stand has a threaded camera attachment, I attached the camera monitor to it instead and positioned it directly behind my webcam so that if I look into the camera, I'm also looking at the center of the camera monitor, which is directly at the person I'm talking to.
- I mirror my computer screen to the monitor that contains the conference call app.
- I bought a bi-directional HDMI switch so that I can switch the monitor between my work computer and writing computer with the push of a button.

That solved the problem completely. I feel so much better about my conference calls now, and they feel more natural.

I recorded a video on my personal YouTube channel about the setup if you are interested at www.authorlevelup.com/eyecontact. The video racked up 375 views in three weeks despite having a good thumbnail and strong production value. People just aren't interested yet.

But one day, when more people decide to solve this issue, my video will be there.

BECOME A WORLD-CLASS MARKETER

FOLLOW-UP THOUGHTS ON BOOK COVER DESIGN

In the last volume, I discussed my concerns around the future of book cover design. In short, I believe that we may be on the cusp of a designer shortage—existing good designers continue to raise their rates (and waiting periods) without providing higher quality in return (because their designs are good), and newer, less experienced designers don't provide a high-enough quality product. The gap between the two is where many authors will find themselves stuck—not able to afford higher quality designers but not satisfied with the entry-level designers. My conclusion was that, unless something changes, the best long-term solution for prolific authors like myself is to design their covers.

I made that conclusion reluctantly. I'm not thrilled about having to learn cover design, but I'm willing to do it to maintain my desired publishing speed if my predictions come true.

I received a wonderful email from a listener of "The Writer's Journey" who offered some advice on how to get started with designing your own covers. He's a designer by trade and has a lot of experience. I wanted to pass his advice along.

First, the companies that provide design software offer the best tutorials, even though the material is dry. He recommended always starting there, especially with Adobe Photoshop and Affinity Designer, which are the two competing apps for most design tasks. Both programs have similar capabilities, but he preferred to work with Adobe for text. In fact, he frequently switches between the two apps because Affinity does other things better.

He recommended always working at print resolution. This means at least 300-350 dots per inch (300 DPI). Fortunately, this is just a setting you can apply once and not have to worry about it.

In his opinion, a curriculum for learning how to design your covers would contain the following "lessons" (learning them at an advanced level):

- Layers
- Layer blending (allows you to adjust the transparency of shapes and create textural and lighting effects)
- Layer-based color correction (helpful for combining multiple photos)
- Selection tools
- Eraser tool
- Eyedropper tool (to transfer colors consistently)
- Color washes (helps bring different photos into a unified color palette)
- Brush-based color correction
- Gradations (for emphasizing one area of your cover over another)
- Text settings; primarily kerning (adjusting the space between letters), ligatures and special characters, color adjustments, effects (drop shadows, embossing, bevels, and so on)
- Exporting a cover design for both ebook and print

What a lesson plan! Master these aspects of your design software, and you'll have the skillset to create a cover, even though you won't have designed one yet.

Once you learn these things, you can ascend to the next level of learning.

I thought I'd pass the advice along as I receive emails frequently from people wanting to do their covers but who have no idea where or how to start.

THOUGHTS ON PERSONAL BRANDING

This chapter is long and meandering, but there is a lesson at the end.

I was invited by Matty Dalrymple to do a guest segment on her podcast "The Indy Author." My message was that branding is everything you do.

I recorded a 2-minute video on personal branding and how authors can improve theirs.

I specialize in personal branding. It's one of my superpowers. Sure, I'm not a good *designer*, so at first glance, my claims might appear to be arrogant and outsized, but consider my qualifications.

In my professional career, I've progressed through corporate America at a rapid rate for someone my age, and I've done it unusually.

First, personal branding is everything you do. The cliché "every day is an interview" is true in the digital age. Every time a reader comes into contact with your brand, you're interviewing for their attention. The same techniques that apply in the working world apply to writing. I'll explain why that's the case and how you can mine your personal experiences to improve your author branding.

How do you find a new job in today's digital age? In the past, it used to be that you had to know someone. That's why people put so much emphasis on "networking."

Today, while networking is still as effective as it always has been, there's a new way to find jobs: playing to search engine algorithms and automation. Many people still don't understand that no one looks at resumes anymore; computers do. A system scans your resume for certain indicators on whether you are a match for the job in question. If your resume matches those indicators, you'll advance to a screening interview. Even if you meet all the qualifications of a job, you'll be declined if your resume doesn't play nicely with the company's software. This means that you must use keywords from the job description and industry lingo on your resume to have a *long shot* at advancing to a screening. Read that last sentence again. Assuming you can get to a screening, then it all depends on your interviewing skills.

I am a *very* good interviewer. Even before I started podcasting and YouTube, I was highly skilled at verbal communication. My original major in college was Speech & Rhetoric (before they killed it—Rest In Peace). I've interviewed and gotten jobs that there was no way in hell I should have gotten. I got them because I knew how to work the system and I have a positive personality.

What do I mean by working the system, do you ask? I don't mean lying. And I certainly don't mean exaggerating my qualifications or experience. I never did that. I landed jobs well above my experience level with a slightly better-than-average work product.

The secrets? I'll list them and then explain.

- Be better than average.
- Learn how to "read" leaders in your organization and predict their future behavior at least three steps ahead.
- Choose your boss, and choose wisely; if your boss is chosen for you and that boss is bad for you, wait it out or find a new job. Refer to step #2. Never stay in a miserable work environment longer than necessary.

- As soon as possible, discern the "professional lessons" each job can teach you, and strive to learn them. These lessons are not what you think they are.
- Focus on my professional development.
- Do no harm.

Be better than average. Most people take the path of least resistance at work (and in life). Yet very few jobs are difficult. The jobs themselves are the easy part.

You can win big in life if you learn to execute on the same level as your peers, but then do little things that they would never think of (or want to do). This takes you from average to above-average.

(Note: In the professional world, you don't want to be the best. The best workers always have targets on their backs, and many would love to see them fail. You want to be good enough to catch the attention of the leaders in your organization while still commanding the respect of your peers. I know, I know—human nature. Please ignore this paragraph when it comes to your writing life.)

When I was a claims adjuster, customers complained that adjusters never called them back. Customers often had to wait days, sometimes weeks, to hear from an adjuster so they could get their cars fixed. I noticed that the longer a customer's voicemail went unanswered, the madder the customer got. (Wouldn't YOU be angry if you went weeks without a car?) That led to *more* phone calls, escalations, and manager involvement.

Yet the prevailing opinion on the work floor was "I have too much crap to do. This angry customer can wait like everyone else."

I made it a personal goal to return voicemails within 24 hours, even if I had to sacrifice performance in other areas of my job. When other adjusters were trying to rush customers off the phone because of heavy workloads, I spent *more* time on the phone with customers. If they asked me about their policy, I'd send them a

PDF and go through the coverages with them. Since I spoke Spanish, I worked with many Latino customers who didn't speak English. I offered to translate for them when they went to retrieve their cars from the impound, or when they went to the rental car company and needed an interpreter. My leaders always told me that I had a good "phone side" manner—I connected with people in ways that my peers did not, mainly because of my voice and my calm demeanor.

My customers were much happier than my colleagues' because I returned their calls. It's easier to settle a claim with someone happy with you versus someone angry at you for not calling them back. I settled claims so quickly, people thought I was cheating.

My manager received fewer complaints, which astounded him. He made me his "fixer"—he would send me the angriest customers and I would make them go away.

Guess who got the best customer compliments?

Not me. In fact, I seldom received thanks. I used to keep an "accolade" folder whenever a customer sent a thank-you note. In my five years as a claims adjuster, I received fewer than 20. Once customers got their cars fixed, they forgot about me and never answered the customer surveys. Many of my colleagues took that as a personal insult; I considered it an indicator that I did my job correctly.

My colleagues chased praise from customers. Some even begged customers to send their manager kind words, or to answer a "10" on the customer surveys. While they were doing that, I just returned people's calls.

At the end of the year, who do you think got a promotion and a pay raise? Me, all because I reverse-engineered the system. I then *built my resume* around those successes, which I could point out in my next job interview.

This method worked like magic. Interviewers would ask me basic questions, and I would come back with answers that shocked them and showed that I thought about things differently. Combine that with good performance results and a glowing manager recommendation, and boom—new job.

I kept building on my successes, and after a few years, I had a resume and a background that looked like no one else's, even though I had a similar work experience.

I consider my work experience to be a portfolio of assets, just like my books. When I net a professional victory, I find a way to package it so I can "sell" it in a future interview.

Before you start thinking that I'm vain, the best experience to sell is one that also develops you professionally because you can speak to how it developed you.

Here's how you sell an experience:

- Identify the pain point (it must be something that YOU uncover, not someone else).
- Tell what you thought about it (and don't mince words).
- Explain how you solved it, who you worked with (job titles), and the result in quantitative terms.
- Explain what you learned and why it's relevant to the job you're interviewing for.

Learn how to "read" leaders in your organization and predict their future behavior.

At one company I worked for, I noticed that news predictably flowed from the top-down.

- Low-level executives often received advance notice of a change at least one year to 18 months in advance. It was then their job to set a strategy within the directive to achieve it.

- Directors received the news around six months before the change. It was their job to operationalize the change, and because they knew the news but couldn't share, they would often "nudge" managers in a certain direction without telling them why.
- Managers received the news around one to three months before the change. By this point, the plan was already finalized and it was their job to deliver the (usually bad) news.

As a low-level employee, I used this knowledge to predict what was coming. Whenever workers received a "survey" about something or were asked to track their time for certain tasks, I could reliably predict when a change would be announced.

Once I knew the "when," I could read between the lines and figure out the "what" and then the "how." If the answers resulted in my job getting harder, I changed my behavior to align with what I thought was coming.

When reorganizations were announced, I studied the organization charts carefully. I observed that in a major company reorganization, there are always one or two "threads" left dangling; in other words, the moves didn't make sense, and if you pulled the threads, you could spot what the next reorganization would be.

For example, once, after a round of layoffs, one executive had 20 direct reports. That was very high for the company—most executives rarely had between three or four. From that data, it was clear that the next re-org would strike that executive's organization because that type of ratio is not sustainable. Or, that executive would get so burned out that they would leave, triggering another re-org! If and when the re-org struck, I mapped out what might happen to me and my boss. "If person A moves here, where would person B go?"

And guess what? I was often right.

This type of calculus was helpful when determining the future of the projects I was working on. *Nothing* kills projects like reorgs. If I sensed one was coming, I'd speed up the work so I could get it done, or sometimes I'd let work die if I knew that the work couldn't get done in time and I would be facing a hostile colleague or executive who'd want to kill it.

By learning to predict the upcoming changes that would impact my work at least 18 months in advance, I was able to plan my work, projects, and career.

Choose your boss (if you can). There's not much else to say here other than many, many people stay in jobs they like but suffer bosses they hate. Or, they think that maybe they can make their boss like them. It'll never happen.

Sometimes, the desire to stay in a job is generational. Sometimes, there are other concerns such as family and finances. But I suggest that this staying in a bad work environment is detrimental to your mental health. You can always find another job, even if it doesn't seem like it.

As soon as possible, discern the "professional lessons" each job can teach you. Most people just want to learn how to do their jobs. That's what I call the "day-to-day experience." This type of experience will help you be successful in the role. It might help you secure another job, especially if it's at the same company, but more often than not, your day-to-day experience is no longer relevant when you leave that job. Day-to-day experience is useful because it allows you to understand others' worldviews. As an executive mentor told me once, day-to-day experience can help you influence and work more effectively with that department in the future, if you ever work with those people again.

But there is another experience that is more valuable—I call it "universal experience." You carry universal experience with you from job to job, and it's applicable anywhere you go.

Let's take the claims adjuster profession. The day-to-day

experience is learning the ins and outs of insurance policies, claims systems, and how to settle claims.

The "universal experience" you gather in claims is learning how to relate to people. By relating to many types of people, you can work more effectively and get what you want out of them. I don't mean this cynically, but practically. If, as an adjuster, you knew this on day one of the job, you would focus less on learning policy language and claims settlements and instead on trying to talk to as many different people as possible to learn what is important to them—happy people, angry people, sadistic people, parents, executives, immigrants, truck drivers, teenagers away at college, doctors, farmers, trust fund babies, and so on. Each person you talk to becomes a blueprint for the next person you meet with a similar personality. When you're at your next job and have to deal with a jerk who talks down to you in a meeting, maybe you have tools to disarm that person based on how you dealt with a similar jerk in the past.

Even though I hated my time in claims, it gave me a masterclass in learning how to work with people, even if they hate my guts.

The writing life is the same. The day-to-day experience of a writer is about learning how to write, publish, and market a book. The universal experience is learning how to communicate effectively in the written word and persuading people to take the action you want them to take: clicking your ad, buying your book after reading the book description, turning the page from the moment they read the first chapter, buying your *next* book, and so on. With fiction, it's about making people feel emotions. The universal experience of a writer is learning *mind control* through self-expression.

Focus on professional development. By committing to your professional development and learning, you'll remain relevant in an ever-changing marketplace.

Do no harm. I don't believe in hurting or backstabbing people. I've somehow managed to survive in corporate America without having to do it or having it done to me.

Let's put this all together. What does any of this have to do with personal branding for authors?

First, every day is an interview. Readers will encounter your brand 24/7/365. You must control the experience, and more often than not, this is done through metadata, search, and content such as videos, podcasts, interviews, and blog posts. Branding is everything you do. If you think about it this way, you'll think about it correctly.

Second, strive to be better than the average author. Do what others are doing, but then do things that they would never do. For example, I respond to all fan-mail. I always take the time to be thorough in my responses. Do something special and do it at a world-class level. Readers will remember. This becomes your brand.

Third, predict, predict, predict. Predict what the market will do. Predict what other authors will do. Predict what your readers will do when they finish your books. Make predictions and update your strategy accordingly. For example, maybe there's a new type of advertising that has promise but no one is adopting it yet. That's an opportunity to create a new touchpoint with a new audience.

Fourth, choose your work wisely, just as you'd choose a boss. If your writing ever becomes like a nagging boss, that's trouble. Choose the projects that you're passionate about and readers will feel it. That may not always translate into commercial success, but I'd rather be successful writing work I love than be successful writing books that make me miserable. That defeats the purpose of writing.

Fifth, focus on your professional development. Keep learning, stay committed to the craft, and keep writing, even when it's hard.

Readers will remember you for being prolific, and they'll respect you for it.

Sixth, do no harm. Don't be a jerk. Don't hurt other people in exchange for your success. The publishing community is smaller than it looks, and the truth always comes out. In an era of #MeToo and social media transparency, it's much more difficult to be an asshole and get away with it. Develop a brand for being a nice author. (When I say "nice," I don't mean pushover.) That will do wonders for your author brand and help you attract more opportunities that will help you grow your business.

I distilled all of this advice into a 2-minute video, which is the main reason I decided to make this chapter so long.

THOUGHTS ON ANIMATED BOOK COVERS

I'm seeing animated covers on the market again. Again...

I'm not a fan of animated book covers. I like how they look, but I don't like what they will lead to.

Imagine that you're browsing a book retailer and all the book covers are animated. Each cover strives to attract your attention with glitter, sparkles, flames, and kinetic wisps. It won't matter what's on the cover—all that will matter is how flashy it is.

It would be like reading *The Daily Prophet* from the *Harry Potter* series while you're trying to buy books. Yikes.

I hope book retailers resist the urge to allow animated covers. It'll just make *everything* harder for authors in a market where winning attention is already hard enough.

I see authors use animated covers on their websites and social media to add flair. Tools like Book Brush now allow you to create animated covers easier than ever before, so I don't blame people for playing around with the technology. I just hope it doesn't get abused if it goes mainstream.

WORKING WITH APPLE

In my capacity as Outreach Manager for the Alliance of Independent Authors, I received an opportunity to work with the Apple Books team to produce a webinar called "Growing Your Sales on Apple Books." The webinar was a 45-minute presentation on why authors should distribute their books to Apple Books and how to maximize their sales on the platform. There was also a 15-minute Q&A. Suffice to say that ALLi members gained great insights into the Apple Books platform and how it differs from Amazon.

I organized the webinars and took care of the little details. The experience was a useful practice session for when I organize a future event for my community.

Here were the steps:

- I met with the Apple Books team to discuss their slides and their specific requirements. Apple has some unusual corporate guidelines, so I needed to understand those so ALLi could comply.
- I met with the ALLi team to discuss a plan for creating website pages, event calendar entries, email communications, and social media marketing for the event.
- I locked in dates with the Apple team for two webinars, each one week apart. Because ALLi's community is international, we created one webinar for authors in the

northern hemisphere and one for authors in the southern hemisphere. Around five to seven weeks from the event, we created the web pages and email communications for the event. Each event had its page, and when authors signed up, they received an autoresponder sequence that set expectations for the event. Due to Apple corporate guidelines, we could only accept 50 people on the webinar. Spots filled up in less than 24 hours.

- After the event, I sent out a survey asking authors what they thought of the event and whether they would recommend it to their friends.

There were other details, but those were the major steps. The webinars went well, and I was grateful for the opportunity.

Speaking of personal branding, you can bet that I built this experience into my resume!

LEARNING MY LESSON ON SERIES COVERS

In the previous volume of this series, I discussed how I screwed up the design on my cover *Dead Rat Walking*. The designer was great, but I gave her instructions that led to rookie mistakes:

- I put a character against a flat background, which gave the cover no depth.
- I used a dark setting, making the hero hard to see.
- I used a dark color scheme, compounding the problem.

Again, this was not the designer's fault. I take full responsibility. But I should have known better because I made these mistakes early in my career. I thought I had learned, but apparently not.

When it was time to order the design for book two, *Rat City*, I explained my concerns to the designer and we worked to create something different that would look better in a thumbnail.

The result was more colorful and a better blend of light and dark. Is it perfect? No, but I'll take it.

It seems that I always find my design stride in the second book in a series. If the series doesn't sell well, I thought about having the cover for book one redesigned by the same designer once I finish the series. It's just an idea, but I still feel that I didn't give *Dead Rat Walking* the best chance it deserved.

Now I just need to publish the series to see what happens!

WHY I HAVE A PRESS PAGE

For several years, I have included a "Press" page On Michael La Ronn.com and Author Level Up.com. The page showcases my public speaking highlights and lets venue organizers know that I am open to speaking engagements. It also contains a press kit with author headshots and a biography. The goal was to both promote me and make it easier for venues to feature more with less effort from me.

This quarter, my Press pages continue to reap dividends and grow my sales and brand. In one month alone, I landed two speaking engagements that specifically referenced my speaking page. The conversations started with "I saw X video on your speaking page and thought a similar talk would be great for our audience."

This is one of the rare instances where I can tell that a marketing technique is working. My Press pages took about 30 minutes each to create and cost nothing. They have provided an amazing return on investment.

BRAVO TO A PUBLICIST

Let me start this chapter by saying that I don't recommend hiring a publicist. There's nothing wrong with the profession, but I've never seen any concrete data that a publicist can help *an indie author*. I've heard too many stories of authors spending thousands of dollars on a PR firm only to see disappointing sales. There's also the problem of fraud; there are always a few scam artists who will gladly take authors' money and provide nothing in return. You have to be careful, which is why I recommend not hiring a publicist unless you're making a lot of money and can hire a reputable firm. (Even then, I still think you're wasting money if you're not strategic about it.)

Otherwise, I don't believe publicists are practical for the everyday author. There are better, more cost-effective techniques to invest your money in.

Now that I've made my position clear, I want to take a moment to extend a bravo to a publicist.

I received an email from a publicist from Wiley (a publisher well-known for informational nonfiction, such as the *Dummies* franchise). The publicist stumbled across my YouTube channel and wondered if I would be interested in reading and reviewing an upcoming book on their roster called *Book Wars: The Digital Revolution in Publishing* by John B. Thompson. It is a historical account of the digital media revolution and how it disrupted the publishing industry. Thompson wrote a similar book in 2012 called *The Merchants of Culture.*

Not only was this book perfect for me, but it was also a great recommendation to my community. The publicist did her homework (or if she didn't, I would have never known).

I expected the book to be one-sided in its coverage, favoring traditional publishing. Quite the opposite. It not only covered the traditional publishing industry, but it also covered self-publishing in astounding detail. Thompson's research was meticulous too. It's a very academic book—not the kind you read on a Saturday night. But if you're a serious professional author like me, this book is a must-read because it gives historical perspective. Younger and less experienced writers often lack the historical perspective and there aren't many books on the history of the publishing industry, so Thompson's book is required reading.

I'm still shaking my head at the fact that a *publicist* made me aware of this book. Does it change my opinions about hiring one? No, but the experience taught me what a publicist can achieve if they do their due diligence.

STUMBLING UPON AD IDEAS

A long time ago, I attended a Q&A session with Joanna Penn. This was before I published my first book, so it was probably in 2012 or 2013. I asked, "I can't find any comparable books similar to mine. What should I do?"

Her answer: "If you can't find a comparable book, you haven't looked hard enough."

Ouchies! Trust me, I had plumbed Amazon and Google for hours, and I could not find anything similar to the book.

Sure enough, two years later, I found a book that was comparable to mine. And it had been published well before I performed my search. For some reason, it didn't show up until then. Joanna was right.

An important lesson I've learned over the years is that you often won't find some comparable books until *years* after you publish your book.

This quarter, I was doing Amazon Ads research for my book *The Indie Author Atlas*. I happened to encounter a book called *The Writer's Atlas*, which was a book of fantasy maps. It was a perfect target for ads, yet I have no idea why I never encountered it when I was doing marketing research for *The Indie Author Atlas*. The world is funny like that.

This incident was a reminder to remain on the lookout for comparable books even after you publish your book.

EVERYONE HAS THEIR TIME

While I wrote this book, I binge-listened to Casiopea, one of my favorite jazz Japanese fusion bands. I've been listening to them since college, but they're mostly unknown in the west except in jazz aficionado circles.

Lately, I've been watching their live concerts. They have recorded more *live* albums than most bands have *studio* albums. Their prolific live discography puts most bands to shame. Even more unusual, you can find videos of all of their live performances. It's fascinating to watch them over the years. I am captivated at how tight, consistent, and prolific they are as a band, especially between 1977 - 1988. Every year during that period, they released *at least* one album. Some years, they did two or three. Recording an album in the seventies and eighties required an extraordinary amount of manpower and planning. Only the most disciplined artists recorded more than *one* per year. Many artists during that period only recorded albums every few years. That's true today too.

At the time of this writing, the main Casiopea band recorded over 40 albums between 1977 and 2021. Its leader, Issei Noro, has recorded 17 albums under his name and various spinoff bands. The band's original bassist, Tetsuo Sakurai, has recorded 21 albums under his name as part of various spinoff bands that he created after leaving Casiopea in 1988. The bassist who replaced Sakurai, Yoshihiro Naruse, recorded nine solo albums *before* joining Casiopea. The band's (most famous early) drummer,

Akira Jimbo, has recorded 34 albums under his name and as part of spinoff bands. The band's (most famous) keyboardist, Minoru Mukaiya, has recorded three albums under his name, as well as over 200 jingles that play at the Japanese train stations. Kiyomi Otaka, the keyboardist who replaced Mukaiya, recorded six solo albums before joining Casiopea.

Add the numbers up, and you have a backlist that is over 130 albums deep. That's hundreds of songs.

If you like one Casiopea album, you'll like most of them. Their style changes from album to album, but their core sound is the same. Even better, unlike many bands, the former members went on to create music that jives well with Casiopea's sound, and their solo careers are worth following.

You always know what you're going to get when you listen to Casiopea: a mixture of progressive fusion and smooth, emotional ballads. The band almost always uses a quartet configuration, but here are some ways they've changed that up over the years:

- They have rerecorded all of their classic songs with reimagined versions.
- They recorded an album where all the members play acoustic versions of their instruments.
- They recorded an album where the chord changes are almost exactly the opposite of what they would normally compose.
- They recorded an album that is best described as stadium rock meets jazz fusion.
- They recorded an album that prominently features horn sections.
- They recorded several albums that predominantly feature vocal tracks.

Yet, no matter what you're listening to, Casiopea is always a guitar, keyboard, bass, and drums. Always.

When I think about Casiopea's sound, I think about oatmeal. There are many flavors of oatmeal and ways you can eat it, but at the end of the day, it's oatmeal. That's part of the band's charm.

Consistency and a prolific work ethic lead to amazing results.

Is every Casiopea album a perfect "10"? No. Is every Casiopea song amazing? No. But with the amount of work they've produced, they have more good albums and songs than your average artist. Also, their experiments are fun to listen to, even when they don't quite work out.

As I think about writing and publishing, I don't see why this work ethic can't apply to writers. We have such a bias toward "taking ten thousand years to write a magnum opus" that prolific writers are often sneered upon. And perhaps it's a matter of preference, but I appreciate the author who writes 100 books, even if many of them strike out. Because I suspect, as is the case with Casiopea, that when that author finds his/her "tribe," they'll buy *everything*.

This is why prolific personalities fascinate me: if you start with their early works and work your way to the present day, you can see their souls in their work. You learn deep lessons about that person and their artistry that you can apply to your work in a way that you just don't get by consuming an artist who only has written one masterpiece.

Here are lessons I've learned from prolific personalities over the years:

- Quantity breeds quality.
- Never settle.
- Every artist evolves, but sometimes audiences don't like it. True courage is continuing to push in the direction you believe in.

- Being fearless comes with a career cost, but it also comes with a greater respect long-term.
- Customer tastes are cyclical; what seemed like a terrible idea decades ago will suddenly find a new life with customers.
- Today's digital age means that styles will never truly go out of vogue anymore; once something becomes popular, it may always be popular with a small group of people.
- Some ideas are ahead of their time.
- Some ideas flop tremendously.
- Every prolific artist has "good" periods and "less inspired" periods.
- Find ways to pay homage to your fans with every new work you do.
- If you enjoy the work you create, readers can FEEL it.

The key is to keep honing your craft. Are you getting better with each new book? Are you developing yourself? If you stay committed, then you'll find success in the future.

What if you found a way to think of your books like oatmeal— with each new series, you delivered something new and unique, but the core reason why readers love you remained? In other words, while the flavor might be different, the taste is similar. What would that take? What would it look like for you?

BECOME A TECHNOLOGY AND DATA-DRIVEN WRITER

THE IMPORTANCE OF BEING NIMBLE

This quarter, I fell in my driveway. I was taking my trashcan to the curb and didn't see a patch of black ice. In an instant, my cul-de-sac spiraled in front of my eyes, my hands pushed out instinctively to protect me, and my glasses went flying. I was on the ground before I even knew what happened.

It took me by so much surprise that I lay there for a few moments. My brain had to catch up with the fall.

I scraped my palms, skinned my legs, and ruined a pair of jeans, but I was otherwise okay. However, the experience got me thinking about the importance of contingency planning.

What if I had been seriously hurt? What if I had broken a wrist? What if my glasses broke? What if…?

The thought exercise led me to reevaluate my contingency plans. More importantly, though, it confirmed that I am on the right path.

I've been intentional with investing in tools and technology to help me write anywhere, in any position, and in spite of injuries.

If I had broken a wrist, I could have switched immediately to dictation as my primary writing method, and I would have racked up *higher* word counts per session.

If my glasses broke, I could have also used dictation, probably with Dragon Anywhere, so I could at least see the screen on my phone as I spoke.

That's what it means to be nimble.

WHY TECHNOLOGY

Since my fall in the driveway, I've been thinking a lot about technology. Technology is my number one investment. To use executive terminology, it's one of my "big bets."

I thought this chapter would be a good opportunity to recap on *why* investments in technology are important to me.

The writer of the future will be very different from the writer of today. As I look at the market, global economy, and trends, I believe that the market conditions won't always be as favorable for indie writers as it is now.

Consider this:

- Amazon will continue its monopolization efforts.
- Traditional publishers will continue to consolidate.
- Artificial intelligence will continue to drive disruption, eliminating jobs and changing the way we work. With fewer people working due to automation, they'll turn to the arts, making the "content creator economy" more crowded.
- We still don't know how COVID-19 will shape the future and customer trends.
- Traditional publishers will eventually get savvy about digital media and find ways to provide a better value for their authors, particularly through AI, thus making them more attractive to authors (but the contracts will still be terrible).

Add all of these factors together and you have an environment where today's entry and mid-level authors will find it hard to stay relevant.

The *only* way to compete in a landscape like this is through technology. Technology levels the playing field. Big companies are terrible stewards of technology; they brag as if they've mastered it, and it drives their expenses down, but talk to their employees and you'll get a different story. Plus, it's impossible to get anything done at large corporations because of bureaucracy. I say this as someone who understands the corporate world very well.

So, if traditional publishers ever get hold of effective AI, I expect that they won't truly get their money's worth out of it, even if it's making them money. That leaves a small opening for indie authors like you and me.

I'm willing to bet that if you look at the average author's workflows, they're almost all manual. This means that the author must initiate each step by hand (rather, keyboard) to accomplish them. Technology can help us eliminate manual processes.

Here's a brainstorming exercise on how technology can help us win.

- Capture your ideas using a capture service like Evernote or OneNote. Install these on all your devices. Use your phone to capture photos, audio, or quick notes while you're out and about. Catalog your notes with tags for easy recall later.
- Use your phone to write books; write when you're on the go to bolster your daily word counts.
- Use dictation to speak your way to higher word counts.
- Invest in a writing app that does the hard work for you, such as Scrivener. When you pick the right writing app, you won't spend time fighting with it; you'll spend more time being productive.

- Use artificial intelligence to assist you with parts of your writing. Authors are experimenting with AI in helping them tell certain parts of their stories, such as randomizing planets or the weather that takes place in the story.
- Automate your editing with tools already on your computer (as I have documented with my automated editing engine).
- Invest in dedicated formatting software instead of doing it yourself. If you own a Mac, Vellum is the best app that money can buy at the time of this writing. It will save you hours of trouble with Microsoft Word. You can reinvest those hours toward writing new stories, marketing, and so on.
- Use the ONIX architecture to create a data feed that will allow you to automate your book publication and any changes. Instead of uploading a book through a dashboard, use your data feed. This is how traditional publishers do it. Outside of a couple of ebook aggregators who offer limited bulk upload, this option isn't available for indies, but the technology is. I predict this will be an option in the future.
- Use existing programming tools to help you track the health of your books and retailer product pages. How will you know if your book is pulled from sale, or if your price is wrong? You can hire someone to write software to "patrol" your properties for these sorts of events. I know because I did it!
- Write highly converting copy with a swipe file tool. (I covered this in a previous volume.)
- Write highly converting copy with an AI copywriting service.

- Use a keyword research tool like Publisher Rocket to find winning keywords and categories for your books.
- Use Microsoft Excel, Microsoft Access, or Microsoft Power BI to aggregate your sales reports into one source so that you can determine your sales. Explore this data for key insights that will inform your marketing decisions.
- Outsource less important tasks to a virtual assistant, and communicate with them using a project management tool like Slack or Asana.
- Use platforms like Upwork to hire freelancers for one-off tasks that you don't have time for.
- Use your email client's rule system to route emails to specified folders, such as expenses or royalty statements. This stops you from manually moving them, which adds up over time. More generally, triaging your emails will save time in other areas.

There are many more ways to use technology to save time, effort, and money. If you haven't yet, start investing now. You'll be shocked at how cheap it is. Almost everything you need is already on your computer.

LIQUID TEXT

While browsing YouTube, I stumbled across a Mac app called Liquid Text. The idea behind it is novel: speed up everyday functions that a user requires with keyboard shortcuts.

For example, if you type in a word and want to look it up on Wikipedia, normally, you'd follow these steps:

- Minimize the writing app window
- Open your browser
- Go to www.wikipedia.com
- Search for the term
- Click the correct search result
- Read the page
- Minimize your browser window
- Return to your writing app

Liquid Text simplifies those steps:

- Highlight the term in your writing app
- Type Command + Shift + two to bring up the liquid search bar
- Enter the R key to bring up the reference menu
- Enter the "W" key for Wikipedia
- This will bring up the appropriate Wikipedia page
- Read the page
- Return to the writing app

While Liquid Text doesn't necessarily reduce the number of steps, it does reduce the time, mouse clicks, and effort.

It's a great idea. You can even program additional search engines into it, such as Google, Wolfram Alpha, Merriam-Webster, Dictionary.com, and more. You can even convert units if needed.

I installed Liquid Text but don't use it to its full potential. However, it got me thinking about what a fantastic tool this would be inside of a writing app.

Consider these ideas:

- Enter a keyboard shortcut to bring up a menu similar to Liquid Text that has a search engine capability, dictionaries, unit conversions, sharing, translation, advanced copy/paste, and so on.
- Access your character profiles with a key.
- Force the writing app into a certain mode. For example, in Scrivener, a keystroke will automatically create a split-screen with the current chapter on the top and the outline on the bottom. Another key will revert to your original view.
- Look up all similar instances of a word or phrase, or get statistics on how many times you've used a particular word.
- Do competitive intelligence on book retailers with a keystroke.
- Share snippets of your work-in-progress to your social media network of choice.

And more!

This could be a killer feature if a writing app developer experimented with it.

PERFECTIT

I discovered a great proofreading add-in for Microsoft Word called PerfectIt.

PerfectIt is an app that allows you to run important proofreading checks:

- spelling and grammar
- consistent hyphenation, proper nouns, and abbreviation use
- proper table/figure numbering

And more.

PerfectIt is *not* like ProWritingAid or Grammarly. Its main function is not spelling and grammar. PerfectIt exists to make sure that your manuscript is *internally* consistent, which is often forgotten.

I bought PerfectIt within 15 minutes of using it because I understood the value. Ironically, PerfectIt isn't marketed at authors—it's marketed at editors! If editors believe in this tool enough to purchase it, then it's a worthy investment for authors.

I reviewed PerfectIt on my YouTube channel, but my audience didn't receive it well.

First, they asked what the difference was between it and Grammarly. That's my fault as I should have anticipated that objection.

Second, they resisted the subscription model. My audience *hates* subscriptions.

Third, I didn't do a good enough job explaining the benefit of internal consistency. It's a professionalism thing. Again, that was my fault.

Maybe I did a better job explaining the benefits of PerfectIt while writing this chapter, maybe not. But PerfectIt is a critical part of my editing workflow, and it has made my work considerably stronger and more cohesive. Readers won't necessarily see it, but I hope that over time, they'll feel it.

AUTOMATOR: MOST UNDERRATED TOOL ON MAC?

For years, I promised myself that I would learn how to use the Mac's Automator app, but I kept putting it off. Not anymore.

I spent a weekend delving into tutorials on how to optimize Automator. I used it to successfully automate my bookkeeping.

I figured out how to move massive amounts of files into many different folders with just a single click.

I also figured out how to automate cleaning my desktop and downloads folders, which both get messy quickly.

Is Automator perfect? No, but it's a hell of a tool if you can find ways to use it for your needs. By understanding how to use it better, I unlocked more horsepower from my computer, which didn't cost me anything other than a few hours of my time and effort.

KOFAX POWER PDF: GREAT LITTLE TOOL FOR PDF WORK

At work, I needed to do some advanced PDF work with a short turnaround. Because of corporate guidelines (and common sense), I'm not allowed to upload company documents to free websites that can do much of this work. That would expose company data, which would probably get me fired. My company doesn't use Adobe Acrobat because it's too expensive.

I called my IT department, and they offered to install a program that the company uses for PDF work. It was called Kofax Power PDF, which is a cheaper alternative to Adobe Acrobat.

I was impressed with it. Not only did it help me accomplish the task at hand, but it also offered a lot of cool features. I found myself playing around with it for longer than I should have. I was supposed to be working, after all!

Kofax Power PDF is also a single perpetual license, which makes it much more attractive than Adobe Acrobat. At the time of this writing, it costs $179, which isn't cheap, but it's cheaper than the $180 *per year* for Adobe Acrobat.

I don't have many uses for PDF work in my writing business, but if I did, I'd buy Kofax Power PDF without hesitation. It's available on Windows and Mac operating systems.

THE RISE OF AI FOR COPYWRITING

Get ready for a wild ride; not this chapter, but a wave of technology that is finally hitting the self-publishing space: AI-assisted copywriting.

This technology has been around for at least a few years—I spotted it in the wild at least as early as 2018 , but most people weren't investing in it. The only people using them were... (wait for it) marketers.

Now I'm seeing startups with slick products that use artificial intelligence to create highly converting copy. (Perhaps those marketers who were early adopters started these companies, but I don't know.) These startups are marketing to the average entrepreneur who hates writing copy. Most businesspeople I know don't like copywriting, authors included.

I'm seeing a shift in that influencers in the self-publishing space are covering these services now, where they didn't six months ago.

I played around with one such service, and I was impressed. I should have saved the results of my experiment, but I forgot.

The service made me fill out a questionnaire with some details about my product and the target audience. It then produced surprisingly good copy. Some of it was obviously written by an AI, but some of it was honestly better than what I could have come up with.

The value of these services is that they can "backstop" you when you're tired or struggling to come up with converting copy. They're not a replacement for copywriting; rather, they're an assistant.

If you're interested, sign up for a free trial for one of these services and see for yourself. The results are scary good, and if they're this good now, just wait five years. Once more people adopt them, the services will build a bigger and better corpus and therefore deliver more targeted results.

One concern I do have is whether the authors that use these services will have a "sameness" in their copy. For example, are the services recommending the same taglines to all authors, or are the results truly specific to each person's project? Although minor, it's a concern.

Another concern I have is privacy. Internet marketers can't be trusted with anything, let alone our data. Remember that when you use these services (especially if they're free), that you're helping a team train their AI. This means they're gathering tons of your data, which puts them in an unfair position down the road where they control a goldmine of information that we'll have to pay to access. The services offer free trials and affordable pricing right now because they need to build a user base and accumulate more data. But what is their endgame? Is it to create amazing copywriting assistants, or is there a bigger (and possibly more sinister) goal?

Call me skeptical, but all you have to do is look at Google and Facebook to see how much power a company can gather under the guise of being helpful to people in their everyday lives.

The AI battle hasn't been won yet—there will be companies that get so rich off data and AI that they will make Google and Facebook look like Mom & Pop shops.

Skepticism aside, I do believe that AI-assisted copywriting is the future.

HOW I SUCCESSFULLY AUTOMATED MY BOOKKEEPING

I've complained about my dislike of bookkeeping in previous volumes of this series. I don't enjoy it, but I recognize that it is critical in the event of an audit to have good books. I try to keep good records—I track all my expenses and keep all my receipts forever because you never know when you'll need them.

In 2014, I downloaded a template from the Internet that another author had compiled. It worked for a few months, but the design of the template wasn't user-friendly.

In 2015, I designed a system of my own that addressed the issues from the template I used. Here's how it worked:

- I categorized all of my expenses: cover design, editing, marketing, business, software, and so on.
- I created a corresponding folder system on my computer that matched the expense categories.
- I created a spreadsheet with tabs for each category.
- When I received an expense, I would save the PDF into the proper folder and also log an entry on the spreadsheet so that it would match the expense in the folder.
- The spreadsheet auto-calculated the categories.

This system worked well for about three years. It took me about an hour each month to categorize and organize everything, and my accountant had no issues tabulating my expenses at the end of the year for tax purposes.

However, my accountant stopped her business. I hired a new accountant who used QuickBooks. I don't like QuickBooks. The software is good at what it does, but I don't like the way it categorizes expenses. I need to be able to look at my expenses and know how they break down for *my purposes.* That said, it didn't make sense to have two systems—one for QuickBooks and one for myself.

With the new accountant, I created a new system that scrapped my categorization system. I let the accountant categorize the expenses, and I forced myself to rely on QuickBooks. I didn't like it, but it saved me time.

However, I still had the issue of saving receipts. My accountant didn't need those, but I still needed to keep records, so QuickBooks only solved part of the problem.

(Yes, I know that QuickBooks can store your receipts, but that added extra steps to my workflow.)

Using Airmail and Automator, I created a system that completely automated the cataloging of my business expenses. Here's how it worked:

- Airmail automatically flags approximately 80 percent of my expense emails and moves them to an expense folder. I move the rest manually as needed.
- I use a one-click workflow that grabs all the emails in the folder and saves them as .EML files to a designated folder on my computer. This takes approximately three minutes.
- I run an Automator Workflow that moves all of the files into proper folders accordingly based on their filenames. For example, PayPal emails have the same naming structure. This is true for all vendors I use, which makes

it easy to identify the filenames with rules. This moves around 85-90 percent of the expenses automatically. I then can move the one-offs manually, which doesn't take long.

- I run a clean-up Workflow that alphabetizes everything within the subfolders.

Total Time Before Automation: 60 minutes per month, with 120 minutes in December for end-of-year stuff, so 780 minutes per year, or 13 hours.

Total Time After Automation: five minutes per month flagging and moving emails. This workflow only needs to be done once per year, so it only takes three minutes to run the Airmail workflow, one minute to run the Apple Workflows, five minutes to do remaining sorting manually, and five minutes for cleanup. Add 60 minutes per year reviewing my expenses each month to see where my numbers are. Overall, that's 79 minutes per YEAR. That's an 89 percent reduction in time spent for $0.

Is it perfect? No. I had to make some major trade-offs. But this frees up a good amount of time to do other things, and it supports my vision of having a business that runs itself.

This isn't a storybook ending, though. Turn the page to see how, despite the efficiency win, this project still ended in flames for me.

I DON'T KNOW ANYTHING ABOUT BOOKKEEPING

Despite reducing my expense categorization process by 89 percent, I still suffered a huge failure this year. I'm sharing this because I hope that you can learn from it.

At tax time this year, I stared at an enormous "balance due" from my accountant and wondered what the hell had happened. It was a *lot* of money and I had *never* owed this much money in my life. What went wrong?

First, I hired the wrong accountant. The individual just wasn't a good fit for my family or my business.

Second, I discovered I know nothing about bookkeeping. The way that I "kept my books" was a joke. The categories I had created confused my accountant, so they slotted my expenses into their own category system based on best practices. That caused massive confusion for us both.

Third, I made some calculation errors in my spreadsheet for the year that threw off my expense count to the point where I couldn't trust my numbers. I had to go back to all my expenses and recalculate everything by hand several times to reconcile the errors. Add to the fact that I couldn't trust my accountant's numbers either.

Fourth, I waited until the last minute to do my taxes due to the pandemic, which made everything much more painful than it should have been. I never do that, but 2020 was a terrible year in more ways than one. I suppose I can be forgiven for that. But nope, I'll never make that mistake again!

Fifth, if I had known anything about bookkeeping, I could have prevented this problem entirely because I would have had a bookkeeper that took care of the expense categorization.

The episode ended well. I hired a new accountant two days before Tax Day who did a great job and shrank my balance due by two-thirds. It's amazing what a good accountant can do. I'm just bummed that I had to learn the hard way.

Anyway, I learned that my bookkeeping is a joke. Sure, I automated my *expense cataloguing*, which was great, but that didn't solve the core problem that I didn't realize I had until everything fell apart: I need a real bookkeeper. Automation can't help me with that.

Here are the lessons I learned:

- Hire the right accountant.
- Pick an expense categorization system, and never change it. Hiring the right accountant will ensure you do this correctly the first time.
- Hire a bookkeeper. Or, if you must keep your own books, take courses on bookkeeping so you can learn how to do it correctly.
- Don't delay in getting your taxes filed. Before the pandemic, I would often get mine done in February after my last 1099 arrived.
- Sit down and review your tax return. It's a pain, but you learn a lot by simply reading it. I don't know why I never did it. I'm embarrassed to admit that.

I learned what I needed to do to start preparing my business for a proper bookkeeper. I need to do a lot of cleanup, but hopefully, I'll be doing things correctly starting next year. This way, I'll be in the best possible position if I ever get audited by the government.

BREAKING DOWN MY EDITING PROCESS

In the previous volume, I discussed my automated editing engine project. I've had the opportunity to refine it since the last volume and wanted to cover each step in the process.

First, I use Microsoft Word's spelling and grammar checker. It helps me catch at least a few errors.

Second, I use the Grammarly add-in. I've found that Grammarly does a good job of policing comma usage. It's not perfect, but good enough. Grammarly also does an above-average job of catching missing determiners, which in my opinion, are the bane of every author's existence because they're so difficult to spot.

Third, I use the ProWritingAid add-in for Word. This differs from advice I've given in the past. I ran tests on both ProWritingAid and Grammarly, and I used to recommend Grammarly for nonfiction and ProWritingAid for fiction. Most authors are on a budget and it doesn't make sense to use both. However, the more I use both apps, the more I understand their nuances and what they're especially good at. Both apps have helped me catch more errors combined than using just one. ProWritingAid is better for fiction. It also catches errors that Grammarly does not, such as missing quotation marks. ProWritingAid can also catch some missing determiners, but not at the same rate as Grammarly.

Fourth, it's time for Word Macros. I use FREdit by Paul Beverley. FREdit is an advanced find and replace macro that can help you catch improper (but not incorrect) spelling errors, inconsistent hyphenation, and more. I can use FREdit to catch errors that my editors have recommended over the years.

Here are some examples of commands I've programmed into FREdit:

- Replace "stormwater" with "storm water"
- Replace "self publish" with "self-publish"
- Always use a comma after "Therefore" when it starts a sentence

FREdit also lets you launch other macros within it, so you can embed multiple macros within one click.

Here are some other commands I have programmed into FREdit:

- Remove multiple spaces (a common error after reviewing tracked changes)
- Highlight duplicate words ("said said" or "do do")
- Auto-insert comments based on usage rules (such as inserting a comment any time I use the word "cadence" to remind myself to use it correctly)
- Hyphenation rules based on my editor's feedback, such as replacing "wrought iron" with "wrought-iron"
- Proper noun check (it will generate a list of all proper nouns in the manuscript and color code any discrepancies)
- Italicize my book titles

Fifth, after FREdit, I have my own proprietary macros. These include:

- Numeral checks (numbers between one and ten are written out and everything higher is numericized)
- Chapter heading check (applies "Heading One" to chapter names)
- Broken link checker
- Repeat word check (looks for repeated words within a certain radius)

I run every chapter I write through this system. It takes me extra time, but it's worth it because I catch a lot of issues before the manuscript goes to my editor.

CHAPTER SCORING FOLLOW UP

In the previous volume, I discussed a new concept that I created called "chapter scoring" as part of my editing engine project. Chapter scoring is separate from the editing process I described in the previous chapter, but it is complementary because it helps me improve my writing through data.

When I look at an editor's edits, I want to know a few things:

- How many edits did they recommend (as tracked changes)?
- How many comments did the editor make on the manuscript?
- What is the breakdown of those edits (spelling and grammar versus continuity and story)?
- How many edits did I receive per chapter?

That's a basic picture that you can glean from your edited manuscript with the right tools. You can accomplish this in seconds with automation in Microsoft Word.

The real insights are at the chapter level.

I created a tool that I called a "chapter scoring model." It sounds fancy, but it's simple: it looks at several data elements present in each chapter and then gives each chapter a score based on how well it underwent my editor's scrutiny.

The model is based on both objective and subjective factors. The data elements for the chapter scoring are:

The total number of spelling and grammar errors. These usually take the form of tracked changes on a Word document. These are the most important edits in the editing engine because you can teach the editing engine to spot them using code.

The total number of continuity and story-related edits. These usually take the form of comments in your Word document. Editors are usually hesitant to change a story issue, but they will point it out. Some comments, however, are spelling and grammar-related, so I filter out comments that don't meet these criteria. Also, I can't teach continuity edits to the editing engine. These are uniquely in the editor's territory.

The total number of spelling and grammar-related edits and continuity and story edits. This is perhaps the most telling number. A chapter with a higher number of total edits means it required more of the editor's attention, which is a bad sign. It's not all bad, though—you get good data and can learn a great deal!

The number of writing sessions per chapter. A chapter with a higher number of writing sessions may indicate more errors, especially if those sessions are spread out over several days. On the other hand, a chapter written in one session may not necessarily be better either.

Duration of chapter creation. If you start writing a chapter in January, suffer writer's block, and don't resume writing until March, that may indicate that more errors are present, especially of the continuity type, since it may take some time to remember the story.

Writing method. Some forms of writing are cleaner than others. Trust me, I would know. I find that text written by hand on my computer tends to be the cleanest, followed by text dictated while seated at my desk, followed by words written on my phone, and so on. Words I dictate using Dragon Anywhere always require the most corrections in self-editing.

These components work together within the model. For the prototype, I gave them all equal weights.

I'll share some of the hypotheses I posed while building this model because the results were insightful. I came up with these hypotheses while digging into the data and used my findings to determine whether they were correct.

Hypothesis: The more sessions it takes to write a chapter, the more errors there will be, especially if those sessions have mixed writing methods or long lengths of time between them.

A "session" is how many times it takes me to write a chapter.

The data showed that chapters with two or more sessions tended to have more edits, with three and four session chapters driving the highest outliers. My conclusion was that I should (try to) avoid dragging chapters out into multiple sessions wherever possible to reduce potential errors for my editor.

Hypothesis: There is a relationship between continuity errors and spelling and grammar errors. The more continuity issues exist, the more spelling and grammar errors are likely to be present.

The data disproved this one. There was no correlation I could find between the number of continuity (story) and spelling and grammar errors.

Hypothesis: The longer a chapter is, the more likely it is to have errors.

This one is intuitive. The more words that exist on the page, the more potential there is for errors. I was certain this hypothesis would be correct, but I wasn't sure how.

The data showed me that chapters higher than 2,500 words had the highest number of edits. Chapters at or lower than 1,000 words had the lowest number of edits. Longer chapters scored significantly worse.

That's insightful because I determined I could build chapter length as a special indicator of areas that need more attention. If a chapter is over 2,500 words, I can automatically flag it in the model for my editor to pay more attention to it. More practically, the data tells me that I should spend more time on longer chapters when self-editing.

Hypothesis: The better I feel when writing, the fewer errors I will create.

I wanted to know if mood correlated with edits. If I'm feeling great about a chapter, how does that show up in the number of edits my editor recommends? What about days where I'm feeling bad? I thought that maybe the data would give me some unique insights into writer's block.

However, the data led me down a different path. I found that the chapters where I felt "good" and "great" drove the biggest outliers of edits, which is an indicator that being in flow could cause more errors. Wow. I didn't expect that.

Two of the four biggest outliers were chapters written in flow. Even more, flow chapters contributed to approximately 25 percent of the total manuscript edits. Wow again. *One in four edits were in sections written in flow.*

This means that flow, while great for productivity, has the opposite effect on my edits. Some people might take a finding like this to mean that flow is bad. Flow is *not* bad; in fact, it's the best thing that can happen to you in a writing session. But if you hit flow and then think, "Oh crap, I'm going to have more errors," that's the danger. Fortunately, I don't think about editing when I'm writing, but others may not be able to separate the two functions. But this finding was earthshaking for me.

Hypothesis: Some writing methods produce more errors than others.

Since I use many different writing methods, I wanted to see which one was the "cleanest."

I assumed that my laptop would be the cleanest writing method and that dictation while multitasking (through Dragon Anywhere on my phone) would be the messiest. However, the laptop drove the highest number of errors. My phone drove the lowest, but my phone contributed the fewest words to the manuscript, so that may not be true long-term.

How is it that my laptop drove the most errors? I'm staring at the screen as I write! When typing on my laptop, my writing app does not catch hyphenation or spelling issues, whereas dictation tends to catch them better. Also, I can catch dictation errors more easily because they are somewhat predictable and best caught by spellcheckers, whereas laptop errors are more difficult to detect.

Hypothesis: A novel has fewer overall continuity errors than spelling/grammar errors.

The data showed me that this hypothesis was true. Eighty-eight percent of the total edits were spelling and grammar-related, and 12 percent of the total edits were story-related edits. Only about 40 percent of chapters received story edits.

The takeaway is that being relentless with programming any

spelling/grammar edits I can find will go a long way toward reducing my overall error count.

Hypothesis: There are more errors in the "murky middle."

This makes sense, doesn't it? The murky middle is a painful time during the writing process.

The finding? Not true. The total number of spelling and grammar and continuity edits stayed relatively stable per chapter throughout the novel. However, if I look at the scores and chunk the novel into quarters, the first and fourth quarters scored the worst. Just as mood is not necessarily an indicator of edits, neither is the "location" of the novel. The murky middle doesn't exist from a data perspective. At least that's what the data says right now.

Those were the hypotheses, and I learned a lot from them.

I shared the data with a fan in my community who is a data analyst by trade. He didn't agree with parts of my approach and helped me refine the model. For example, he felt that using components that are not inherently in the data is problematic; he thought the way I structured writing methods assumed that some methods were better than others, which was true. That's not a proper way to work with data. Additionally, he took an alternative approach with the data; he looked at each edit in terms of how many words were impacted. He assumed that each edit impacted three words on average.

His findings: "Chapters where five percent or more of the words were impacted accounted for just over half of the novel, with the worst chapter having nearly 23 percent of the words impacted and the best having less than one percent."

That's another interesting way to approach this.

Overall, the chapter scoring engine is an interesting prototype that helps me own my data and make data-driven decisions with my editing. It doesn't interfere with my writing; rather, it becomes a talking point for my editor.

ARE YOU DATA BLIND?

Data is the future. The authors with the most data who can make the smartest insights will win.

Yet no one thinks about data in self-publishing.

Data can help you:

- understand how your books are performing and why
- figure out what books to write next
- uncover ways to sell more books
- learn how to best to connect with your readers

Data can be very, very powerful.

I've been thinking about a few key questions this quarter.

- What data do I have access to?
- How can I connect data sources?
- Can I automate these connections somehow?
- Can I create a database of *all* the data I have access to?
- Can I query that database to create the reports I need?

Let me give you some examples of how these questions connect.

As an author, I have access to many sources of data: sales reports, expenses, marketing (such as Amazon Ads), Google Analytics, email marketing analytics, trackable links like Genius Link and Bit.ly, YouTube data, publishing industry statistics, to name a few.

What if, instead of viewing each data source on its own, if I wanted to connect them for better insights? For example, what if I wanted to know how much a book has "earned out" in terms of expenses? If you invested $1,000 in a book, what percentage of that have you earned back? If you advertise that book, how much are you spending, and how much money are you making on that? You can do this manually, but you can also do it in a more sophisticated way.

Other questions you might ask of your data when connecting the sources are: is there a relationship between the amount of editing you spend and your sales? How are a particular editor's edits reflected in your sales data? What about a cover designer? How many sales can you attribute to email marketing? Would it be possible to assign a dollar value to your "organic sales," ad sales, email marketing sales, affiliate sales, and more? What might that tell you about your revenue streams?

Anyway, I believe owning your data and delving into it for insights is important. You have more data than you realize—it's your job to connect it in ways that help you figure out how your author business is performing.

Are you data blind? In other words, are you ignoring the data that's all around you?

Remember, the authors with the most data and the best insights will win in tomorrow's game of publishing. Being able to own your data will become especially important when traditional publishers start adopting artificial intelligence to help them mine insights from their backlists in ways that we can't imagine.

WHAT PUBLISHING INDUSTRY STATISTICS EXIST, AND WHAT MATTERS?

If it's not obvious by now, I've been thinking a lot about data. What kind of data do I have access to as a self-published writer? I discussed much of that data in the last chapter, but I also want to know about industry data. What is the market doing? What are other authors in my genre doing? This information is vitally important.

In other industries, we call this "competitive intelligence." In the publishing industry, authors aren't technically competing against each other, so I would consider it "cooperative intelligence." What works for one author can work for you, and you can both make a lot of money doing it. If you're successful, other authors in your genre can be just as successful without stealing readers from you, because readers are voracious. If they like your book, they'll probably want to read your author friends' books too.

In the insurance industry where I work, I have access to some great competitive intelligence tools:

- I can access public filings to see what types of products other insurance companies are filing.
- I can access stock performance, earnings reports, and other competitive data on competitors.

- I subscribe to a competitive intelligence service that sends me a daily newsletter on what competitors are doing. For example, I know early if there's a new product coming to market.
- My company has a competitive intelligence department that archives any proprietary competitor data that employees happen to find (all insurance companies do this).
- I have access to a website called AM Best that provides financial snapshots of competitors among other helpful tools.

I share all of these tools without you not because I want to geek out about insurance, but because these are exactly the type of tools that we could use in the author community. Imagine with me for a moment what proper "competitive intelligence" in the author community would look like.

Here's what I can already do today:

- I can use K-Lytic reports to obtain high-level information about certain genres *on Amazon.*
- I receive news updates from The Hot Sheet by Jane Friedman with holistic industry insights.
- I use Publisher Rocket (formerly KDP Rocket) by Dave Chesson to research keywords and ad ideas for my Amazon Ads. Other tools like this also exist and are readily available.
- I subscribe to a few publishing industry blogs that provide data on bookstore sales.
- Now, let's pretend that the following opportunities exist:
- I receive a list each morning (or week) of new titles in a particular genre. The email contains the cover, link to

the book, a link to the author's website, price, book description, current sales rank, review average, retailers published at, and snippets from reviews. The same service might even allow me to download an Excel sheet with all books in a genre released in a given year. This would give me the ability to pivot, add my data, and review trends.

- I can access data on the entire publishing industry that *includes* self-publishing. I can see how sales are performing for the ebook sector, for certain genres, and for certain countries. Most data that exists right now is skewed toward traditional publishing, and it is very generic.

- I receive a weekly (or monthly) briefing that contains a digest from all the major self-publishing podcasts, blogs, and YouTube channels. Since my time is limited, I'd love a two- or three-paragraph summary of interviews. Then I can decide which content I want to explore. This would be extremely time-consuming for someone to do manually, but with artificial intelligence and advancements in natural language processing, I believe a product like this is possible within the next few years.

We'll see what types of data sources arise in the future.

Remember that traditional publishers have access to far more data than you and I. Their problem is bureaucracy and old ways of thinking; they have mountains of data, but they haven't figured out how to use it. Our problem is that we haven't learned how to own our data yet. We have to think future-forward and stay a few steps ahead of publishers—they're not our competition, but when they unlock artificial intelligence and book discoverability, they will be.

A STORY ABOUT YOUTUBE PERFORMANCE

I discovered a "happy accident" with my YouTube channel.

I released a new video on Friday and realized that I forgot to promote it. I usually promote videos right at noon when they release, again at 1 PM, and a few tweets throughout the rest of the day.

This particular video didn't do well on the first day. It was ranked six out of ten in terms of views and watch time.

On a whim, I decided to promote the video on Saturday. I did the *same things* that I normally do: tweet on Twitter, make a Facebook post, and mention the video on my blog and YouTube community tab.

To my surprise, the video jumped from six to one in just one day. I've never seen that before. Usually, if a video languishes in the first 24 hours, it languishes forever.

The lesson? I started promoting my new videos on Fridays and Saturdays. My watch time and views jumped.

Sometimes, accidents lead to great successes.

LEARNING PYTHON

Now that I've finished my law degree, I've decided that I want to learn another practical skill: Python.

Why Python? It's the language of artificial intelligence. It's also the most popular programming language. By learning Python, I will learn a lot.

I don't want to become a programmer. I just want to understand how a programmer thinks. I want to know what the possibilities and limitations are in code. That helps me when I'm daydreaming about new projects and chapters for this series. It's one thing to say, "I wish that X service exists," but if it's not feasible given current technology, then I'm wasting my time. It's another thing to say "I wish that X service exists" because I understand the technology and know (at a high level) how it would work. That's powerful.

Over the last year alone, I've proven this. I said that I wanted to automate my sales, and I did that using existing technology. I said that I wanted to automate editing, and I did that. So much is possible if you understand technology and data. I believe that learning Python will open up a world of possibilities for me. Hell, it might also help me get a job in the future.

I'll probably take a class at a community college or use LinkedIn Learning.

Python is a bet that I hope will pay off for me in the future. It won't cost me very much, and I'll learn a lot.

BECOME THE WRITER OF
THE FUTURE

IF I BECAME A MEGA-BESTSELLER TOMORROW, WHAT TEAM WOULD I BUILD AROUND ME?

In my book, *Mental Models for Writers: 73 Ways to Improve Your Writing, Elevate Your Thinking, and Capture Success*, I discuss a mental model called "You are the Creative Director of Your Career," which is taken from Orna Ross, founder and director of the Alliance of Independent Authors. Orna believes that, as a self-published author, every decision is up to you. No one is going to make them for you.

If you became a mega-bestseller tomorrow, you would NOT be able to do everything yourself. You'd have to build a team around you. What would that team look like? It's an interesting thought exercise.

In the book, I wrote:

Framed another way, you could also argue that you are the CEO of your creative career.

In a corporation, everything starts and ends with the CEO; therefore, they have to know a lot about a lot of different things. So congratulations! You're now a CEO for the rest of this chapter!

Imagine that you're in a board room and you've assembled your C-suite for the first time.

The top executives in your writing business are staring at you, ready for orders.

Your goal is to give them instructions about how to get things done so they can carry out the day-to-day affairs of the business.

Your C-suite officers are as follows:

- Chief Marketing Officer. Where should they focus their time and what emotions do you want your books to instill in readers?
- Chief Operations Officer. How can they help your company write better books faster? What will your book covers look like? How should they find the right designers? Editors? What should the working relationships be like?
- Chief Information Officer. How will your writing business adopt new technology? How will you maximize the technology you already have?
- Chief Legal Officer. What types of publishing contracts will you sign? What happens if you get into legal trouble?
- Chief Financial Officer. How will you make money and reinvest your profits back into the business to stay sustainable?

After I wrote *Mental Models for Writers*, I thought of a few extra team members.

- Product Manager. This person would patrol book retailers regularly to spot errors such as typos in book descriptions, incorrect prices, and so on. They would also be responsible for updating the packaging.
- Administrative Assistant. This person would help me with emails at scale and possibly oversee a team of admins who serve various purposes.

- Programmer. I'd keep a developer on retainer for items on my website that need to be done.
- Media Professional. This person would make me look good and sound good as well as edit my audio and video.
- Personal Stylist. Call me vain, but if you reach mega-bestseller status, your looks will be scrutinized. This person would make sure that I'm always looking good for the camera.
- Accountant. This person would be on retainer and report directly to the CFO. They'd do my taxes and help me minimize my tax liability.
- Financial Investor. This person would help me manage my financial investments and assets.

Here's the thing. It was a fun thought exercise to imagine this team. The responsibilities I listed are damn near what an author's job description should be. Turn the page to read more about that.

AN AUTHOR'S JOB DESCRIPTION

I also wrote this in *Mental Models for Writers:*

———

When I was a manager in corporate America, I had to hire people. Hiring comes with a ceremony of many rituals, one of which is writing a job description for the role you're hiring for.

Job descriptions serve as reminders to employees and bosses about what the employee is supposed to do. In many cases, it's also an important legal document.

If you were going to write your job description as an indie author, what would it look like?

- What are the core elements of your job?
- How will you divide your time between those core elements?
- How will you handle the non-core elements? Will you simply not do them, or will you outsource them?
- How will you assess yourself to gauge your progress? In other words, how will you know if you're doing a good job?
- How often will you reassess your priorities?
- What are your "other duties as assigned"? Do they take up more of your time than they should?

When you write your job description, it forces you to think

hard about the limited time and resources you have.

For example, I have discovered over the years that I'm an idea guy. I like to conceive ideas and build stuff (such as books, videos, and courses). But when it comes to maintaining the things I build, I'm not good at it because it's not my passion. Some people are the exact opposite—they want nothing to do with idea generation or building a product, but they enjoy maintaining something, making rules, enforcing those rules, and contributing to a community.

My job description would focus on content creation and engaging with people in my community around my ideas. It would not include a Facebook community, for example, because I don't have the energy or patience to run a group like that. At the end of the day, it's my career, and I'm going to do it my way.

Remember: it's your career.

———

Let's have some fun with a job description based on the "mega-bestselling team" I built around me in the last chapter.

JOB DESCRIPTION FOR A SELF-PUBLISHED AUTHOR

The self-published author provides their strategic direction about the types of books they want to publish. This position is responsible for strategic leadership, content production, and overseeing every process of publication. It also proactively participates with editors, cover designers, and other freelancers to accomplish projects and meet business objectives.

- Writes amazing books.
- Manages existing books and content and ensures they are always up-to-date and effectively marketed.

- Identifies target audiences and the best ways to market books to them.
- Aggressively pursues new marketing opportunities and manages ad campaigns to drive revenue and growth.
- Finds new ways to produce content faster and more effectively, leveraging technology and automation.
- Collaborates regularly with editors, cover designers, and other freelancers.
- Responsible for all legal contracts.
- Oversees the business and manages the day-to-day financial operations.
- Responds to emails and fan-mail promptly.
- Updates website as necessary.
- Produces audio and visual content to support the author brand.
- Actively supports the self-publishing community through mentoring other authors.
- Pursues continuing education to continue honing the craft.
- All other duties as assigned.

That, in my opinion, is a multimillion-dollar job description!

I don't know about you, but when I list all of these responsibilities on paper, it makes me truly understand how desperately outsourcing is needed in our community, yet most authors can't afford it. In a previous volume, I wrote about how authors can pool their money to make virtual assistant services affordable. I believe that is a winning strategy.

This description also shows you that it is unacceptable *not* to outsource once you start making real money with your writing. There just isn't enough time in the day.

What I've done over the years is to look at this job description and determine my priorities. Pick your top five, focus on those, and do the rest when you can. You already know my top five:

- Become a world-class content creator
- Become a world-class marketer
- Become a technology-driven writer
- Become a data-driven writer
- Become the writer of the future

I spend at least 80 percent of my time in these areas. What does *your* author job description look like?

FOLLOWING AN EDITOR'S CAREER PATH

Authors work with editors regularly. Aside from cover designers, editors are the most frequent freelancer that authors work with.

In the last chapter, I discussed the author's job description. What about an editor?

More importantly, what does an editor have to do to become an editor? As executives in the corporate world would say, "What's the career path?"

Does an author have a career path? Not really. Usually, it involves reading a ton of books as a kid and then waking up one day and saying that you want to be a writer. The moment you write your first book, the career pathing is done. After that, it's about developing yourself.

Editing is different. A good editor goes through some level of training, either by sheer experience or by taking classes.

I don't care if an editor has a college degree or if they've worked for a publishing house. I also don't (necessarily) care about their years of experience, as long as my manuscript isn't the first one they've ever worked on. I just care about the result. And I know what a good editing product looks like after working with around a dozen editors in my career.

What would it be like to step into an editor's shoes? What if, to understand our editors better, we said, "Let's follow the career path of an editor"?

That's fascinating to me. The only problem is that there is no uniformity. There's no "editing school." Every editor's experience is different. But what do many editors have in common?

I saw some training courses on the American Copyeditors Society (ACES) and the Chartered Institute of Editors and Proofreaders (CIEP) in the UK. These are societies dedicated to cultivating editing talent. They offer memberships, training classes, and other resources to help editors become better editors and find work. If anyone would know what an editor needs to learn to become competent, it would be ACES and CIEP. (If you don't live in the US or the UK, check if your country has an editing society. They probably do.)

Here are titles of classes from the ACES Academy website at the time I wrote this article:

- Microaggressions in Editing: Understanding Biases in Editing and Undoing Harm
- How to Master the Business Side of Editing
- Respect: How Editors and Writers Build Great Relationships
- Let's Get Technical: How to Plan and Edit Content About Technology
- When Words & Design Collide: How to Write and Edit with Design in Mind
- Perspectives: People of Color in the Editing Community
- What's New in the APA Style
- The Invention of the Modern American Dictionary
- Grammar Arcana

When I checked the CIEP website, I found a jackpot: a document called "Curriculum for Professional Development" for editors.

Here's what the curriculum contains:

- Professional practice and ethics
- Business management and practice
- Equipment and file management
- Production knowledge and practice: workflows, schedules and budgeting, editorial processes, production processes, design, typography and typesetting, printing and finishing, ebook formats, tables and illustrative materials, different models of publishing, principles of accessibility, and so on
- Editorial knowledge: grammar, punctuation, usage, spelling, voice and tone, citations, references and bibliographies, numeracy, use of languages, sources of information, indexing, and so on
- Editorial judgment
- Editorial practice: markup, editorial standards in context, errors, omissions and other problems, house style, project style sheets, and so on
- Specialist skills in knowledge: medical, technical, legal, music publishing, and so on.

This list is interesting. From comparing the ACES class list and the CIEP curriculum, we can say at a high level that an editor's career training would contain:

- Professional practice and ethics: how should an editor conduct themselves?
- Business: How should an editor conduct their business, market themselves, and price for their services?
- Equipment and file management: How should an editor archive writers' documents? How should they protect their writers' data?

- Editorial knowledge: How can an editor rapidly improve their knowledge of the rules of English and its style manuals?
- Editorial judgment: How should an editor learn to think like an editor and challenge inherent assumptions in a work?
- Editorial practice: What are the best practices for how an editor should mark up a manuscript and conduct communications with writers?
- Specialist skills: What areas should an editor specialize in, and what are the rules of those special areas?
- Equity: How can an editor ensure that an author's work is free of implicit bias?
- Technology: How can editors become masters of the software they use?

With this curriculum in mind, if you wanted to understand editors better, just take appropriate classes and talk to editors about the different items. Pretend that you're going to become an editor, even though you'll never edit a single manuscript.

Let's run through this list again and discover the benefits we can learn by learning to think like an editor. Imagine that you are searching for a new editor and you're evaluating someone who seems like a good fit.

- Professional practice and ethics: Is this person conducting themselves according industry standards?
- Business: Is this editor underpricing or overpricing their work? Are they a competent business person? Are their contracts fair?
- Equipment and file management: More generally, how might this editor store their documents? Is there

something I can learn about this to store documents more effectively in my writing business?

- Editorial knowledge: Is the editor competent at editing? (I know, I know...it's shocking how little knowledge of spelling and grammar factors into this curriculum, but that's true of the writing profession too.)
- Editorial judgment: Will this editor help me improve the clarity in my work?
- Editorial practice: How does this editor prefer to work?
- Specialist skills: Does this editor specialize in my book's genre or subject matter?
- Equity: Does this editor have the proper knowledge to help me avoid implicit bias in my work that might be distracting to readers?
- Technology: Is the editor competent at Word?

Some of these questions are basic, but others can help you to truly understand the editing profession. Considering that most writers want to be writers for a long time, it only makes sense to understand your editor.

Now that I'm done with law school (which I'll discuss in the next chapter), I've been thinking about exploring the editing career path for my own knowledge.

LESSONS LEARNED FROM LAW SCHOOL

In May 2021, I finally graduated from law school. It took me four and a half years, but only because I had to take a couple of semesters off for personal reasons. I probably could have finished in three years.

My degree is a specialized Master's in risk management and compliance. It's insurance-focused.

Law school is an amazing experience. I didn't get the "full" experience, though—I only took one class at a time in the evenings, but I was just as busy, if not busier than your average full-time law student. I was raising a toddler, working 50 hours a week as a manager at a Fortune 100 insurance company, taking law school classes, traveling the state and teaching insurance classes, writing books at a prolific pace, hosting three podcasts, running a YouTube channel, doing public speaking engagements, and managing a video editor.

I look back at the last five years and wonder how the hell I did it.

I admit to people all the time that law school slowed my productivity down immensely.

I attended law school between the fall of 2017 and the spring of 2021. During that time:

- I wrote 26 books novels (11 novels and 15 writing books).

- I recorded around 700 podcast episodes for all of my podcasts combined.

Most people would read those numbers and say, "What do you mean law school slowed you down???"

For each class (at least in the beginning), I spent approximately three to six hours per week in class, and an additional three to six hours week studying. If I'm honest, I studied much, much less after the first year, but hey...

That's 12 hours per week dedicated to just law school.

I've analyzed my writing output over the years and I've learned that it takes me approximately 40 hours to write, edit, and format a novel.

Twelve hours per week for 12 weeks is 144 hours, which equals 3.6 novels per semester. That's how many novels I could have written during that semester in a perfect world.

I attended law school for seven semesters, so that's a net loss of 25 novels during my time there. I've written around 60 books now, so if I hadn't gone to law school, it's not insurmountable that I could have had *around* 85 books to my name at the time of this writing.

I could do some more math about how much each of my novels earns me, and you would see how much time and long-term money I lost throughout my career. It's a *big* number. It's akin to cashing out your retirement investments before you retire—it doesn't seem like a lot of money, but you're missing out on the future value of your money.

That begs the question of why even go to law school? I just explained that I lost an incredible about of time and money, and that I robbed myself of the ability to write books that I would have enjoyed. Also, I did not go to law school to be an attorney, and I will never practice law because my degree doesn't allow me to.

Huh???

I went to law school to improve my knowledge and professional development. I wanted to learn how to "think" like a lawyer, how to use that knowledge to avoid legal pitfalls in my writing business. Also, because the degree is technically a Master's degree, that provides me more earning power in my professional life. I also attended because I enjoy legal studies and thought it would be interesting.

I went because my employer paid for 95 percent of it. I just had to pay for books, which was around $200 each semester. I graduated debt-free.

I spent about $1,400 on the degree out of my pocket. Just having the degree on my resume helped me land three different jobs while I was in law school, including a new job as an executive one month before graduation, which resulted in a salary increase well above the $1,400 that I invested. The degree produced a very good ROI for my career.

Here are the lessons I learned from law school.

- I can handle a lot of pressure. I already listed the concurrent activities I managed while attending school. There were a few points where I exceeded my capacity, but ultimately, I thrived under the high pressure. I emerged from law school without any substance abuse issues, with my marriage still intact, and with a promotion at work. My appetite for risk and high pressure is higher than most people's, and I've learned that it serves me well.

- I learned how to read (and negotiate) contracts like a lawyer. One day, if I'm ever staring at a film deal or a licensing agreement, I'll know how the terms will impact my career, and most importantly, I'll know when to call a lawyer.

- I took Employment Law. The information will be very, very helpful when it's time to hire people full-time into my writing business.
- I took Copyright Law. Since authors make their money off copyright, this class was worth the cost of the degree alone.
- I have a knack for spotting opportunities that others overlook. A "Masters's" law degree is usually a laughingstock of the law community. No one in the legal profession takes you seriously. I knew this before I even applied. Yet I had no desire to practice law and knew that the degree, while not helpful in the legal world, would help me immensely in the corporate world. This type of degree is still so new that corporate people have no idea what a law degree in risk management and compliance is—they just see the law school on my resume and that I have a law degree. I don't hold myself out as a lawyer and never will, but just by having this degree, my portfolio looks different to recruiters and hiring managers because most people at my level have MBAs. I think MBAs are boring and would have never attended school for one. I knew that this unique law degree could become a talking point in interviews and I could sell it. Plus, it's good insurance if I ever get laid off because I have a Master's level degree. Additionally, I knew that the degree would benefit my writing business. I knew all of this before pursuing it. I'm proud of myself for recognizing these opportunities, and it paid off.

Now that I'm done with law school, I suddenly have 12 hours per week that I can devote to my writing again. I'm excited about that. I got what I needed out of the experience, and now it's time for the next thing, whatever that may be. But one thing is clear: I'm done with traditional education and will not be spending any more time or money toward degrees.

LESSON FROM A SHAOLIN MONK

This quarter, I stumbled upon a TED Talk that encapsulates almost every problem new writers have. It so neatly sums up the problems that I hear from writers weekly that I wanted to share and summarize them. The talk is given by a Shaolin monk, Master Shi Heng Yi.

Writing is about knowing and mastering thyself. Master thyself and you master your surroundings. Master Shi Heng Yi speaks about this:

"To bring meaning to your life
to bring value into your life
you need to learn and master yourself and
don't let the hindrances stop you."

In his TED Talk, Master Shi Heng Yi discusses the Five Hindrances to Self-Mastery.

#1: Sensual desires. Master Shi Heng Yi refers to this as anything you can experience in the five senses: touch, sight, taste, smell, and hearing. He uses the example of climbing a mountain and suddenly discovering that there is an amazing restaurant carved into the mountainside. The smell of the delicious food lures you off track, and you stop to eat in the restaurant. You never leave because it is comfortable and you can't imagine climbing the mountain when you're in the pleasure of delicious food and good company.

To put this into context:

- Many writers in the community come for the writing but stay for the community. They talk about writing and enjoy other writers' company, but they don't ever get around to writing.
- Many writers in the community seek out everything there is to learn about writing but never get around to writing.

#2: Ill will/aversion. Master Shi Heng Yi refers to this as discomfort. If you're climbing the mountain and it starts raining and you don't have an umbrella, you turn around and go home. But the rain is exactly what you need to temper your spirit. Just because it's uncomfortable doesn't mean you should stop; it means you should keep going. Seeking comfort means missing out on clarity.

To put this into context: how many people start writing but quit because it's too hard? How many people finish their first book but never publish it? How many people publish their first book and quit because the marketing is too hard? How many people publish several books and quit because of lack of success? Writing is expensive, time-consuming, draining, and if all you can see are the negative parts, you'll miss out on so much.

#3: Dullness/heaviness. Master Shi Heng Yi refers to this as your mind being locked in a cell. You tell yourself you can't write well, or you fall for the movies your critical voice plays inside your head. What you don't realize is that while you *appear* to be locked in a cell, the door is unlocked and you can leave at any time. You just have to have the courage to do so.

To put this into context, read anything I've written about self-doubt. I talk about how so many writers get trapped in the theaters of their minds. They tell themselves they can't do something, or that their writing isn't good enough, or (insert any excuse). It stops them from making progress.

In my opinion, this is the biggest problem that writers face. Everyone, without exception, gets locked in a cell for a time. Not everyone escapes, though. I've been locked in the cell many times, but never for long.

#4: Restlessness. If you're too focused on the future or the past, you cannot be focused on the present. You cannot enjoy your writing journey or appreciate where you are. That's deadly.

To put this into context: so many writers want to be rich overnight. They want to write one book and become immensely successful. Everyone wants notoriety yesterday, and they're in a hurry to get it. Who doesn't want more book sales?

Instead, could you focus on where you are right now and be appreciative of it? Sure, it may not be where you want to be, but every time is a special time, and there's always something to appreciate about where you are in your journey, even if you don't have an audience.

#5: Skeptical Doubt. This is self-doubt. If you doubt yourself, then nothing is possible until you set those doubts aside. The scary part about self-doubt is that it's the last hindrance that Master Shi Heng Yi talks about, the last one before you reach the mountaintop.

To put this into context: so many writers are closer than they think to the next level of their writing career. They just have to have the courage to keep going. The closer they get to the summit, the louder the "skeptical doubt" (self-doubt) gets.

FACING THE HINDRANCES

Whenever you face a hindrance in your life, Master Shi Heng Yi recommends a four-step process he calls "letting it R.A.I.N."

1. Recognize the hindrance. Figure out how you are feeling in response to it, and where those feelings are coming from.
2. Accept the situation. Hindrances never go away completely; understanding their nature and accepting it is key to defeating them.
3. Investigate. Ask how you got yourself to this point. What will you do about it, and how can you avoid this next time?
4. Non-Identity. If you believe in Hindu philosophy, it's the same as "being attached and unattached at the same time." Separate yourself from your body and set your emotions aside. Then keep going.

I could explain more about Master Shi Heng Yi's philosophy, but you should check it out. I find it amazing how non-writing philosophers and spiritual guides offer advice that applies to writing.

Master Shi Heng Yi's talk offers the answer to every writing problem that exists if you're willing to listen.

The big one is dullness/heaviness. Just because you're locked in a cage doesn't mean you can't get out. No one can hold you. Remember that the door is always unlocked.

TOM CRUISE DEEPFAKE

Earlier this year, a video of a Tom Cruise deep fake went viral. It shows footage of Tom Cruise talking to the camera, but it's not Tom Cruise.

Watch the video; it's eerie and disturbing at how far deepfake technology has become. Many experts are calling the Tom Cruise video a watershed moment for the technology.

If you're an influencer, that should scare you.

Why Tom Cruise? He's a celebrity and there is a *lot* of footage of him. The guy has made tons of movies and given hours and hours of interviews. Artificial intelligence needs copious amounts of data, and that data exists for Cruise in the form of videos that probably total hundreds of hours.

Guess who else has lots of videos that can easily be downloaded for free to create deepfakes? Influencers!

My YouTube channel alone has over 300 videos. I'm the only subject in the frame for most of my videos. Someone could create a deepfake of me easily. This is true of many YouTubers, especially as the technology becomes more sophisticated and needs fewer video data to be effective.

The concern many people have about deepfakes is that we're headed for a world where it's hard to know what is truth and what is fake, deception, or misinformation. Imagine a deepfake of a president or world leader saying something that incites war, or a "sex tape" with an influencer's face on a model that looks real. (This already exists, but the results look fake.)

Technology doesn't yet exist to "spot" deepfakes, and if it doesn't come to pass, that's scary.

Influencers are a target, and I believe it will be a good idea for influencers to think about how they can protect themselves against the threat of deepfakes. They should have a plan in place about what to do if they find themselves the victim of a deepfake that threatens their career. They should communicate that plan with their fans too. The future might usher in the rise of two-factor authentication for influencer content; an influencer might upload a video to a site like YouTube, but they would also publish a certificate of authenticity on their website so that if the video doesn't match the certificate, then it gets flagged. This way, someone can create a deepfake, but additionally, they would also have to hack the author's website. This would only protect an influencer for the content they personally create, though. If a difficult future unfolds where people cannot determine the veracity of videos, I can see some influencers restricting appearances to their official channels or the channels of people they trust to prevent potential deepfakes.

Technically, YouTube's Content ID system can flag videos that infringe copyright. I suppose that the technology could be evolved to spot deepfakes too.

But I'm not an alarmist. I also believe that deepfake technology has great promise for writers:

Cover designs with people of color. Writers who want to put a person of color on the cover have a major problem right now: it's difficult to find suitable models of color. For example, when I was searching for a model for my *Magic Trackers* series, I needed a strong African-American heroine. My designer and I searched royalty-free photo sites such as Shutterstock and Canstock, and we only had a few options. We needed a model who had many different poses; we found that many of the models only had a handful of poses, and not all of those were suitable for a book cover. Deepfakes can eliminate this issue by creating models of color that are a composite of many different models. You simply pay the models whose images are used to create the composite, and you'd do this through Blockchain and cryptocurrencies.

Character art. Currently, it is expensive to create character art. You have to find a designer. Imagine deepfake technology that makes a composite of multiple artists' work to create character art that you can share with your fans. You could even do this with photography. Want a hunky twenty-something male leaning against a motorcycle in a dark alley? You got it!

Author photos. Imagine a deepfake program that can review every photo ever taken of you and create a composite author headshot that never actually existed. You'd never have to worry about taking headshots ever again, and you could just update them every few years, and your headshots would age with you.

So the technology is not all bad. Like any emerging issue, it's up to us to decide if it will be good or evil.

Q2 PROGRESS REPORT

In the previous volume, I shared the progress I was making toward my 2021 author strategy. This strategy will guide me for the next several years. I wanted to provide an update for Q2 2021.

I've shared a detailed mind map about this at www.authorlevelup.com/2021strategy.

MY STRATEGY

My mission is to educate and entertain my audience in the genres I write, and to remain nimble in an ever-changing industry.

I will achieve my mission through five strategic priorities:

- Become a world-class content creator
- Become a world-class marketer
- Become a technology-driven writer
- Become a data-driven writer
- Become the writer of the future

WORLD-CLASS CONTENT CREATOR

Goal: 64 books published by 12/31/2021. I'm currently at 55 books written (including this one). That means I need to write nine more books this year. I'm in danger of missing my plan, so I'll need to do another "beast mode" challenge in Q3 to catch up.

Develop a way to ensure consistency across my platform. This is just a fancy way of saying that I need to ensure that my work is consistent and that readers are receiving a consistent experience. In the Q1 update, I said that my editing engine was part of this initiative because it will go a long way toward ensuring a better reader experience. To date, I have not yet thought about other ways to do this across the rest of my platform.

WORLD-CLASS MARKETER

Grow my Amazon Ad imprint. My sales continue to rise from my use of Amazon Ads.

Improve my copywriting skills. The sales copy builder I created continues to work well for me. I even used it to write a book description for a family member who is making his debut self-published poetry collection this year.

Reduce my tax liability. I made progress in this area and then suffered several steps backward. That said, my knowledge of tax law is substantially improved compared to last quarter due to the tax debacle that I described in this volume.

BECOME A TECHNOLOGY-DRIVEN WRITER

Develop an automated way to enforce consistency. My editing engine project this quarter satisfies this requirement. All of my manuscripts now go through it before sending to my editor.

Redesign my Book Wizard tool on Michael La Ronn.com and "Author Level Up".**com**. Still no progress on this goal. It'll be a focus in Q3 and Q4.

Implement a flexible book database that houses all the metadata for my books. Still no progress here. I may punt this to 2022.

Automate my bookkeeping. I've talked enough about this topic in this book that I don't need to cover it anymore here, but I satisfied this goal.

BECOME A DATA-DRIVEN WRITER

Make minor enhancements to my sales database. No progress.

Invest in learning the basics of Python, Webhooks, and Application Programming Interfaces (APIs). This is good knowledge to understand for the future. I'll probably sign up for a class starting in Q4.

BECOME THE WRITER OF THE FUTURE

Read 50 books. I'm about 50 percent toward the goal, with around 20 books read this year.

Implement direct print and audiobook sales on my website. No progress here yet, but I do have an audiobook distributor lined up.

Complete my law degree. Completed.

Complete 12 WMG workshops to improve my writing craft. I'm in danger of missing this goal. I'll have to make it a focus in Q3 or Q4.

BRINGING IT ALL TOGETHER

My final law semester and my new job put a dent in my goals for the year, but I'm still making progress.

The editing engine is a gigantic win, and I should still hit my book production goals, even if I fall behind.

I'll have to focus on the other goals in the upcoming quarters. My goals are solely my own; no one will die if I don't achieve them, but I'd like to have a killer goal year this year so that I can start reducing my goals in future years. I've benefited from my investments in production, technology, and data, so I don't need to be so aggressive with goals moving forward.

I'll share more progress on my strategy in the next volume so I can keep myself accountable, but you can view the details of my 2021 + strategy by visiting www.authorlevelup.com/2021strategy.

IDEAS YOU CAN STEAL

OPEN-SOURCE COMPUTER VISION IDEA

Computer vision is a type of artificial intelligence that recognizes images. A classic example of computer vision is the lane detection technology in automobiles; the car can detect the lane and notify you when you accidentally change lanes without your turn signal on.

Advancements in computer vision have implications in every area of our lives. This is also true in publishing.

What if you could train computer vision software to identify book covers?

I was doing some competitive intelligence on the urban fantasy genre on Amazon. If you've ever browsed bestseller lists on Amazon, then you know that it's an exercise in frustration. Authors frequently misclassify their books to get visibility. It's not uncommon to look at, say, an urban fantasy bestseller list, and see it overrun with titles that aren't even urban fantasy. But I digress.

Computer vision is object recognition. Just imagine what software could do when the answers to the questions below are YES:

Can it detect urban fantasy covers?

Can it detect subgenres of UF? Such as cozy mystery?

Can it detect the gender?

Can it detect hair colors?

Can it detect emotions on a character's face?

Can it detect magic?

Can it detect objects such as swords?

Can it detect fonts?

Can it detect colors on the cover?

A book cover is just an assembly of symbols. Computer vision can and should be able to read book covers easily.

What if someone created computer vision software that crawled book retailers and identified books based on genre? What if it could detect urban fantasy covers, sort those covers into subgenres, and then pass that data to a report, such as some of the ones I mentioned earlier in this volume? Imagine receiving a report in your inbox that says, "Per your request, here are newly published urban fantasy detective novels about werewolves." Wow.

Why would you care about this? Let me tell you a story. In 2019 , I released a series called *The Good Necromancer*. It's about an ex-necromancer named Lester Broussard who made a pact with a demon that went wrong, and the demon killed his family. Ridden with guilt and shame, he's trying to live a normal life and atone for his sin. When an old friend asks him for help, he finds himself delving back into the dark art of necromancy.

When I wrote *The Good Necromancer*, there weren't many urban fantasy novels featuring necromancers. I only found three series that were comparable to mine.

But what happens if necromancers become hot five years from now? I want to know when that happens! A service like the one I described would ensure that I stay up-to-date with any necromancer novels that are published after mine. This way, I can run ads toward the new books, collaborate with those authors, and figure out what readers like about the new books. Maybe I'd need to update my covers or book description to adapt to a new trend.

When you have as many books as I do, you simply cannot keep track of what is happening on the market. I've written in around a dozen genres—I can't research all of those genres all of the time. A tool like this fills in a critical gap that prolific authors need.

THOUGHTS ON MENTORING: AUTOMATED MENTOR SELECTION AND REVERSE MENTORSHIPS

I obtained a new mentor this year in my professional life, and the experience got me thinking about mentorships in the author space.

The company I worked at had a prestigious program where you had to fill out an application that was reviewed by the Office of Human Resources, and they assigned you a mentor at least one level above your title based on your goals. The mentor also filled out an application so there was a detailed matching process.

Because of expense reductions, the company hired a vendor who automated the mentor matching process. The entire process worked without a single human involved.

Here's how it worked:

- I set up a profile and filled out an application that detailed my goals.
- Based on my answers, the program showed me a list of mentors it thought would be a good match.
- I reviewed the mentor's profiles and picked my top three candidates; the mentors did the same thing.
- The system matched you based on preference.
- Both the mentor and mentee received an automated email explaining the process and expectations.

I was skeptical. In the corporate world, any time the company brings in a "vendor" to do something that used to be someone's job, the results are almost always lackluster. This program was one of those rare exceptions.

I was matched with a mentor who, quite frankly, was like a kindred spirit. She had the same level of ambition as me, and she was only a year older than me. However, she was a director and I was a manager.

We were a great match and I learned a lot from her.

That got me thinking about why we can't have something like that in the author space.

A few years ago, the Alliance of Independent Authors facilitated a similar program using Facebook. I was a mentor through that program.

I believe a website that matches successful authors with author mentees would be effective. Authors tend to be shy, and in the digital age, it's not exactly easy to approach someone you don't know to ask them to be a mentor. A website like this removes friction because both parties are willing to participate.

I wouldn't be surprised if something like this doesn't already exist, but I haven't seen anything specifically for authors.

The second thought I had around mentorships was around reverse mentorships. I've heard of mentorships where the mentor-mentee relationship is the opposite: the mentor is the junior employee and the mentee is the senior employee. For example, an executive might want to learn more about a particular business unit, so they enlist an entry-level employee to help them learn. The entry-level employee also gains the benefit of working with a more experienced employee. I also don't see why this can't apply in the author world.

Bestselling authors and more experienced authors lose touch with emerging trends. Today's hot new authors will inevitably be tomorrow's opponents of new processes and technology. I'll bet money on it. Although new authors lack experience in publishing, they contain a wealth of information. Publishing a book in 2021 is vastly different than 2012. The marketing tactics are also different. An experienced author can learn a lot from newbies, even if the newbies aren't successful in their endeavors.

While I have experience as an author, I still think of myself as a newbie. But as the years go on, it makes a lot of sense for me to establish a reverse mentorship. The person I'd like to learn from probably hasn't graduated high school yet, honestly.

I want to be "forever young" when it comes to publishing. I want to capitalize on new trends to reach new readers, and I want to make sure that my books are always speaking the language of relevance. A reverse mentorship can help with that.

GENRE-SPECIFIC BOUTIQUES

I've said for a while that when you're hiring freelancers, it's best to hire someone who has experience in your genre (if you can). Assuming the same level of competence, an editor who has extensively edited in your genre is almost always better than an editor who has not. The same is true with cover design.

I see value in a "boutique" that only services authors of a certain genre.

For example, you could hire an "urban fantasy boutique" whose editors and cover designers specialize in urban fantasy. When you work with them, you're guaranteed to create packaging that will be relevant for urban fantasy readers because the freelancers specialize in it.

There are economic reasons why this might not work, namely scale. Most freelancers are generalists because they might only edit a few manuscripts in a certain genre a year. But a boutique service could work well for successful authors or newbies with means who are willing to invest in a higher level of quality.

Imagine hiring a firm that would:

- Assign you an editor and cover designer who specializes in your genre
- Provide genre-specific marketing services and advice
- Update you about trends in the genre

This is almost like a traditional publisher, but they don't take your copyright. You simply pay them for their proven expertise.

80/20 YOUR 80/20

I picked up this idea from James Altucher in his new book *Skip the Line*.

Altucher discusses the 80/20 rule (also known as the Pareto Principle), which says that 80 percent of results come from 20 percent of the causes. For example, if you write 100 books, 20 of those books will drive 80 percent of your income.

Altucher's idea is to 80/20 your 80/20 results. In his reasoning, if it's true that 20 books will drive 80 percent of your income, then it might also be true that 20 percent of those 20 books will drive 80 percent of that 80 percent. It's a very meta idea, but the gist is that instead of focusing on 20 books that drive your income, you should focus on four. If you put your energy into those four books, you'll reap the benefits faster.

This is a fascinating idea because you can apply it anywhere the 80/20 rule applies.

IDEAL DAY

What's your ideal day as a writer? After reading Bertrand Russell's *The Conquest of Happiness*, I thought about what mine would look like. I wrote down my thoughts and I'm inviting you to think about your ideal day as a full-time author.

I'd wake up at 5:30 AM to exercise, eat breakfast, and get an early-morning writing session in.

At 7:30 AM, I'd leave to take my daughter to school.

At 8:00 AM, I'd return home and start writing again.

At 11:30 AM, I'd eat lunch, get another workout in, take my dog on a nice long walk, and watch some YouTube videos.

At 1:00 PM, I'd sit down and work on business and marketing items.

At 2:00 PM, I'd devote the rest of the afternoon to reading and consuming content.

At 4:00 PM, I'd pick my daughter up from school. Then it would be dinner time and family time.

At 8:00 PM, I'd spend more time reading and preparing for the next day.

At 9:00 PM, I'd go to bed.

On a perfect day like this, I'd probably write anywhere from 3,000 to 5,000 words. That's 21,000 to 35,000 words per week, 1.82 million words per year, and a whole lotta fun writing!

Not every day would be the same, and I'd weave in other tasks such as podcast interviews, research for a new book, or simply running to the post office if I need to do that. My day would be structured around whatever I need. If my daughter is sick, I can take a day off. If I need to go to a doctor's appointment, I can take an afternoon to do that. And despite what I do, the words continue to add up, the money continues to hit my bank account on schedule, and my happiness is unbound. I suppose this is the definition of freedom.

That's my ideal day. What's yours?

WRITER ASSISTANCE PROGRAM

Many companies have Employee Assistance Programs (EAPs). EAPs provide confidential services such as counseling, mental illness assistance, and provider recommendations for childcare, eldercare, and other issues that employees face that inhibit them from doing their jobs to their fullest potential.

EAPs are popular with employers because there is a direct correlation between employee's personal distractions and their work product. As a manager, I can attest to the fact that employees who were having problems at home were not productive. That causes stress for both the employee and the manager.

I'm not praising corporations. They don't provide EAPs out of the goodness of their hearts—trust me on that. The motive seems optimistic on the surface, but corporations are corporations, and that often means capitalistic. And capitalism has a very ugly side. However, I do believe that employees should take advantage of EAPs, assuming that the employer ensures confidentiality. It's free, and it can be effective. I used my company's EAP to seek therapy for the issues I had with my biological father, and it helped me tremendously.

Anyway, this quarter, my 93-year-old grandfather sustained a life-changing injury that required him to move in with my parents. It was completely unexpected and a difficult adjustment for everyone in my family.

I called my employer's EAP to see what recommendations they had for caregiving providers. They sent me an eldercare kit with some great information that my parents were able to use to give my grandfather better care. All free, and all confidential.

I love the idea of a Writer's Assistance Program. I know that such things do exist; the state of New York used to have a hotline that artists could call for mental health issues and advice regarding their profession. I don't know if that still exists or not.

Writers are all alone with no assistance. Consider that, as a group, we:

- suffer from mental illness and substance abuse at a higher rate than the general population
- have a higher rate of repetitive stress injuries
- struggle to get access to healthcare if we're not employed in a full-time job
- may or may not have spouses and family members who understand our art
- endure money issues because writing doesn't exactly pay the bills for most authors
- have a more difficult tax situation that is truly hard to appreciate until you've experienced it firsthand
- have bills, family obligations, and issues just like everyone else

Yet, what assistance do we receive? None unless we seek it out ourselves.

I envision a Writers Assistance Program that assists writers in their personal lives to help them write to their fullest potential. When writers write more, they make more money.

Such a program might provide:

- programs for substance abuse, addiction, and mental illness, such as a set number of sessions with a certified treatment provider

- resources to help authors reduce repetitive stress injuries, including discounts on equipment
- a referral network of financial advisors, attorneys, and tax accountants who understand authors
- connection to a suicide prevention hotline

This *feels* like something where an existing EAP service provider can tailor their offerings for writers, possibly through a nonprofit organization. It depends on the cost. I believe that authors would gladly pay a slight increase in dues if they knew that the money was going to authors in need, and that the same benefits would be available for them someday. That's how we take care of each other as a community.

COMMUNITY-SUPPORTED AGRICULTURE...FOR BOOKS?

Community-supported agriculture (CSA) is a way for consumers to buy local, seasonal food directly from a farmer. Typically, you pay a flat fee for a season, and then the farmer delivers food to your home. Or you pick it up at the farm.

There are many CSAs in my state of Iowa. This year, I bought a "salad" package, and every week I had a random green delivered to their doorstep—kale, lettuce, arugula, etc. I ate a lot of salads, but the produce was fantastic. CSAs are a great way to support local agriculture.

What about doing something like this for publishing?

Enter community-sourced publishing (CSPs). Pay a charge, and you'll receive hot new self-published books every week with bonuses. Imagine something like this tailored for a genre, like space opera, mystery, or urban fantasy. The titles could even be exclusive to the CSP for a short time.

I'm sure someone has done this. It's similar to a book club but without discussions.

You can handle the book fulfillment with a service like Book Funnel or Story Origin for ebooks. You can even have a paperback or hardcover option for higher rates, and the paper editions can be fulfilled through automation and drop shipping. You just need a human or two to handle the website, curation and customer service, and author payments.

WATCH THE MASTER AT WORK

I've been spending time on Twitch lately. It's such a fascinating platform—people will watch a streamer for hours, even if that person isn't doing anything. I watched a livestream of a writer working on their novel draft in Microsoft Word. The camera wasn't even directly pointed at him. He didn't say a word on the stream. He just sat there typing, sighing in frustration, and staring at his computer. That's intriguing to me.

Here's an idea: every day at the same time, go live and share your screen. Tell people what you're working on and then do it. Then answer a few questions here and there. Let people see you outline, research, write, edit, format, publish, and market your book.

Imagine a mega-bestselling author doing this and what aspiring and new authors could learn from simply watching someone's screen. How much time does it take? Not much more than going live and answering a few questions. After all, they're going to be sitting at their computer anyway...

Imagine what amazing instructional lessons an author could build over just a few years. I'm a fan of "documenting" your process and your journey. Let people see how you work and how your writing methods evolve. Sure, you might spoil some of your work ahead of time, but I doubt anyone will care.

This would be captivating even if the author spends time staring at the screen. If it wasn't, then Twitch wouldn't be nearly as popular as it is today. It's no longer a platform for just gamers. I believe someone on YouTube could be successful doing this too.

AMALGAM FOR
SELF-PUBLISHED WRITERS

In the nineties, Marvel and DC Comics organized a collaboration called *Amalgam*, which was a crossover in both universes. The series took place in an alternate universe where Marvel and DC characters were merged.

For example, they took Wolverine and Batman and merged him into a character called Logan Wayne, also known as the Dark Claw. This character is a mixture of both characters; his parents are murdered at a young age, he goes to live with his uncle in Canada, and is the victim of a scientific experiment gone wrong. He swears to use his powers to avenge his parents and fight crime. He has an adamantium skeleton with claws, regenerative healing powers, a utility belt, and is a martial art specialist. And he solves crimes.

The villain of the story was a merge between Sabretooth and the Joker.

Wow!

The *Amalgam* comics were popular among fans because of their creativity. Plus, they were great marketing.

I've often thought about this for my fiction. What if I took two of my fiction series and amalgamated them together? What if I merged both series' heroes, villains, supporting characters, worlds, and plots together?

I imagine that if the right author did this, their fans would lose their minds. But more practically, it would just be a lot of fun.

The story would take you in different directions too so it would feel familiar but probably end unexpectedly.

How cool would it be if the series became a discoverability tool? Maybe some readers don't know about one of the series that contributed to the amalgamation, and they rush off and buy it. You'll look like a marketing genius if you're successful.

I love this idea! But you can steal it if you want.

REVERSING YOUR SERIES

What if you took a series that you already wrote and reversed it?

Turn your hero into a villain but keep the core elements of their personality the same. Transform them from male to female. Change the mood from optimistic to pessimistic. Turn the setting upside-down (if the original story takes place in summer, make the new one in winter, for example) . What would happen?

Do this with an already popular series and it would be a fun experiment. What would readers think? What would happen if the "reversed" series was *more popular* than the existing one?

KINGDOM HEARTS FOR SELF-PUBLISHED WRITERS

One of my favorite games for the PlayStation two was *Kingdom Hearts*. It was a Japanese roleplaying game crossover between the *Final Fantasy* series and the Disney universe.

In the story, the main character, Sora, lives in a peaceful place called The Destiny Islands with his friends, Riku and Kairi. One day, a rift opens, and monsters called Heartless arrive and destroy the islands. Sora is separated from his friends and sucked into the void. He mysteriously lands in a place called Traverse Town, where other people end up as refugees because their worlds were destroyed by the Heartless too. Those people in Traverse Town happen to be characters from the *Final Fantasy* and Disney worlds. Sora meets two characters named Donald and Goofy who are trying to find their king who has gone out to search for a way to defeat the Heartless once and for all—King Mickey Mouse!

Sora travels across the universe to various Disney worlds to protect them from the Heartless. Tarzan, Aladdin, Mulan, the Lion King, and so on. In each world, the Heartless appear and change the timeline of the original Disney film. The game is an epic crossover, possibly one of the most original of all time.

Much like the *Amalgam* idea, wouldn't be interesting if an author did this with their writing?

Imagine a prolific author with many series who creates a new storyline where an original character visits the worlds of the author's most popular series and works with the readers' favorite characters. That's my idea of fun.

An idea like this might not work, but if it does…you'll create raging fans because the series will be a figurative billboard for your entire body of work. It's incredible marketing. Readers will go on to read the worlds represented in the series.

I've been thinking of doing this too, but you can steal it if you want.

STREAM DECKS FOR PUBLISHING

I recently purchased an Elgato Stream Deck for use in my livestreams. The deck sits on my desk and has 15 gel buttons that I can press that activate features on my computer.

In video conferencing programs, I can use Stream Deck buttons to go live and end broadcasts, change scenes, mute and unmute, turn my webcam on and off, bring in guests, share my screen, and more.

In Microsoft PowerPoint, I can control the flow of my slides.

In Google Chrome, I can map bookmark websites to a button. I can even launch multiple websites with a button.

Even better, I can use hotkeys and map those to buttons on my Stream Deck so I can use it with any program as long as it supports hotkeys. This got me thinking about how a Stream Deck can be a helpful productivity tool:

- While researching my novel, I can bring up websites such as Wikipedia, dictionaries, YouTube, or more with the click of a button. This saves time.
- While writing and editing my novel, I can map simple functions like copy, paste, cut, split-screen, word count revealer, and export into a single key. Again, this saves me a few fractions of a second because I don't have to type the hotkeys. I just push a button.

- When I'm ready to publish, I can launch all of my retailer dashboards with the push of a button. I can also use this to review my sales.
- If I want to see how a certain book is performing, I can launch the book's sales page at all retailers.
- When I'm doing Microsoft Excel work, I can map macros to a button. This will save clicks.

Is the Stream Deck the ultimate productivity tool? No. It has limitations, but it can save time. I've never liked hotkeys on the Mac; I find them too difficult to execute without having to look down at the keyboard. It's easier to press a button. It's not ergonomic, but I don't use the Stream Deck often enough for it to be an issue.

THE OPPOSITE YEAR CHALLENGE

What if, every day, for a year, you did the exact opposite of your publishing instincts?

When your critical voice says, "Don't write your novel without outlining," write without an outline.

When you tell yourself you can't do something, do it anyway.

When a marketing idea sounds repulsive to you, try it.

What would happen? What would you learn?

I believe our instinct exists to protect us and guide us in the right direction. I also believe that sometimes our instincts can be wrong. In my experience, I find that my instinct is right around 90 percent of the time when it comes to major decisions. What about that other 10 percent?

I bet many of your choices wouldn't work out, but what if one amazing thing happened? What if it changed your career? What if it brought in readers and money in ways you never dreamed? That's why this challenge intrigues me, and I believe it would be great for introverted writers who lack confidence in their publishing endeavors. Nothing gives you confidence better than doing something that turns out well unexpectedly.

MEDITATION MP3S FOR WRITERS

Last year on my YouTube channel, someone recommended that I do meditation MP3s. I always liked the idea but never got around to it. It's not high on my priority list, so I'm releasing it to the public.

Here's the idea: do a series of MP3s that help writers build their confidence and focus on their stories. In five minutes, state affirmations and give them prompts to think about their story.

"Imagine that you have published your book and that you are successful. Your family is proud, readers are sending you fan-mail every day, your bank account is overflowing with money. All the negative emotions you feel right now will be a distant memory, and you won't remember them."

"Visualize your self-doubt as a wispy ball of energy. Inhale, and when you exhale, imagine that energy dissipating like salt evaporating in water."

"Think back to the last section in your novel. What did you write? As you think about it, let your mind drift…"

Sync your voice to calming, royalty-free music and create MP3s for different tasks: one set for writing, another for editing, etc. Writers can use them before they start writing for the day or whenever they get stuck.

ROADMAPS

Every app has a "roadmap" these days. Over the past few years, developers have created pages on their websites that show what features they are working on. Some developers even allow users to vote on what they want next, and the developers prioritize accordingly. I've always thought roadmaps were a good transparency tool and a great community builder.

What if an author created a roadmap tool? Create a page on your site with works-in-progress and the next books you plan on writing. Let readers vote on which ones they want to see and prioritize your workload accordingly.

I like the idea because it lets readers participate in your vision for your portfolio, but you're always in control. After all, they're voting on books *you already want to write.* That's the magic behind a tool like this. If you let readers tell you to write books you're not passionate about, then this idea will fail.

COFFEE AND TEA BRANDS
FOR AUTHORS

I've always wondered why influencers in the writing space haven't been more aligned with coffee and tea brands. Coffee is the patron saint of writers.

If you're a popular influencer, why not:

- Cultivate a sponsorship with a coffee or tea brand.
- Approach a coffee or tea brand about partnering on a line of blends geared toward writers and creatives.
- Collaborate with a coffee or tea label to create your brand of writing coffee or tea.

There's some risk, of course. Sponsors come with demands. Any time you put your name on a product, you can be sued for products liability if someone gets sick (so you'll need insurance). There's also the problem of trademarks. But liability and legal concerns aside, it's a great idea and one that would make an influencer a lot of money. I've only seen one influencer on YouTube do this, so there's an opportunity here.

BRING ESSAYS BACK

I've always loved essays. Not high school essays (boo), but traditional essays in the spirit of writers like G.K. Chesterton and James Baldwin.

An essay is an author's opinion about a certain topic, written in a highly stylized form. One of my favorite examples of an essay is *In Praise of Shadows* by Junichiro Tanizaki, which is a celebration of the Japanese aesthetic.

I like essays because they memorialize the times in which they're written. They're also an amazing way to broaden your perspective on an issue. Imagine how much better our world would be today if people wrote well-reasoned essays in favor of their opinions and refuting others'. That's a far better world than the one we currently inhabit, where people just yell at each other on news shows and social media. Writers like James Baldwin changed the world by channeling thoughts that many black people had about racism but couldn't articulate. Throughout history, there have been countless other men and women who changed the world with well-reasoned arguments on the page.

Essays are still alive, but they have fallen out of favor in shaping the culture. No one talks about essays around the watercolor at work. That said, you could argue that certain YouTube videos are a continuation of the modern essay in video form. Casey Neistat is a good example of this kind of YouTuber. He published a video about how irritated he was with a New York City bike lane on the Williamsburg Bridge, and the video went so viral that the city did something about it.

And, of course, writers everywhere are familiar with the classic essay collections *On Writing* by Stephen King and *Bird by Bird* by Anne Lamott. Essays are alive and well, but I wish that they were more popular, that's all.

I've had an idea for a long time to write a collection of formal essays on self-publishing. Maybe I'll do it someday, but in the meantime, I believe essays will come back in the future.

IDEAS THAT HAVE WORKED WELL FOR ME IN THE LAST DECADE

I thought it would be a good idea to cap this book with an analysis of ideas that have worked well for me over the past eight years as a self-published writer. Also, it's my attempt to show that I come up with crazy ideas all the time, and some of them work. Maybe these ideas will work for you, or maybe they won't, but you never know unless you try.

Hermetic behavior. I don't do very much when I'm not working other than write or think about writing. I've given up almost every hobby except for listening to jazz and video game music. And I do watch a lot of YouTube. But other than that, writing is my sole focus. I've paid a price for it in other areas of my life—namely I don't have much of a social life—but the price was worth it.

Pilot series. Once upon a time, I had two ideas for series and couldn't decide which one to write, so I asked my readers to help me. I wrote two series "pilots" with one chapter each and shared them with my readers. Readers voted on the one they liked best, and I turned that into a series. The winning series was *Android X*, which was my first fiction success as an author.

Crazy series. I wrote a series about the wackiest idea I could think of: a gang of anthropomorphic vegetable terrorists fighting to take down a civilization of processed foods. This was my *Moderation Online* series, and it was a spectacular flop. However, the readers who like it really like it. The concept is always good for a giggle, and people regularly pick it up because it sounds so ridiculous that they have to see it for themselves.

Treat your work like an ant colony. In 2015, I had an infestation of carpenter ants in my home. Strangely, the experience taught me to think of my books like ants. Every book you write is an ant that you send out into the world. Some ants never return; others return with money and opportunities. Every piece of media you create is an ant too, such as blogs, videos, and podcasts. But you don't start seeing ants return until you send a *lot* of them into the world. Being prolific is a smart long-term strategy.

Treat your portfolio like a portfolio. Every book you write becomes part of a portfolio of assets. Treat your book like you'd treat real estate. Every few years, you need to update your covers, book descriptions, and metadata. Some assets are worth more than others, but they all contribute to the overall value of your portfolio.

Be first. In 2015, I published a book called *Indie Poet Rock Star: The Poet's Guide to Ebooks, Marketing, and the Self-Publishing Revolution.* It was a courageous book because I predicted that self-publishing would transform the poetry world. Around this time, poets and poetry readers were resistant to ebooks and self-publishing. Many of the predictions in the book came true. I didn't care if anyone read the book, but it turns out someone important did, and it led to amazing opportunities to work for The Alliance of Independent Authors, which led to getting introduced to Writer's Digest, which led to getting face-time with Apple Books, which led to…you get the idea.

Be last. Sometimes, you don't want to adopt something right away. Let other people figure it out.

Nonprofit outreach. I devote time each month to The Alliance of Independent Authors, and it has led to amazing opportunities. But most importantly, I love giving back to the author community by contributing to a cause I believe in.

Unified branding. In 2016, I decided to go with a similar look all of my book covers. I created a design for fiction, nonfiction, and poetry. That went a long way to improving the overall look of my portfolio.

Be willing to talk to a wall. If you look at my multimedia efforts (YouTube, podcasting, blogging, etc.), I started with nothing. My very first podcast was a 10-minute show where I talked about what was on my mind while I drove to the gym every week. For later podcasts, I talked to a wall and published that conversation. Slowly, people started paying attention. That never would have happened if I didn't dare to put stuff into the universe with no expectation of return.

"The Writer's Journey" Podcast. I did a podcast for two years, and it was immensely popular. The only content was about me and the issues I was dealing with. I learned that people love to see behind the scenes how others work and what they're thinking.

"Writing Tip of the Day" Podcast. For two years, I released a podcast that shared a crisp writing tip in five minutes or less. At the time of this writing, it was my most popular show of all time.

Set a clear strategy. I'm not saying that people have to follow my strategy, but taking the time to craft a clear strategy helped me win big in 2020 during the pandemic. I learned that when you take the time to be clear about what you want out of your author career and work toward your goals, the universe will reward you for it.

Writing in public. I learned this from Dean Wesley Smith. He publishes a daily journal blog post on his website every day and tells people what he did to move his writing business forward every day. I did the same thing, and it worked very well for me.

Float test ideas. I've had ideas that I felt strongly about but my audience didn't like. Whenever I have an idea, I "float it" to my audience on my blog to see what the response is. If it doesn't connect, I'll float it again. If it fails twice, then it's not something they want. I did this with my editing engine and it saved me time and effort—I thought maybe people would be interested in building something similar for themselves, but they weren't.

Blue ocean strategy. I've built a name for myself in the writing space by tackling ideas that others won't touch. My *Writing Craft Playbook* is a series of drawings that show writers how mega bestsellers write their fiction. I was inspired by watching a football game one day. I'm willing to go places no one else will go, and I've been rewarded for it.

Collaboration. I wrote a series (*Modern Necromancy*) with my friend Justin Sloan. It was successful and it grew both our audiences. I would collaborate with someone again if it was the right project.

Beast Mode. I made a public goal of writing as many books as possible in 90 days, and my community loved it. I called it my "Beast Mode Challenge." It increased my portfolio count and brought great engagement to my platform.

Synergizing my personal, professional, and writing life. I see my insurance work, writing, and personal life as harmonizing forces. My goal is to ensure that they're playing a great song. Many people hate their jobs and don't want to think about them outside of work. I happened to enjoy my work and used many benefits that my employers offered to further my writing business. My employer paid for law school, therapy, and so on. I applied lessons I learned at work to my writing, especially with data and analytics. I kept getting promoted, which afforded me better opportunities and more time to write.

Writing on the go. Pre-pandemic, I owed 40 percent of my word counts to writing on my phone. At first, I didn't like the idea of writing on my phone, but it was so successful for me that I relearned how to write novels. I consider it one of my superpowers along with dictation.

Use speaking engagements to pay for technology. Every time

I land a paid speaking engagement, I use that money to reinvest in my technology. I believe this is a competitive advantage. It allows me to upgrade my online presence cost-free.

Capture ideas like Pokémon. I'm religious about writing ideas down. I have notebooks full of ideas, and that ensures that I never run out of ideas.

Practice idea sex (also known as idea calculus). I learned this from Claudia Azula Altucher in her book *Become an Idea Machine*. I come up with new ideas every day and mix ideas in unusual ways.

Test runs. When I take on projects, I do it because of what I will learn. I often "test" a project on a small scale. When I created my first course, *Write to Market*, I did it as an experiment. I broke a lot of rules and figured out how to create a course. The next year, when I created my course, *Writing in Hard Times*, I did it in a third of the time, at a much higher production level. That taught me how to make a seriously good premium course. To date, I have made very little from my courses, but I was willing to invest that time and energy to learn how to create them.

Be willing to go down rabbit holes. I like to explore ideas just to see what happens. Most people are far more pragmatic than I am; they'll decline anything that doesn't suit their immediate needs. I'll dissect an idea for the idea's sake even if I know it possibly won't go anywhere. I do it because of the knowledge. Knowledge is power. When you accumulate knowledge, you can use it to inform your strategy and aid your tactical execution. For example, I saw someone use a Microsoft Excel macro once, and a voice in the back of my head told me to explore it. Dozens of hours later, I had created an automated sales report process. I had no idea where the journey would take me, but I'm glad I took it. Several months later, I successfully automated parts of my editing. All because I was willing to explore an idea that most people would have written off because they either weren't interested or willing to learn how it could help them.

To give you another example, I provided a consultation to a Silicon Valley company for a tool that can help authors manage their intellectual property. The project lasted several months. We hit a dead-end, but the knowledge I learned was extremely valuable because I know how to build a tool like this in the future. The project was a masterclass in working with developers and shrewd businesspeople.

To be fair, most of my expeditions don't end this way, but I'm willing to go on 100 expeditions if 20 of them produce treasure. Each treasure is a competitive advantage in the long term.

Those are just a few of the ideas that helped me get where I am today. Feel free to steal them for yourself. If you do, I hope they work for you as well, if not better than they did for me.

CONTENT CREATED WHILE WRITING THIS BOOK

Author Level Up YouTube Channel - Highlights

Watch at youtube.com/authorlevelup.

New Studio Setup. See Michael's new YouTube setup in action.
Scrivener 3 for Windows: First Impressions. Now that Scrivener 3 is available for Windows, hear Michael's thoughts.
How I Deal with Overwhelm as a Writer. Hear Michael's thoughts on how he approaches stressful times.

Interviews & Appearances

"The Curiously Effective Power of Drifting." Article in the print version of Writer's Digest, May/June 2021. Look for it wherever you get your magazines.

INDIE AUTHOR CONFIDENTIAL

Secrets No One Will Tell You About Being a Writer

VOL. 6

M.L. RONN

VOLUME 6

INTRODUCTION

In the last volume, I wrote about how a major life change kept me from writing for a brief time during Q2. I'm making up for it with this volume, as I'm back to normal. In fact, I'm better than normal because I'm doing another "Beast Mode Challenge" this year, with a goal of writing at least 10 books in 90 days.

In Q2 of this year, I wrote the *Indie Author Confidential* volume book late in the quarter. In Q3, I decided to write the volume early in the quarter so I could focus on Beast Mode. I technically wrote part of this book during Beast Mode, and I'll be publishing it in the middle of the challenge.

By writing most of this volume before the busiest days of the challenge, I'll stay on schedule. Last year, a lot of items fell off my radar during Beast Mode. This year, I don't want the *Indie Author Confidential* series to be one of those things.

I'll share the results of the Beast Mode Challenge in the next volume, but in the meantime, I've got a great volume for you that ventures into both familiar and new territory.

My Core Strategic Priorities

As a refresher, my mission is to create content that entertains and/or educates my audience, preferably both, and to remain nimble in an ever-changing industry. I do this by focusing on five strategic priorities:

- Become a world-class content creator
- Become a world-class marketer
- Become a technology-driven writer
- Become a data-driven writer
- Become the writer of the future

I believe these five priorities are most important for me to have a long-term, sustainable career.

What's in This Volume

As usual, you'll find sections for each of my strategic pillars, though Technology and Data and have been combined.

In the World-Class Content Creation section, I discuss my preparation for Beast Mode, why I don't write every day, and some thoughts on wrapping up teaching insurance classes, which helped me become a better public speaker.

In the World-Class Marketer section, I discuss experiments with permafree and pricing psychology. I also write about my most ridiculous pitch of all time.

In the Technology and Data section, I discuss thoughts on the new writing app Atticus, artificial intelligence and why authors aren't interested in hearing about it, and more nuanced thoughts about backing up my data.

In the Writer of the Future, I discuss more adventures in AI as well as a new segment where I look back at my writing career one year, five years, and ten years ago. I also discuss the potential ramifications of big tech legislation in the United States and it will almost certainly impact indie authors in the short and long term. And, in a series first, I discuss thoughts on death and what it means to be an author after the death of my grandfather.

2021 has been a decent year so far and I'm hoping that the progress I made this quarter will help me finish the year strong.

Enjoy this volume.

M.L. Ronn
July 15, 2021
Des Moines, Iowa

BECOME A WORLD-CLASS CONTENT CREATOR

HOW I MASTERED REPURPOSING (AGAIN)

The previous volume of this series was the last to contain an "Ideas You Can Steal" section.

I had an idea to create a new book with just the "Ideas You Can Steal" from the first five volumes of this series. My goal was to use them to compile a fresh book that would have separate marketing potential and a life of its own.

Good ideas should be shared. I don't know if the ideas I posed in this series are good or not, but I figured I might as well send them into the world to find out. There was also the slight chance that this book could bring new readers onto my platform, but I didn't design the book with that goal in mind.

The book was titled *Authors, Steal This Book: 67 Business Ideas for the Writers of the Future.*

I made the book permafree to make it easier to spread the ideas. However, I had to accept the major downside of permafree: bad reviews. Readers who get books for free are far more likely to leave harsher reviews. But if there was any book where I welcomed bad reviews, it was this one.

I knew in advance that some people were going to read it and say, "This book didn't make me any money. I wanted actionable strategies to sell more books that work TODAY, not visions of the future." There are always going to be those people who completely miss the point of a book, even though you beat them over the head with it.

The reviews I care about are the ones that say, "This was an engaging book of ideas, but I agreed/didn't agree with the ideas because..."

We benefit when we engage in meaningful dialogue about what we want the author profession to be in several decades. Whether readers agree with me or not, if my book makes people start thinking about this and assert their own opinions about what they want the future to look like, then the book will have done its job.

When you write as many books as I do, your goals change. I've never written a book that advances a philosophy (for free) before, so this was a fun experiment.

Also, you never know who will read your books. It could create opportunities for me, or even better, one of the ideas might become reality! If that happens, we all win.

Will it work? It's too soon to tell, but I'm glad I published the book.

Authors, Steal This Book was stunningly simple to create. It required almost no effort to produce.

It took me an hour to write the introduction. I slipped it in with my manuscript for *Indie Author Confidential Vol. 5* when I sent it to my editor.

It took an hour to research a good image for the cover.

It took three days to get the cover designed.

It took 30 minutes to compile all the ideas from the previous volumes in this series into Vellum (my formatting software), and another 30 minutes to proof everything.

And boom—new book with minimal cost and effort. Fully edited and with a cover quality that my readers typically expect. And it fits right in with the other books in my writing guide series.

That's how you can take content that you've already created, repurpose and repackage it, and use it to reach a new audience. If there's anything I've learned in this business, it's that you NEVER know who is going to come into contact with your books out in the wild. If you understand that, then you understand that it's in your best interest to put as much out there as possible. If, from time to time, you can repackage something with minimal effort, it's a smart win. (But remember, don't nickel and dime your audience, and don't be deceitful about it. A lot of marketers give repurposing a bad name.)

At the end of 2021, the *Indie Author Confidential* series will be a substantial property with seven volumes, two omnibuses (Volumes 1-3 and Volumes 4-7), and a spinoff book with the ideas. Pretty amazing what you can do if you get creative.

If you're interested, you can grab *Authors, Steal This Book* at www.authorlevelup.com/stealthisbook.

WHAT IT LOOKS LIKE WHEN YOU HAVE AN INTERESTING IDEA

In the previous volume, I wrote about "amalgamating" a series, which meant mashing two series together to create a new one. The new series would contain hybrids of the characters, worlds, and settings. I was fascinated by the idea.

As I reflected on it, I realized that this was a rare idea with a clear provenance.

Often, my ideas have multiple sources and it's weird how they come together. I don't often stop to think about HOW my ideas are formed, but this one is pretty fun.

- I was reminiscing on old-school comic books, and I remembered the *Amalgam* series by DC and Marvel. They fused their iconic characters into one. Batman + Wolverine = Dark Claw. Superman + Captain America = Super-Soldier. And so on.
- A few days before that, one of my series suddenly spiked on Amazon. It rose to #1 in its categories and it came out of nowhere. To this day, I still have no idea what precipitated the sales boost.
- In a recent livestream on my YouTube channel, someone asked me if my ideas are inspired by real-life or if I just make them up. I answered that I get inspiration from my personal life.

- Around this same time, I had some construction done at my house and the contractors tore up my grass pretty badly. They laid down sod, so I had to water it every day. The roots started "establishing," which means they were digging into my soil, which is a major step in the development of sod because you can mow it and reduce the watering.

PUTTING IT ALL TOGETHER: A NEW SERIES IDEA

Idea 1.A: What if I took two of my existing fiction series and mashed them together? Take both protagonists and fuse their personalities and timelines? What if I did the same with the supporting characters, villains, and settings?

Idea 1.B: What if I used this new "amalgamated" series as a marketing tool for my existing two series? In other words, if it becomes popular, it will automatically increase the sales of my existing series. If any of my existing series become popular in the future, readers will LOVE the amalgamation!

Idea 1.C: Because both worlds are already written, do I need to write into the dark or is the story more of a creative exercise? In other words… do I need to OUTLINE THIS SERIES to stay true to both worlds while also pushing them in a new and original direction?

In theory, readers already know what happens in at least one of the worlds, but not the new one. The new one will always "feel" familiar, but it won't quite be.

With Writing into the Dark, the key philosophy is that "If you don't know what will happen, then readers won't either." Fusing both worlds would achieve that goal.

I can use outlining as a STRATEGIC TOOL to deliver maximum fan service. It's also an example that every writing technique is merely a tool. If you've followed me for a while, you know that I have strong feelings about writing into the dark, and I haven't outlined in years. But maybe this is the right time to pull out the tool and use it unusually. All I care about is telling a great story and taking readers on a fun ride. I'm not above using any tool to help me do that.

Will I outline my novels moving forward? Heck no, but this could be an interesting experiment.

Idea 1.D: Maybe I just need to outline the series up to a certain point, and then the "roots" of the series (i.e. reader expectations) will be established, allowing me to write the rest of the series into the dark.

That's how this idea formed. I haven't written the series yet, but it's high on my priority list because I'm excited about it. If it fails, it will at least have been fun. If it succeeds, it could make an amazing amount of money and grow my readership exponentially.

You can steal this idea too.

A NOVEL WITH NO CHAPTERS

Many book ideas come to me when I listen to jazz. In the previous volume, I wrote about Casiopea, my favorite Japanese jazz fusion band. I was listening to their 2004 *Marble* album, which was the last studio album before the band went on a hiatus. The first track, "Universe," is a 25-minute-long magnum opus that takes you on a journey through the universe. There are no breaks, and the band plays the song in one take. There are complicated chord changes, complex rhythms, and very technical solos. The entire song is a tour de force in jazz fusion, and every time I listen to it, I'm amazed by the band's musicianship.

That got me thinking about an interesting idea for fiction. What if I wrote a novel with no chapters? What if it were a story told in one continuous take? What kind of character would this be about? What craft techniques would I have to use to keep readers engaged?

Readers expect chapters. Almost every book is written using them. I think it would be fun to write a book that didn't.

I know I'm not the first to try this, but it would be a fun challenge.

When I wrote poetry, I used to challenge myself to write in different poetic forms. I would pick a form and then figure out what the poem would be about. Sometimes it worked, sometimes it didn't, but I find that I am a content-first person. Typically, I decide what type of story I'm going to write, and then the form follows. It's fun to do it the other way around sometimes.

I'm still mulling this idea over, and it may be a long time before I implement it. You're welcome to steal it.

BOOK COMMENTARY

In 2014, I created a reader bonus that I forgot about until now. I called it "book commentary."

This makes me feel old, but I used to collect DVDs. One of my favorite bonus features was director commentary. It was an audio track that, when chosen, would play over the movie or television show, and the director would talk about the inspiration to the story and how scenes were filmed. The commentary was always fascinating to me. I don't understand why it stopped in the streaming era. Netflix and Hulu's failure to implement it was a blow to the creative arts.

I still owned DVDs in 2014, so commentary was fresh on my mind. For my novels *Theo and the Festival of Shadows* and *Food City* (formerly *Eaten Season 1*), I recorded author commentary and linked to it from special sections of the book. *Theo and the Festival of Shadows* is an interactive novel, and the commentary was a bonus feature that the reader unlocked if they beat an interactive board game.

I listened to the commentary again after all these years, and it was fun to relive it. I sounded stiff behind the microphone. I didn't have good gear, and my execution could have been better. Almost no one listened to the commentary.

What if I brought this back for my novels again, and linked to a five-minute video where I talked about the inspiration behind the novel? What if I did this with my writing books? It's an interesting thought now that I have a bigger readership.

HOW I BUILT A SUCCESSFUL WRITING BUSINESS (WITHOUT WRITING EVERY SINGLE DAY)

On my nightly blog, I report my daily word counts, even if I don't write any words for that day.

Last quarter, there were several days where I wasn't able to write. I posted my zero numbers, and I didn't make any excuses for them. Rather, I felt it gave my audience a realistic view of what the part-time writing life was like.

I don't remember the exact number of days, but in May, I probably only wrote on 10 days. The rest were zero-word count days.

Why? I started a new job, I finished law school, and I had some other personal issues to attend to. Those things prevented me from writing.

That's okay. I want people to know that you can have a prolific writing career even if you don't write every day. Many people (including aspiring writers) think they are failures if they don't write every day. They have quotas, and if they don't hit those quotas, their day is ruined.

Don't get me wrong—I'm not against quotas. Prolific writer James Scott Bell advocates for them, and I agree with his reasoning that prolific writers who write day in and day out will have long careers.

I just don't believe in hard quotas. I don't get angry if I want to write a chapter and fail to do so. That's the key.

In my book *Be a Writing Machine*, I talk about the law of averages. Let's say that I only wrote on 10 days every month of the year, and let's say that I wrote 1,000 words each day. That's 10,000 words per month and 120,000 words per year. If you write 50,000-word novels, that's 2.4 novels per year, which is a respectable number. In a decade, that will net you 24 novels, which is more than many writers write in their entire careers.

Keep in mind that those numbers are based on writing only 10 days per month. I happen to think that those numbers are fantastic.

If we bump up our daily word count streak to 20 days per month, that gets us 20,000 words per month and 240,000 words per year, which equates to 4.8 novels per year and 48 novels in a decade. Again, those are fantastic numbers, and we are merely assuming a small word count per day and a 66 percent daily writing rate.

Multiply those numbers by a 30-year-long writing career, and by the time you die, you will have published 144 novels. That easily puts you in the upper echelon of the most prolific writers who have ever lived.

Increase your daily word count numbers and you will become exponentially more prolific—and you're only writing 20 days per month.

Increase the number of days per month you write, and you'll also become more prolific—and you're only writing 1,000 words per day.

That's how the law of averages works. As long as you continue to sit down in the chair, it will work in your favor. Most people don't see it that way, though.

The numbers I described are inspiring and cumulative, yet writers still beat themselves up because life happened and they couldn't write on a Saturday afternoon.

I've written over 60 books while raising a family, working a demanding job in the insurance industry, and attending law school classes in the evenings. If I can write this many books (as a part-time writer) and be considered prolific, then you can too. You can even do better than me if you follow the advice above.

But remember your priorities.

First things first: your family comes before anything else. If you have small children (or big children for that matter) and they need something, take care of them. Same with your spouse, aging parents, relatives, and so on. Your children will only be in the house for so many years and you only have your parents and grandparents for so long.

Second, your day job also takes priority. Why? Because if you're a new writer who is paying out of pocket for producing your books, if you don't have a day job, you can't afford to publish at the quality readers expect. Once you have more books, this changes. If you hate your day job, find another day job.

I'm now an executive at a global insurance company, yet here I am still writing books. There are a lot of days when work makes bigger demands of me than the regular 9 to 5. That's okay. I have a very high tolerance level when it comes to working. I thrive under pressure. My path is not for the faint of heart.

If that's not you and you can leave your work at work, then do that.

Third, you don't have to write every day to have a career as a writer. I've written almost 60 books at this point, and I didn't get here by writing every day.

Sometimes, I had family obligations or work obligations or law school, or something else. I didn't write every day. Many weeks, I did, but there were some weeks and months where I didn't write at all. Or, I'd eke out 100-word days. Yet, I still managed to write 60 books and make pretty good money with my writing. The key is that I always kept at it, even if I failed some days.

I never get upset or worried if I don't write on a certain day.

And trust me, with Beast Mode coming up, I'm going to miss on some days. Any deadlines in this business are self-made. No one will prosecute me if I miss a quota.

Don't worry about zero-word count days. Take that energy and focus it on whatever made you miss because that's where your attention should be *anyway*...then pick yourself back up and try again.

(And no, I don't care what anyone says about NaNoWriMo— no one will die if you don't write a 50,000-word novel in November. Use challenges like NaNoWriMo to motivate and inspire you, but they aren't worth it if you stress yourself out. In all the public challenges I have done, I've had tons of fun whether I succeeded or failed. Big difference.)

I'm not saying that you should never write, or that you should be lazy and find excuses not to write. You all know that I believe the exact opposite, and I hopefully have led by example in this area.

This is why I'm such an advocate for writing on your phone or dictating. Sometimes that can mean the difference between a zero-day and a productive day. Add enough of those days together and you have a career.

Be intentional about your writing. Write as much as you can when you can, and remember the law of averages. Even if you miss a few days or weeks, you'll more than likely have word count days that even out your yearly word count.

If you never thought about your yearly word count, then you should. A career equals many years, hopefully decades if you're young enough. Some years, you'll be down. Some years, you'll be up. In 2017, I wrote 12 books, and 9 of those were novels, which is insane. In 2020, I did 10 books, mostly nonfiction, but it was still an equally productive year. In 2018, I only wrote 5 books. 2021 will probably be somewhere between 10 to 12. Take advantage of the good years and good times and wait out the bad ones. Despite what you think, no one's watching, and no one cares except you. I find that freeing.

And take care of yourself. There's no point writing 10 books a year if you burn yourself out. The reason I don't burn out is that I keep my writing fun.

Sure, it's true that if you write every single day without fail, you will write more books and (maybe) even make more money. But I'd rather write as much as I can (with zero days from time to time) if it means I'm balanced in all areas of my life instead of writing every day and burning out. Life happens. Even with the best plans and organization, you're going to get knocked down. Just roll with it.

I've been a published author for almost a decade, and I've met a lot of indie authors. I don't know any who can sustain a breakneck pace for very long without burning out. Not a single one.

There are people in the community who believe in writing every day without fail, and if that works for them, fine, but that doesn't mean YOU have to do it. Sure, aspire to it, but don't be angry if you fail at it.

"But, Michael! If I take too long between publishing books, readers will forget about me!!!!!!"

Do you think anyone forgot about George R. R. Martin between *A Game of Thrones* books? If he can get away with taking two decades to write that series, then you can get away with anything. Build your email list and your community, keep in touch with your fans, and stay diligent.

"But, Michael! If I don't publish often, the algorithms will send my first books to hell!!!"

So be it. Again, as someone who has been doing this for almost a decade with a lot of books and sales to show for it, I can tell you that a book isn't worth sacrificing for the other areas in your life.

Your writing will always be there. That's part of its charm. It's something you can always escape to and turn to in hard times. No matter what happens to you, you will always be a writer if you write.

Your writing will always be there. That's not necessarily true about your spouse, children, or your health.

We aren't immune to the influence of hustle culture in the indie community. Don't let someone talk you into doing anything that doesn't work for you. Anyone can talk a good hustle game, but at the end of the day, you're the one that has to live your career.

THE ULTIMATE GUIDE TO WRITER'S BLOCK

I published the following chapter in my *Writing Tips* series, and I thought it would be great to include it here since a lot of people are always thinking about writer's block and how to beat it. Enjoy.

Ah, the dreaded writer's block. Every writer must learn to deal with it in some form. While it would be awesome if the words flowed from our brains to our fingers in one smooth motion, it often doesn't happen that way. It can feel like a downright battle to beat writer's block, especially in difficult parts of a book like the murky middle.

You can never banish writer's block, but you can minimize its impacts. This chapter is dedicated to helping you beat writer's block every time it comes around.

The Root Causes of Writer's Block

Writer's block is a response, not an emotion. I believe it's your spirit (or the universe, or God, or whatever you believe in spiritually) telling you that something is wrong. Not with you, but with your story.

Dean Wesley Smith, a prolific writer, often says that your brain (or your creative voice) knows everything about writing a story;

when you read, you learn subconsciously. When you write, much of that subconscious learning flows out automatically. The key is to be aware of what you're learning so you can recognize what your creative voice is doing. I agree with that assessment.

Your creative voice knows everything about writing a story; it also knows when something is wrong. When it can't continue, it throws up a roadblock, stopping you from continuing. At that point, it's *your* job to figure out what's wrong and to give your creative voice what it needs to continue.

To understand what your creative voice needs, it's helpful to understand the three root causes of writer's block.

The first root cause is fear. Everyone deals with fear to some extent. You might be afraid that you can't tell a good story, or that you'll never be able to finish your book, or that readers won't want to buy it, or that you'll receive bad reviews, and so on. Fear is especially difficult to deal with because it changes based on the context. A new writer deals with fear in the same quantity as a mega-bestseller, but the *type* of fear is different. That's what people misunderstand about it. Many think, "If I could just finish my book or become a full-time writer, my problems will go away forever." That never happens.

When you understand that fear will always be with you, you'll have a healthier and more realistic toolbox to beat it. If you treat fear as an ever-morphing foe, you'll be able to recognize it every time it appears.

Fear creates writer's block, and in my opinion, it is the predominant root cause. The best way to address fear is to fight it.

The second root cause is a lack of inspiration. Sometimes your creative voice needs inspiration to keep going. If you've ever driven a car and ran low on gas, you can probably relate to this: you're driving a car, and suddenly, the low gas light comes on. You start panicking about whether you can reach the nearest gas station before your car shuts off. If you're on a road trip, you become especially nervous. Every mile feels like ten until you see the tall, bright sign of a gas station on the side of the road. You pull up to the pump, fill up the car, and drive off, relieved.

Suffering from a lack of inspiration is the same way. Writer's block is like the gas light that switches on suddenly. It changes the tenor of your drive until you fix it. You're running out of figurative gas, and you need it fast.

The best way to combat this problem is to keep reading regularly. This way, you're filling up your writer's tank so that you always have a rich pool of ideas to draw from.

The third root cause is personal circumstances. Sometimes life happens, and it can take you away from writing for a time. Stress, sickness, death, financial issues, loss of a job, and other personal circumstances can halt your writing efforts. Even if you sit down to write, you'll find that your mind is elsewhere. The best way to deal with this cause is to address life head on. Once you take care of your problems, you'll find that the writer's block will go away.

Those are the three root causes of writer's block, but we won't stop there. Now we need to design some strategies to help you win the war.

Developing Strategies Against Fear

First, don't believe anything fear says.

I have a theory: when you write, you become a child. You transport yourself back to your childhood, where everything was possible and there were no bad ideas. Being able to "play" is an essential part of being a creative, and writers know how to access their inner child for maximum benefit.

When readers read, they become children too. Action, adventure, love, and thrill takes them back to their childhoods.

In my mind, writing and reading is just a conversation between children.

However, when you become a child, you invite all the baggage from your childhood to the surface too. So much trauma happens in childhood, and it's easy to push it aside and not address it. For example, if you had difficult relationships with your parents as a child, that will manifest itself in your personality when you become an adult. If you were bullied on the playground, that will have an effect too. We all have our traumas, and sometimes trauma doesn't look like you think it will look. Sometimes it's merely someone saying something to you, and you don't realize the damage until years later.

When you become a child and return to the land of writing, where everything is fun and possible, trauma is never far away. It follows you like a whispering shadow. Sometimes it overtakes you, and that makes you freeze.

The best way to deal with trauma is to face it. If you don't know what your traumas are, you have to find them. But more often than not, you know what they are. Whatever your inner critic says to you when you write is a trauma. Things like "You'll never finish because you don't know how to tell a story," or, "No one will buy my work because..." or "I'm incapable of writing a love story because..."

Whatever excuses your critical voice throws at you, they're probably rooted in your childhood. This is my theory—if I'm right, then the solution is just a matter of human psychology. Once you face the trauma, it becomes easier to manage. It'll still follow you, but you'll ensure that the shadow never engulfs your inner child. Healing your traumas will make your inner child feel safer.

If you struggle to deal with your traumas, I recommend that you seek therapy. Don't listen to people who say that therapy is bad. Therapy is amazing—you get to talk to a stranger who is trained to listen and reflect your thoughts and feelings to you so you can understand yourself as you are, not who you *think* you are.

Understanding yourself and engaging in self-healing is one of the healthiest and most effective ways to fight fear. Fear thrives on a lack of awareness of oneself. When you don't understand *why* something throws you into an emotional rollercoaster, fear will take advantage of that.

To use another analogy, let's use a common fact of pest control. Pretend you have an opossum living under your porch, or a family of mice in your attic. Generally, pests don't like the presence of humans. They try to find places where they can live without interruption. If a pest lives in an abandoned house, and suddenly people move in and start living there, the pest is going to leave and find somewhere else to live. They preferred darkness where there is now light, and quiet where there is now constant noise. Fear is the same way.

Illuminate the darkest spaces of your heart, and fear will have fewer places to dwell.

Developing Strategies Against Lack of Inspiration

As I mentioned before, reading and consuming content regularly is the best inoculation against lack of inspiration. Your creative voice loves it when you're constantly exposing yourself to new stories and ideas.

To use another cheesy analogy, it's like putting hair food in your hair. It makes your hair richer and look better.

I find that capturing ideas is also another effective way to combat a lack of inspiration. For example, I use Evernote to write down ideas that come to me during the day. I write the idea down, file it away, and whenever I suffer from a lack of inspiration, I can refer to my Evernote account for a quick boost. I've accumulated thousands of ideas over the years, so much that I rarely deal with a lack of inspiration anymore.

I take pictures of interesting sights, write down unique things that people say (especially in dialect), scribble ideas that come to me at three AM, and so much more. Over the years, those notes have added up in a big way.

Let's express treatment to lack of inspiration with an equation: Regular consumption of content + capture + catalogue of ideas over time = reduced lack of inspiration. You can almost never go wrong if you follow this equation.

Other smart strategies to combat this root cause are meeting new people and visiting new places regularly. There's nothing like the rush of new people and new places to inspire your writing.

More Strategies to Beat Writer's Block

Now that we've covered tactics to help you beat each root cause, let's talk about advanced strategies. These tips are most effective once you've published a few books, and they can help you fight writer's block and fear as they morph.

The first strategy is to understand where you are in the process. Where does writer's block hit you the most? I find that it typically likes to visit at certain parts of a novel more than others, and that might be true for you too. For example, I tend to encounter writer's block without fail around the 20 to 30 percent mark of my novel. This is right around the point where the "honeymoon phase" and infatuation with a new project wears off. Writer's block strikes again around the 50 to 60 percent mark, usually in the darkest part of the "murky middle." Because I know this, I can plan for it. Usually, at the end of each writing day, I'll tally up my total word count for the novel and try to *predict* when the writer's block will probably come. For example, if I write 1,000 words a day and my novels are usually 50,000 words, I can expect to run into writer's block sometime around 10,000 to 12,000 words. So, if it's Monday and I'm at 7,000 words, I can almost certainly expect to run into a rough patch sometime before the weekend.

Planning is the key. If you treat writer's block like a rainstorm, you'll treat it differently. If you planned a party in your backyard, you'd move it indoors for a rainstorm, right? If you expect writer's block to arrive within a few days, you might reschedule some of your life so that you can be ready for it.

The second strategy is to visualize the future and what will be once you've conquered writer's block. If you can visualize a problem, you can solve it. I like to imagine the problem as a physical ball of tangled yarn, and I imagine myself untangling the yarn. That helps.

The third strategy is to lean into writer's block when appropriate. It's like driving a car and skidding out of control. The best thing to do is to lean into the skid; it's counterintuitive but works every time. Sometimes you should lean into writer's block. Set the writing aside and "drift" for a few days, always on the lookout for inspiration. Just make sure you return to your manuscript!

The fourth strategy is to listen to the writer's block. Is your creative voice trying to tell you something? Is there something else you should be doing instead, such as dealing with a personal crisis? This seems odd, but I find that writer's block often happens a day or so *before* life strikes. It's like it knows when things will go awry. I've learned to listen and be a student of my creative voice, always attenuating myself to its needs.

Remember, writer's block is an emotional response.

The fifth strategy is to approach writer's block like a United States Navy SEAL. Navy SEALs are some of the toughest soldiers in the world, and they endure training that would be unbearable to most people. During boot camp, the most successful seals are those who can adopt "microfocus." Instead of focusing on finishing boot camp, they focus instead on moving their arm while they're crawling through the mud in a thunderstorm. You too can develop microfocus. Instead of focusing on the book, focus on writing the next sentence.

The sixth strategy to develop amnesia about your writer's block. If you're dealing with writer's block, just forget it. Pretend it doesn't exist. A year from now, when your book has been published for a while, you won't even remember the sections that gave you the most trouble.

Also, your editor can't tell when you have writer's block. Once they're done with the book, everything will be so smooth that no one will even know where you struggled. Adopt that perspective while you're writing.

The seventh strategy is to think of writer's block as an experience that will make you a better writer. Every time you beat it, you're better for it. Adopt a curiosity mindset whenever writer's block appears and you'll be shocked at how your perspective changes. Be intentional about fighting it, keep sitting down and writing, try to keep momentum, and there will come a point where you will break through and you'll return to smoother writing sessions. You just have to have the courage to keep going.

You can win the war against writer's block. Fortunately, I have a lot of books that will help you.

How to Write Your First Novel is about helping you finish your first book.

Be a Writing Machine is about writing faster and smarter, beating writer's block, and being prolific. I delve into many of the strategies I discuss in this chapter.

Mental Models for Writers is about small mindset shifts that can make a big difference in your career.

The Indie Author Bestiary is a manual for conquering the "beasts" of the writing life, such as fear and self-doubt.

You can find all of my books for writers at www.authorlevelup.com/books.

TIME TO DO A CLEANUP

Last quarter, I published two books: *Indie Author Confidential Volume 5* and *Authors, Steal This Book*. As I was publishing them, I realized that the major retailer dashboards have changed slightly. Amazon introduced some new functionality on its pricing screen, and Google Play made some minor changes too.

I realized that it's time for another "patrol." I needed to review my books' sales pages to check:

- Metadata
- Prices for all formats
- Book descriptions (typos and formatting breaks only)
- Availability

I don't like doing this, but it's necessary. Things happen over the years. However, when you have over 60 books, these types of tasks become more challenging. I had to develop a plan.

- I can't do all of this by myself. I need help, which means I have to hire someone.
- I need to develop a checklist that covers the items that need to be reviewed.
- I need that checklist to stay mostly the same from year to year.

- I need to develop a "report" that the assistant can give me. I need to retain that report for future years so I can remember what was done for each book.

This is important so that I ensure:

- my books are available widely
- each format of my books is available widely
- the correct version of the book is available for sale
- my books are priced correctly across currencies
- no typos exist in the book description

This is going to be a lot of work, but I will try to accomplish it before the end of the year.

MAKING MINOR MODIFICATIONS TO THE PACKAGING OF THE INDIE AUTHOR CONFIDENTIAL SERIES

While we're on the topic of cleaning up my work, I noticed two minor issues with the *Indie Author Confidential* series that needed immediate rectification.

The first issue was that, when placing all the covers of this series side-by-side, I noticed a color mistake.

Volume 1 of this series had my author name in black text. Volumes 2 and onward had my name in white text. The white text looked much better and more appealing. When you looked at all the titles together, Volume 1 stood out in a bad way.

Most readers probably never noticed. I'm surprised it took me this long to see it. Normally, I catch these errors before the designer is done with the design. I should have caught this with Volume 2, but sometimes things happen. (Do you see why I believe in intellectual property management now?)

Having one author name in the series in a different color is a very minor issue that other authors would have ignored and fixed later, but for me, it was a matter of professionalism.

The second issue was that I forgot that Volume 1 had a call to action page called "Read Next: Vol. X." That page had the picture of the next volume in the series, two sentences of copy, and a link. I forgot to do this with Volume 2 onward. This is even less of a minor issue that I'm certain that almost no one observed.

However, adding CTAs to the series is a smart sales tool. I was smart enough to do this for Volume 1, but somehow I forgot with the rest of the volumes.

Here are the steps I took to rectify both issues.

- I worked with my designer to update the color of the author name on Volume 1. I had him update the ebook cover, paperback cover, and source file so that everything was consistent. It cost me $10.
- For Volume 1, I updated the cover within the Vellum file and regenerated new editions of the book. I also updated the version on the copyright page to 2.0 and logged a note in my versioning system.
- For the omnibus containing Volumes 1 through 3, I included the covers as full-page spreads so the reader knows when they've arrived at a new volume. I changed Volume 1's cover here too. I regenerated new versions of the book and updated my version log.
- I updated the image of the cover on my website: on my books page, on the series page, and the individual book page.
- I updated the CTA for Volumes 2 through 5 so that they have links to the next book in the series when the reader finishes reading. I regenerated fresh versions of the books and updated my version log.
- I uploaded the new versions to all retailers. I went slowly and was extremely careful!
- One week later, I spot-checked the retailers to make sure the right versions were uploaded. I didn't check them all because I'll be doing this as part of my next "patrol."

The entire update process took me approximately two hours.

The result is that the series looks even more professional and it's poised to sell more copies.

This is the behind-the-scenes, unglamorous part of managing your books after publication.

LONG-FORM AUDIO CONTENT

I believe long-form audio content can do well. When I started podcasting in 2014, everyone said, "Keep your shows less than an hour. People are busy." It was rare to see any podcast in any industry go longer than an hour. Occasionally, a show might stretch to 90 minutes if the topic was popular.

Now more podcast episodes are two or three hours long. Podcasters are making longer content on average and people are tolerating it. I believe it's because people are more comfortable with the medium and willing to listen to personalities they love.

I also believe that there is no such thing as cycles in podcasting. Long-form content isn't going anywhere. It will coexist with short and medium forms. All forms have value.

People like short-form content when I need information. This is why my show, "Writing Tip of the Day" was popular. I delivered a writing tip in five minutes or less. It was my most popular podcast.

People like medium-form content because it fits neatly within the time it takes to complete many tasks. If you think about it, in the United States, the average commute is around 30 minutes one-way, so listeners can easily consume a 45- to 60-minute show during that period. It takes, on average, the same amount of time to prepare a meal and clean up the kitchen. It also takes that amount to cut your lawn. And so on. Medium-form content is amazing for when you are multitasking. My show, "The Writer's Journey," was a medium-form show. It was also very popular.

Long-form content is good for multitasking as well, but I believe that people are mostly watching or actively listening to the content. It has their full attention. It is entertaining *and* informational. Livestreams are a good example of long-form content. My Writing Power Hours on my YouTube channel are an example—they run approximately 90 minutes in length, sometimes up to two hours.

We only have a few influencers in the self-publishing space who have ventured into long-form territory. I believe that the right person could find success if they're intentional about it.

THE DEATH OF THE OPEN RATE

Apple released a new iOS update that effectively kills the email open rate as we know it. I discuss this in detail in the next section.

However, because of this massive change, I needed to figure out if I had any sections in my writing books that talked about open rates so I could update them.

The following books needed updating:

- *150 Self-Publishing Questions Answered*
- *250 Writing Tips, Vol. 1*
- *Indie Poet Rock Star*
- *Mental Models for Writers*
- *The Indie Author Atlas*
- *The Indie Writer's Encyclopedia*

I updated the books accordingly to make them current. It took a few hours, but it's one less thing I have to worry about in the future.

That's what happens when you stick around in the writing world for a few years. Things change, and you have to change with them.

LESSONS FROM TEACHING INSURANCE CLASSES

I taught my last insurance class, which closes a five-year-long journey that made a big impact on my personal development.

In this chapter, I wanted to recap the lessons I learned.

In 2016, I was a commercial underwriter. My job was to review businesses to verify if they were eligible for my company's commercial insurance products: general liability, commercial property, business auto, crime, cyber liability, and more. My manager at the time suggested that I go to a CIC class, which stands for Certified Insurance Counselor. It is a designation that insurance agents obtain to help them become more knowledgeable in insurance policies.

Before the pandemic, CIC classes were usually held in hotel conference rooms. For three days, you'd learn about the ins and outs of insurance policies, with a test at the end.

These days, the classes are mostly held online.

I didn't mind a change of scenery and it sounded like it could help me do my job better. Plus, my manager paid for it.

I attended the class and was blown away by the presenters. They made the most boring topics in the insurance world exciting. The speakers would present their material with wonderful stories rooted in their experience, and they held the audience spellbound. And best of all, their examples were clear and easy to understand.

I also met local insurance agents and other insurance industry professionals, which was a great networking opportunity.

(And, the hotel had *amazing* pretzels and cheese for the afternoon snack. I dream about those pretzels from time to time.)

I went to five classes and, in less than a year, I obtained my CIC designation. I asked one of the event organizers about becoming a faculty member, and they told me to apply on the website. The organizers were kind enough to give me a recommendation, so I landed an interview.

My interview was a phone call with the academic coordinator of the nonprofit organization that put on the events. I had no idea what to expect. The coordinator called me, and the interview started immediately. No small talk.

The interview questions they asked are forever burned into my brain.

"Please explain how limited worldwide coverage works on the general liability policy."

"Exclusion j4. What does it exclude?"

"Let's say, for the sake of argument, that one of my employees is driving their personal car on an errand for my business, and they get into a car accident. Would there be coverage under an unendorsed ISO business auto policy?"

Thank God I have an encyclopedic memory. I didn't have the insurance policies in front of me, but I aced the questions.

It went on like this for at least thirty minutes. They told me that I passed, but that I would have to undergo training, which took approximately one year. Then the coordinator explained the rules, which were quite strict.

My first assignment was a 200-slide PowerPoint in which I had to prepare clear examples for each slide. The slide went through the entire commercial general liability policy, line by line. I had a month to complete this assignment…in addition to working my job and writing books.

I came up with examples that explained the general liability policy as simply as I could. All of my examples were rejected. Over the course of several conference calls, the coordinator helped me craft examples that were better than anything I could have done myself. My PowerPoint slide deck went through at least three iterations until my examples were so clear and simple, they were almost childlike.

The next step was to practice my presentation. I prepared my remarks and practiced delivering them in front of the coordinator and a mentor. It seemed like every 10 seconds, they would stop me and try to stump me with a nuanced question.

"Michael, what about the exception to the exclusion you just mentioned?"

"Michael, X company offers Y product. That contradicts what you just said."

They would even ask me trick questions to knock me off-balance.

Honestly, the practice sessions were more like interrogation sessions. I met with them for two hours at a time, and after every session, I wanted to go home and take a nap. Somehow, however, I did well enough to move to the next phase, which was to teach a course under the tutelage of the mentor.

My first course went pretty well. I taught it in person, and I passed the evaluation with top marks. I was officially approved as a faculty instructor.

It was a crazy ride, and there were times I didn't think I would make it, but I persevered and joined the ranks of some of the most accomplished insurance industry speakers in the country.

The lessons I learned:

- Make your examples so clear that even a child can understand them. This is harder than it sounds.
- Prepare more examples than you need. Know when to pull them out.

- Anticipate people's questions ahead of time. You won't always be right, but when you are, you'll deepen your credibility with the group.
- When you give the same presentation over and over, you learn the material so well that your brain goes on autopilot. At the same time, this makes it much easier to read students' faces. When people look confused, that's when you slow down and ask if people understood what you just said.
- When people ask questions, always repeat the question. Always.
- Never tell students they're wrong. Soften your response by going through the material with them again. Otherwise, they will be defensive and they won't learn.
- Be as gender-neutral as you can. Even an innocent phrase like "guys" will upset some people.
- When presenting long-form content, take breaks every 50 minutes. Ten-minute breaks work best, and it's even better if you take breaks at the same time every hour. This way, people can plan around your breaks.
- To take care of yourself when speaking, eat breakfast but make sure you don't eat anything too cold or too hot, as it will strain your vocal cords. Oatmeal is a perfect breakfast before you speak.
- Drink one water bottle every two hours. At each break, suck on a lozenge to protect your throat.
- If teaching from home, set up an essential oil diffuser and use a blend of eucalyptus and lemon to moisten and soften the air; this will make a huge difference in how long your vocal cords last. (Do not set up an essential oil diffuser if you are teaching in person.)
- Print your slides and always have paper copies. Sometimes Internet connections will derail you.

- Keep the webinar phone number handy in case you need to call in by telephone.
- At some point during an eight-hour course, your vocal cords are going to hurt. There's no way around it. The longer you can delay the exhaustion, the better. When I first started teaching, my voice would start hurting in the morning. Once I took better care of myself, my vocal cords wouldn't get tired until the course was almost over.
- For business-focus topics, it helps tremendously if you begin a talk with current events. Nothing gets people to pay attention more at 8 AM than something they probably heard about on the radio while driving into your class.
- The words you speak matter, but so does the tone.
- Try to be as engaging and personable as possible. It makes for a better class.

I learned many more lessons, but those are the ones that jumped out at me the most because I applied them immediately to my YouTube channel when I did live streams, and the techniques worked just as well on live streams as they do in the classroom. That's why I believe so much in liquid knowledge.

I may teach more classes someday. I enjoyed the people I worked with and I also enjoyed the students. I had an average faculty rating of 9.5 out of 10, and many students noted in their evaluations that my courses were some of the best they had ever attended. That makes me proud.

As I move to the next chapter of my writing career, I will carry these lessons with me.

WARMING UP FOR BEAST MODE

In the weeks leading up to my Beast Mode Challenge, I decided to practice and warm up to higher word counts.

There were also some events planned during Beast Mode that I needed to prepare for:

- A family vacation, so I had to prepare for writing on the go.
- Four speaking engagements during the 90-day Beast Mode period.
- A new school routine for my daughter in August, which would drastically change my household daily routine.

Since it had been a year since the last challenge, I figured I would start warming up early.

How did the first day go?

I normally start writing at 5:30 AM. I didn't start writing until 5 PM. I got a late start.

After I logged off work, I turned on my microphone and started dictating. I did 1,000 words in around 20 minutes, all clean. I ran the text through my editing engine and got it super crisp and editor-ready.

Then, it was time to water my sod, so I put in my Bluetooth headphones and opened Dragon Anywhere on my phone. I dictated another chapter while watering my lawn. That took about 10 minutes and it netted me 700 words. But boy, they were sloppy. Dictation gets you considerably worse results when you can't see the screen. I spent 15 minutes cleaning up those 700 words, which expanded it to about 900. I didn't like that, but I'll take the 700 words, even if they were bad.

After watering my sod and eating dinner, I did another dictation session and got another 1,500 words in about 30 minutes.

I did a final session by hand (typing) and got a remaining 800 words in about 20 minutes.

(And then I wrote an 800-word blog post. But I don't count those in my daily word counts. However, I did repurpose that blog post into this chapter, so I suppose I can count that blog post for a change.)

That's 4,000 words in one day. Not bad for a day with a late start.

That's how I warm up for Beast Mode: create a seamless transition between what I'm doing so that I can pick up my manuscript anywhere.

If I'm getting in an Uber? I whip out my phone and write.

If I gotta water my lawn? I dictate while I do it.

I dictate like my life depends on it when I'm sitting at my desk.

When I'm typing, I try to go as fast as I can without creating errors. I go faster than usual because I have a quiet urgency.

I did 4,000 words in an evening. Just think of what I can do with a morning that starts at 5:30 AM, and a lunch break. With perfect conditions, I could have easily hit 6,000 to 7,000 words without trying. In 2020, I hit 10,000 on at least one day during Beast Mode.

Of course, the words never come that easy except on a handful of days, and my word count days are considerably less when I'm writing fiction. But you can see how they add up. All you have to do is be intentional and just keep showing up. Amazing things happen when you do that.

BECOME A WORLD-CLASS MARKETER

IOS 15 AND EMAIL MARKETING

Apple announced iOS 15, which introduces new email privacy settings for iPhone and Apple Mail users. Users can opt in to hide their email and IP addresses, and they can also choose to block tracking pixels. This means that marketers will no longer be able to track reported open rates for Apple Mail users. It's being called a watershed moment in email marketing, and many marketers are freaking out.

When users open a newsletter, their email client downloads a pixel image. The pixel tells the person who sent the newsletter about whether the email was opened, in what email client, what device type, and where. Email pixels have been subject to privacy concerns for many years.

I don't think this will end email marketing. Open rates have always had issues. Users have been able to block images from emails for years, regardless of the email client. Some people prefer to read email in plain text to save Internet bandwidth. I've always known that if I achieve an open rate of 50 percent, the real number is higher than that because of pixel blocking. So, open rates have never been truly reliable anyway. This iOS update just exacerbates the problem.

I read somewhere that around 93 percent of email opens came from phones in 2020. If that's true, then customer preferences have changed significantly. People aren't tied to their desktop computers like they used to be.

That said, it's important to remember that this change is only for iOS users, who, while numerous, do not constitute the entire email universe. To my knowledge, Apple is the first to do this. They may not be the last, but for now, they're the only ones.

Also, my understanding is that click rates will still be tracked, and you don't need a pixel for that. Click rates are the ultimate metric that track engagement, and we still have it.

Many marketers are advising to do baseline tracking for subject lines, headers, calls to action, and so on. This way, they can track what's working and what's not after the iOS update sweeps across the world.

Here are my takeaways:

- Subscriber habits aren't changing per se; it's just that we won't be able to track them. It means that we'll be operating somewhat blindly with subject lines, for example. Candidly, I always thought A/B testing subject lines was always a pain in the ass anyway. While I don't like that I'm losing a data point, it does lessen the burden somewhat.
- Other email providers may follow Apple. If Google joins this trend, the open rate will be effectively dead.
- List hygiene will now be more difficult.
- This won't be the last assault on email marketing, but for now, there's no reason to change your behavior. Strong subject lines, well-written copy, and clear calls to action will still be effective.

I hoped that this would have a minimal impact on my email marketing, but approximately 21 percent of the people who open my emails do so with Apple Mail. That means that I need to stop looking at open rates, period. If I treat them as dead now, that will help me in the future.

To address the issue, I reviewed my open reports and culled

anyone who had not opened my last three campaigns. I hope that I reduced my list down to the most engaged people…while I still can use open rates to track them. After the iOS update, I'll no longer be able to cull my list based on open rates. I'll just have to keep doing what I'm doing and hope for the best. Sometimes, that's all you can do.

RECENT MARKETING FAILINGS

This is one of those chapters where I talk about lessons I learned this quarter for which I should have known better.

My podcasts were great marketing vehicles. I would come up with an idea, float it on my podcasts to test its viability, and then, when I published the book, I would announce it on my podcasts, my email list, and my YouTube channel.

A nice amount of sales came from my podcasts. Yet, because life is interesting and beautiful, I stopped podcasting, even though I knew it would diminish my sales.

When I released my books *Indie Author Confidential Vol. 5* and *Authors, Steal This Book*, I could only rely on my email list and my YouTube channel. My YouTube audience is not interested in my high-concept books.

I announced the book to my audience in my newsletter, but I know the book would have done better if I had still been podcasting.

This is the negative consequence of living your truth, but I don't regret it for a second.

I made some technical errors in sending out the newsletter. This was because I was so used to relying on my podcasts for much of my marketing exposure. First, Amazon hadn't price-matched the book to free yet, so it was $0.99 on Amazon but free everywhere else. That wasn't a huge deal, but I forgot to include a link to where Amazon readers could download the book for free without paying the $0.99. After all, that would have been the right thing to do.

Several people emailed me asking when the book would be free on Amazon. That's when I knew I'd made a mistake. I had to email my list again with a new link that included a direct download on Book Funnel. It's never a good idea to send your readers two emails in a day. I had a few people unsubscribe because of it. So yeah, that lost me money and engagement. There's always a price for your mistakes.

Even worse, I included the book for free on my website, but I didn't mention that!

Oh, Michael...

That's what happens when you don't send out an email list regularly. You make little mistakes like that, and your communication becomes lackluster because you're not writing email copy regularly. I need to be better about emailing my list monthly, but it got away from me. Now that I have more time, I'll try to do better.

MY GENERAL MARKETING STRATEGY (OR LACK THEREOF)

I've been thinking about marketing lately, though not much. Becoming a world-class marketer is one of my core strategies, yet you would be shocked how little time I spend thinking about marketing. It should probably be a crime.

But even though marketing is a key strategy for me, I'm more interested in marketing my way.

I believe that a writer in today's age has three potential strategies to make money:

Strategy #1 is to write books that target a specific audience and do as much as possible to please them. Sometimes this includes writing to market, but more often than not, it just means writing books that you love that serve a chosen audience. This writer can also create a bonanza with their backlist if they write continuously in one genre.

This strategy maximizes profit in the short term, and if a writer is smart at business, they'll set themselves up nicely for the long term. This strategy may involve writing a lot of books quickly or it may not. It depends on the author.

The first downside of this strategy is burnout. They may get tired of writing the books that make them money. This can lead to the second downside, which is the "golden handcuffs" problem. This writer may wake up one day and decide they don't want to write the books that make them money. They may be unable to do this without losing a substantial amount of their readership.

To summarize the choices in this strategy:

- Write books "in the pocket" of the market.
- Maximize income with every new title and with your backlist.
- Decide whether you want to write at a high volume or whether you want to produce at a slower pace. The faster you write, the more money you make, but the higher your risk of burnout.

Strategy #2 involves writing what you want. You focus less on the market and more on writing the books that make you happy. You write as many books as you can, but only a few will make the majority of your money. The 80/20 rule applies (20 percent of your books will drive 80 percent of your income). This strategy is riskier than the first strategy because you may never find a proper market for your work or build an avid readership. The risk of burnout is the same, but the burnout is different; whereas the first writer burns out over writing books they are no longer passionate about and cannot seem to change direction without destroying the career they built so far, the second writer burns out because they feel that their career will never take off. This strategy sacrifices short-term profit for long-term resiliency. If this author is persistent enough to keep publishing, they may eventually hit a series that does very, very well. If that happens, then readers may be interested in the author's backlist. But only if the backlist has titles in the same genre.

The biggest downside to this strategy is the cost. The author spends a lot of money on titles that may never make it back.

To summarize this strategy:

- Write books you're passionate about.
- Maximize income with a small core of books that make money. The more books you write, the more the core grows.

Strategy #3 is to write a few books as a launchpad for another career, such as public speaking. The majority of marketing comes from social media or a platform such as podcasting.

My strategy is a mixture of #2 and #3. Strategy #1 has never appealed to me.

I write the books I believe in, even though they may not do well. I write a lot of books quickly, and one or two out of ten do better than the rest. I take that money, reinvest it into the business as smartly as I can, and keep writing. It's a very expensive strategy, but I've been fortunate enough that strategy #3 has helped me. Ironically, I don't look for public speaking events—I've only pitched a speech twice in the eight years I've been doing this. I'm lucky that speaking engagements come to me, which helps me grow the business.

I enjoy this path. Early in my career, I thought that strategy #1 was for me. I wanted to write to market but always found myself not doing it and feeling guilty about it. I felt as if there was something wrong with me for not being a more market-focused writer. I saw so many authors making boatloads of money, and wished I could join them. But no matter what I did, I physically, emotionally, and spiritually *could not* bring myself to write books that I didn't believe in. I landed on strategies #2 and #3 by default. Over time, I've learned that it's the perfect path for me.

I don't do anything that makes me uncomfortable with marketing and promotion. My big bet is that by developing an insanely large and high-quality portfolio of books that have stellar packaging, consistent branding, and good content, then whenever I write "the big one," it will pour gasoline on the rest of my catalogue. With my writing books, I've tried to be intentional about positioning them so that if you like one, you'll buy the rest.

With the *Indie Author Confidential* series, my early goal was to create a deep series as early as possible, which is why I started with a quarterly cadence. After two years, I will have eight volumes, which is a crazy number. Even though I'm decreasing the frequency after 2021, it's not hard to imagine this series going on endlessly.

My fiction is a slower burn. I've committed to the urban fantasy genre, and the more I write in it, the more success I'll see eventually. I also have the cyclical nature of the market going for me. For example, I have two series about necromancers. Necromancers aren't "in vogue" right now, but I'm sure there will be a day in the future when they will be. When they are, I'll be ready. Therefore, a large portfolio affords you more interesting opportunities long-term. If you follow strategy #1 and you only write in one genre, and that genre falls out of favor with readers, you will have to wait until those books are back in style, if they're back in style. While strategy #2 carries more risk, it's safer in the long term if you understand the market and how your book fits. I've written several books that were ahead of the market and I reaped the rewards for being early. But, you never know what will work.

Those are my current thoughts on my marketing strategy or lack thereof.

MY MOST RIDICULOUS PITCH EVER (SERIOUSLY)

I received an invitation to speak at a writing event that paid well. I had a short turnaround time to give an answer and a pitch for a topic.

It was 6:45 AM, and I had to log in to work at 7:30 AM. After work, I had to get ready for a family vacation. If I didn't come up with a pitch in 45 minutes, it wasn't going to happen.

I was half-asleep and needed to come up with something fast.

I came up with the following idea.

Title: Writing App Speed-Dating

Is your current writing app "the one" or are you ready to find another? With so many writing apps on the market, it's hard to choose the best one! In this session, writer Michael La Ronn will demo the hottest writing apps for writers in 2021 and show you their top features. Discover cutting-edge advancements in outlining, writing, and book formatting. After this session, you just might find the writing app you'll want to spend the rest of your writing career with. Featured apps include Atticus, Scrivener, Ulysses, Dabble, and more!

I sent the pitch at 7:25 AM with time to spare! And trust me, I was laughing the entire time.

Funny enough, I wrote the following in this chapter before I heard back from the venue:

Whether the pitch lands me a deal or not, I'm proud that I could pull out copy in such a short time. If I land the event, I'll refine the copy, as I think it could be better, but I think the "spirit" was there.

There is such a thing as too clever copy. If the idea fails, that will probably be the reason. But if it succeeds, then it'll probably be because I went right up to the line between "good" and "clever," but I didn't cross it.

After writing that, I heard back from the venue. It turns out that I landed the event!

Wow—just wow. Sometimes you never know what will work. The pitch was accepted as-is with only a minor modification. While I can't announce the venue just yet, it's definitely a big one—and in-person!

USE A REVIEW IMAGE FOR MARKETING

I worked with a designer on Fiverr who engaged in a marketing tactic I had never seen before.

He designed a set of icons for me. He sent me a photo of all the icons against a blue background and asked that I post the image in my review so others could see the quality of his work.

It was such a great idea that I wondered why no one on Fiverr asked me to do that before.

I thought about adapting this for my writing business but couldn't think of a good way. My initial thought was to ask reviewers to include quotes from the book but I decided against that.

Still, it's such an intriguing idea that I'm capturing it here in case I develop a need for it.

To whatever extent you can control the marketing first impression without violating ethics, asking readers to share something you've prepared that they enjoyed and benefited from is a smart idea.

MEETING A READER UNEXPECTEDLY

A receptionist at a place I frequent surprised me by pulling out a copy of *Be a Writing Machine*, asking me to sign it.

I was humbled. It is always surreal to see my books in the wild. This is why you should publish your book in paperback. You never know when events like this will happen.

Also, this is another reason why you should update your email signature to include a link to your books and a mention that you're an author. That's how this reader learned about my books because I had to email the company a few times. I've been including my author info in my email signature for years, and every once in a while, I see proof that my email signature is working, selling books for me while I sleep. You never know when people will click your signature and buy something. They might even recommend your books to their friends. Just make sure the signature isn't obnoxious. You want it to intrigue people enough to click. Then what happens is up to them.

LETTING MY READERS VOTE ON MY NEXT WORK

I pulled out my early career playbook and used one of my successful strategies.

For my Beast Mode 2021 challenge, I came up with four ideas for writing books. I only had a vague concept of the content.

I asked my patrons on Patreon to vote on which one I should have written first.

The ideas were:

- 250+ Writing Tips, Vol. 3
- Dictation for Writers
- Strategy for Authors
- The Writer's Guide to Writing Apps

My patrons wanted me to write The Writer's Guide to Writing Apps idea, which surprised me.

When I finished that book, I opened the voting up to my community. Once I passed the 75 percent mark of the book I was working on, I opened up a poll that contained all of my ideas, and I wrote whichever book won the majority of the vote. If there was a tie, I broke it with my preference.

When it was time to release my Beast Mode Collection at the end of the quarter, I knew that it would contain the ideas my readers most wanted to read. I also believe this project was good for the long-term profitability of my portfolio because the books I wrote during Beast Mode were proven concepts that connected with hundreds of my readers.

DESIGNING COVERS FOR THE INDIE AUTHOR CONFIDENTIAL SERIES

When I launched my *Indie Author Confidential* series in 2020, I treated it as a separate brand. I wanted the book covers to look familiar to readers who read my flagship writing books, but I also wanted the books to have their own style.

I worked with my nonfiction cover designer to create a new brand. I found some images on royalty-free sites that I liked; black vector objects with a door opening within them. They had a mysterious look, as if a secret were behind the door.

I found a group of images by the same designer: a lock, a puzzle piece, a book, a heart, and a keyhole. These were the images for the first five books of this series.

Then there were no more.

I wanted to continue with this aesthetic, so I hired an illustrator, sent him the images for the first five books, and told them to design objects in the same style:

- Typewriter
- Pencil
- Dollar sign
- Safe
- e-reader/tablet
- Chess piece
- Coffee cup

- Notebook
- Light bulb

Overall, I paid the illustrator about $150. It was an easy job for him. I paid higher than what most people pay for this type of service because I wanted good work.

Now I have images I can send to my designer to continue the same look for the series. I have enough images to last me a few years.

PRICING PSYCHOLOGY

When I wrote *Authors, Steal This Book*, I struggled with how many ideas to include in the book. I like including numbers in book titles and subtitles because they signal value.

I knew that I would include every idea from the first five volumes of the *Indie Author Confidential* series, but I didn't want that number to be awkward (like 69).

I started with 64 ideas. Was that the right number? I did some basic research on number psychology, and I found some interesting opinions. I didn't verify whether scientific data supports these assertions, but they are at least thought-provoking.

The number one signifies a beginning.

Odd numbers are considered to be masculine and even numbers are feminine.

Seven is a lucky number. In Judaism and Christianity, God created the world in seven days. There are seven continents on Earth. Pricing that ends in seven just works for mysterious reasons.

Ten is considered to be a practical number and a "complete" number. Eleven is one more than ten, so it is above and beyond.

Thirteen is unlucky.

But what about 64?

According to Google, six means harmony. Four means the number of justice.

Justice? Nah. That didn't match the theme of the book.

What about 67? According to Google (emphasis is mine), "The essence of the number 67 is focused on family and home issues and *providing a long-lasting security for the future*. The number 67 in numerology also signifies foundation, focus, family, *idealism, introspection, and pragmatism...*"

I could have picked 68, which is also an idealistic number, but I liked a number ending in seven. I wrote three extra ideas so I could hit 67, and voila! That's how I arrived at the right number.

PRICE DROP FOR THE INDIE AUTHOR CONFIDENTIAL SERIES

I have now published six volumes of *Indie Author Confidential.* I decided it was time to use a new marketing tactic: dropping the price of the first book to make it a loss leader. I dropped Volume 1 from $4.99 to $2.99, which is a 40-percent decrease.

I include Volumes 1 through 3 in an omnibus edition. That costs $9.99. When each of the volumes was $4.99, the true value of that collection was $14.97. When I dropped the price of Volume 1, the true value also dropped slightly to $12.97, which is still a good deal, given that it sells for $9.99.

At the end of 2021, I'll be creating a second omnibus that contains Volumes 4 through 7. When that happens, I may drop the price of the first omnibus so that it is a slightly better deal.

When I have so many volumes, I can afford to lose a couple of dollars on the first volume.

I plan on continuing this series as long as possible, so I will continue to refine the pricing of the individual volumes and omnibuses as the years progress. One day, if I have 30 or 40 volumes available, this may well be the most valuable piece of intellectual property that I own, especially if I become a popular bestseller and a full-time author. At speaking events, I'll be able to point people to a gigantic series that has all my secrets.

AN UPDATE ON MY PERMAFREE SITUATION

I mentioned that I made *Authors, Steal This Book* permafree. It's the first writing book I've ever made free. I figured it would be an interesting experiment.

Permafree is a slow burn. The last time I did this was in 2015 with my book *Android Paradox*. That book did extremely well as a permafree title, with tens of thousands of downloads and a healthy number of sales for books two and three.

When I published the book, I was able to set it to free on every retailer except Amazon, since Amazon doesn't allow free pricing. However, Amazon will price-match your book from another retailer if it's free there.

Amazon must follow Apple's pricing because it did not price-match the book until it was for sale on Apple for 48 hours. Apple had a significant delay in publishing my book for some reason.

Once the book was free, it racked up a couple of dozen downloads a week. I pushed some Amazon Ads to it and that improved the number somewhat. At the time of this writing, it didn't have any reviews.

I didn't expect anything crazy to happen with the book, and so far, nothing has. But it's good to know that permafree is still a viable strategy in getting a book to readers.

WHAT'S YOUR DEFICIENCY?

I needed my gutters cleaned. I have a contractor that I normally hire, but he didn't return my calls. I gave him three weeks, and nothing.

I went online to find an alternative company. Almost none of them called me back. A few did, and what ensued was a pathetic parade of contractors.

One guy charged me four times what I typically pay. I declined him outright.

Another said he was backed up for several months. Declined.

And then, I called a final gutter cleaning company and seemingly tripped into another universe.

First, the website was odd. They were a gutter-cleaning service in my area, but the website looked like a marketing scam. I'm making the following text up, but hopefully, you can see why I was suspicious: "Gutter Cleaning Des Moines. The countrywide gutter cleaners. Call 1-800…" There were also several hundred 5-star reviews from customers on the website, but if you looked up the site on other websites, it had 1- and 2-star reviews.

A local contractor with a 1-800 number. That never turns out well.

I'm picky about contractors, but I was pretty much desperate at this point, and if I didn't do something, I'd have water issues around my foundation. I called the 1-800 number, and someone answered who wasn't from my area. She wasn't from Des Moines because of the way she said the name (It's pronounced "Duh moyn," but out-of-towners always say "Duh-moyns." It's a dead giveaway.) I don't think she was in the United States either, but you never really know.

The representative was very professional and took my address, asked me a few questions, and gave me a quote over the phone. She told me to expect a phone call within 7 days when the contractor would be on the way. Payment would be facilitated by email.

So far, so good.

I got a confirmation email that confirmed the price, deadline for the work to be completed by, and a courtesy notice of which credit cards they accepted.

We had several days of thunderstorms, and she even called me to let me know that they had to reschedule. She gave me a new deadline. Very, very professional.

Yet, the entire experience was giving me anxiety. On the day the cleaning was scheduled, I thought, "This is either going to be excellent, or it's going to be a dumpster fire." I had no idea who the hell was liable to show up at my doorstep.

I received a phone call at 11:30 AM from a guy who told me he was on the way. He was friendly and pleasant. When he arrived, it was in a giant, unmarked van with two ladders strapped to the top. The guy was careful and even rinsed off a mess he made on my driveway.

He did a phenomenal job. As soon as he left, I received an email with an invoice and I paid it.

That's not how I expected this to end. I paid a little more for the service, but I got what I paid for.

I kept waiting for the "gotcha." Afterward, I searched again to see if this company was a scam or a front for a burglary operation. But no, it turns out that they were legit after all.

It got me thinking about how every business is a radar chart between speed, quality, and price. My first boss taught me that.

Customers can only choose two of the three.

- They can get a high-quality experience for cheap, but it will take a long time.
- They can get a cheap experience very quickly, but the quality will be average.
- They can get fast service with quality, but it will expensive.

I'd say the gutter experience was quick, cheap, and above-average quality. That's incredibly rare. This company defied the laws of business, which is why I was fascinated by the exchange.

That got me thinking about the business of writing. Now I don't think it is fair to say that readers should only be entitled to two out of the three attributes. They deserve all three. But every writer has their deficiencies.

To frame this better, let's say that the real attributes are craft, business, and marketing. Every writer is good at two.

As for me, I learn craft quickly and I have a business sense for publishing. Marketing will always be my deficiency.

Other writers I know are phenomenal marketers and amazing craftspeople, but they're terrible at business. Others are good at business and marketing, but their writing skills need serious work. Some writers excel at all three, but they are rare, just like the gutter-cleaning business I hired.

I challenge you to consider these strengths and weaknesses whenever you discover a new author.

As a writer, what are your deficiencies?

BECOME A TECHNOLOGY AND DATA-DRIVEN WRITER

TWO BOOKS IN ONE

I was watching a YouTube video about finance and accounting. I watched a boring video about life insurance, but at the end, the YouTuber pulled out a book and said, "If you want to learn more about the strategies I've used to build wealth, I've got a book for you. It's called *X* and I've written it two ways. The first way is for the data-minded, but if that's not your thing, just flip it over and I give you the same information in story format."

My head exploded. After I got over my initial shock of what an *amazing* idea this was, I tried to figure out how the heck he did it.

I thought, "Surely, Amazon's Kindle Direct Publishing program would never allow this." And I was right. Their website says, "All pages and content must be oriented the same way. Pages can contain some upside-down text as long as the rest of the page contents are right side up (e.g., a book of riddles with answers printed upside-down on the page)."

Maybe Ingram Spark allows this. I doubt it, but I couldn't find anything on their website about it. I think you'd have to hire an offset printer, honestly.

Technically, I stepped through how one could accomplish this feature:

- You'd need a print cover that had two front covers. You'd have to have one cover for Book A, a regular spine, and then another cover for Book B. The second cover would have to be upside-down.

- From front to back, the text for Book A would need to be right-side-up, but the text for Book B would need to be upside-down and in reverse order. You would need a clean delineation within the interior so that readers wouldn't get confused.
- The "middle ground" of the book poses an interesting design and usability opportunity; you could use some sort of page design on the edges of the page to indicate where both books end.
- The page numbers, headers, and footers for Book B would also need to upside-down and in reverse order.

I'm intrigued by the idea. That said, it'd be difficult for a self-published author to pull off. But if they did, there would be unique use cases:

- A two-sided novel, with one book told from the perspective of the hero and another told from the perspective of the villain. (Or, two characters of the author's choosing.)
- An "A/B" novel, with the first half being the novel in its original format and the second being an "author's cut" with extra scenes.
- A "what if" novel with the first book being the original novel as the author intended, and then a "what if" novel where it branches down a different path around the middle, with an alternative ending.
- A two-sided self-help book, with the first book written for analytical people and the second book written for creatives.

- A double feature, with a novel from two different but complementary authors as a cross-promotional tactic. This could also be done with nonfiction and poetry.

There are lots of opportunities with an idea like this. Maybe one day it'll be easier for indies to pull off.

SECONDHAND BOOK SALES: ANOTHER REASON TO BUY ISBNS?

I encountered an article in *The Guardian* about an effort underway in the United Kingdom to pay authors for secondhand sales of their books.

In international copyright law, the "first sale doctrine" has always dictated that authors can make money on the first sale of their book but not subsequent sales. This keeps used book sales in demand and makes it easier for books to be sold without having to worry about licensing.

I have mixed feelings about the first sale doctrine; on the one hand, I would love the ability to make money off secondhand sales, but on the other hand, I also understand that whether I make money directly from them or not, I still make money. Readers who buy a used book and love it will go on to explore more of the author's backlist, and maybe even buy books on the frontlist too. It's possible that putting an additional burden on used bookstores could reduce book sales for authors across the board, so I suppose we have to be careful what we wish for.

In the UK initiative, two used booksellers partnered to create a royalty fund for authors whose books are sold secondhand. With each sale, the retailers contribute to the fund. Each author receives a payout of up to £1,000 (which is approximately $1,400 USD at the time of this writing). The payments are facilitated through the Authors' Licensing and Collection Society (ALCS) in the UK.

Here's how the ALCS describes themselves on their about

page: "We make sure you receive the money you're entitled to as a writer when someone copies or uses your work. We collect money from all over the world, then pay it to our members. So far we've paid a total of £570 million."

Authors pay a £36-lifetime membership fee. ALCS puts the author in a database, and if they find a match on dues owed as a result of a mass licensing deal or another project, they pass the money along to the author after taking a 9.5 percent commission. Anyone in the world can join, and I presume that this includes indie authors since they are not excluded in their eligibility guidelines.

Back to the subject of this article, I have some concerns. £1,000 is merely a token amount after taxes and the ALCS's commission. Also, I doubt something like this would ever happen globally, though it would be nice. US retailers are in too dire straits to do something like this.

However, this paragraph grabbed my attention (emphasis is mine):

"*Participating retailers will share their sales information with the ALCS*, which will match the works with their writer members and pay them their royalties as a lump sum twice a year."

Let's say that something like this *did* go global. How would retailers facilitate payment? This is predominantly a data concern.

Book retailers would probably collect sales data based on ISBNs. If a secondhand book doesn't have an ISBN, it technically won't exist and that book's author won't be covered in the fund. Hence, if an author wants to participate in a program like this, they would need to use ISBNs. Otherwise, the fund gets to keep that money, which means it earns interest and can be invested.

If something like this were to happen in the US, then ISBNs would be required to participate. This would be yet another reason to invest in ISBNs...if it happened!

But again, let's do some math. Even if my books were sold secondhand, which I imagine that they are, I'd have to sell a lot to reach the $1,400 cap. But even if I did, I'd have to account for taxes.

How much do ISBNs cost in the US? $575 for a pack of 500 and $1,500 for a pack of 1,000.

Still not worth the money.

ATTICUS: THE APP I PREDICTED

In Volume 2 of this series, I laid out my vision of the writing app of the future. I'm reposting the article here in its entirety because I am going to brag at the end.

The writer of the future needs a unified command center. Not a writing app, a formatting app, a spelling and grammar app, and the myriad other software we use.

My workflow today is as follows: I write my books in Scrivener, then export them to Microsoft Word so that my editor can edit using track changes. I review the editor's edits in Microsoft Word, run the manuscript through ProWritingAid, copy/paste the book back into Scrivener, then export to Vellum for formatting.

I despise the workflow, but it's the best we have right now.

It's unreasonable to expect one app to execute on the level of Scrivener, Microsoft Word, ProWritingAid, *and* Vellum, but it is reasonable to ask that the writing apps of the future work together seamlessly.

I'd like to write my novel in Scrivener and be able to send it to my editor, perhaps by granting the editor permission to edit my Scrivener file with tracked changes (if Scrivener ever supports that). Preferably, I should never have to leave my writing app for anything, even formatting.

The bestselling writing apps on the market are extremely vulnerable for disruption. Writers just don't realize it because the writing app as we know it hasn't changed in forty years and we can't conceive of how it can possibly evolve.

If a new writing app functioned similar to how I describe the following narrative, it would render the current landscape of writing apps irrelevant. Let's call it Shapeshifter.

Shapeshifter is a writing app that offers an interchangeable interface that supports WYSIWIG (what you see is what you get) writing interface a la Microsoft Word, or a markdown experience like Ulysses. With one click, you can change its appearance and therefore its layout. It's two or three different writing apps in one. That's the app's headlining feature. It "shapeshifts" extremely well, molding itself to suit the writer instead of asking the writer to adapt to it.

The desktop version is available on Windows and Linux. Mac users were originally left out, but they quickly learned that they could run the app by installing Windows on their computers—a deliberate and intelligent choice on the developers' part that allowed them to seize the Windows market, which was ripe for a new, modern competitor. Given the benefits you're about to hear, Mac users will have no qualms about upgrading their computers to quickly abandon their current writing app. Ironically, the app is available on iOS, iPad OS, and Android, with good feature parity so that users can write on-the-go no matter their phone or tablet.

Shapeshifter is also available in the browser, with an optimized writing experience.

No matter where you are or what device you are using, Shapeshifter will shift to suit your preference.

If that were it, Shapeshifter would be remarkable. But here's what makes it the writing app of the future: out of the box, the app itself is not terribly robust. It has a few key features such as a word processor and the ability to import and export.

However, the app has way more features available; you

purchase what you need. If you don't need a distraction-free mode, you don't have to pay for it. If you ever want it, you pay a one-time fee of $5. The app and its features are like LEGOs that you can snap together based on your preferences. Every writer's app will look different; in fact, writers are encouraged to share their "space," which is linked to a generous affiliate program that rewards them for every referral they make.

Shapeshifter is also the first writing app other than Microsoft Word to offer third-party developer integration. The app's in-house features are comparable to most other writing apps, and without any integrations, it looks rather vanilla. Third-party integrations are where the app shines. Developers can create new kinds of writing tools—outlining features, dictation support, macros, and integration with other apps, like voice assistants. All of these plugins help you become a better version of yourself. This also allows the app to stay on at the forefront of advancements in operating systems.

Shapeshifter offers a Discord or a Reddit community where users can request new plugins and developers can create them. The app gathers a cult following that quickly becomes mainstream.

Now, let's talk about the biggest selling point: the price.

Shapeshifter's developers wanted to create an affordable writing app and avoid the ire of the community by switching pricing models. For a one-time fee of $30, you pay to own the app. The developers keep the prices low because you pay a la carte for additional features such as cloud syncing between mobile and desktop and WordPress blog integration, for example. You only pay for the features you'll actually use. Overall, you might pay around $200-300 over the lifetime of the app, more including plugins, which can range from a couple dollars to a few hundred dollars depending on the plugin.

And that's not all…

Shapeshifter is just one app in a suite of apps for writers.

Shapeshifter Writer handles the writing. You see, the developers figured out that it's impossible to do everything well in one app, so they modeled their app suite after the Adobe Creative Cloud so that all their apps work together seamlessly.

Shapeshifter Writer is an app and marketplace for *writing*.

When it's time to edit, the writer can, with the click of a button, "shift" the app into Editor mode, which is technically a separate application in its own right that you can also purchase.

Editor is optimized for editing. Shapeshifter Editor is a pioneering editing app that is designed solely for back-and-forth between a writer and editor. Drawing inspiration from apps like Google Docs and Asana, a writer and editor can collaborate on a manuscript without the manuscript ever leaving the Editor ecosystem. All the author has to do is invite the editor to join a given project. The editor can edit the book in a browser and does not need to purchase the software, though doing so under an Editor's license will grant them unique benefits.

All edits that the author accepts in Editor get pushed to Writer so that the manuscript is in sync everywhere. The author can of course revert and rollback changes at any time.

Editor also supports third-party integration, such as Grammarly, ProWritingAid, and anything else a developer can dream of in the editing process. Editor would also encourage and support artificial intelligence plugins.

When it's time to format your manuscript, you can "shift" to Shapeshifter Formatter with the click of a button. With just one click and a smooth wizard, you can have a publish-ready ebook and print edition. It offers the power of Vellum but also third-party integration for formatting templates and special features such as indexes. You could even grant access to a formatter who could upload HTML that the app would accept. Changes you make in Formatter are automatically synced with Writer and Editor.

Formatter even integrates with book retailer APIs so you can publish without having to leave the app.

Shapeshifter's holy triumvirate of Writer, Editor, and Formatter succeeds because it streamlines the process of writing and helps writers do more in less time. It takes advantage of the fact that some writing apps go years without receiving updates as well as writers' frustration with subscription-based apps. It leverages the power of Adobe-smooth integration between the three apps, with the ease of use and customization of Reaper (a very popular sound recording app among musicians).

While the future of writing apps may look different than the narrative I've written, consider that writing apps as we know them haven't changed much in forty years as I mentioned earlier. With emerging technology, writers will have such a need to evolve that it will be a no-brainer if someone offers them the ability to move to the cutting edge of technology and writing.

I wrote Volume 2 of this series between July and September of 2020.

Here we are in July 2021, and now we have an app called Atticus, created by Dave Chesson of Kindlepreneur fame. Atticus is still in beta at the time of this writing. Dave is one of the brightest tech minds in publishing, and I don't say that lightly.

I have no idea if Dave read Volume 1 of this series. I'm willing to bet he didn't. Yet, consider Atticus's feature set:

- It is a web-based writing app that (in the future) will allow you to use it on any device.
- It has a writing mode that rivals most top-tier writing apps.
- It has a formatting mode that matches much of Vellum's functionality, including paperback formatting.

- In the future, it will support an editing mode where your editor can edit your book within the app itself. You just give them a link and the necessary permissions.

Wow. It happened just like that: we are now looking at the writing app of the future. While it doesn't have ALL the features I mentioned, it has the most important ones.

If Atticus takes off, it will rapidly erode Scrivener's market share. Scrivener's biggest weakness is that you cannot edit your book effectively within it; most people export to Microsoft Word or Google Docs and work with their editor there. Then they import the work back into Scrivener, or into a separate formatting app like Vellum. Scrivener also does not excel at book formatting. It is possible to create good-looking ebooks with it, but not paperbacks.

If Atticus can pull off the "one-stop shopping" approach by offering a single ecosystem that the book never has to leave, the entire field of writing apps will have to play catch-up. Some will never catch up.

Will I migrate to Atticus? Not yet. When the following things happen, I will consider it:

- I want assurances that my data is protected in the browser, with the ability to back it up to another source in case of a hacking attempt.
- I want the ability to write on my phone with the same ease as Scrivener and Ulysses iOS. Atticus currently functions as a progressive web app on iOS, but that's not good enough for my needs.
- The editing mode needs to work smoothly and eliminates back and forth within Microsoft Word between my editor and me (and my editor has to rave about it).

Atticus is the writing app to watch. It has a special blend of features that can change the writing process as we know it.

THOUGHTS ON ARCHIVING DATA

Every few years, I reflect on my data archiving strategy. Data changes with the times, and if you're not careful, you'll lose your data.

(When I refer to data, I'm talking about your books. Your books are data, but most people don't think of them that way.)

I was cleaning out my basement and stumbled upon some physical photographs that I had taken long, long ago with a disposable camera. I used to buy disposables at my local drug store for $10, take 30 photos, have them developed at a photo lab, and then receive a pouch with 30 photos and a roll of negatives. It's amazing how far camera technology has come.

How do you archive those old disposable photos? The photo quality degrades over time unless you protect them in an album. It's probably best to digitize them. But how do you do that? You buy a scanner and upload them to your computer in the highest quality possible.

Once the photos have made the migration to your computer, how do you ensure that they outlive your computer? Most people either use digital hard drives or cloud services. What happens when those hard drives fail in five years, or the cloud service gets acquired or goes out of business? If you care about your data, you're always engaged in a constant battle to keep it available and preserved.

The same is true with our books. Have you thought about what data standards will be popular in 2041 ? I think about it all the time.

Today, writers currently use some combination of the below formats:

- Microsoft Word .DOC or .DOCX
- Rich text file (.RTF)
- OpenOffice (.ODT)
- A proprietary format such as Scrivener (.SCRIV), which is a bundle of .RTF files
- Plain text (.TXT)
- Portable Digital File (.PDF)
- Electronic Publication Format (.EPUB)
- MOBI Pocket (.MOBI)
- Google Docs format

Let's examine each format, its strengths and weaknesses, and the challenges that will exist in 2041.

Microsoft Word. It's hard to argue that Microsoft Word *won't* be around in 2041. It is the program of choice for just about every profession when it comes to writing letters and correspondence. But what if political winds shift against Microsoft (as they did in the nineties)? In the next section, I write about a potential antitrust problem brewing in the tech sector, and that could affect Microsoft. What if Moore's Law becomes true and the processing power of computer chips stops doubling every two years? What if Silicon Valley, a shining beacon in the tech world today, becomes a rust belt and an economically depressed region? (Yes, I know Microsoft, along with Amazon, is located in Washington, but follow along.) If Silicon Valley goes the way of department stores such as Sears and JC Penney, then it's not unreasonable to think that Microsoft could sell assets that don't perform. It's also possible that a competitor could release a new technology that renders Word obsolete and irrelevant. Of course, these events may not happen. More practically, though, it's certainly possible that Microsoft will *at least* update the Word format between now and 2041, just like they did when they created the .DOCX format. That means that .DOCX will likely become obsolete in the future.

Rich Text File. This format was also created by Microsoft in 1987 as a way to create cross-compatibility between Windows and Macintosh versions of Microsoft Word. Microsoft discontinued it in 2008 but it is still widely used.

Just by its association with Microsoft, I'd put RTF in the same category of concern as .DOCX.

OpenOffice. I'm not too familiar with the OpenOffice format, but I know it's popular among writers who can't afford (or use) Microsoft Word. OpenOffice is open-source software, so there's always a chance that people in the community will stop supporting it in favor of a new format.

Proprietary formats. Will Scrivener be around in 2041? I hope so, but it's a safe bet to *assume* it won't. Therefore, if the .SCRIV format is the only way you're backing up your work (which is just a bunch of .RTF files), you're asking for trouble in about twenty years. I hope Scrivener will continue to flourish, but Literature & Latte is a small business, and small businesses fall on hard times. Its founder won't be around forever, and who knows what will happen after that? Scrivener could get acquired or discontinued. And once that happens, it's anyone's guess. I believe that it's a smart strategy to export *all* contents of your Scrivener binder to formats that exist outside of your Scrivener file. This includes:

- Research
- Outlines
- Manuscript
- Any other materials used in the creation of your manuscript

Save those files separately in addition to your .SCRIV file. This way, if you wake up one morning and Scrivener is gone, your work will persist. Don't be one of the writers who say "that will never happen" and then find themselves scrambling.

Oh, and this also applies to Vellum. Just because Vellum is doing well now doesn't mean it will in 2041.

This applies to *any* writing app. I'm just singling out Scrivener and Vellum because they're the most prominent right now.

(Much love and respect to the people at Literature & Latte and 180g, but I'm being a realist. No one is immune to the inevitable tide of life and death.)

Plain text. If there's one format that is sure to be around in 2041, it's plain text. It's a universal format. That said, it's not helpful for working with books. If you back up your work in plain text, I hope you'll never need it, because you'll have to do a lot of work to reproduce your book in the format that you intended.

PDFs. I believe PDFs will still be around in 2041, but they might be a legacy format. Saving your book as a PDF is required anyway if you publish paperbacks, so most authors are already using this format. An issue with PDFs used to be character recognition—if the PDF you used didn't allow for text manipulation, you couldn't convert it without using some type of optical character recognition (OCR) software. Authors don't have that problem.

ePUB and MOBI. ePUB and MOBI are the predominant ebook formats. Will ePUBs be around in 2041? I think so. Amazon discontinued support for the .MOBI format for new titles in 2021, though it is still accepted and read by Kindle devices. An ePUB is just a bunch of HTML files, and I don't see HTML going anywhere any time soon. This is good news for authors. ePUB is probably the most reliable format we'll have moving forward, assuming that nothing bad happens to Microsoft.

Google Docs. Google will never kill Google Docs, right? Right? Consider the website Killed by Google, which is a graveyard of all the projects Google has scrapped. Google doesn't care if a product is popular; it has its own reasons for ending projects, and it ends them all the time. While I'm optimistic about the future of Google Docs, I don't forget for a second that Google is capable of killing projects in a moment's notice. That makes Google Docs less reliable, and I would not include Google Docs in my long-term data preservation strategy.

Am I an alarmist? I hope not. I'm just trying to be real about the advancement of technology.

It's not enough to think about the data. You also have to think about how it will be stored.

No one stores their data on floppy disks anymore, and almost no one uses CDs or DVDs for data storage either.

What about external hard drives? The research I've done suggests that rotations per minute (RPM) drives may be the most reliable, but they still fail and break down like any other hard drive. I've also seen people argue that solid-state drives (SSD) aren't much better. And regardless of which one is "better," is there any guarantee that computers will contain them or be able to read them in 2041 ? Of course not! After all, how many new computers have CD and DVD drives in 2021? None! Ah, technology…

There is no clear answer here except to update your external hard drives every three to five years and migrate your data to the new devices to account for new advancements in technology.

After this exercise, I refined my data preservation strategy.

1. I save all my books in .SCRIV, .DOCX, .RTF, .EPUB, and .PDF. I'm already doing this today.

2. I store all my books on my computer, in the cloud, on an external hard drive, on external USB "thumb" drives, and on an automatic backup service.
3. I update my external hard drives every three to five years.

I spent a Sunday afternoon reviewing my book files and filling in any gaps. I forgot to save one series as an .RTF, for example. I also never exported my outlines, research, and so on. That's all done now, and backed up across all my different backup locations.

That's all I can do. I'm confident in knowing that no matter what happens in the future with file formats and storage technology, I'll see it coming before others, and I'll be able to make the migration without too much difficulty.

BACKUP BEST PRACTICES WEBINAR

I attended a webinar sponsored by Backblaze, the company I use for automatic data backups. I highly recommend Backblaze because they saved my data when my other backup sources failed a few years ago. It is my safety net—I never hope I have to use it, but when I do, I'm glad I had it.

The webinar was called "State of Backups 2021" and I learned some new concepts that I wanted to memorialize here because the Backblaze team said the same things I've been saying on my platforms for years. If anyone knows about how to protect your data, it's Backblaze.

Here were the takeaways.

- They did a study with a data firm and did a broad sampling of people across the United States. They asked them about their backup habits. Only 11 percent of participants backed up their work.
- Eleven percent of participants backed up their work weekly, 11 percent backed up their data monthly, 58 percent of people did it yearly or every few years, and 20 percent *never* backed up their work.
- Sixty-two percent of participants have lost data at some point, 76 percent deleted something by accident, 51 percent have had an internal or external hard drive crash, and 61 percent had a security incident such as

ransomware or a virus. Twenty-five percent of those incidents happened within the last year.

- They did a "best backup persona" of the ideal person who exercises best practices based on their sampling. That persona is a female 35 to 44 years old.
- They explained the difference between cloud syncing and true backup. Cloud syncing (used by services such as Dropbox, Google Drive, and iCloud) merely makes sure that your files are the most up-to-date versions. The cloud keeps everything current. True backup saves every version of your work (naturally, Backblaze offers true backup).
- They recommended the 3-2-1 backup method, which means saving *at least* three copies of your files, with two copies kept onsite in your home (i.e., on your computer and external hard drive) and at least one off-site (using a service like Backblaze or with a bank safety deposit box).
- They recommended testing your backups regularly. The worst time to figure out if your backups work is when something happens. Test your backups regularly so that you'll know how to use them in a crisis.
- If a ransomware attack happens, kiss your files in the cloud goodbye; the software may corrupt or infect the most up-to-date files without a way for you to restore older versions (in most cases; some cloud services do support limited versioning). True backup can protect you against ransomware because even if an attack locks your computer down, the bad guys can't access older versions of your files. Just log in to your backup service from a secure location, select your last backup, and download it. (See why backing up multiple times a day is smart?) They'll even ship you a hard drive with your data if needed.

It was a great webinar and I hope participants learned how to protect their data better.

To distill these best practices down so that you become a "best backup persona" (with some added tips of my own):

- Invest in a backup service that backs up your work *at least* daily, but hopefully more. Backblaze can do this for you, but there are other competitors such as Carbonite that do the same thing.
- Use cloud services for the syncing benefits they offer, but don't expect them to save you.
- Learn how to spot phishing attempts. Many computer compromises happen because someone clicks on an attachment in an email.
- Be careful when browsing the Internet and visiting sites you're unfamiliar with. If you get hit with a ransomware attack or debilitating virus, it might happen while you're researching your book or when you're troubleshooting a computer problem. Be extraordinarily careful these days when you're researching your books.
- Use the 3-2-1 backup method.
- Develop a written plan for ransomware attacks. They're on the rise. I've been talking about them since 2019, and unfortunately, I was correct in predicting that they would start hitting average consumers (and writers) more frequently. A sound ransomware strategy will detail what to do to recover your data, diagnose the problem, and what to do with the infected computer. If you do your job correctly, you won't have to pay the ransom because you'll never lose your data. Start planning now.
- Follow these best practices, and you'll never lose your data. If you do, you'll severely minimize the amount of

data you lose. Whether it be a ransomware attack or an honest mistake that deletes your manuscript permanently from your computer, you'll be protected.

I'll keep talking about this until people listen.

WIRELESS HARD DRIVES

As I mentioned in the previous chapter, it has been approximately three years since I upgraded my external hard drives, so this year, I was in the market for new ones.

I was pleased to see that wireless hard drives have become more affordable. The disk emits its own Wi-Fi network. You can plug them into your computer or transmit files to it via Wi-Fi. This comes with its own problems—namely, it's one more thing that can go wrong in the hardware—but it's a convenient feature.

I have limited desk space, and new computers come with fewer and fewer USB ports these days. Being able to transmit my files to a hard drive wirelessly is a godsend. Also, as a security measure, I can turn the hard drive's wireless functionality on and off, which helps prevent access to it in a hacking event.

I always buy external hard drives in groups of two because they can and do fail. For Amazon Prime Day, I got a great deal on two drives: a SanDisk 32GB Connect Wireless Stick Flash Drive and a Samsung Portable T5 SSD drive.

The Samsung SSD drive will be plugged into my computer all the time. It will take over when my current hard drive fails, which will be any day now, as it has been acting funny. The SanDisk will not be plugged into my computer. It will be my wireless backup, but I will only turn on the wireless functionality when I'm backing up my work. Otherwise, it will be turned off for security purposes.

Investing in both hard drives cost me approximately $200, but it was money well-spent to protect my work and preserve it for the future.

MY EXPERIENCE WITH COWORKING SPACES

I took a new job last quarter as an insurance executive, and the job is 100 percent work from home.

Before the pandemic, I worked from home one or two days a week already, so I had an easier transition into the new lifestyle. When you're working from home, certain amenities that you take for granted in an office setting can be detrimental in your home environment if they stop working. Of course, I'm referring to the Internet!

If your Internet goes out when you're working from home, you're screwed. All you can do is get down on your knees, pray, and then hope it comes back on as quickly as possible. If that doesn't work, you have to call your Internet service provider. By that point, your absence may be noticed by your employer, especially if your Internet went out during an important conference call. (As is the case with me. My Internet *always* goes out during an important conference call when I'm the one leading the meeting.)

Internet outages are unacceptable. Sure, they happen. When you work from home but your employer has an office nearby, employers understand this and will often accommodate you by offering you a desk to work at while your outage gets resolved. But the nearest office my employer owns is six hours away in Chicago…

When you work from home and your Internet goes out, you

have to make choices quickly. If the outage is for a few minutes, or even an hour, you can make up the time. Hopefully, you have a boss who understands (and even better, they're experiencing the outage too!) If the outage is longer or you have a boss that is less lenient, you have to use your paid time off (and in the United States, we don't get much PTO, even though we overwork ourselves). If you don't have any time to use, you will get fired. For this reason, my Internet presence needs to be up and operational 99.99 percent of the time, 24 hours a day, 7 days a week. I'm not getting fired because of a public utility's incompetence.

I wrote in a previous volume about how I invested in Ethernet ports in my home so I could use a hardwire Internet connection for my podcast interviews and work calls. That worked extremely well and almost completely eliminated my Internet issues.

However, I also made another contingency plan. What would I do if my neighborhood suffered a power outage? In August 2020, a derecho blew through Iowa and most of the state lost power for at least a week. If a mass Internet outage happened again, what would I do?

I signed up with a local coworking space to rent office space on an as-needed basis. It's five minutes away from my home, so I can get there quickly, it has reliable Internet, and it's affordably priced. Even better, they have satellite offices across the Des Moines area, so it's unlikely that all of them would be impacted in a future derecho. I planned that if anything happened to my Internet, that I would immediately get in my car and go to the coworking space.

Sure enough, this quarter, my home Internet became unreliable. It went out two or three times per hour, making it impossible to get anything done. I called the Internet company and it turns out that my neighborhood was experiencing an outage that would take several days to fix.

I hopped in my car and went to the coworking space, where I had a desk, reliable Internet, access to conference rooms, and free beer on tap. My employer never knew that I had an Internet issue, and I damn sure wasn't going to tell them.

My service provider fixed the Internet and everything was back to normal in a few days. This kind of outage doesn't happen very often, but it does happen.

This is yet another reason why I advocate for contingency planning. A few minutes of forethought and asking "what if?" saved my butt. During the week my Internet went out, I had to give an important presentation to a senior executive. Thank God I signed up for that coworking space. The meeting went smoothly and no one even knew that I was in a different space because I kept my webcam turned off.

Another great benefit of coworking spaces is that they're similar no matter where you go. To use a US example, it's like going to the Hampton Inn. Whether you're in Iowa, Florida, or Arizona, the Hampton Inn is the Hampton Inn. Same prices, same amenities, same service, same terrible breakfast.

I went to Orlando on a family vacation. I can do my job from anywhere, so instead of using a day off, I found a coworking space two minutes from my hotel. They used the same booking and payment program like the one in my city. I flew into Orlando late Wednesday night, worked all day Thursday, and logged off to enjoy a nice three-day weekend. Anyway, I digress, but I'm a big fan of coworking spaces.

I've been referring to my day job to explain the benefits of coworking, but that's not the point of this chapter. If you're a full-time author, you need a reliable Internet connection too. Imagine your Internet going out for a week when you have a major book publication and marketing campaign planned. Or, imagine that you're speaking at an important event and need a trusty Internet connection. Full-time authorship is also 100 percent work from home. The problems are the same. If you're serious about your writing business, then you need highly dependable Internet too.

I viewed this entire episode as practice for the full-time writing life one day.

BALANCING DATA AND FEELINGS
(A RANT)

Recently, I had the unfortunate displeasure of listening to an unbearable webinar. The topic isn't important, but it was related to data science, and it had nothing to do with my job or writing. I attended merely out of curiosity.

The person presenting on the webinar was a jerk. I didn't like them from the moment they opened their mouth because they were unfriendly to the moderators. They said something that, if I could have responded, I would have refuted.

They were talking about the importance of making data-driven decisions. They said, "A person without any data to back up their opinions is just a person with feelings." I wish I could have captured the condescending, arrogant tone in which the person said it. The underlying assumption was that in the business world, people who make decisions with data are better than people who don't, which is total bullshit.

If you've read this series, then you know that I believe in making data-driven decisions whenever possible. Data is extraordinarily important to the writer of the future—I don't need to say that again because I've said it a thousand times. And you've read chapters in this series where I dug deeply into data. But numbers are not the only thing that matters.

I've worked with many "data heads" in my professional and writing life. My experience is that people who make decisions *solely* based on data usually end up making decisions that are just as bad, if not worse, than people who make decisions with no data at all.

The "feelings" that this speaker spoke so poorly about are underrated. It's why in virtually every company in America (and probably the rest of the world), you have leaders at the top who make decisions based on data and analytics, but those decisions often are not what employees would recommend (if employees were ever in a position to counsel their senior leaders, which never happens). Companies sometimes make decisions that are contrary to their customers' interests as well.

Take Google. How many apps and services do they kill that *their customers and employees love*, but they don't serve Google's interests?

Or your local utility. I recently disputed a charge on my Internet bill. They tried to charge *me* for asking for a technician to visit my home and diagnose Internet issues when the outage was *their fault*. I called to complain, and the representative told me that the company had implemented a new service charge, but that they always waived it if customers called to complain. She even told me—on a recorded line—that employees didn't like it because it increased the number of phone calls and angry customers. But a bean counter executive somewhere was probably looking at the number of service calls the company was incurring, and they did some voodoo math that justified charging customers for service calls to recoup costs. I guarantee you that whoever made this decision did not consider the company's reputation. At some point, someone probably said, "This is a terrible idea because it's not fair for customers," and the bean counter probably replied with, "Fair doesn't pay the bills," not understanding the root cause of the increased service calls to begin with. It's always better to fix the root cause than to charge the customer for it, but hey, nobody listens to me.

When every decision you make is about numbers, then your

customers become numbers too. No one likes being a number.

I once worked for an insurance company that handled customer complaints and segmented them into different "buckets." Once, I overheard a colleague tell a customer "I'm sorry, ma'am, you got put in the wrong customer bucket." I would have loved to know how that woman felt about being "put" in a bucket.

Feelings *must* be a part of any major decision. If I had to attribute a percentage, I'd say that any decision regarding your writing business (or any business for that matter) should be 80 percent data-driven and 20 percent feelings-driven. It's the feelings that allow you to connect with your audience and serve their interests. The data exists merely to help you determine the best way to do that. But too many people lose sight of that.

I look forward to the day when people will demonstrate a more balanced approach to solving the world's problems.

So, if I had been able to respond to the jerk who said, "A person without data to back up their opinions is just a person with feelings," I would have responded with, "A person with no feelings to back up their data is an asshole."

CREATING A BOOK WALLET

In Volume 1 of this series, I wrote about the idea of a "Book Marketing Plugin" that stores the metadata for your books so you can recall them easily when you are marketing.

I wrote:

I envision a browser plugin that gives you easy access to all of your book metadata so that if you need it, you can select the book in the plugin, and the plugin will auto-populate most of the book's info for you. The plugin might also automatically take you to any folders on your computer for that specific book so you don't have to click around to find the right folders.

Think of it like a password wallet like LastPass, LogMeIn, or the Safari keychain, but for your books. Pick the book you want, and the plugin auto-populates as much data as it can. If desired, you could export data from the plugin too. You could also integrate the plugin into a database so that the database feeds the plugin.

Database idea aside, I don't believe this would be too difficult to program.

In 2020, I did a lot of database work when I was creating my automated sales database. Part of that work *was* creating a database with all of my books and their metadata. I abandoned that because the sales database was more important (and more difficult) at the time. Now that I have some more free time, I wanted to revisit this initial database work.

What does a book database need to have to fuel a plugin like the one I described?

It would need:

- Title
- Subtitle
- Author name
- Series name
- Series number
- Names of other contributors
- A low-resolution image of the book cover
- Price in each major currency (for each format)
- Date of publication (for each format)
- BISAC categories
- Keywords
- Book Description
- Unique identifier such as ISBN, ASIN, and other retailer-specific codes
- Print page count
- Print trim size
- Audiobook narrator
- Audiobook length
- File size
- Formats available
- Major retailers that stock the book (with links)
- Number of Reviews
- Review average
- Testimonials

The database would store all of these fields for every book you publish. I call the database a "book wallet," because that's what it really is.

I would also include a few extra fields based on my preferences, such as versioning for my book's interior and book description, as well as fields that capture price changes and when I changed them.

This data can be filtered, pivoted, or manipulated in virtually any way because it's a simple spreadsheet. Each book has a unique ID, and that ID indicates all of the fields above for that book.

I can create a database like this over a weekend. I could also pay someone to compile it for me. Once it's built, it becomes a powerful tool that can help me:

- Feed a marketing plugin like the one I described
- Build an ONIX data feed
- Review the actual metadata for my books compared to what exists in the database (for when I'm doing a "patrol," as I mentioned earlier in this book)

And more.

DEAR AMAZON, APPLE, GOOGLE, AND OTHER BOOK RETAILERS

I'm writing this open letter to you as players who have immense sway in the publishing industry. You have the power to shape the future of the author profession.

Your action (or inaction) will determine the trajectory of publishing as we know it. And you have the power to do some tremendous good, and it won't cost you very much money at all.

My demand is simple: create a book publishing-specific application programming interface (API) for authors to use.

As you know, an API allows a developer to interact with your servers and download data in a manner that you dictate. Controlling the dispensation of your data through APIs is better than allowing developers to "scrape" data from your servers. Web scraping is unethical.

Amazon, you know this better than anyone. How many people have you banned because they scraped data from your website? Data scraping is done to create a competitive advantage, and it can be difficult on your servers.

Amazon, you also know that you offer one of the best APIs in the world: the Amazon Product Advertising API. With clean documentation, easy-to-use instructions, you have set the standard for how APIs are created. Apple and Google, you didn't do a bad job in this area either.

You're probably wondering, "Why is an author asking us for a publishing-specific API?"

Authors need API access because:

- As we become more prolific, it is cumbersome to log in to several different dashboards to upload and manage our books. Being able to interface with an API would make this easier.
- We are finding increasingly sophisticated ways to think about our books. One of those is thinking about our books as data. We need ways to see how our books are performing across all retailers. When I say "performing," I don't mean sales (although that would be nice if you could help us with that too), but metadata. Is my book priced appropriately on Amazon and Apple? Which version of a book description did I upload to all retailers? Did I even upload the right book? These are questions that authors will soon have as more authors become super-prolific. I define "super-prolific" as anything over 50 books. At that point, those authors are practically publishers. If they need to make changes to multiple books, those changes can take hours.

I understand the concerns from your perspective. Do you really want to give API access to authors who, as a class, are not terribly tech-savvy? After all, APIs are not for the faint of heart and the transmission of data cleanly and correctly is important. You need a competent developer to work with APIs; this task should not be left to regular people.

But consider this: you control the standards. You don't have to make the API so that any author can use it. You just need to make it available. Authors who don't understand it will just hire someone who does. And when they do, a new cottage industry will emerge: publishing metadata experts. As you're aware, this already exists in the traditional publishing sector. Publishers use the

ONIX standard to publish and manage books on your retail platforms. I even suspect that your biggest book aggregators are using ONIX too. The ONIX standard is written so that authors can use it too if they have the right software. It's so complicated that most authors will run away screaming, but those who need it and can afford it would use the standard. But they can't do that if you don't allow them.

The ONIX standard is not perfect, but it's a suitable alternative for writers of the future.

You may also be thinking, "We already offer APIs." But it's not that easy.

Amazon, your API can only be used to direct traffic to your website and to make sales. It's available in your Amazon Associates Program, and any affiliate who does not make sales through the API can be choked off from access. You don't allow API access for non-sales purposes. You would need to develop a publishing-specific API for authors, or permit authors to use your product advertising API for other purposes, such as monitoring the metadata of their books. Sure, metadata monitoring doesn't make sales per se, but also consider that if an author accidentally lists a book at the wrong price and doesn't realize it for several months, you lose money too. If an author has an accidental typo in a book description, you also lose money. Allowing authors to manage this information at a global level helps to improve the quality of self-published books overall, which is something that I hope you would support.

Apple, I have the same concerns with you as I do with Amazon.

Google, maybe your API is okay to use for metadata management, maybe it's not. You don't offer any official documentation.

If you'd like to take the next steps, here are my recommendations:

- Create a clear publishing API so authors can hire developers to create automated publishing solutions. Or, permit authors to use your existing API for non-sales purposes. Or, allow authors to use the ONIX standard to publish and manage their books.
- Reduce reliance on your dashboards to make changes to books.
- In your existing API documentation, explicitly permit users to gather data for non-competitive purposes, such as monitoring their metadata. You have the power to monitor and restrict access accordingly. I'm not asking you to allow bad actors to use your platforms. I'm merely asking you to allow me to use your API to manage my intellectual property.
- Provide resources to help the new cottage industry of metadata experts to help authors help themselves and reduce the burden on your servers and support staff.

Again, you have the power to change the trajectory of the author profession. Allow API access and you will change the author profession as we know it. Imagine a world where an author can upload a book to your platform with the click of a button, and it's perfectly conditioned and meets your quality and data standards. I dream of a world where books (data) flow easily between authors and retailers, and everyone makes more money as a result of this efficiency.

If you have any questions, call me.

ARTIFICIAL INTELLIGENCE: REQUESTS FOR COMMENT AT ALLI

The Alliance of Independent Authors released a request for comments around artificial intelligence. Depending on when you read this, the comment period is probably over, but I recommend that you read the article and comments anyway, if only to see how little activity there was.

ALLi wanted to know authors' thoughts on artificial intelligence so it can advocate on their behalf. Almost no one responded. Does this mean that authors don't care about AI, or was it just bad timing?

I don't know, but I suspect the former.

When you're an indie author trying to make it, you've got a thousand other things to think about. You're worried about how you're going to pay for editing and cover design. You're worried about whether your work is any good. You're fighting the noble war on book formatting and learning how to produce paperbacks that pass quality assurance. You're worried about the fact that your books aren't selling at the level you want. You're seeing everyone else doing better than you and wonder if you're doing something wrong.

And then there's self-doubt, writer's block, and the emotional aspect of being a writer. And your family. And your job. And then, if you're lucky, there's business and taxes!

Artificial intelligence just isn't high on the list of most authors right now, and that's understandable.

Consider this multi-part test that might explain why authors aren't interested.

- **Is it relevant to beginners?** New writers need to understand the process of publishing by going through it *at least* once. Otherwise, they won't be interested because, in the early years, the process consumes all of their attention and resources.
- **Does it interfere with the writer's need to be comfortable?** Writers who have published at least a few books move on to the intermediate level, which can last a long time. They need to be *comfortable* by making enough money from their work. I define "enough" as enough to recoup the costs of production plus a little profit. Once the money isn't a worry, writers' awareness expands. If they're making money, they're less preoccupied with craft too, which frees up some of their attention.
- **Is there social proof?** Writers need to feel that a subject they are pursuing "belongs" in the writing life. They might be interested in something conceptually, but it doesn't become real until they see others making money with it and believe they can too.
- **Is it easy to use?** Writers must be able to use a tool or technology easily. Even non-techy writers must be able to use it.

Emerging technology can meet one or more parts of the test, but it won't become mainstream until it meets all the parts.

If you consider the test, then you can see why AI is not taking off for writers yet. So many writers are just worried about finishing their first book, or making enough money to feel comfortable, or understanding how to run a better business.

For a technology to matter, it has to have social proof and ease of use. We aren't there yet. Most AI tools (with a few notable exceptions such as copywriting tools) are *not* easy to use and require programming knowledge. That won't do.

However, this creates an opening for authors who can see opportunity; if they're willing to adopt technology that doesn't meet all elements of the test, they will be early adopters. If they're fortunate and smart about how they use it, they will be rewarded.

That said, it's still unfortunate that ALLi didn't receive much participation. As I'll discuss in the next section, authors' disinterest in AI will probably cause problems for us as a whole in the near future.

AI FOR CONTENT SUMMARIZATION

In Volume 4 of this series, I wrote about an idea called a "Publishing Content Curation Service."

Well, I stumbled across a developer who created something very similar. Before I discuss that, here's what I wrote:

———

Ever since 2010ish, authors have had to navigate a never-ending amount of information on how to be a better author, marketer, and businessperson. There are services such as "The Hot Sheet" by Jane Friedman and The Writer's Knowledge Base by Elizabeth Spann Craig that curate self-publishing knowledge and each of these services is great in their own way. But there is no single service that I know of that can capture everything.

Eight years ago, I would have recommended that someone do this manually, but even a full-time curator would be embarking on a fool's errand. These days, I believe artificial intelligence can solve the problem. An AI can consume blog posts, books, podcasts, YouTube videos, and even comments on social media and contextualize them.

So many news articles these days are written and created by artificial intelligence, so AI already has the capability to consume content and create context. If it can do that, then it can also organize and recommend content based on what you are looking for, and aim to recommend the "right content to the right user at the right time."

Imagine wanting to know the hottest marketing trends. The service could spin a narrative about what people are doing right now based on recent content. It could even spin you a narrative based on how a certain marketing technique has evolved, such as Amazon Ads. As such, it might be able to warn you about certain practices that are either out of favor or no longer effective.

————

I also went further and discussed how technology like this can help with the discoverability problem, but I won't go into that here.

I was searching for a developer to help me with an unrelated project, and I encountered one who had a project on his resume that caught my eye.

It was a "Financial News Summarizer," which, in his words, was "a system that intakes financial news articles and simplifies the article into a quick and easy-to-read summary. This program uses NLTK, BeautifulSoup, and Flask."

On Github, the documentation reads as follows:

"FINS (Financial News Summarizer) uses a combination of web scraping, extractive summarization and Flask-RESTful to create a simple API that summarizes financial news articles. Extractive summarization works by assigning weights to the sentences through a series of tokenization. This program is built to create summaries by only using sentences with a weighted score above three standard deviations from the mean weight, capturing only the most important content."

Wow. Tech jargon aside, this is fascinating. Imagine receiving an email update weekly with a summary of major events in the self-publishing space:

- Who did your favorite podcast interviewers talk to this week, and what tips did they offer?

- What's happening at the Alliance of Independent Authors' blog?
- Are there any industry statistics you need to be aware of that are in the news?

You can certainly look up the developer's tool, as he was a nice guy and more people should know about the work he did in this space. I share it merely to prove my earlier point that this technology already exists, and it's available for us to use. It's just not easy yet. Someone can make it easier.

MORE AI SUMMARIZATION EXPERIMENTS

In the last chapter, I discussed AI content summarization and how a developer I networked with created a tool that created financial summaries.

I couldn't help myself in researching other tools that could do this, just to see how good they are.

I took the previous chapter and ran it through two free AI tools to see how well they summarized the main points of the chapter. Does the technology produce usable summaries?

One tool was called Sassbook. Here's the summary it provided me:

An AI can consume blog posts, books, podcasts, YouTube videos, and even comments on social media and contextualize them. The service could spin a narrative about what people are doing right now based on recent content. It could even spin you a narrative based on how a certain marketing technique has evolved, such as Amazon Ads. As such, it might be able to warn you about certain practices that are either out of favor or no longer effective. It can also organize and recommend content based on what you are looking for, and aim to recommend the "right content to the right user at the right time."

Nope. It just took the sentences that it thought were the most important.

I also ran the chapter through TLDR, another tool. Here's how it did:

In Volume 4 of this series, I wrote about an idea called "Publishing Content Curation Service."

Well, I stumbled across a developer who created something very similar.

So many news articles these days are written and created by artificial intelligence, so AI already has the capability to consume content and create context.

This program is built to create summaries by only using sentences with a weighted score above three standard deviations from the mean weight, capturing only the most important content."

Imagine receiving an email update weekly with a summary of major events in the self-publishing space?

I share it merely to prove my earlier point that this technology already exists, and it's available for us to use.

Even bigger nope.

Hmm...perhaps the technology is not as advanced as I thought. Or, premium programs are doing a better job. I'm not willing to pay to experiment.

Does that mean this technology will never work? No, but it's not where it needs to be yet. Give it a few years and it will be dangerous.

AI CHARACTER GENERATOR

I stumbled upon LitRPG Adventures, which is a service by LitRPG author and developer Paul Bellow that provides AI-generated characters, stories, and worlds to use in their tabletop gaming and LitRPG stories.

Paul's service isn't the only one. There are other apps such as Sudowrite that provide a similar service.

Paul writes the following on the website: "Save time and money with our AI D&D generators and library. Members of our growing community get instant access to our fantasy RPG generators powered by GPT-3 from OpenAI. Members also get access to our growing RPG library full of all sorts of tabletop RPG content."

Tabletop gaming and LitRPG are all about character data and statistics. In the RPG world, characters have "strength," "defense," and other characteristics that determine how well they will do in battle.

To relate this to authors, you can use Paul's content as fodder for your novel. If you need a character, use one from his library. The character comes with a backstory, a profession, a race, and other elements that make them fully fleshed out and ready to import into your story.

Licensing issues aside (which Paul addresses in the terms of service), this is an interesting concept. I heard an interview with author Yudhanjaya Wijeratne on "The Creative Penn Podcast," where he talked about using artificial intelligence as a co-writer. He used software to help him write scientific elements in his bestselling book *The Salvage Crew*. It seems that this method, while still among early adopters, will soon seep into the mainstream.

I also see immense value in a tool like this when writing short stories. Sometimes, I like to write about random people. A character generator could help with that.

Three years from now, more people will be doing it, especially if more services like Paul's make it easier for authors to benefit from AI without having to be a programmer.

BECOME THE WRITER OF
THE FUTURE

THE FUTURE OF KDP: THOUGHT EXERCISE

As I write this, there is chatter in the United States about Congress (finally) passing bills that will limit the power of big tech companies like Amazon, Google, and Facebook.

The US barely has a functioning government right now. Both political parties never agree on anything, so it's odd to see them agree on something now.

Reasons this is a hot topic right now include:

- Facebook lost trust after the Cambridge Analytica scandal in the 2016 election, which almost certainly contributed to Donald Trump winning the election to become a Republican president. I suspect that Democratic Party wanted revenge.
- Tech companies have faced growing criticisms for antitrust practices. Examples include Facebook buying WhatsApp and Instagram.
- Social media platforms and YouTube have faced criticism for silencing far left and far right political voices for various reasons, some legitimate, some not so legitimate. This reached a crescendo during the pandemic and the 2020 election cycle.
- Social media platforms en masse permanently banned Donald Trump after the riots at the US Capitol on January 6, 2021. Now Republicans wanted revenge.

- Congress held a series of testimonies with big tech giant CEOs. In one of these sessions, Jeff Bezos, then-CEO of Amazon, admitted that the company had potentially used third-party seller data to create new private label products to compete in the marketplace, among other serious antitrust violations. Also, during these testimonies, Congress revealed how woefully out-of-touch they were with the advancement in technology. (Is it in any surprise with the average Congressional age being 59 to 62 years old? Our representatives frequently die in office, and since they get such great healthcare, they live a long time.) Anyway, Congress didn't want to look stupid again, so they did their homework.
- Amazon keeps making the headlines for all the wrong reasons; its suppression of workers' right to unionize in Bessemer, Alabama, stories of drivers having no time to take bathroom breaks, and more.

Now, here we are. Tech companies have pissed off both political parties in the United States, and they have lost trust with American citizens (and the rest of the world). At the time of this writing, they're staring at six potential antitrust bills that will change their industry as we know it. The United States isn't the first to take action against them. Other countries have been attempting to curb big their power too.

Here's how that could affect self-published authors.

One of the bills is called the American Online Innovation Act, and it attempts to regulate and/or break up tech companies, including Amazon.

In reviewing the House of Representatives' first draft of the bill, it reads (with enumeration and formatting removed for readability), "It shall be unlawful for a person operating a covered platform...to engage in any conduct...that advantages the covered platform operator's own products…over those of another business user; excludes or disadvantages the products…relative to the covered platform operator's own products…or discriminates among similarly situated business users."

In short, this is saying that companies like Amazon can't disadvantage third-party sellers by prioritizing its own products in search. This could also be interpreted to apply to books too. Amazon won't be able to promote Amazon Publishing titles as rampantly as it does now. Kristine Kathryn Rusch points out that this could apply to Kindle Unlimited titles too. If that's true, then all of the marketing advantages of KDP Select will disappear overnight.

Kristine Kathryn Rush also quotes Michael Cader of Publishers Lunch and offers some additional insights.

"For Amazon," Cader writes, "that would likely mean divesting most arms of their publishing octopus, including much if not all of Audible, plus Brilliance, Amazon Publishing, Kindle Direct Publishing, and probably CreateSpace. It might apply to divesting AbeBooks as well.

"Sit with that for a moment. Amazon might have to get rid of everything that makes their indie publishing arm possible. Amazon could do a few things with it. They might sell the pieces. If those arms aren't making a lot of money (in corporate terms), they might simply shut them down."

What would happen if Amazon divested itself of Kindle Direct Publishing?

The best-case scenario would be if they spun their publishing arm into a separate company. It might operate with increased regulation, but we'd still be able to self-publish.

The worst-case scenario would be if Amazon shut it down. The Kindle reading division would probably continue, but (self) publishing on it would not. Self-published authors would lose a giant chunk of revenue. Authors exclusive to Amazon would lose everything. Everything. More likely than not, traditional publishers would be able to continue publishing on Amazon. My understanding is that the Kindle Direct Publishing division does not oversee traditional publishers.

The doomsday scenario would be if Amazon sold KDP. Who would they sell it to?

Consider if Penguin Random House (PRH) bought it. Overnight, you'd be at the mercy of a traditional publisher who would now have a near-monopoly on the self-published market. Don't forget that PRH also owns Author Solutions, a notorious vanity publishing company. Might we be folded into Author Solutions and be forced to pay to continue publishing on the platform, for a reduced royalty and tougher publishing rules? That's really, really scary.

And if you're thinking "But that would be a monopoly, right?", consider that Congress is only focused on big tech. For all other industries, Congress (and our Supreme Court) has done very little to curb antitrust operations. In Iowa, our Internet is run by a duopoly. If you don't like one, you have to go to the other, and they both engage in the same bullshit tactics. I don't see the federal or state governments doing anything about *that*. I digress.

But, no matter what happens, I predict that if traditional publishers are smart and learned *anything* from the ebook revolution, they'll seize on the opportunity. If they get around to embracing AI and data, then they'll have tremendous advantages that I've been warning about for the last few years. The current boom cycle indies are experiencing will be over, and authors will believe that they have no other way to make money but to sign horrible contracts again.

Everything is cyclical. Traditional publishing is out now, but it won't always be. It'll be back, just in a different form. It's just a matter of time, and the breakup of Amazon and the divestment of KDP Publishing could facilitate it.

Do I want Amazon to be broken up? I don't know. I would hope that they can comply with regulations and play fairly. I would also hope that if Congress does something for a change, that they will do it right and empower government agencies to regulate. But I recognize that that has consequences for my author career, my livelihood, and my future as an author.

The good news? If you're not reliant on Amazon for all your income, then you'll be less impacted by such a change. That's why it pays to start building an audience on other platforms now so that you aren't forced to later.

Such an event would be a mass extinction event for indie authors. The authors who survive will do so because they had a sound long-term strategy.

Will any of this happen? I don't know. Despite Congress's rare bipartisan agreement, I'll believe the bills when they're passed and enforced. Too many things can happen. The bills could get watered down. A major political event could force Congress to pay attention to something else, and this moment will fade away. Or, Congress didn't really want to implement these bills, and they were just sending a warning shot to big tech companies and it could be several more years until we see true antitrust legislation.

In any case, it pays to think ahead and be prepared if the scenario comes to pass.

GOOGLE'S AI NARRATION INITIATIVE

I learned that Google has started a beta for artificial intelligence narration for audiobooks. I've written at length in previous volumes about my thoughts on AI narration, so I won't rehash them here, but I am intrigued.

Google now sells public domain titles on the Play Store with AI narration, which, as far as I know, is the first time this has been done outside of China. As with all betas that Google does, one has to watch with bated breath and a healthy dose of skepticism.

That said, I downloaded a few public domain titles and listened to them. The narration wasn't good, but it wasn't bad either. It clearly sounded like an AI was reading the book, but it sounded a hell of a lot better than current voice-to-text software on phones and computers. The voice still reads too fast and doesn't handle sentence breaks or proper nouns well. Still, it's promising.

With any new technology, people are quick to judge or write it off without understanding the rate at which technology advances. I'd give Google's effort a C-. In five years, however, if they continue the program and continue improving the technology, it'll be a B+ or an A-, enough for customers to start paying attention. Then, overnight, the technology will be mainstream and everyone will be using it.

Of course, it's hard to know how this specific technology will work, but that's usually the story.

Being able to publish your books on Google Play and then

check a box that makes AI narration available along with your ebook edition will be a winning proposition. You could get your book into audio without any extra effort on your part. Then, you could also create a traditional audiobook with a narrator. It's not an "either/or." It's an "and."

The watershed moment will occur when AI narration is almost indistinguishable from an amateur narrator. If the AI edition is cheaper than a traditional audiobook, customers will split into three groups.

The first group will *never* listen to AI audiobooks, much like some readers today who will never read ebooks and prefer print.

The second group will *only* buy AI audio, forgoing traditional narration in favor of cheaper prices and convenience. These readers probably listen to audiobooks only for information, or they listen at two- or three-times' speed, so the performance of a narrator isn't as important to them.

The third group will prefer traditional narration for the authors and narrators they love but will buy AI audio for authors they're less sure about. AI audio will become a way to test an author's work, and if it's good, they'll buy future books in traditional audio format.

That's an interesting future. Will Google shape it? I doubt it, but we'll see.

WHY I LOVE COPYRIGHT LICENSING

I recently licensed an article that I wrote for money. Cool! I signed a contract, wrote the article to spec, and got paid.

Here's why I love copyright: there was a clause in the contract that said, "If we reprint the article, we'll pay you again."

One morning, I woke up to an email from the company saying that they liked the article so much that they were going to reprint it in a book, and that they would be depositing a tidy sum into my bank account. It was on a Monday morning too, which made it a great start to my week.

Ka-ching!

That's the beauty of copyright. It will keep making you money for your entire life plus 70 years, and if you're smart about the contracts you sign and the people you do business with, you'll wake up to unexpected but pleasant paydays.

CONVERSATION WITH AN ASPIRING AUTHOR

I spoke with an aspiring author by telephone early this quarter. This person wanted to publish their first book but was paralyzed and overwhelmed by the sheer amount of information out there. They didn't know whether to use a traditional publisher or self-publish, but they leaned toward a publisher because (insert every publishing myth you can think of).

"A publisher taking a chance on me will want me to succeed."

"Having a publisher behind me makes me more legitimate."

"A publisher will get my book into bookstores."

"A publisher will take care of everything so I can just write."

This was just in the first five minutes of our conversation.

I talk to authors all the time, and I've learned that some people are going to do what they're going to do even if it hurts them and you try to warn them. Therefore, I don't give advice. I just give people information and they can do whatever they want with it. I try to give people a realistic expectation of what the writing life is actually like, not what they want it to be. New authors are too hard-headed to listen to common sense sometimes. I say that out of love and respect because I was hard-headed at the beginning of my writing journey too.

I discussed the pros and cons of traditional and self-publishing with this author. Their biggest objection to self-publishing was that they had low self-esteem. I explained that feelings of low self-esteem are prevalent in the community and that it was okay. That freaked the author out. Then I tried to dispel some of the myths around traditional publishing, then I discussed the downsides of self-publishing. I tried as much as possible to paint an accurate picture for this author. That's what they needed, not advice.

I have no idea which path the author will choose, but that's ultimately their decision. However, it got me thinking about how I desperately need a book in my catalogue that I can point beginners to. My book *The Indie Author Atlas* sort of does this by creating a curriculum of things to learn, but not quite.

The conversation was helpful for me because it kept me grounded with the issues that aspiring authors continue to face. It's important for me to stay connected with those so that my books remain helpful to people, even though I'm much further down the road.

ENTERPRISE SELF-PUBLISHING

Mike Shatzkin published a blog article about what he feels will be the next wave of self-publishing: self-publishing enterprises. You can find it by searching his blog for "enterprise self-publishing."

Shatzkin is a traditional publishing industry veteran who sometimes gets flak from the indie community, but he offers valuable (if sometimes a little too romantic) insights into the history of traditional publishing.

His thoughts on enterprise self-publishing were half "he's onto something" and half "he's a little late to the party."

He writes, *"What I believe we are on the verge of seeing is that waves of entities will discover that they can clearly benefit from publishing books. Think of this as enterprise self-publishing. Every law firm, accounting firm, consulting firm, retailer, political campaign, cause organization, charity, and church, synagogue, or mosque is only a bit of imagination and effort away from books that can promote any variety of missions. These will be books delivered by a vast unaffiliated network of entities doing publishing as a "function", not publishing as a "business."*

Shatzkin foresees a second tsunami of books on the market, this time by corporations who realize they can create a book with value for cheaper than they can pay a marketing campaign. Shatzkin isn't the first to express this sentiment; I've heard others talk about this as well.

On the one hand, I agree with him. He envisions an industry where books are published by *businesses*. He uses the examples of small businesses, but that's where he gets it wrong. Small business owners are already doing this, using books as calling cards for their businesses. This is especially prevalent on YouTube. Sean Cannell and Benji Travis of Think Media (a YouTube channel and digital media company) published a bestselling book about YouTube strategies. While they are savvy influencers, publishing isn't their main goal; but their book made them a lot of money and helped them serve their audience, which was already over one million when they published. YouTube, LinkedIn, and other social media sites are full of stories like Sean and Benji's, with entrepreneurs, executives, and small business owners sharing books about their personal experiences.

I believe it's more likely to see big enterprises entering publishing. KFC experimented with this in 2017 during a Mother's Day marketing campaign by writing a steamy romance novel called *Tender Wings of Desire* starring Colonel Sanders. The book cover showed a muscular Colonel Sanders atop a stormy moor with a swooning woman and—wait for it—a bucket of chicken. Despite how cheesy it sounds, the book was *surprisingly* well-written and garnered great reviews and marketing buzz.

KFC released the book around Mother's Day because that's one of its biggest sales days. The company actively targets moms in its marketing.

It's not hard to see companies like KFC hiring a skilled ghostwriter (like they did with *Tender Wings of Desire)* and publishing a romance series that is written to market. Taken a step further, this would become, as Shatzkin correctly pointed out, a function of KFC's marketing department. They'll do it until it stops working.

Or, imagine Taco Bell (owned by Yum! Brands, the same company that owns KFC) publishing a military science fiction series to reach a male demographic.

Companies may try this because it's a different type of revenue stream. Invest $1,000 in the creation of a book and it becomes an asset that generates income every month. They never have to unpublish it. That's appealing, but only if it works. In the case of KFC, the books will need to get people into their restaurants.

The pandemic has businesses looking for ways to rebalance their portfolios. One sector where this is happening is in real estate, with private equity buying up housing stock since the stock market is so volatile.

Companies also may not try this because there isn't a huge return and there are other ways they can make more money faster.

But Shatzkin's sentiment is accurate. I do believe it could happen, but not for a long time. Eventually, businesses will find something else to chase.

If it does happen, though, a smart indie could position themselves to major brands as an enterprise novelist or nonfiction writer. All it takes is for one or two brands to hire you for your writing and publishing expertise, and you'll be paid handsomely in what may ultimately be a small window of opportunity. If I'm wrong, it could become a nice freelancing avenue.

HITTING BESTSELLER LISTS

Benjamin Franklin said that two things are certain in life: death and taxes. I'd like to add a third to the list: indie authors trying to find a way to hit a bestseller list, even just for a day so they can have the coveted "Bestseller" or "USA Today Bestseller" behind their name. Every few years, this comes back in full force, and droves of authors, as if mind-controlled, start clambering for the titles.

I remember early in my career when authors would use box set schemes to hit bestseller lists. One author in particular offered a buy-in program where authors could pay to get into box sets that were guaranteed to hit lists. Not only did venues learn about it and try to police the behavior, but many of those authors also got their accounts terminated at retailers because the actions required to hit the list bordered on unethical and violated terms of service. And still, authors want that title behind their name more than anything. You can't reason with them.

The *New York Times* has made it more difficult to land on their bestseller lists, primarily because of scammy indie authors. I'm surprised other bestseller lists haven't done the same.

If I was an author with six-figure sales who, all math considered, could easily hit a list with a little help, would I consider it? Sure, but only because I would be so close anyway, and only because I'd have the fan base to do it.

But the people who most often want to do this do not have stellar book sales, and they think that having an illustrious title behind their name will help that.

I've seen studies over the years that have shown that authors with a major newspaper behind their names tend to sell more books. Maybe that's true. But I believe in authenticity and integrity above sales. If your name even has the distant smell of impropriety, that's not worth it in my opinion. I'd rather readers buy my books based on their inherent value, not because I gamed the system. If that means I never achieve a fancy title, so be it. Writing has never been about titles to me.

I always shake my head every time I see these schemes pop up again.

AUTHORS ARE TIRED OF AI

I talked to a few influencers who expressed concern that discussing artificial intelligence was hurting their audience engagement. Because artificial intelligence doesn't help writers write books faster or sell more books, they just aren't interested in it.

I predicted this from the beginning. I've said many times on my channels that authors won't be interested in this technology until it can provide something concrete and tangible for them. In other words, "What's in it for me?"

However, that's not how artificial intelligence works. If you talk to any data scientist who specializes in this technology, they will most likely tell you that artificial intelligence is about incremental progress. It is not about short-term profit. But so many companies and people approach it wanting immediate profit from it when the real profit is long-term.

How can we discuss the emerging technology in a way that will be engaging to writers so that they can see the vision of the type of world they can create with it?

I see this vision clearly: authors can use artificial intelligence to become near "cyborgs," using technology to assist them in accomplishing every task of the writing and publishing process faster and more accurately. They can also use tools to own their data and make more targeted decisions that will make them money, improve the quality of their books, improve readers' enjoyment of their books, and even improve the quality of their lives because AI will permeate every aspect of our society.

Alternatively, how can we communicate the dangers of this technology so that we can proactively seek to prevent its dystopian aspects that are sure to come about if we do nothing?

I also see this clearly: a society of haves and have-nots where authors and publishers with the most money can afford to take advantage of sophisticated technology, and authors who failed to embrace the technology will be deprived of opportunities and therefore quit or make less money. Just as I mentioned previously, AI will permeate every area of our lives, and not being able to succeed in the writing space will make these writers miserable. They will be left behind, forgotten, and mocked for not embracing the technology earlier. Traditional publishers will figure out the technology too, and they'll be so good at it that authors will have no choice but to sign their contracts again if they want to sell books.

I don't mean to be alarmist, but I do believe that if we do not put ourselves in the driver's seat to shape the kind of future we want, others (read: corporations) will shape the future for us. We won't like what we see.

But people still aren't interested in this technology, even if I use sharp imagery. Why?

It doesn't make authors' production processes smoother yet. It doesn't help writers write books. It doesn't help with marketing right now outside of copywriting. It doesn't offer any other efficiencies.

In short, it's merely entertaining to watch and muse about, but it doesn't yet bring about any real change for an author who is just concerned about writing their book and marketing it. Watching amusing doesn't pay the bills and it doesn't build platforms. So what are we to do?

I don't know, but I don't believe it's fair to blame authors for not being interested. Sure, they should be, and sure, we would be in a better place as a profession if we did, but it's human nature not to care about something until it affects you.

I wish I knew the answer. If I did, I would offer some solutions and a roadmap. But I fear that if the apathy continues, we will either see stunting of growth of artificial intelligence in the author space or we're not going to like what's coming.

I don't have any solutions for the community at large other than for influencers to keep talking about it. But I do have some advice for YOU.

Every author can take steps to understand this technology, its promise, and how they can weave it into their platform.

I suggest that it is up to you to figure out your artificial intelligence strategy. At this point, no one is going to do it for you, and I don't see anyone dedicating themselves to creating advanced tools to help authors as a whole. If they do, they'll do it without too much input from the authors who need it most—those who will be left behind.

That means that it's all up to you. Your choices will be limited. But if you keep following the technology and keep your eyes open to opportunities, you will find benefits, and you will gain long-term advantages.

In this series alone, I have discussed many tools that you can be on the lookout for in the future to become the writer of the future.

The future arrives daily. The future of artificial intelligence for your writing career is unfortunately up to you and you alone. Some may see that as a burden, but I see it as an amazing responsibility to explore a future that will look drastically different from today. You can win in that future if you become a student of the technology. That learning begins today.

PUBLISHER CO-OPS?

It's not a proper volume of *Indie Author Confidential* without mentioning a co-op of some kind!

I was watching a series of interviews with Marxist economist Richard Wolff, and he was explaining a concept he believes in called "Democracy at Work."

I don't ascribe to either United States political party because I believe they're both terrible. I consider myself a populist and anti-establishment. I agree with many liberal progressive policies, but I agree with some conservative ones as well.

I believe the United States is in a transition period because capitalism isn't working. What we're transitioning to, I have no idea, and that's what makes the current times we're living in scary.

But anyway, I digress. I like hearing people's ideas because the exchange of ideas, whether you agree with them or not, makes our society better.

Professor Wolff's "Democracy at Work" idea is fascinating. It's a type of socialism, but without the baggage of socialism.

It's not Scandinavian socialism, which many Europeans are familiar with in some form.

It's not Communism, which many countries in the world have unfortunate experiences in.

Instead, it's a reform of capitalism that allows it to remain intact, but with some major changes.

Today in any corporation, the CEO, senior executives, and the board of directors make the major decisions. Orders flow downward. Entry-level associates have no say in how the company is run. If you're an employee and you don't like the direction the company is moving in, you have to find another job. If you're an investor in that company and you don't like what they're doing, you have to sell your shares. You have no power.

The principle behind "Democracy at Work" is to create a cooperative sector where companies are co-ops. In a co-op, employees decide how the business is run, not executives. Employees decide about the products, suppliers, customers, marketing, and more. They decide how decisions get made too.

There are cooperatives in the United States currently, but they are not a popular way to run a business.

I'm sure that you've worked for a company in which you vehemently disagreed with a decision your boss or senior leaders made while wondering at the same time what it would be like if managers listened to their employees. If you worked in a co-op and you were able to convince your colleagues that a decision was wrong, you might be able to stop the company from doing it. You can't do that in today's capitalistic society.

Professor Wolff's vision is a market where the capitalist sector that we have today competes with a cooperative sector. Let's see what happens. Maybe the capitalist companies will do better in a certain industry. Maybe co-ops will do better in others. Maybe co-ops will offer better benefits such as more time off or other benefits that allow people to spend more time with their families. But either way, they will compete against each other. By empowering employees to change the workplaces in which they live, they have the power to improve their lives. After all, they spend more time with their coworkers than they do with their families. Shouldn't it be an enjoyable experience?

We have democracy in our civic lives, so why not in the workplace?

Professor Wolff's strategy isn't perfect. No economic strategy is. And I'm sure there are trade-offs that haven't been considered. But as someone who wants to see our society rebuild crumbling infrastructure and create better opportunities for prosperity for everyone and not just the upper classes, I believe it's a better strategy than doing nothing or continuing the same tactics from the past seventy years.

This got me thinking about what the publishing industry would look like with a cooperative sector.

On one hand, you'd have the Big Five publishers and small presses as we know them today, and on the other hand, you'd have something interesting.

Let's pretend that there exists a publisher called Walrus (Walrus...competing with Penguin. Get it?). Walrus is a publishing co-op run by its employees. Instead of an acquiring editor, the employees of Walrus determine which books to publish. The employees decide which authors to bring on board, the company's general contract terms, and its marketing strategy for its books. They decide who gets marketing dollars too.

What types of decisions might they make? Would they end up aligning with traditional publishers? Maybe.

They might also decide that they don't want to create a portfolio of long-term assets. They only want portfolios of authors' books that sell. If an author doesn't sell and the company can't find a way to fix it, they give the rights back as soon as possible.

A publishing co-op might also have a better idea of what readers in certain segments want because, as a smaller company, they can keep in better touch with booksellers and reader habits.

They might also be better stewards of the Internet and emerging technology.

They might also give their authors some voting rights in how the business is run. That would be interesting...when an author signs with Walrus, they're incentivized to treat the business like they own it. That might lead to some interesting twists on how publishing businesses are run. It might also lead to disaster, but nobody knows.

Co-ops might also give their *readers* a say in how the business is run. Hmm…imagine being a voracious reader in a certain genre and being able to buy shares in Walrus. You, the reader, get a say in the type of books that get published…so you can read them.

You might think, "This could be a bureaucratic nightmare," but remember that employees decide how the company is run and how decisions are made. They would decide if authors and readers can vote, and what those voting rules would be. When we think of bureaucracy, we think of it in terms of hierarchy. This is because everything that goes on in an organization must be approved by leadership. People in the "middle" of a company have their agendas for making sure some things don't get done. I've worked in corporations for a long time—trust me, I would know.

Employees would be incentivized to make their business as efficient as possible. Some of that might involve doing business as usual per capitalistic companies. But the fact that they *don't* have to do the same old tiring, disengaging things is infinitely intriguing and worth exploring in my opinion.

Another thing worth considering is that you can make an argument that a business in the hands of its employees could be more ethical. They might not sacrifice human capital for short-term profit, especially if the collateral is in the very communities they live in. A co-op that runs a manufacturing plant would be less likely to pollute the drinking water in their town, for example.

It's an idea worth exploring, at least in the publishing sector.

A SAD MEMORY

When I was writing an earlier chapter on my marketing strategy, I remembered something sad.

Sometime between 2016 and 2017, I saw a Facebook ad in my newsfeed for a company that wanted to buy the rights to self-published books. I'm paraphrasing the copy on their website, but it read something like, "Are you tired of publishing books that don't sell? Maybe you've spent thousands of dollars of savings and retirement on a dream that never came true. We'd like to buy your books and help you replace those expenses. Select how many books you have in the drop-down below and get a quote. We'll take the books and breathe new life into them, and you can rest assured they are safe with us."

I'm not kidding. A wave of sadness rushed through me as I read it, and I felt it again when I was writing about how authors who write their passion are more likely to burn out when their career doesn't happen.

The company paid absurdly low amounts for books too. If I remember correctly, they paid around $100 per book. Sell the copyright to the hard work you created for $100 so you can pay your bills…

I think about how some authors were probably stupid enough to fall for it. They might have spent thousands of dollars on a career that brought out their self-doubt, alienated them from their spouse, or caused money issues. They might have just had a fight with their spouse about money the night before, then saw this website and decided to sell their books.

The worst part is that the company paid a fraction of what the books were worth. Even the most poorly edited, typo-ridden book is worth more than $100. For the cost of an editor, a new cover, and better positioning, the book might be able to sell better. But authors can't see past the current moment, unfortunately. That book could be worth tens of thousands if not millions. Sure, maybe not, but no book I know of is worth just $100. A book is the output of the human mind, and that's worth a lot of money.

It always comes down to self-esteem and self-doubt. Writers who can't suppress self-doubt always lose. Moreover, writers as a class suffer from self-doubt. It's an occupational hazard.

The people at this company knew this, and they used it to exploit authors. I have less respect for them than I do for scammy marketers. I like to see my scammers coming. These types cloak themselves in authors' emotions and make it seem as if the author is making a choice that will empower them, when all the author will do is regret the decision down the road. Regular scammers just want your money. These people want your soul, and your book is the clearest expression of it.

I hope that this company is no longer around and that their business failed. I also hope there is a special place in hell for them where their punishment is refreshing their sales dashboard every second and seeing that all the work they stole isn't there because the rights were reverted to the authors.

SOME THOUGHTS ON DEATH

"We're all just passing through."

Al Jarreau, one of my favorite jazz and R&B singers, said this while giving a eulogy for George Duke, another jazz legend. That wisdom always stuck with me.

A few years ago, I was a manager. I had a team of 13 great people, a group of peers with whom I got along very well, and I genuinely enjoyed the work. Yet I was unhappy.

I became a manager before I was ready. I thought I knew what I was signing up for, but I didn't. The only reason I did it was because my director at the time believed in me and thought it would be a good growth opportunity. He was right, but probably not in the way he expected. Shortly after hiring me, he left the department, and things were never the same afterward.

I didn't succeed as a manager. Not from a business perspective. I'm not a manager—I'm a leader. I don't find any joy in managing people or situations. I prefer to develop people and help the business meet its goals.

The experience taught me a lot about myself and what I am (and am not) capable of. The truth was that the role was a bad fit for me. When I learned *why* and gazed upon my soul, I discovered that I was capable of being a leader, but not in that environment. That said, I was grateful for the experience because of what it taught me.

The department had a tradition of slow-clapping out people who leave. I got a slow-clap as I carried my box to the elevator that would take me to my new department on the top floor of the building. I appreciated that, and it was bittersweet to leave colleagues I liked.

I entered the elevator, and as it carried me to a new job and new future, I had a strange feeling of cosmic self-awareness, when you connect to the universe for a split second. I was alone—intensely alone despite *just* having been enveloped in respect and love. And waiting, watching the numbers above the elevator doors shift and beep. A brief shiver ran through my body.

I realized that a phase in my life was ending and I was preparing for another. I was standing in that elevator with my box, waiting for the next phase of my life.

Then the doors opened and ended the brief moment of cosmic awareness, and I walked into what was a very fruitful transitional period in my life. During that period, I sought therapy, entered a period of deep self-reflection, and I grew my writing endeavors exponentially. I also became a better father, husband, and son. When COVID-19 hit, I was centered and more equipped to deal with it than most. As I reflect on that moment, only now can I fully appreciate those thirty seconds in the elevator for what they were.

That waiting period in the elevator…maybe that's what death is like.

Life is just a department. You're put on this Earth to do *something*. Whether you're aware of your purpose or not, you accomplish it. When you're done, you get slow-clapped to an elevator that carries you to the great beyond.

We're all just passing through.

While you're here in this "department," how will you spend your time before the claps start?

No one knows when they're going to die. Some people are fortunate enough to live a long life and see it coming, like my 93-year-old grandfather. He spent his final days in hospice. Hospice is one of those rare moments in life as well where you can see someone preparing to leave this world. It's terrifying at the time, but once it's over, you can see the moment for what it truly was.

Others don't see death coming, like the uncle I lost in the Vietnam War who stepped on a landmine and lost his life in an instant.

I don't know whether it's better to see death coming or to die instantly, but I do know that however it happens, I want to make a difference with my time here before the worms get my body.

For me, I can make a difference in several ways:

- Be a good father.
- Be a good husband, brother, and relative.
- Do what I can to make a positive impact in the companies where I work. For me, positive impact doesn't mean profit necessarily. It means making connections with colleagues and making their lives easier.
- Be a good citizen of my community and my country.
- Write novels that educate and entertain people.
- Write books and create content that makes a difference in writers' lives and pushes the profession forward.
- Put good vibes into the universe.

Are those things my purpose? I don't know. I don't think anyone truly knows their purpose. You can choose something that you believe your purpose is and put your energy into it, but that doesn't mean you will have been right. Maybe the purpose we think we are serving isn't the actual purpose. Humans want "big purposes" like changing the world, but maybe our true purposes are micro. Something as subtle as smiling at someone down on their luck or taking the time to help your cousin with a high school project that will ultimately lead to an amazing passion—that could be what we're meant to do. Instead of a big purpose, our purpose might simply be to *be here* on this planet and transmit a certain frequency of attitude that impacts and influences others. That frequency is our personality. Whatever we choose to do within the confines of that frequency (and it has a very wide range) is up to us, but our waves transmit everywhere we go, and others' waves wash over us.

Dr. Cornel West says the kingdom of heaven is within us and we should leave a little piece of heaven everywhere we go. I've always agreed with that.

Books are a wonderful way to transmit our frequencies. They are little pieces of heaven and time capsules that offer a look into the times in which we live.

Books are a celebration of life. Every book is a monument to the author. They too can emulate the elevator. Some books transport you to a different realm of thinking, like *The Conquest of Happiness* by Bertrand Russell did for me.

I am confident that when I leave this world, I will be leaving behind a lot of beacons that will continue to transmit long after I'm gone. Not many professions can say that.

I know what I want to do before my time is up, and I do my best to live with passion and purpose every day.

How are you living your passion and purpose for the time you're just passing through?

SIGNPOSTS ALONG THE ROAD

Dean Wesley Smith wrote a wonderful blog post about a concept he called "signposts along the road."

At the time, he was preparing to move out of a condo in downtown Las Vegas to a bigger high-rise penthouse with better views, and he stopped to reflect just how far he'd come in his life as a writer. I'll let you read the article because I thought the way he wrote about it was very touching.

We often don't stop to think about our progress. We're so busy thinking about what's next, how to sell our books, and how to make more money. But there are times when life asks us to stop and reflect on where we are and how we got there. It's our choice whether we listen or not.

Another thing Dean said that I appreciated was that he focused on looking for signs on where he was in his career in his first two decades. Now he doesn't care, but the exercise is amusing to him.

I despise giving out ugly links, but I'll break my rule. You can read his post at

www.deanwesleysmith.com/a-signpost-along-the-road/.

The post got me thinking about the signposts in my life.

The first signpost for me was vivid. It was 2014, and my wife was pregnant with my daughter. We were living in a tiny studio apartment, and my "writing space" was our living room couch. One night, I had gotten my manuscript back from my editor for my second novel, *Theo and the Festival of Shadows*. I stayed up late into the night working on my editor's edits and formatting the ebook version. I remember a great feeling of joy spreading through my body, and I remember saying to myself what a special time this was. Sitting on my couch, working on a second book—how many writers ever got that far? I loved my protagonist, a steadfast and prickly teddy bear with a sword and shield who fights tirelessly to save his owner from a nightmare dimension (think "Toy Story" meets "David Bowie's Labyrinth"). I loved the *process* of writing and publishing a book, even though there was a lot to learn. I think about that moment from time to time because there was something special about it; thinking about it now, it was a signpost.

The next signpost was in 2016 when I was writing *Old Dark*. It was the first book I wrote on my phone. One week, I attended an insurance seminar at a Holiday Inn Express. It was for an insurance designation called the Certified Insurance Counselor (CIC), and the class was about general liability policies. The instructor was *amazing*, probably one of the best public speakers I've ever seen.

The class took breaks every hour for ten minutes so people could go to the bathroom and refresh their coffee and snacks.

On *every single break*, I power-walked to a nook near the hotel lobby, sat in a plushy chair, whipped out my phone, and wrote *Old Dark*. I probably wrote 5,000 or so words over three days just at the hotel on my phone—all during ten-minute breaks. I had a blast writing that novel. I passed the test at the end of the seminar too, which wasn't easy. After that seminar, I decided that if I was half as good as the teacher who taught that course, I'd be somebody.

(In a very ironic twist of fate, I became an instructor teaching the same material, and I even became an assistant vice president of general liability at a global insurance company. The passion started at the same time I was writing *Old Dark*. And even more ironic—I wrote *Old Dark* into the dark, which is a method of novel writing without outlining.)

When I look back on that moment, it was a signpost too. It cemented my ability to write on my phone. That conference forever broke my brain and changed my future. I learned how to execute on high levels with both writing and insurance. This is the point where both careers began to feed off each other.

In 2019, a brief minute I spent in an elevator was another. (I wrote about this in a previous chapter). That was the moment I learned to start owning the spiritual side of being a writer, and when I worked on my mindset and emotional baggage.

And now, in 2021, I've just passed another road sign. I reversed my focus from inward to outward after reading *The Conquest of Happiness*. Now I've landed an amazing job, published a metric ton of books, finished law school, and have a lot more time on my hands to shape my future. That's really exciting for me.

What are signposts saying? Hell if know. All I know is that I'm enjoying the ride, and at the very least, I'm not spinning my wheels.

What are your signposts?

THIS TIME LAST YEAR

I thought it would be fun to start a new segment that looks back at previous volumes to see how I have advanced and how the industry has changed. It's hard to believe that I'm already six volumes deep into this series and I am already forgetting what I wrote in earlier volumes.

What was happening a year ago in Q3 2020 ? Some of the things that were important for me:

- The world was still in partial lockdown due to the COVID-19 pandemic, but many in the US were starting to emerge for summer.
- The uncertainty about future events was palpable. It was impossible to plan for *anything*.
- Riots erupted all over the US after the murder of George Floyd.

Content Creation

This time last year, I was in the middle of my Beast Mode Challenge. Because I couldn't control current events, I focused on what I could control. I wrote over 100,000 words in August, even while a derecho (an inland hurricane) hit Iowa and knocked out power for several days.

I also did my second interview on "The Creative Penn," and

my Internet connection crapped out on me during my chat with Joanna, which was a major embarrassment. Afterward, I immediately had Ethernet ports installed in my studio.

I also hired a video editor.

I also successfully narrated my first audiobook and got it approved on the first try.

Marketing

I implemented a new email signature with a headshot, title, and link to my books. That little decision (which cost about $40) is still paying off.

Technology and Data

I finished my automated sales database and was finding ways to visualize my data using Power BI.

Artificial intelligence was also top-of-mind. I wrote about natural language processing in that quarter's volume, which was the first step toward building my automated editing engine.

Writer of the Future

I wrote about the writing app of the future and how the writer of the future needs an app that functions as one command center, merging outlining, writing, editing, and formatting into one app so that the author (and editors and formatters) never have to leave the ecosystem. Today, one such writing app has emerged and is now in beta—Atticus (which I covered earlier in this book). While I wrote about this concept in 2020, I talked about it as early as

2019 on "The Writer's Journey" podcast. It's gratifying to see that someone else arrived at the same idea independently, especially one of brightest minds in publishing (Dave Chesson).

And, of course, I was still writing about bold new ideas that you can steal!

And here we are in 2021. What a year.

THIS TIME FIVE YEARS AGO

I was thinking about how far I've come compared to five years ago. I'll continue my trip into (not so) old memories.

In July 2016, my writing life was very different. I only had 17 books to my name, my YouTube channel was on a hiatus, and I was still struggling to figure out what direction I was going to take my writing business.

My most popular books had yet to be published: I had just finished *Old Dark (The Last Dragon Lord, Book 1)*, but I had no idea how successful it was going to become.

I had just stopped outlining novels too. I wasn't making much money from my writing either. I hadn't started law school yet.

When I reflect on July 2016, I remember my processes and technology clearly:

I was using Scrivener two for Mac to write my novels.

- I was using Dragon for Mac to dictate. At this point, I had become proficient in dictation, using it to write *Old Dark*.
- Scrivener iOS had just released, allowing me to write on my phone. I was just starting to experiment with it.
- I was still using Scrivener's Compile feature to format ebooks.
- I gave up on paperback formatting because there wasn't a good formatting solution for Mac users. I had been

playing around with professional templates, but none of them worked for me.

- I tracked my bookkeeping and sales manually. I don't even think I tracked my sales reports once in 2016 because it was such a pain.
- Artificial intelligence was just a buzzword. Everyone was experimenting with Facebook Ads, and they were the cheapest they would ever be.
- My book covers were all over the place. The designs were drastically different and I had inconsistent branding.

Yet I did a lot of things right in 2016, even though I wasn't aware at the time. Writing on my phone and dictation would lead to amazing word counts and the ability to continue my writing career. That year, I began a three-year campaign to create consistent branding on my book covers, finishing in 2019. Now all my covers have similar "shells." That was a huge leap forward.

Now Vellum is my formatting app and it has improved my paperback quality immensely.

I'm using automation in ways that I never would have dreamed of in 2016, although the technology was on computer and available back then.

Five years later in July 2021, I've come a long way and I have a lot to be proud of.

THIS TIME TEN YEARS AGO

Since we're on the topic of traveling back in time, I might as well look at the last decade...

The year was July 2011. I had been out of college for a year and was working a crappy job as a claims adjuster. The silver lining was that I had become bilingual in Spanish on the job. My Spanish was very good.

I was writing poetry at the time, and I had just started meeting with a writer friend at a coffee shop on Tuesdays. We shared our work and talked shop.

I despised self-publishing. Sometime around this period, I went to an open mic night and heard a poet who delivered a fantastic poem on stage. He ended by saying that he had a book on Amazon. I loved the poem, so I bought his collection. A week later, a monstrosity of a book appeared in my mailbox. The cover looked as if it had been designed in Microsoft Paint, the text was full of typos, and the formatting was unprofessional. I swore that I would never buy another self-published book, and I believed that an author *needed* a publisher behind them.

I know that's hard to believe that I was ever anti-self-publishing, but I wrote an entry in my journal about it, and I'm embarrassed to share it with you, but here it is:

I have known a few people to self-publish their work. I recently had a friend who published a novel. Finishing a novel is to be commended. Everyone wants to write the next great novel, but most of us aren't writers, most of us can't do it, and most of us shouldn't even try. However, I respect those who do it and give it their all, no matter what the quality of their work. But self-publishing is the worst way to celebrate the finishing of your work...

Authors who self-publish are driven by the belief that their novel is going to be epic, and that it's going to change the world. Unless you've got an editor and an audience, it won't. For the aspiring author, it's one of the most foolish things you can do. First, self-published books brand you as an amateur. Second, self-publishing a novel ensures that it especially won't be picked up by a publishing house—publishers want to be the first to publish a work. Don't make it hard on yourself. Self-publishing is essentially the same as tossing your book into a river.

Keep in mind that this was a private journal entry, and I was so smug and condescending...and also keep in mind that I had barely written a few poems around this time. It's embarrassing, but we all have said and done things in our past that we believed at the time but disavow now. I find the passage above embarrassing but also an indicator of how I've evolved over the years.

I had no idea that I would have a near-death experience one year later in July 2012, and it would change my perspective on writing forever. I was a year away from a paradigm shift.

It's amazing how far you can go in a decade. That's why I like to think in terms of years and decades. It's easy to overestimate what you can do in a year while also underestimating what you can do in a decade. What types of goals would my 2011 self have made for 2021?

I might have wanted to write 100 poems thinking that it would take me 10 years. That's 10 poems per year. I was a perfectionist back then. With a perfectionist mindset, it's not hard to see how you could limit yourself to such a small number...and still not get published in magazines. I suffered from self-doubt too. I rewrote *everything* and took advice from anyone and everyone who read my work, even people who didn't even like poetry.

Again, it's amazing what a difference a decade makes.

As I think about my progress through 2031 (ten years from now), what are my goals?

I have no idea what will happen throughout the next decade. But if I'm able, I plan to keep writing. If I write 10 books per year, I'll have published *at least* 160 books by then. Who knows, maybe I'll increase my writing output dramatically and be well over 200 by that time. Or maybe I'll suffer a setback and be at a significantly lower number. Or, maybe everything I wrote in this paragraph will be hilariously wrong.

If I'm lucky, I'll be a full-time writer by 2031, with no debt, house paid off, and a fair amount saved up for retirement. My parents will be aging, so I will have the responsibility of taking care of them, something I started preparing for in 2014. My daughter will be in high school and I'll be looking at an empty nest very soon—and booooy, if you thought I was a fast writer now, wait until I don't have to worry about kids in the house anymore...

I hope this series will continue for ten years so I can verify if anything I wrote was correct.

Q3 PROGRESS REPORT

In the previous volume, I shared the progress I was making toward my 2021 author strategy. This strategy will guide me for the next several years. I wanted to provide an update for Q2 2021.

I've shared a detailed mind map about this at www.authorlevelup.com/2021strategy.

MY STRATEGY

My mission is to educate and entertain my audience in the genres I write, and to remain nimble in an ever-changing industry.

I will achieve my mission through five strategic priorities:

- Become a world-class content creator
- Become a world-class marketer
- Become a technology-driven writer
- Become a data-driven writer
- Become the writer of the future

WORLD-CLASS CONTENT CREATOR

Goal: 64 books published by 12/31/2021. I'm currently at 58 books written (including this one), which is approximately 89 percent to plan. I'm writing this in July and have approximately half the year left. Beast Mode will help me exceed my plan this year.

Develop a way to ensure consistency across my platform. Not started.

WORLD-CLASS MARKETER

Grow my Amazon Ad imprint. **Completed.**

Improve my copywriting skills. Completed.

Reduce my tax liability. Successfully failed (and completed). See the previous volume for more information.

BECOME A TECHNOLOGY-DRIVEN WRITER

Develop an automated way to enforce consistency. **Completed.**

Redesign my Book Wizard tool on Michael La Ronn.com and Author Level Up.com. Not started. Hopefully, I'll achieve it in Q4.

Implement a flexible book database that houses all the metadata for my books. Not started. I may not accomplish the goal this year, so if that happens, I'll push it to 2022.

Automate my bookkeeping. Successfully completed.

BECOME A DATA-DRIVEN WRITER

Make minor enhancements to my sales database. **Not started. Invest in learning the basics of Python, Webhooks, and Application Programming Interfaces (APIs).** I took an API course in Q1, which was very helpful and informative. I will complete this goal in Q4. I should accomplish it easily.

BECOME THE WRITER OF THE FUTURE

Read 50 books. I'm still at 50 percent toward the goal, with around 20 books read this year. I may fall just short of plan.

Implement direct print and audiobook sales onto my website. Not started.

Complete my law degree. Completed.

Complete 12 WMG workshops to improve my writing craft. I'm in danger of missing this goal as I still haven't started yet.

BRINGING IT ALL TOGETHER

I wrote this volume early in the quarter, so my progress is a little thin. I expect to have more completed in Q4.

I don't have all my goals listed here, but for the ones I do, I have achieved 6 out of 15, which is 40 percent.

I'm on track to completing two others, so that brings my completion to 53 percent.

For me, I'll have a rock-solid year if I hit around a 75 percent completion rate. I always set more goals than I can accomplish to help me stay motivated. The goals I accomplished are pretty big ones too.

I don't care if I miss goals. I prefer to set many goals; if I accomplish half of them, I've had an amazing year. I'm not stressing over them.

I'll share more progress on my strategy in the next volume so I can keep myself accountable, but you can view the details of my 2021+ strategy by visiting www.authorlevelup.com/2021strategy

CONTENT CREATED WHILE WRITING THIS BOOK

Books

Authors, Steal This Book: 67 Business Ideas for the Writers of the Future

In this book, M.L. Ronn breaks down 67 radical ideas that might just change the future of the writing profession as we know it. This book is free because ideas are meant to be shared. You might find something on these pages that could change your writing career.

Buy at www.authorlevelup.com/stealthisbook.

INDIE AUTHOR CONFIDENTIAL

Secrets No One Will Tell You About Being a Writer

VOL. 7

M.L. RONN

VOLUME 7

INTRODUCTION

As 2021 comes to an end, I realize that this year was finally a "normal" year—as normal as things can get right now given the COVID-19 pandemic. This year flew by compared to 2020, which was like a decade packed into a year.

I started 2021 off strong but then faltered a little in Q2 as I changed jobs and finished my final semester of law school. I made up for lost time in Q4, which was my most productive quarter ever.

As I write this chapter, I'm nearing the end of my "Beast Mode" challenge, and I wrote 10 books between July 1st and October 15.

Now that I've finished law school, wrapped up podcasting, and am no longer teaching insurance classes, I have a lot more time on my hands, and it's showing up in my productivity. I have more focus than I ever had at the beginning of the year, and that feels great!

This volume concludes a great year for me, and a year where I got a lot done to put myself on solid footing in the future.

My Core Strategic Priorities

As a refresher, my mission is to create content that entertains and/or educates my audience, preferably both, and to remain nimble in an ever-changing industry. I do this by focusing on five strategic priorities:

- Become a world-class content creator
- Become a world-class marketer
- Become a technology-driven writer
- Become a data-driven writer
- Become the writer of the future

I believe these five priorities are most important for me to have a long-term, sustainable career.

Stay tuned for significant changes to my strategic priorities for 2022.

What's in This Volume

In the World-Class Content Creator section, I discuss the lessons that "Beast Mode" taught me this year as well as some major editing victories that drastically reduced the number of errors in my books.

In the World-Class Marketer section, I discuss lessons learned in public speaking engagements as well as some other miscellaneous topics. Also, due to updating my strategic priorities, this will be the last volume where I discuss marketing ideas.

In the Technology and Data-Driven section, I discuss some issues I had with data this year as well as experimenting with emerging tech. I also finally resolved to learn cover design.

In the Writer of the Future section, I discuss problems with being prolific, clothing that can potentially help you become a better writer, and major lessons learned in 2021.

Moving forward, I've decided to keep the series quarterly for now. I'll also be making some updates to the format of the book, which I'll discuss in the final chapter. These changes will streamline my process of creating the *Indie Author Confidential* series while improving the quality.

Enjoy this volume.

M.L. Ronn
October 15, 2021
Des Moines, Iowa

BECOME A WORLD-CLASS
CONTENT CREATOR

LESSONS FROM RAT CITY

This quarter, I embarked on what was my most difficult writing task this year—restarting a novel that I left off in the middle of.

That novel was *Rat City: The Chicago Rat Shifter* Book 2.

The worst part about this novel was that when I stopped writing it, I was in a murky spot, and wasn't sure what was going to come next. That made it much more difficult to restart because I had to first remember what I wrote and then try to figure out where to take the novel.

I don't like doing cold restarts, so here's what I did to prepare for writing the story again:

I reread the first few chapters and the latest chapter.

For the first few days, I wrote 500 words, followed by rereading a chapter. I rinsed and repeated until I reread everything, which made it easier to push the story forward.

That worked so well that I didn't even notice when I was having regular word-count days at first.

However, my first few weeks had low word-count days. Normally, I write around 2000-3000 words per day when I'm writing fiction; for the first few weeks after restarting, I was lucky if I wrote more than 1500 words per day. The novel was slower than I am used to.

But *Rat City* taught me some valuable lessons:

At 76,000 words, it's my longest novel ever. My second-longest novel, *Old Wicked,* is 67,000 words.

When you write a novel that is beyond your stamina level, it's an intense exercise, especially when you're writing every day. I experienced several days of sheer mental exhaustion. This happens when you write consistently over your daily average. For example, during the last two weeks alone, I was writing well over 4000 words per day.

This story was the ultimate test of writing into the dark. It's extraordinarily complicated, with many plot twists. I continue to be amazed at how my creative voice stitches stories together.

There were many times when I thought I was coming up on the end, but I was nowhere close in retrospect. My mind kept playing tricks on me.

I rediscovered the joy of writing with a quota. I haven't historically been a quota guy, but implementing a 2000-word per day quota in the last quarter of the novel helped me finish it. I may revise my thoughts on quotas moving forward.

This story is the darkest story I've ever written. Sure, it's tame compared to a lot of authors, but I go into very weird territory: intense rat scenes, necromancy, demon possessions, and so on. There are serious consequences at the end of the story and it's not a happy-go-lucky ending like I normally write. It's a depressing ending, actually. The funny thing is that I didn't realize how dark the story was until I was self-editing it.

Normally, writing into the dark (without an outline) has a predictable series of events: you start off knowing absolutely nothing about the story, and as you progress, you slowly see where your brain is steering you. At some point around the 80- to 90-percent mark, there's the "glimmer," which I call the moment in the novel-writing process when you know exactly how the story is going to end. Once you see the glimmer, finishing is just a foregone conclusion and you just have to go through the motions. *Rat City* had a glimmer, but it was a very faint one, and this novel kept me on the edge of my seat until the final scene. I had no idea what would happen, which is scary for a lot of people, especially when you're writing a 76,000-word novel.

My "current tolerance" level for writing novels without outlines is around 60K. Under that amount, I can usually remember most details and keep all the threads together easily. I discovered with this novel that once I write over 60K, this task gets twice as hard. To be honest, I struggled to keep everything straight. It was a learning experience that taught me how to manage bigger novels. I don't have any difficulty with keeping the plot together; it's the little details that get me. For example, I remembered that my hero needed to meet a friend for ice cream. I forgot that my hero told the friend to meet her at a park. I just had the hero show up at the ice cream parlor. Little stuff like that adds up in a big way throughout a long novel. My current workflows aren't designed for big novels, and I need to change that.

I owe much of my success for this novel to waking up early in the mornings. Whether I was inspired or not, I woke up and wrote, and there's something to be said about that, even when I was staring at a blinking cursor for longer than I wanted.

I had a bout of "writer's block" around the 75-percent mark and I dissolved it very quickly with a new technique. My heroine needed to solve a problem, but I didn't know how to get her past it. I walked away from the computer and mowed the lawn. I told myself that I would listen to something—anything—and whatever I listened to, I would make it contain the answer. I happened to resume an audiobook about death called *The Five Invitations* by Frank Ostaseski. He wrote something in the book that triggered an idea. When I finished mowing the lawn, I returned to my chair and charged full-speed ahead.

I tested out at least ten experimental writing techniques in the novel. With one, I switched from the third-person POV to the first-person; with another, I "bookended" an entire scene within a conversation between the hero and his mom, where the middle scene is an encounter with a villain—it all happens at the exact same time; I also wrote a scene that the hero imagines but doesn't actually happen, but the reader doesn't realize it until the scene is over; I wrote several scenes between two villains who are brothers, and the POV switches between them so that the reader can't directly see what's happening, but instead experience it through the brother who is also experiencing it secondhand. This novel was a training ground for a lot of fun techniques. Whether they work or not is another matter entirely.

Anyway, there are many more lessons that *Rat City* taught me, but I'm grateful for the experience it gave me.

LESSONS FROM COLD HARD MAGIC
(OR, A LEVEL UP)

In the previous chapter, I discussed my experience with *Rat City (The Chicago Rat Shifter, Book 2)*. Two days after finishing that novel, I started writing another: *Cold Hard Magic (The Good Necromancer, Book 2)*.

Both novels have a lot in common:

- I started writing them in a blaze of glory, but then had to stop for some reason or another.
- I stopped writing both novels at exactly the 50 percent mark.
- Both use a lot of experimental story techniques that readers will love or hate.
- I had zero idea what I was supposed to write next.

In *Cold Hard Magic's* case, I stopped writing the novel in late 2019, just before the pandemic started.

This novel had many similarities and differences with *Rat City*.

The biggest similarity is that I started the novel cold. I just sat down and started writing. That's extremely difficult and taxing, and because you don't always remember what you wrote before and you don't always know what to write next!

However, I did it anyway because I knew the only way to finish was to start, no matter how painful. The difference with this novel was that I started with a quota. It took me several days to ramp up to "ground effect" with *Rat City*. It's amazing how, because I set a 2000-word quota for *Cold Hard Magic,* that I managed to exceed that quota every day for a week, which led me to finish the novel expeditiously. I had more zero word-count days than I would have liked with *Rat City*, but I didn't have any with *Cold Hard Magic*, though there were times when I had zero clue what to write.

That's the power of quotas.

Overall, though, *Cold Hard Magic* was an easier and shorter novel to write. It clocked in at about 50,000 words. It was easier to keep the different plot threads straight too.

This novel also reinforced a concept that I learned early on when I learned how to write into the dark: the best answer may be behind you.

Much like *Rat City*, this novel took a few left turns that I didn't see coming.

It was such a left turn that I second-guessed myself. Late last night, I was lying in bed thinking, "This is crazy. I don't know about this."

I kept thinking that maybe I overwrote part of the final battle—sometimes when you write into the dark, you go down avenues that you don't ultimately use, so you have to throw some words away. It's part of the process. I wondered if this had happened. I was in the middle of the final battle and hit a wall. I had no idea what was going to happen, and that's unusual this late in a novel.

So, I slept on it.

The next morning, I decided to review the entire novel. I gave it a quick read to see if there was anything I forgot when I was writing the last quarter of the novel.

Sometimes, when you write into the dark and don't know what to do next, the answer is most often behind you.

It's like when you're on an airplane and the flight attendant says, "Please note that the nearest exit may be behind you." In a crisis, people don't always remember that.

Anyway, I reviewed the novel, particularly a few sections that I wasn't sure about. Sure enough, my creative voice remained true. It had planted ALL the seeds for the final battle. I was just too stubborn to realize it. In fact, some of the lines I write very early in the first couple of chapters were almost eerily prescient when you read what happens in the final battle. I had zero idea where this story was going, and it's still awe-inspiring to me how your mind will tell a story if you let it. Your first job is to simply get out of the way and give your mind what it needs. Your second job is to listen.

In my case, the answer was familiarizing myself with what I wrote.

I returned to the final chapter, and the next thing I knew, I was typing the final sentence.

So, remember, if you get stuck in a novel while writing into the dark, the answer is probably behind you. *Cold Hard Magic* helped me re-learn that important lesson.

ONE OF THE BEST PARTS ABOUT THIS JOB: THE FAN MAIL (OR, A PERMAFREE UPDATE)

Last quarter, when I published *Authors, Steal This Book: 67 Business Ideas for the Writer of the Future*, I had no idea what would happen. The book is now successfully permafree at most retailers and it is starting to accumulate anywhere from a dozen to two dozen downloads per day. I'm seeing a slight increase in sales of my other writing books, and that's a good thing.

However, the real test of success is whether my ideas have an impact.

I received an email from a *New York Times*-bestselling author who was in his mid-seventies and just starting on his self-publishing journey. (Yes, you read that right.) He was fed up with traditional publishing and wanted to reach readers directly. While this author isn't a household name, he wrote a book that many avid book readers in his genre would recognize. Random circumstances led him to my book and he downloaded it. When he read my chapter on "Pilot Series" (series where you have readers give you feedback on whether to write it or not), it inspired an idea that he felt so passionate about, he emailed me on the spot. He's going to be testing that idea with a new series he's writing.

How cool is that?

Sometimes I'm amazed at where my books travel. I'm honored when people reach out and let me know how my writing has impacted them. I hope that the pilot series idea works well for him.

Now, if one of my books could just land in the hands of a celebrity who wants to feature me on their platform...

WHAT MAGIC MUSHROOMS AND WRITING INTO THE DARK HAVE IN COMMON

I've been watching news stories discussing the use of psychedelic drugs. There have been studies that have shown that they are effective in treating PTSD and ameliorating terminal cancer patients' conditions, among other things.

I listened to several interviews with psychedelic experts who discussed the benefits of the drugs in certain situations.

(No, I'm not going to do magic mushrooms. However, what they said was intriguing. I won't pretend to be an expert on this topic, but I'll summarize some of the takeaways as I understood them.)

One of the effects of psychedelic drugs is what is called "ego death," which is defined as a detachment of the soul from the body. Some people report it feels as if you are actually dying, but it's ultimately a transcendence that helps people explore themselves and become more self-aware. Terminal cancer patients who undergo ego death can become more comfortable with dying for real. Ego death can help someone with PTSD move past trauma.

When one takes a psychedelic, it is recommended to do it under the watch of an experienced guide, someone who understands what the drug will do to you so they can help you through the process. You also want someone with you to "hold space"—someone who will not be taking the drug, but will be there to provide you emotional support. You also need a safe space.

The result of an effective psychedelic session is mind expansion and self-awareness, among other things.

What does this have to do with writing?

I've been getting many questions about writing into the dark lately, and I happened to receive a question about it on the same day I was listening to an interview about psilocybin (magic mushrooms). That got me thinking about how writing into the dark and consuming psychedelics have a lot in common:

- They're both illegal ("pantsing" is frowned upon in the writing world).
- They provide deep insights into yourself that is hard to put into words.
- They're best experienced under the tutelage of a guide and someone who can hold space for you.

Writing into the dark is exactly that: writing into the dark. You start a story with no idea how it will end, and you keep sitting down and working on it until you finish it. I can't overstate enough how extraordinarily difficult this is for writers to do. I glamorize it and make it look easier than it actually is. It requires self-confidence, courage, and faith in yourself.

I suspect that many authors fear writing into the dark because they don't have a structure. It feels scary to them. This was true for me until I read Dean Wesley Smith's book, which served as a guide for me.

In my monthly power-hour livestreams, I frequently field questions about writing into the dark. I often end up giving advice to writers about how to get through their manuscript because they're stuck and aren't sure how to proceed. I've become sensitive to the feelings that people experience throughout the process as well as my own feelings when I'm writing without an outline. Most of the questions I receive are about the emotional side of writing into the dark.

I've learned a lot, mainly that:

- Writing your first book into the dark is always the hardest; it gets much easier after the first time (but the first time is a bitch, let me tell you).
- Every book is a test. Every book will test you in different ways. If you finish the book, you pass, even if the story fails to resonate with readers.
- Every book requires a different approach when you're in the dark. Once you've done it for a while, you intuitively know what the book needs, but this knowledge comes with experience and it is difficult to explain to beginners.

I've decided to write a book about my process of writing into the dark. I will talk about the technical, emotional, and practical sides of it. I hope that the book will be a guide for writers and hold space for them as they go through the process.

It's amazing how unrelated ideas come together and result in a book idea.

TWO EDITING VICTORIES

I sent the manuscript for my novel *Cold Hard Magic (The Good Necromancer Book 2)* to my editor.

Cold Hard Magic is technically the first novel to benefit from the efficiencies of my new editing workflow. It took me two previous novels to tweak it.

My benchmarks for editing are approximately 275 edits per novel, which is around 1 edit per 200 words or so.

To my surprise, this novel came back with 179 edits! That's 34 percent lower than my average!

It wasn't an accident. It was a culmination of the process I created (and discussed in the previous volumes of this series). It's also a testament to the power of owning your data and using it to become a world-class content creator.

Cold Hard Magic is officially the cleanest novel I have ever sent to an editor. At 50,000 words, it's a standard-length book for me. To put it into perspective, my writing books are usually very clean when I send them to my editor. *Cold Hard Magic* was cleaner than some of those, which is a feat. Most people agree that it's harder to write clean fiction than nonfiction.

Then came the second victory.

My novel *Dead Rat Walking* (The Chicago Rat Shifter Book 1) is 60,000 words. It received 384 total edits. This is not an apples-to-apples comparison to *Cold Hard Magic*. This novel went through a copyedit and a proofread, whereas *Cold Hard Magic* only received a copyedit. This was also the first novel I used my editing workflow on. It is also a more complex novel, which is why my total edit count is higher than my average of around 275 edits.

Here's where things get interesting. *Rat City (The Chicago Rat Shifter* Book 2) is considerably longer at 76,000 words, but it received 370 total edits despite being 27 percent bigger!

That's amazing. It is evidence that my editing process is working.

I'm pretty proud of these accomplishments. Will my next novel demonstrate the same results? I don't know, but this appears to be a positive sign that my editing analytics approach is working, and it's making a real difference in how clean my manuscripts are.

All of this happened because I was lying in bed one night and had this idea that I couldn't let go. I kept exploring it because I didn't know how, but I felt in my gut that it would take me somewhere. Funny how that works.

The work isn't over. I need to keep using insights and following the data to find additional ways to cut down on repetitive edits. But this is definitely a moment for celebration!

WRITING AT GROUND EFFECT

I read a blog article by Kristine Kathryn Rusch, who talked about "ground effect" in writing. I recommend you read her blog article, but here is a summary of the idea:

- "Ground effect" is an aviation term for when a plane is landing, but it does not seem to want to land; instead, it feels as if it could keep traveling forever, using the ground as a cushion.
- In writing, Kris talks about how her husband Dean Wesley Smith and writer friend Matt Buchman adapted "ground effect" as a way to describe their writing productivity. When they wrote for several days in a row, they'd achieve "ground effect," and it would be much easier to write on subsequent days. However, whenever they missed a day, it was a lot harder to get back to ground effect.

In some respects, this reminds me of Newton's First Law: an object at rest will remain at rest and an object in motion will remain in motion until acted upon by a net external force. It's a lot of work to roll a boulder up a hill, but once you get going, it's easier. But heaven help you if that boulder comes to a full stop.

I've been thinking about this blog article and how it's also true for me. Historically, I've been so busy that I simply could not write every day. It was impossible when I was working a full-time job, raising a family, and attending law school classes in the evenings. Now that my calendar is emptier, I'm finding that it's easier to write every day. More interestingly, I'm finding that every day I write breeds another equal or better writing word count the next day.

When I wrote my novel *Rat City*, I hit ground effect very quickly at the beginning but lost it around the 25 percent mark and didn't recover until the 75 percent mark. Roughly half of the novel was me struggling to get back to ground effect. Some of the low word-count days were because of circumstances outside of my control, but I noticed that whenever I missed a day, I would miss for several more days until I could hit ground effect again.

There's something to be said about momentum. I've said for a while that good word-count days are almost always followed by bad word-count days. That's true for me.

This got me thinking about some observations on writing (at least for me):

During any given novel, the very high and very low word-count days almost cancel each other out. The real progress is in the days where you're writing closer to your average.

Good writing days breed more good writing days and writing days where you "miss" breed more misses.

Once you have written a certain number of words, you will hit ground effect, which makes it easy to write for a long period.

It's always interesting to read about how other writers think about their productivity.

HOW I'M TRYING TO READ MORE

In writing the chapter about ground effect and writing, I realized that this is true of other areas in my life.

For the last few years, I've struggled with balancing writing and reading. With my crazy schedule, I often had to choose whether I would write, market, or read for any given day. Since I'm trying to grow my writing business, I often chose to write.

My experience is that it's never a good idea to pit writing and reading against each other. If you're an ambitious author like me, reading will almost always lose. That's why I listen to audiobooks—they help me continue reading books quickly.

I still read more books than the average person, but I don't read anywhere near the level I used to, which was one or two full-sized books per week. I desperately want to get back to that, but I know that it won't be possible as long as I work a full-time job.

Anyway, I noticed that when I have long streaks of reading every day, reading is easier. When I've been away from a book for a while, I struggle to get back into it. This is a basic observation, but something I've been aware of lately as I reconfigure my life to a new "normal" after scaling back many of my activities.

CREATING A HARDCOVER BOOK FOR THE FIRST TIME

Earlier this year, Amazon KDP introduced the worst-kept private beta of all time: hardcovers. I've had access to it for a while but didn't say anything because of a non-disclosure agreement (which was the worst-kept non-disclosure of all time). However, now the NDA is lifted, and just about everybody knows about the program…

I still think it's a better idea to go with Ingram Spark for hardcovers, but I do like that Amazon provides the option now. I don't want to be tied to Amazon's ecosystem, so I decided to break down and buy ISBNs (more on that later).

I decided to test out hardcover editions with my *Chicago Rat Shifter* series. The first book is 60K and the second book is 76K, so they're great candidates for a hardcover edition.

I simply emailed my designer and asked them to design a new hardcover print edition. It cost $50.

I signed up with Ingram Spark, who offers a special deal for members of The Alliance of Independent Authors (ALLi). Normally, they charge you to set up a book in their system, and they also charge for every revision. ALLi members get those fees waived. (Have you joined ALLi yet?)

I ordered proof versions of the hardcovers just to test them out and see the quality.

Not bad. I'm happy with how they turned out.

Finally, I published them. It's pretty cool to have hardcover editions for sale. They look great on a bookshelf. I should have done this a long time ago, but hey, it's never too late to do anything in self-publishing.

Moving forward, I'll create hardcovers for my books when it makes sense. I'll probably do it for all books over 50K—I don't think smaller books look good in hardcover, but that's a personal opinion.

A NEW APPROACH TO OUTLINING (IN THE DARK)

In a previous chapter, I discussed lessons I learned while writing my novel *Rat City*. It is the longest novel I have written to date, and it taught me some valuable lessons.

One of those lessons is that my current outlining process doesn't work for longer novels.

I write my novels "into the dark," which means that I write them without an outline. However, as I finish chapters, I document what I wrote. This is the outline I'm referring to. A plotter used an outline to help them figure out what to write; a writer who writes into the dark uses an outline to capture what they wrote. This, outlining when you're writing into the dark, is a practical tool, and your outlines are always 100 percent accurate (compared to plotter's outlines, which may not be).

Before *Rat City*, my outlining processes were as follows:

- I wrote a chapter.
- I created an outline that listed the POV, characters present, location, summary, and any character details.
- Rinse and repeat.

However, with *Rat City*, that process didn't work. I started noticing problems.

The first was that my outline, while accurate at the macro level, wasn't helping me keep track of *micro* details in the story. For example, there is a character who has chains running down his torso and legs in Chapter 20. Those chains become very important near the end of the story…but I accidentally described them as ropes instead! Naturally, I caught the problem and corrected it, but my outline should have helped me avoid that. It didn't.

The second problem was my characters' actions. In one chapter, I had my hero agree to meet a friend for ice cream. When I first wrote the draft, he tells her to meet him at a park entrance and they'll walk over to the parlor. But when it's time to meet, I had him show up at the parlor instead, where she was waiting for him. In another scene, my heroine agrees to meet his mom for a birthday gathering, but her mom shows up at her house!

In other words, the characters' actions didn't reflect their words. There were lots of little problems like this that I easily fixed during self-editing, but there were more of these issues than I like to see. Usually, my drafts are clean. *Rat City* was not.

There are also other elements that need to be closely tracked during drafting, such as any injuries characters sustain, wardrobe changes, and so on.

I thought about my outlining process. Is there a way I can manage details more precisely so that I don't create these sorts of issues moving forward? Nothing makes a reader put a book down faster than continuity errors.

Is there a way I can use my outline better so that I can write the story consistently? I am fine with spending a little more time on the outline if needed.

I recently switched to Microsoft Excel for my outlines. I like Excel better because I house my Editing Analytics Chapter Scoring Model there (see previous volumes for more information). I thought, "Since I'm using Excel for outlining, what if I used it to improve my outlining process?"

Most importantly, I wanted to find answers to the following questions:

- How can I outline so effectively that I don't need to read the novel again?
- How can I use an outline to help me keep the *series* consistent?

My initial idea was to create a form macro that would capture the important details and store them in a database that I could refer to throughout the novel (or series). The database would help me manage my story more globally. However, that was too complicated and would have required time and money, which I didn't want to spend.

I ended up amending my outline so that I captured more of the micro details.

Here was the result.

I tested the method by redoing the outline for *Dead Rat Walking* and capturing micro details. Not surprisingly, I found some very minor issues that needed correcting. Nothing serious—just little details that most people won't notice.

The outline also lets me see the story not as a story, but as a series of data points. For example, I can filter the outline down to all the chapters with a certain character and then track their appearance over time.

For example, the hero's sister in *Dead Rat Walking* has a distinct look: blonde ponytail, starry-night bandanna, stud in her cheek, dragoon tattoo on her arm, and a camo tank top.

When I filtered down to her chapters, I noticed that I described her well in the first couple of chapters, but then I failed to describe her in the middle of the book. Using the Excel sheet, I quickly found the chapters where she needed a little characterization, and I used this knowledge to surgically add some details that were consistent with the description above, like the hero seeing her ponytail bob across the bar, or her untying her bandanna and tying it again in a messy knot over her head. Or coffee stains on her camo tank top because she owns a coffee shop. Just a little characterization is all the reader needs. My new outline method helped me identify surgical gaps like this one.

There's no doubt in my mind that this outlining method is much better. It's effective for small *and* large novels. It takes me a little more time with the outline. Before the new method, it took me approximately two minutes to jot down the events and details of each chapter. This new process will take me approximately seven minutes per chapter. That's around 3.5 hours outlining for a 40-chapter novel.

But consider the benefits:

- By forcing myself to *write down* the micro details in summary form, I'm more likely to remember them later.
- The micro details are well-organized, succinctly written, and easy to sort and filter on the spreadsheet.

This minor enhancement to my workflow should help me write cleaner first drafts faster and more effectively.

ANOTHER OUTLINING TEST

My new outlining method worked so well for my *The Chicago Rat Shifter* series that I wanted to apply it to my current *The Good Necromancer* series.

The two series couldn't be more different. *The Good Necromancer* is written in the first-person POV and the books are shorter and easier to manage. *The Chicago Rat Shifter* series is written in the third-person POV and the books are much bigger and have more details.

More importantly, the flow of information in the novels is different. When you're writing in the third-person POV, you divulge details about characters and settings in a traditional, matter-of-fact way. They're presented as facts. In the first-person, information is presented as an opinion—the character will say something and then make an opinion about another character. The result is that first-person novels tend to be richer with world-building information, at least in my experience.

This is a problem when you're building an outline for writing into the dark.

Let me give you an example. In *The Good Necromancer* series, Lester's friend CeCe is a lich, which is a supernatural warden of the dead. He says in the novel, "In supernatural terms, CeCe is what we call a lich. A lich is an immortal warden of the dead, and a necromancer of the highest degree. They control the dead and prepare them to either ascend to the next plane or shatter from existence. Everything that happens in the spirit realm happens under the watch of the liches. They're smart, organized, and vengeful—not supernatural beings you want to cross. If you steal from them, they'll steal from you, only two times as bad. And if you delay their retribution by running away, they'll place a doom and a curse on your soul, wait patiently for you to die, and harvest you into the worst kind of undead servitude.

"When a necromancer of extraordinary ability dies, they can become a lich if they so choose, but only with the permission of the Lich King, who is tough to please. Trust me, I would know."

How does one classify the information that Lester shares? These aren't character details per se, and they're not setting details. It's simply lore of the world, which is very hard to capture systematically.

I found that my new outlining method didn't work as well with *The Good Necromancer*. The original outlines are pretty good. That said, I can see forgetting details in this series just like I did with *The Chicago Rat Shifter* series.

Here's how I decided to address the issue:

- Use the new outlining method for the series, including *Cold Hard Magic (Book 2)* because it's still useful.
- When I pick up Book 2, I'll read the outline first, followed by the first three chapters, ending with the last three chapters that lead to the current point where I left off. Then I'll start writing.
- When I start writing, I'll do a master loop. For example, if I pick up on Chapter 18, once I finish the chapter, I'll loop Chapter 18 and then review Chapter 1. Once I finish Chapter 19, I'll loop that chapter and then review Chapter 2. And so on.
- Every time I finish a chapter, I will review the same chapter in the previous books. For example, once I

finish Chapter 18, I'll review Chapter 18 in Book 1 and Book 1.5. This will help me connect more dots as I stitch the series together.

We will see how this goes. The more books you have in a series, the more work you have to do to keep everything consistent.

A THIRD OUTLINING TEST

This summer, I wrote a book about writing apps. I designed the book to be an edition-type book, meaning that it would be one that I revisit every few years because some of the information might be outdated.

Normally, I try not to write books that have a shelf life. It's not a smart long-term strategy to have to keep updating your books' content. However, I felt I had no other choice with this book, and the content demanded it.

When I write fiction, I outline my novels as I go. The outline becomes a reference document that helps me remember what happened.

Occasionally, I'll outline nonfiction. Mostly, I create a short table of contents of the different benefits I want people to get from the book, but it's not anything elaborate.

With my writing app book, I had to *plan* for obsolescence. I had to predict, as much as possible, which sections would most likely need to be updated in the future, and then I had to capture that information so I could access it. My goal is to make any needed edits as quickly as possible. How do I accomplish that?

I created an outline in Microsoft Excel. My worksheet had two tabs. The first tab tracked snippets of content that might need to be updated.

The second tab tracked all images in the book. This book has a *lot* of images (also another thing that is against common wisdom). I numbered each image on the spreadsheet, which corresponds to the image's file name. This way, I can identify which images need to be swapped quickly.

Thus concludes how I "outlined" a writing book for the first time. Will it work? No idea, but we'll see. It's better than doing nothing!

SOME QUICK MATH TO SUPPORT DAILY WRITING QUOTAS

I've often discussed how I have not been a writer who writes every day. I discussed this a little in a previous chapter.

Now that I have more time in my day, I've come around to the power of word quotas.

James Scott Bell said something that has always stuck with me over the years: to paraphrase, he said the only reason he is a career writer is because he adheres to a strict quota every day, rain or shine. I love that sentiment and want to do the same thing.

The question I asked: what should my quota be? I don't want a number that's too low, but I also don't want one that is too high.

I settled on 2000 words no matter whether it's fiction or nonfiction. My quota is in effect for six days a week, with a slightly easier 1000-word quota on Sundays.

Two thousand words a day of nonfiction is doable for me and 2000 of fiction is a slight stretch, particularly when I'm starting a new book or in a rough spot. How would my habits change with a quota? How would that affect writer's block?

At the time of this writing, I've been on a three-week streak and I've exceeded the quota every day.

A quota gives me great flexibility: on days where I hit the quota early, I don't have to continue writing—I can market, read, or do something else related to the writing business and know that I'm on a good path. Or, I can keep writing as if I have no quota. Either way, I benefit from having a day where the foundation is built on a solid word count.

Two thousand words per day is:

- One 50,000-word novel approximately 25 days
- 12.48 novels per year (assuming one month off)

That's only if you meet the quota! Imagine what these numbers would be with a consistent, healthy number of higher word days. It wouldn't be hard to exceed one million words per year, which is out of this world.

Those numbers add up fast. They have inspired me to keep a quota. This is a break from how I've conducted my writing business in the past, so we'll see how it goes.

QUALITY ASSURANCE CHECKLIST

At almost every job in the world, there is someone who checks your work. Quality Assurance (QA) is one of the most anxiety-inducing and infuriating terms you can ever utter to someone on the job.

Some workplaces dangle QA scores over employees' heads like carrots, making them chase the impossibility of perfection. In other jobs, QA exists to sabotage and destroy people's prospects of success.

Everybody wants to get better at their jobs, everybody makes mistakes, everybody accepts that they're human, and (almost) everybody will graciously forgive the mistakes of others, but *nobody* likes being called out for their own mistakes. In some ways, QA is as human as humanity itself—full of contradictions.

What does QA look like for an author? For starters, there's no one breathing down your back, waiting for you to screw up. In my estimation, we already come out ahead based on that fact alone.

We can use QA truly as a way to get better, because we know that releasing better books will lead to better sales.

Here's how I'm thinking about QA across my writer platform. I want to eliminate:

- typos and spelling errors in my books, book descriptions, and website
- inconsistent story details

- broken links in my books and on my site
- anything that creates a poor reader experience

What if I put together a checklist of items to check for? Each item would be a pass or fail. I could give that checklist to an assistant who could do the checking for me so that I have a neutral third party reviewing my platform. It would cost a little money, but any mistakes they find are probably costing me money anyway. This would be akin to an "audit" at a workplace. (I know, I shuddered when I wrote that last sentence, but you can't deny that this is a legitimate problem that an "audit" can fix!)

I could hire an assistant to do a platform audit every year or biannually. It's a great idea and a smart use of money.

ESTIMATING E-BOOK DELIVERY FEES

With my book *The Writing App Handbook*, I put a lot of images in it.

Images are a big no-no in e-books. The common wisdom is to not include images or think twice about the ones you do. I usually agree with this wisdom.

However, this book needed images. You can write a book on writing apps and not show people how they work! Honestly, a book is not the most elegant format to showcase this information, but I had an idea and I wanted to see what would happen if I executed it.

The Writing App Handbook has 73 images. All of them are screenshots from different writing apps on different operating systems.

The book is organized by features. Each chapter explains what the feature is generally and how it often shows up on different apps. I then illustrate this point by using screenshots of the feature in action.

It's a unique concept that I haven't seen in the writing space. I have no idea if it will work or not.

Anyway, with that many images, I have to worry about e-book delivery fees on Amazon. They charge $0.10 per megabyte, and the fee is subtracted from the commission of the book.

First, I made sure I compressed my images using free online websites. That reduced my average file size per image by about 50 percent.

Second, I estimated the delivery fee to help me pick the best price for the book. Did I need to charge more for this book to offset the delivery fees?

I used a quick Excel spreadsheet to make a rough estimate of what the delivery fee would be for each price point.

I estimated that my file size would be around 4 MB, and it ended up being 3.3 MB, which is actually pretty good, all things considered. At $4.99, I'm still clearing $3.00. With a more modest delivery, I would usually clear $3.30.

So, I decided that $4.99 was an appropriate price point. I was willing to sacrifice the additional $0.30.

We'll see how this book does, but this was an exercise I've never had to do before. My first novel had over 100 images, but I wasn't wise enough to think about compression, delivery fees, and price points before I published it.

LESSONS FROM MICHAEL CRICHTON

This year, I've been studying the works of Michael Crichton. I considered him a "virtual mentor," one whose work I learn from at my own pace, even though I don't know him and will never be able to meet him because he passed away in 2008.

Michael Crichton is the author of hit novels, such as *Jurassic Park*, *The Andromeda Strain*, and *Timeline*. He was also a producer and director of movies like *Westworld* and TV shows like *ER*. Crichton was and is considered by many to be a master of the written word, and he single-handedly shaped pop culture in the nineties. Everyone in the nineties watched the "Jurassic Park" movies and *ER*. It's undeniable that Crichton had a magic touch. A former doctor turned writer, he practically invented the technothriller genre. I consider him to be the Robert Louis Stevenson of the twentieth century. Every few hundred years, a writer comes along who captures the public's imagination with a novel that becomes part of the zeitgeist. For Robert Louis Stevenson, that novel was *Treasure Island*. For Crichton, it was *Jurassic Park*. In fact, I believe you can draw a straight line from Stevenson to Crichton. They're that similar, and Crichton said several times that Stevenson was an influence (they even both write novels that took place during the Middle Ages, for example).

In many respects, Michael Crichton is a kindred spirit for me. From what I could tell from his interviews and his nonfiction writings, we have very similar personalities and thought processes about how we approach the craft of writing and life in general.

Crichton was a man of controversy. People frequently point to sections in his work that they claim are racist, sexist, and xenophobic. I've read enough of Crichton's work to conclude that I don't think he was any of those things. If anything, he was a man of his times just like we are people of ours, and we can just agree to leave it at that.

And, we could also talk about his opinions on global warming, which I strongly believe were wrong. But we can only speculate on what he would have believed if he were alive today to see what's happening around the globe.

I believe that if Crichton were alive today, cancel culture would have come for him hard. Maybe they still will at some point. That's unfortunate. I don't care what anyone says about Michael Crichton as his legacy ages—I still admire the man. His work ethic, outlook on writing and humanity, and his contributions to the literary world were long-lasting and life-changing for a lot of readers. His contributions to Hollywood were equally so. There won't be another writer like him for a few hundred years. Writers like him are rare comets.

The older I get, the more I appreciate how nuanced people are. When I was young, I went out of my way to avoid the works of writers whose worldview contradicted my own. My mother would often watch biographies and read thick, doorstop books about historical figures' lives. I always asked her why she did it, and she told me it was to help her understand how to live her own life better. I thought that was ridiculous, and it never clicked with me until I got older and did a lot more living. Now I find myself more interested in biographies than I ever was as a young person.

As I studied Crichton, I found that I learned an immense amount from him while also disagreeing with him at the same time, often in the same sentence. That's such an interesting dynamic to have with someone. It's also a perfect mentorship.

In this chapter, I'll share some of the major lessons I learned from studying Crichton and his novels, interviews, and memoirs.

COUNTLESS CRAFT TECHNIQUES

Crichton was a master of the written word and I've learned and integrated some of his techniques into my own fiction.

Crichton taught me little things that readers never notice but that make a scene extraordinary:

- How to treat a conversation between two characters on the phone
- How to paint a three-dimensional character in less than 100 words
- Summary/abstract openings
- Pacing intensity
- How to create unlikable characters (because many of his heroes are unlikable)
- And so much more

GO PULP

Like many mega-bestsellers of his generation, Crichton started writing pulp novels under a pen name, John Lange. He wrote these novels while he was in medical school.

GATHER STORIES

In one of his final interviews, Crichton was asked about how he prepares his case when he wants to make a point about something (like spreading awareness about a disease). He talked about the process of "gathering stories."

For example, if I wanted to share the importance of proper strategic planning, I would start with the story of someone who didn't do it. John Smith, age 58, a data architect who wrote over 20 novels on the side and landed a hit novel that allowed him to quit his day job. When he suffers a heart attack and dies, he leaves behind a wife and three children in their 20s. Because his work was selling well, a court determines that the value of his estate is over one million dollars and his heirs have to pay taxes on it, which bankrupts them. They have to put up the family house for sale. When they declare bankruptcy, the bankruptcy court seizes John's books and sells them to the highest bidder. Now the family no longer has the rights to his books and they associate the books with pain instead of love. All because he had no idea that a court would do this. If he had, he would have made different choices.

Or, I could talk about Betty Anderson, a Generation Y writer who just graduated from college and wants to be a writer. She wants to write novels for a living but has no idea where to start. When a literary agent emails her, praising her work, she fawns and sells the copyright of her novel to a traditional publisher. Now she can't publish another book again because the book performs terribly and the publisher now owns the copyright to her book. Even worse, she can't publish another book without sending it to her agent for first right of refusal. Her dreams of making a living from her writing are severely hampered, and now she's in a depression because she listened to common wisdom.

That's how you might start gathering stories and present them if you want to open people's minds to something. It's a technique I will use in my nonfiction moving forward.

SCIENCE OVER CHARACTERS

Crichton said several times that the science in his novels always took precedence over his characters, and it's true. To paraphrase him, he said that emotional depth in writing is something that can't be done when there's a dinosaur outside your window. He believed that his characters were in a bigger, more important catastrophe, and individual traits were not as important.

It's such an interesting take on fiction that it made me think. Do I believe characters are less important in a story than the idea? I suppose it depends on the story.

It comes down to a debate between "important character" versus "important idea" debate. Do you care more about the characters or more about something else? I don't believe there is a wrong answer.

In an interview with Charlie Rose, Crichton expressed this view, and Charlie called him out on it, saying that Crichton himself was an interesting and memorable man—he was a doctor, wrote bestselling books, made Hollywood movies, had several wives, and traveled all over the world. Charlie asked point-blank why he didn't want to make his characters as interesting as he is in real life. Crichton gave a non-answer that didn't really answer the question in my opinion.

Yet, even though Crichton says that his characters aren't as important as the science in his books, he created some unbelievably memorable characters. Dr. Alan Grant from *Jurassic Park* comes to mind. The characters in *Timeline* were also very memorable. His other novels? Maybe not so much. I still enjoyed them.

That got me thinking about how maybe there is a time and a place to have memorable characters. Maybe they don't have to be memorable in every book you write. As long as you're telling a good story and getting what you want to get across, and readers are buying it, then it doesn't matter. Many writers would see that as sacrilege, but I find it intriguing. It takes some of the pressure off your writing when you don't force yourself to create insanely memorable characters.

PEOPLE DON'T KNOW WHY THEY DO WHAT THEY DO

Crichton had a fascination with Sigmund Freud. On the one hand, he admired him. On the other hand, he didn't believe a word the man wrote. He called him the greatest fiction author of the twentieth century.

In an interview, he said something that I've believed all along: people don't know why they do what they do. He didn't know why he did the things he did in life. I wrote these exact words in my book *Mental Models for Writers* in 2017, and I was surprised to hear a mega-bestseller say them decades before me.

GET THERAPY

Crichton talks about getting therapy in his interviews. He also writes about how he sought a therapist in his memoir *Travels*. Much of his need for therapy came from his difficult relationship with his father, but he also talked about how he used a therapist as a sounding board for mundane things that somehow helped him navigate his life. At the time of this interview, Crichton was one of the richest authors in the world. If he needed therapy, then we all need it.

DON'T DIE WITHOUT AN ESTATE PLAN

Crichton died without updating his author estate plans, which created a mess for his fifth wife, who was pregnant with his child.

Estate planning will be a focus for me in 2022. Crichton taught me that.

PLOT HOLES

Crichton's work, love it or hate it, was filled with plot holes. Readers conveniently passed over many of them, but some were too obvious and headshakingly bad...even though I still enjoyed the novels very much.

Take the novel *Timeline*, about a group of graduate students who travel back to the 14th century to rescue their professor, who is trapped there because of the evil machinations of a corporate CEO. (Spoilers ahead.)

In the novel, Crichton presents time travel as space travel instead. The characters aren't going back in time; they're traveling to another universe that happens to mirror our own. Makes sense.

However, then the characters do things in that universe that affect the present day, which completely contradicts the premise of time travel to begin with.

When it was published, *Timeline* was a blockbuster hit. All Crichton fans read it. It generated an awful Hollywood movie.

Furthermore, Crichton had a traditional publisher. Did no one at the publisher say, "Wait a minute. This doesn't make sense." You're telling me that his agent, his developmental editor, copyeditor, line editor, proofreader, and oodles of other people who probably got their hands on the book didn't see this plot hole? Get outta here...

There are really only a few explanations for a plot hole this bad:

- Everyone missed it.
- Crichton had an iron will and kept it in to protect the science. He says in every interview that the science is more important than the characters, and by inference, the story.
- He/they did it on purpose to get people talking. It was a sales tactic.
- His books were so full of plot errors like this that the editors cleaned them up considerably, and what we ultimately got was a miracle.

I don't know, but if anyone tries to argue that traditionally-published books are better-produced than self-published books...

WRAPPING IT UP

Michael Crichton taught me a lot and I will forever be a fan of his work. If I'm ever half as successful as him one day, he will have taught me some important lessons that will no doubt have contributed to that success.

DICTATION COURSE

With my book *How to Dictate a Book*, I wanted to do something different.

I did competitive intelligence on all the books about dictation on the market. My biggest disadvantage is that the popular dictation books right now came out several years ago, and they were synonymous with "dictation books."

The current books went in-depth into Dragon, covered the "why" of dictation, and answered the most common questions. What else could I add to a body of work where everything has already been said?

I spent quite some time trying to figure out my "angle." What was my value proposition? Why should someone buy my book on dictation when they could buy everyone else's that have already been on the market for several years?

After some time, I figured out the angle. If I am a new writer wanting to know how to dictate a novel, is a book really the best way to learn dictation?

In other words, should I really be writing a book about this?

I decided that a book still made sense. Instead, I decided to do something that I've never done: I created a video course as a companion to the book. No email address required, no upsell other than a mention of my YouTube channel and writing books at the end of the course, and no other BS. Just click and watch. I nested the link to the companion course after the downloadable sample so people wouldn't download the sample, watch the course, and leave me hanging.

In the video course, which was approximately 10 videos with each video being up approximately less than 10 minutes each, I showed people how to dictate. I went through my dictation setup, let them see and hear several of my dictation sessions, and answered many of the common dictation concerns in video format. My rationale was that dictation has a steep learning curve, and it would do someone well to see another person practicing the art. For the cost of a cheap e-book, a writer could get all of the dictation information they needed in a 100-page book and/or a 90-minute course.

Did I leave money on the table? You betcha. But I was more curious than anything else how people would receive the book. Would they say that I was full of crap or what they find it helpful?

Detractors of the current books on the market often attacked them because the books were very short. Frankly, I think this is unfair. There just isn't that much to cover about dictation. I would be far more suspicious of a 300-page book on dictation than I would of a 90-page book on the topic. I find that beginners want more information than actually exists. Would my course help satisfy those demands?

Most creators would never create a companion course for a book and give it away for free. I've got that lane all to myself. I just charged a little more for the book than usual. I know that if I write a compelling book and offer good value for the money, it will pay dividends for me in the future because I'll have a reader who trusts, knows, and likes me. Plus, video is a natural medium for me and I know I can do well there if I can just get readers to click the link to the course.

Also, I built on the knowledge that I learned from my previous courses. It took me approximately six days to write the dictation book, and that also included filming, editing, and uploading the videos for the course. It took me almost no time at all.

We'll see what happens.

BEAST MODE RECAP

On July 1st, I began my "Beast Mode" challenge. I've decided to do it annually because it's a lot of fun.

During "Beast Mode," I write as many books as humanly possible for 90 days. I rack up big word counts and have a lot of books to show for it at the end of the challenge.

This year, I changed up the challenge:

- I introduced fiction into the mix (last year was only nonfiction).
- I let readers vote on which books they wanted me to write. Once I reached the 75 percent mark, I opened up voting for the next book.

I had some significant challenges with Beast Mode this year: There were also some events planned during Beast Mode that I needed to prepare for:

- Two family vacations, so I had to prepare for writing on-the-go.
- Four speaking engagements during the 90-day Beast Mode period.
- A new school routine for my daughter in August, which would drastically change my household daily routine.

The first family vacation fell on the first week of Beast Mode.

Yikes. We went to Orlando and West Palm, and I had to rely on writing on my phone. That worked very well, and I wrote on every day of the vacation—if you looked at my word counts alone, you would have never known I was on vacation.

The second family vacation was over Labor Day. We drove from Iowa to Wyoming. Fortunately, I didn't drive the whole way, so when I wasn't driving, I was writing on my phone.

The speaking engagements were tougher. I did have to take a week off writing to fulfill them, since they were paid engagements and I signed contracts. However, I decided to extend the challenge by two weeks to accommodate that. Problem solved.

Here is what I accomplished for this year's "Beast Mode" challenge:

- Nine books (three novels, six nonfiction books), which will be around 250,000 words
- Two additional published books that were written before the challenge
- A Writing App Database designed and developed from scratch
- A 90-minute free video course on dictation
- A 90-minute free video course on Microsoft Word macros and editing
- One article for an upcoming issue of *Writer's Digest* (which was accepted and will be appearing in Jan/Feb 2022)
- Two podcast interviews
- Four speaking engagements (*Writer's Digest*, ALLi SelfPub Con, Inkers Con, and Jessica Brody's Writing Mastery Academy)

I just love "Beast Mode."
Here are the lessons I learned:

- I applied the lessons from the 2020 challenge to this year—namely, how to write while on vacation and amid a natural disaster.
- In 2020, I wrote seven books in three months. This year, I wrote nine (which included three novels). That's 28 percent more.
- In 2020, I wrote approximately 220,000 words for the challenge. This year, I wrote over 250,000. That's 13 percent more.
- A daily minimum helped me considerably during the challenge. I implemented it halfway through. If I had maintained daily minimums throughout the entire challenge, I would have written even more.
- Much like last year, my email response time suffered during the challenge. Otherwise, my writing business worked pretty well on autopilot.
- If I kept the writing pace I maintained for the challenge, I would write over one million words.
- I also took all the books published during the challenge and compiled a limited-edition *Beast Mode Collection* and sold it directly on my website.

The big lesson I learned this year was that my writing speed is getting faster, but the quality has remained the same (editing-wise). That's powerful. It means if I keep practicing the craft and keep doing what I have been doing, interesting things can happen.

And then I thought, what if every month in 2022 was "Beast Mode"? What if I made my "Beast Mode" speed my regular speed? I am confident I can do it. What would next year look like if I did that?

Barbara Cartland is considered to be one of the most prolific authors in the English language. When she died in 2001 at the age of 99, she had published 723 books. She started publishing at 23, which is right around the same age I started (25). That means she wrote approximately 9.5 books per year. I'm doing that already—better than that most years, actually. Why not shoot to publish 724 novels before I die so I can beat her record?

I don't care what critics and snobs say. ("Anyone who writes 9.5 books per year must be a hack…") Screw them and the horses they ride on. I care about getting ideas out of my head, having fun, and building a legacy I am proud of that will provide for my family and heirs when I'm gone.

Of course, there's the issue of burnout, but I'm about as far from burnout as a writer can get. Every day, I'm having so much fun when I write, and I can't wait to sit down at the keyboard and see what's next in my stories…even when I'm not making enough money to make a living at my writing yet. Writing remains fun, and so long as it remains fun, I hope to maintain my current writing speed.

There's the issue of health and dying too, so hey, I might as well write as much as I can while I'm here.

But, back to the idea of 2022 being a "Beast Mode" Year…that's such a fascinating concept that I just might do it.

BECOME A WORLD-CLASS MARKETER

WHY TAKING TIME TO HELP PEOPLE MATTERS

My father-in-law will be ready to retire soon. In the United States, that means it's time to enroll for Medicare (senior healthcare) and Social Security (senior income). Enrolling in both programs can be a nightmare to manage on your own, so many people hire advisers who take care of the hard work. This way, you can rest assured that you will be enrolled correctly and will receive your benefits.

My wife met with a Medicare adviser who helped her navigate this process for my father-in-law. She knew nothing about Medicare or Social Security, so all of this was new and challenging for her.

The adviser, an independent agent, met with her on Saturday morning and spent an hour with her, explaining everything and how to get started. At this point, my wife hadn't committed to him and it was a pure sales call.

When she came home, she was surprised at the fact that this unknown stranger spent so much time helping her.

When it was time to buy, my father-in-law went with the adviser's services.

What does this have to do with writing? Maybe it's true that spending time with people with no expectation of a return is a helpful sales tool.

Most people are so busy that they run their schedules like despots. "I'm too busy," or "I can't spare the time to help them with that," or "I," "I," "I"...But what about *them*?

What if a reader emails you a heartfelt email?

What about a speaking event that is at a convention that has absolutely nothing to do with your genre, your career, or your ambitions?

What about that book that readers keep asking you to write?

What about giving a book away for free?

Do you have the time?

When you take time to help people with no expectation of a return, then people may choose to work with you more. That doesn't mean you should give your time away to everyone who asks, but sometimes doing things that others would never do is a smart business strategy.

TEACHING BRANDING

I spoke at this year's annual *Writer's Digest* Conference. One of my talks about was branding. It was called "The First Impression: Building a Magnetic Author Brand." The goal of the workshop was to teach authors how to think about their branding, how to build it, and how to create lasting relationships with readers.

To my surprise, it was one of the most difficult talks I've ever prepared. For starters, I was a little out of my element; I tend to do better when I am teaching writing, productivity, or apps, but I chose to do this topic because it interested me and I'm pretty good at personal branding.

I struggled to prepare material for the talk. Usually, I can find the "angle" for any talk. The "angle" is when you have an intuitive sense of what both the venue organizer and the audience want. When you nail the angle, you give a talk that crushes it on every level. The preparation is easier, the audience is more receptive, and it's more fun. When you don't nail the angle, it's painful.

I scrapped the material for the talk several times, electing for a different angle, but I don't think I ever found it.

The talk wasn't bad by any means; I delivered on my promise and I certainly think I gave people some good information. However, it wasn't my best, and that bothered me.

I discovered that branding is extraordinarily difficult to teach.

In my personal life, I excel at personal branding. I've talked about my professional career in this series many times, so I don't need to rehash it. My YouTube channel is also an exercise in personal branding. So I get it.

But it's so hard to teach because so much of branding is about your intuition.

The first lesson I taught in the talk was to figure out your story and your "why." Some people know their why, but they struggle to put together a story around it. My message was to figure out how to create a story and fail your way to the right message. That didn't resonate.

The next lesson I taught in the talk was to draw upon your work experience to build a brand. I talked about how most people know how to interview for a job (which is the ultimate exercise in personal branding), but even though the skills are the same, they can't translate that to *selling* to readers.

In a job interview, you have to:

- Explain how your experience relates to the job at hand by telling clear and powerful stories
- Write a résumé that gets past automated resume scanners and the scrutiny of Human Resources and hiring managers
- Ask for the job

To relate this to selling a book, you have to:

- Explain to readers why your book is for them by telling a clear and powerful story (in your description)
- Create packaging that gets visibility in algorithms and catches the attention of readers browsing tiny thumbnails
- Ask for the sale

The similarities are uncanny, but no one thinks about that. When writers enter the writing world, they leave their professional experience at the door, which is a shame.

This lesson *really* resonated with the audience, and I received the most questions around it.

Finally, we talked about the "common" branding stuff, like picking colors, author websites, and so on. I personally didn't like this part, and I don't think the audience did either.

When I reflect on the talk, I realized that I made a basic mistake: I was too scattered. If I ever get the chance to do this presentation again, I'll retool it.

HOW A COVER EVOLVES

I taught a masterclass for *Writer's Digest* called "The Ultimate Self-Publishing Masterclass." In it, I walked students through the process of self-publishing. I taught them how to find an editor and cover design, how to think about business, and how to market their books.

One section was on cover design, which was the most popular part. I dissected the major parts of every book cover:

- Foreground
- Background
- Title
- Subtitle/Tagline/Series Statement
- Author Name

My premise was that if you learn to think of a book cover as a series of signals, it's easier to get it right. Each of the elements I listed above gives off a reader signal. The key is learning *what* signal each one should give off, and the best way to learn that is by studying other successful self-published books in your immediate subgenre.

If you learn to isolate book cover elements, you can also provide better feedback to your designer. I shared the evolution of my book cover for my novel *Old Dark*. I shared the first draft of the cover (which was not good) and each subsequent draft until the final one, which is one of my more successful book covers. I also shared emails from which I demonstrated how to communicate with my designer.

Here is the first draft of the cover:

Here is the feedback I gave the designer:

"There's so much to love about this design, but it didn't immediately jump out as fantasy to me. At first glance it felt more like a crime/thriller cover.

I liked:

- The fact that the dragon element is the first thing that you see
- That you took an abstract approach to representing the dragon (superb) The prominence of the author name

What didn't work for me:

- The fonts Background
- Also reminded me of The Hunger Games."

Note how I broke my feedback into short bullet points based on each element of the cover. I didn't say very much either.

Here was the next draft:

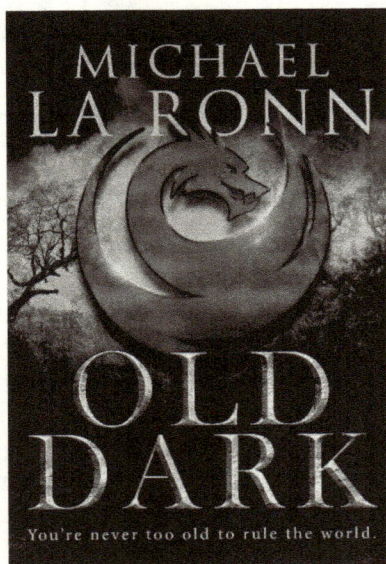

And here's what the final draft looks like:

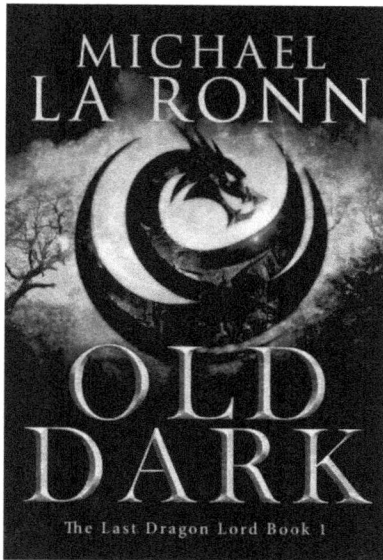

I found that the students loved to see this evolution.

I took the exercise one step further and made it interactive: I taught them how to do market research. I asked for a volunteer. I asked everyone to share a one-sentence description of their book and the subgenre. I picked one with a very clear premise and subgenre: historical fantasy based in ancient Greece. As the students watched, I went to Amazon and found several book covers that were similar to what she described. Then I took the best one and broke it into its respective elements, with feedback from the students.

Overall, the exercise was successful. It helped students think about book covers differently, and it made cover design less overwhelming for them.

The exercise was so successful that I plan to do it again.

NEVER ASSUME

The more public speaking events I do, the more I re-learn the importance of never making assumptions.

When you're speaking, never assume anything.

Never assume that your audience knows anything about your topic.

Never assume that your audience understands jargon or acronyms that are obvious to you.

Never assume that you can skip out on providing basic context.

If you do, it creates friction. When you're at an event in person, you can see friction in people's eyes and body language. Online, it's harder.

While teaching my "Ultimate Self-Publishing Masterclass" for *Writer's Digest*, my audience ranged from beginners who knew almost nothing about self-publishing to published authors. When explaining basic self-publishing concepts, I had to slow down and provide more context than usual.

I developed a rule of thumb for myself when I'm public speaking called ABC—Always Be Contexting. Sometimes all it takes to provide proper context is a few seconds. But I know when my ABC is successful because there's no friction in the room. If there is friction, it means that I need to stop and revisit my ABC because I must have said something that confused people.

Anyway, during the presentation, I found myself doing a few things that ultimately led to success:

- I never assume that people can see my screen well when I'm screen-sharing. I installed a "mouse locator" tool that puts a blue ring around my mouse, making it easier to see and follow.
- I never assume that people can see where my mouse is right away, so any time I was talking for more than a few minutes without moving my mouse, I wiggled my mouse first to help people find the blue ring.
- Whenever I wiggled my mouse, I told people I was wiggling my mouse.
- I found myself saying simple, almost childlike statements when explaining self-publishing concepts.
- I found myself reading the audience's comments and knowing what they were thinking. After a while, you learn how to read the room and adjust your speech accordingly.

The experience helped me re-learn that if you think about marketing, it's very much the same. You should never make assumptions about what your readers will do. When a reader encounters your brand for the first time, the best rule of thumb is to pretend that:

- they've never heard of you before
- they don't know what book to buy
- they don't know why they should buy one of your books
- you need to explain your value proposition to them

If you approached marketing through that lens, then you'll make different decisions about your book description, book cover, website, email communications, social media, and other marketing channels. It's a useful framework that can grow your sales.

THE POWER OF REMINDER EMAILS

I don't do a good job of promoting my Writing Power Hour livestreams. I've spoken about them in previous volumes of this series.

On a whim, I sent an email to my list letting them know about one of my livestreams. I sent the email the morning of the event, approximately 30 minutes before it started. To my surprise, I had record attendance because people saw the email and joined the link. Several people said thank you for letting them know about the event.

I did the same thing for the next livestream, and it worked again. Several people again said that they appreciated the reminder emails.

My livestreams don't make me money, and I don't get anything out of it other than a nice word count and a great time engaging with my community.

Moving forward, if I can remember to do it, I will time my monthly email communications around the power hour; that way, my audience knows that if they get an email from me, the power hour is coming up soon.

HOW I LAND SPEAKING ENGAGEMENTS

Someone wrote me recently and asked how I land so many speaking engagements. They wanted to know what I did to land them.

I had to think about it. I don't really hunt for speaking events. They usually find me.

I've only made a pitch to speak at an event once. Once, and that was for 20Books Vegas. Other than that, my strategy is to let the venue organizers come to me.

Why has that strategy worked?

First, my YouTube channel. I have over 300 videos on writing and self-publishing, and every minute of every day, someone is watching one of my YouTube videos. My entire portfolio of YouTube videos is like a sales force. They're constantly engaging, selling, and networking with people without me having to do a thing. It helps that I have decent video production, though it's not perfect. It also helped that I had two podcasts for several years; those were also excellent promotional vehicles.

Inevitably, organizers reach out to me because of videos I did years ago. As long as I keep making videos, I can keep deepening my pipeline. I like to think that every video I make is a demo of what it will be like if I speak at an event.

The second reason I attract speaking events is my speaking page. When an organizer sees one of my videos (or books) and goes to my website, I have a page called "Press" that highlights my accomplishments and recent speaking events. When possible, I include links to my prior events. I treat every speaking engagement as a calling card for the next one.

The third reason I attract speaking events is that I do my very best at every event, paid or not. I treat unpaid engagements as if they were paid, and paid engagements as if I were getting six figures. If you impress venue organizers, they'll invite you back, or spread the word about you to their friends.

That's it. I spend shockingly little time looking for speaking events. Perhaps one day the opportunities will dry up; that doesn't bother me because it just means I'll be able to spend even more time writing! Speaking is not an active part of my strategy. I love doing it and I'm good at it, but I don't want to build a career on it. I anticipate that a problem moving forward will be that I'm invited to speak to *too many* events and will have to cut back. That's why I don't hunt for events. If you look at the career of many successful influencers, they follow a predictable pattern:

- When they start, they'll speak at any venue to get exposure.
- Once they become successful, they're so in-demand, they have to start saying no to events; they're speaking frequently, traveling, and making good money.
- At some point, they burn out and stop speaking because it's too much money and effort and it takes them away from why they started speaking in the first place: the thing they're speaking about. They walk away from a significant chunk of income and opportunities for their own mental health.

I'm somewhere between steps 1 and 2. I'm not in any hurry and would prefer not to follow the path to step 3.

THINKING UNIVERSALLY
ABOUT MARKETING

I've been thinking lately about how many elements of marketing connect to form a bigger picture.

Sure, we want to sell as many books as possible, but it's quite amazing how we can integrate marketing into so many aspects of our platform.

I have been focused on the holy triumvirate lately: the book cover, book description, and first chapter of the book. Get those right and marketing becomes easier.

Here are some ways I'm trying to unlock the power of the triumvirate.

First, write a great book.

Second, commission an effective cover design using reader signals. I've discussed reader signals in previous volumes.

Third, integrate the book cover and first chapter with the book description. The first chapter is everything; the book description should reference it and the book cover should match the feel of that first chapter. Then you can also reference and match the feel with your ad copy and email marketing.

When I do market research, I only focus on the first chapter. How does the first chapter of the book compare to other similar books? What about the cover and book description? Beyond that, I trust my story to do its job.

It's easy to focus on advertising and promotion to sell books, but so much of book sales is in marketing, and so much in marketing is about little decisions around positioning and branding. My experience is that the most important marketing decisions don't cost any money other than your book cover. Thinking universally about your books can help you improve your sales.

INDIE AUTHOR = E-BOOKS AND PAPERBACKS (MINIMUM)

I was working with a family friend to help him prepare their first book for publication. He just graduated from college, and he's three years younger than I was when I discovered the joys of self-publishing.

That's encouraging. It's amazing to see young people interested in self-publishing, but there are still a lot of myths and misinformation out there.

Our first conversation went like this.

Friend: I'm going to publish a book.

Me: That's awesome! How will you be doing it? Self-publishing or finding an agent.

Friend: Self-publishing for sure.

Me: Great. How can I help?

Friend: I found an editor and cover designer, but I'm not sure how to format the book.

Me: I can help you with that.

Friend: Yeah, I really want to hold this book in my hands.

Me: [Explains how to create a paperback version of a book]

Friend: I'm almost at the finish line.

Me: Yes, you're close. Have you thought about KDP Select?

Friend: What's that?

Me: It's a program on Amazon where you can be exclusive in exchange for visibility benefits. It's a short-term tool for new authors to promote their e-book versions. From what you're describing about the book, I believe you should give it a try.

Friend: e-books? You can create e-books?

[Record Skips]

The conversation was going great, and then suddenly, we were in the Twilight Zone. He was so focused on creating a print book that he missed the biggest opportunity to make money as a self-published writer: e-books. I'm not surprised about his preference for print books (nothing wrong with that), but the fact that e-books *weren't even on his radar* was a little scary.

For the record, my friend is also a newly-minted English major. That no one even mentioned publishing e-books in an English program in one of the biggest colleges in the Midwest US should tell you something. When I graduated in 2010, no one was talking about e-books in academic circles. It sounds like very little has changed in academia in 10 years...

None of this was his fault. I coached him and brought him around to what needed to be done.

But it just goes to show you that even though *you and I* think that self-publishing is relatively common, and *we* know that e-books are essential, and that we can publish our books on great places like Amazon, Kobo, Google Play, and more, most people don't.

Self-publishing is a growing club, but it's still an exclusive club.

This chapter is a public service announcement that self-publishing properly requires an e-book *and* a trade paperback edition, minimum. I'm glad I got the opportunity to help my friend on his journey.

BECOME A TECHNOLOGY AND DATA-DRIVEN WRITER

DEAR RETAILERS

Dear Amazon, Apple, Google Play, Kobo, Draft2Digital, Smashwords, StreetLib, PublishDrive, and every other retailer on the planet that sells e-books and paperbacks,

I have an urgent request.

I recently published a bunch of books, and the experience made me keenly aware of an issue that is present on your platform. If you fixed this issue, it would make many authors happy.

The issue? Setting prices!

When I upload a new book, I have to specify how much it costs in each currency. That's great, and I have no problems with that. However, why can't I designate a default amount for each currency?

Instead of rounding up to the next dollar per the current exchange rate, I believe it would be much more useful to designate currency defaults.

For example, if I price a book at $4.99 USD, your platform always uses current exchange rates to round to the best estimation of other currencies, like £2.68 GBP.

What if I want all of my books at $4.99 to be priced at £2.99 instead of £2.68? I can't do that. Instead, I have to type in £2.99 every time, which, naturally, poses the danger that I might accidentally type in the wrong amount, like £299 GBP. (That's if I even remember to type in the same amount. I suspect that many authors don't price their books consistently, and that's another part of this problem.)

Please allow authors to set pricing defaults so that all they need to do is set a price in their home currency and it automatically defaults to the author's chosen price points everywhere else in the world. This would eliminate work on the author's part and make the publishing process much smoother. If an author enters the wrong price, that affects your retail sales too.

This is something that authors have needed since the advent of self-publishing, and scores of them would adore you if you implemented this feature, myself included.

If you have any questions, give me a call.

HOW I BUSTED MY WEBSITE

Readers have been asking me to update authorlevelup.com to include Secure Socket Layer (SSL) for a while now. I'm just now getting around to it. It's good to update your site with SSL because Google penalizes you in search results and your site appears "unsecure," and this is no good when people are purchasing books from you directly.

To my surprise, it didn't take long at all! It was a rather pleasant surprise. I was ready to invest several hours in the task.

All I had to do was click a few buttons on the dashboard of my hosting provider.

It was that easy...and then all hell broke loose.

Readers emailed me to let me know that links on my site weren't working. The oddest part about it was that they were links that I *knew* should have been fine because I did a sweep of my site earlier this year.

It turned out that all the links and images on my site were broken. I didn't realize that SSL affects them.

Ugh...

I had to hire a developer to help me fix the issue. I have tons of links and images on my site and I didn't have time to fix them all myself.

It took a week to fix. It sucked.

And guess what the worst part is? I still haven't updated michaellaronn.com yet!

I know what to do now, and if I could have done it all over again, I would do it differently:

- I would have hired a developer to help me with this from the beginning. They would have handled the broken links and images issue.
- The morning of the update, I would have put a banner on the top of my home page that explained I'm doing some construction on the site and to pardon my dust for a few days. I would ask people to use my contact form if they need help (and I would prioritize any emails from readers).
- After the update, I would have checked every single book page for any issues. I would have used a broken link checker plugin to help me catch any broken links. Broken links are bad news.

Anyway, that's what I would have done. The good news is that this strategy will be exactly what I do when I update michaellaronn.com with SSL!

Lesson learned.

BUILDING A CORPUS

Most forms of artificial intelligence (AI) I know of require big corpus sizes. A corpus is a body of text that is used to train the AI software. You can't train an AI with little data sets. You need very, very big ones. Like millions of words big.

That got me thinking about what it might be like for an author to have an entire corpus of their own work.

I have almost 2.5 million words published.

What if a developer could treat my entire corpus as a training ground for an AI tool they build for me? Sure, the more data the better, but I love the idea of my and only my data. No privacy issues, no copyright problems. My data is like my land—I own it and can do whatever I want with it.

I envision a tool that helps me with my editing. It reads my work, compares it to the changes an editor recommended to make recommendations tailored to my work. This is the opposite of how modern spellcheckers work—they compare your work to other users around the world, using the collective power of a network to improve its quality.

What if I could designate certain elements of style that I wanted an app to check for? Or, what if I wanted it to search only for comma issues? What if I didn't care about other people's comma usage, and I wanted to set my *own* rules?

This is possible if you could train software with your own work. We're probably a few years away from that being possible. There will be a day when developers can train AI software with smaller corpora.

But guess who has the biggest corpora of all? Traditional publishers. Since the beginning of the *Indie Author Confidential* series, I have stated that that if traditional publishers figure out AI, it will increase competition with indies.

When you think about marketing, traditional publishers own the rights to their corpus and can use it for whatever they want. They have treasure troves of data, and fortunately for them, they've digitized most of their books. They're uniquely positioned to take advantage of AI, but I haven't seen much activity yet. Probably because it's expensive, they can't see the value in it yet, and because, well, capitalism and short-term thinking.

They won't be clueless forever. When they start exploring it, it will be very clunky because they'll struggle with bureaucracy and misguided strategy at first, but eventually, they'll figure this out. It's inevitable.

But for now, I'll keep dreaming about my corpus.

EDITING DATA DEEP DIVE

This is a long and meandering chapter on editing data and there is *not* a lesson at the end. I'm just capturing my thoughts about some work I recently did on my editing analytics project.

I have my edited manuscripts for all but seven of my novels. The seven I don't have are my earliest novels. I wasn't as savvy about backing up my work then as I am now.

The previous chapter on corpora got me thinking a lot about the work I do have. I have 25 novels' worth of editing data—copyedits and proofreads. It's probably at least 5,000 edits, maybe more.

What if I could load all my manuscript edits into Excel, with each sentence in a cell? What if I could (quickly) categorize each edit by its type: spelling, grammar, format, and story?

It would be fascinating to create a chart that showed you the percentage of edits you received in each category. It would be even more fascinating to dig deep into each category. What types of words drive your spelling errors? Which punctuation marks give you the most trouble? Does your editor give feedback on certain elements of your story? How have you improved in different areas over time?

This knowledge alone would be sobering for a lot of people. Most people would say, "How can I do better than this?"

Next, I would love, love, love to overlay my edits with Word's Editor, Grammarly, ProWritingAid, PerfectIt, and my Word macro set to determine which edits each of these apps could have caught versus my editor. I didn't start using Grammarly regularly until about two years ago, and my macros are only a few months old. I believe there would be power in knowing what edits you could have caught before sending them to your editor. That's how much time you could have saved your editor.

I would also love to experiment with self-editing. I had the idea to write a novel in Word and track my self-editing changes. What percentage of the total number of edits would my self-editing account for? My hypothesis is that the number of self-edits would eclipse the number of *all* other edits by several times. I believe that the bulk of all editing happens in self-editing, which is why improving your manuscript *before* you send it to an editor is so critical.

Let's take this even further. What if, during this experiment, I could track my manuscript's progress through time by seeing how many edits each phase of editing generates?

For example (and to use simple numbers):

- Self-editing results in 1 edit per 75 words
- After Word's Editor is done, it improves to 1 edit per 77 words
- After Grammarly, it improves to 1 edit per 100
- After ProWritingAid, it improves to 1 edit per 101
- After PerfectIt, it improves to 1 edit per 102
- After copyediting, it improves to 1 edit per 200
- After proofreading, it goes from 1 edit per 225

This example goes from 75 edits per 100 to 225 edits per 100, which is a 200 percent improvement.

DEEPER INTO THE RABBIT HOLE

My next goal would be to subdivide issues down to a root cause.

Take commas. In 2018, they represented approximately 55 percent of my edits. In 2021, they were 28 percent. The reason for the difference? Grammarly—it has fantastic comma accuracy, but it's not perfect.

How can I go from 28 percent to 14 percent? What would it take to bring the number of comma-related errors below 10 percent?

When I was creating my editing workflow, I played around with the idea of a comma checker app. The *only* thing the app would check for would have been commas. I wanted to know if it was possible to program the rules or comma usage into an app.

The short answer, after speaking with several data scientists, was probably not. The best tool for this is natural language processing (NLP), which is a type of artificial intelligence. One weakness with NLP is that it isn't good at sentence clauses. While there are some workarounds, it's not easy to have software determine independent and dependent clauses. If you want to program comma usage, then you need to know the clauses. This is why I believe that apps like Grammarly still haven't mastered comma usage.

Anyway, the ideal version of a comma checker isn't possible yet, but maybe it will be in the future.

For now, it's still worth thinking about because there is a potential solution.

Let's look at my novel *Dream Born*. It's 40,000 words and it generated 245 edits from my editor. One hundred thirty-six of those edits were commas (55 percent).

There are 2,841 total commas in the book, so approximately 7.6 percent of my commas have issues. Put another way, I'm using commas correctly 93 percent of the time. Is 93 percent good? I think so, but wouldn't 97-98 percent be better?

Looking at the trends, the most common errors were with coordinating conjunctions and serial commas. I can't catch the former, but software can definitely catch the latter.

I came up with an idea: a macro that could extract every sentence with a comma to a table with the chapter, page, and line identified. I could review the sentences in rapid succession and even filter in Excel to spot problems faster.

Should I look at EVERY SINGLE COMMA in my manuscript? God, no. That would take an eternity. Like I said, I'm using commas correctly 93 percent of the time, so a sampling is best. This can easily be accomplished with a quick filter in Excel.

But what commas should I look at?

There's something else I know from analyzing my data and creating a chapter scoring model (discussed in previous volumes): I am more likely to make errors in chapters that have certain indicators (flow, important character introduced, 2500+ words, and the existence of writer's block in a chapter). What if I reviewed only THOSE chapters, and what if I did a random sampling of commas within those chapters to review (like every 10th comma).

For example, if I have 2841 commas, then I would want to look at 7 percent of them. That would be around 200 commas. Or, maybe around 100 sentences since many sentences have more than one comma.

The idea is that I might catch enough to impact the number of comma-related edits I receive.

That got me thinking about another crazy idea: what if I hired an editor *solely* for commas? It's a very silly idea, and not terribly practical by common wisdom. But what if I hired an editor to look at, say 1000 commas, which would represent the most predictively problematic chapters? How many comma-related errors would they catch?

I decided to pretend I was a comma-only editor to find out.

First, I hired a developer to write a macro that identified every sentence with a comma, extracted it to a table, and identified the chapter name, page number, and line number. I then copied that table into Excel and used a simple formula to calculate the number of commas in each sentence.

I took a random sampling of 61 sentences and read through them. In this review, four sentences needed to be corrected because there were bona fide errors. That's approximately 6 percent, and pretty consistent with my earlier stat that I used commas correctly 93 percent of the time.

I did a second sample. This time, I found 60 sentences, and five required updates. That's around 8 percent. Again, very close to the original sample and strangely consistent.

Let's talk about these results because they're impressive. I caught nine commas that needed to be corrected. If my average number of edits for a novel is 275 edits, and 28 percent of my edits on average are commas, then commas would represent approximately 77 edits. If I caught nine commas, that brings the number of comma-related edits down to 68. That's a 12 percent decrease in comma edits, and a 3 percent decrease in edits overall.

All in a trial that took me approximately 35 minutes (because you know that I love to time everything). *Nine* commas can make that much of a difference. Hot damn!

I was so stunned that I did a third trial, but with this one, I followed a hypothesis. I reasoned that the higher number of commas in a sentence, the more likely I was to make an error. More commas equal more complexity.

I took a third sample, but this time I pulled all sentences over four commas (the most was eight). There were only 30 sentences that met this criterion.

The result? Ten sentences had errors. That's 30 percent of the total!

So, in the third trial, I had fewer results, but I caught the same number of errors. That lends some credence to a rule that I should at least check sentences with greater than four commas, as they have a higher error rate. Intuitively, that makes sense. That hypothesis is probably correct.

If I wanted to make a real difference in my editing moving forward, I would:

- Do a random sampling of say, 100-150 sentences with fewer than four commas.
- Analyze ALL sentences with greater than four commas.

If such an exercise netted me approximately 19 errors (like this one did), here's where I would end up with my editor:

- 256 edits per novel (down from 275, or a 7 percent decrease)
- 58 comma-related edits (down from 77, or a 25 percent decrease)

Wow, what a difference an hour makes! When have you ever heard a writer say that something they self-edited resulted in a 25 percent decrease in edits caught by their editor? That's how you use the power of data to become a cleaner writer.

I could drive a 25 percent decrease on my own, and as I said before, I could hire a comma-only editor and push that number even higher. And I could do it at an affordable rate.

These are the types of conversations we should be having about editing in our community.

WHITEBOARDING: MY NEW TEACHING METHOD

In a previous volume, I discussed how I purchased a Wacom pen and tablet to try out a unique teaching style. This quarter, I was able to test it.

I spoke at the 2021 Annual *Writer's Digest* Conference. I did a four-hour workshop titled "The Ultimate Self-Publishing Masterclass." Students paid a fee to be there, and I covered the basics of self-publishing.

I started the session with a few PowerPoint slides, but then I switched to OpenBoard, my whiteboarding software. The whiteboard (in combination with my pen and tablet) allowed me to draw on the screen, insert images, and even do interesting things like use a magnifying glass!

Here's what I learned.

Teaching insurance classes worked wonders. In a previous volume, I discussed the lessons I learned from teaching insurance classes to professionals across the country. All the tactics I used in those classes translated to this event.

OpenBoard is phenomenal. I still can't believe this software is free. I used every inch of it, from sketching to shapes to screen-sharing to the on-screen calculator to the magnifying glass to the export feature that let me share my whiteboards with the students after the event.

The Wacom pen and tablet paid for themselves. The money I made from the event more than justified the purchase. It was a smart gamble. And, of course, I can claim them on my taxes and amortize them if I wanted.

I mimicked a technique from a comedian. I love the US comedian Sinbad. He made a courageous decision early in his career to stop cursing and make his comic routines family-friendly. In an era where comedians are expected to have dirty mouths, that's saying something. I like raunchy comedians too, but I've always respected Sinbad for that decision.

On one of his comedy specials, he did a segment where he told the married couples in the audience he would help them with marriage advice. He took questions from the audience and turned them into jokes. He did this for at least 30 minutes, in the middle of a planned routine. He had no idea what the people were going to ask, and he improvised. It was the most masterful comedic improvisation I've ever seen.

I tried something similar. During my section on cover design, I asked for all the students on the webinar to give me a description of their book. I told them I would take one of the descriptions and do market research for them live on the call so they could get some ideas what to put on their cover.

I selected one student from the list. She had a Greek historical novel. I went to Amazon and found some similar books to hers using some basic keyword searches. I then annotated the cover and taught the students how to think about covers. This exercise went over very well with the students.

People are funny about money. This isn't related to whiteboarding per se, but people criticized me when I shared editing costs because they felt my numbers weren't true to their experience, even when I caveated it. People also got mad at me for telling them about how low editor rates can go, which is baffling to me. If *you* don't want to pay a certain rate, don't criticize the messenger for sharing facts. Oh well.

If you share numbers, they criticize you; if you don't share numbers, they criticize you for not sharing numbers. Basically, you can never win.

The audience appreciated freebies. I gave them two books from my catalog and a guide that compiled all the resources I mentioned in the class. As discussed in previous volumes, I don't ask for email signups. I just give the books away. Some people do eventually join my email list, though.

The style was professional and polished. I received positive feedback from the students and the venue organizers, which is ultimately what matters.

Overall, I learned a lot from this event that I can apply to future speaking engagements.

INTERVIEW ABOUT EMERGING TECHNOLOGY

This quarter, I sat down with Matty Dalrymple on her show, "The Indy Author Podcast." We talked about emerging technology for writers. My message was that emerging technology is important and writers should be watching for watershed moments that will make technology easier to use, but that they should also maximize the horsepower of tools that already exist on their computers.

I shared how I developed my editing workflow and my sales tracking macros. I also talked about the power of thinking of books as data.

Will the message resonate? I have no idea, but it was fun to do the interview. I recommend you check out Matty's show.

AUTOMATIC RIGHTS LICENSING

When you die, who will take care of your estate? This is a huge problem that indie authors will have. It's a problem today, but it will become worse the more authors make a living from their work.

What if you provided an automated self-service rights system that lets people license rights to your work?

Here's how it would work. Before you die, you load all of your work into a database where you can designate which rights are available, and at what price.

If a magazine anthology editor, agent, or other rights buyer wants to know if your work is available, they click a button on your website that takes them to an automated portal. They can see what works are available, which rights are available, and which rights have been sold. Some works, such as short stories, might have a set price—the rights buyer selects which rights they need, enters their credit card info, and the short story is delivered to their email inbox along with the author's bio, headshots, and other marketing materials. The email also would include legal language indicating what the buyer can and cannot do with the work. The estate would receive a separate email notification. The reasoning is that for some rights, the estate doesn't need to be involved in the affairs unless there is something complex that requires their time.

The estate might even use "make your best offer" pricing, where the buyer puts in what they're willing to pay, and if the offer is below a certain minimum, the system would reject it or make a counteroffer. All of this would happen in minutes.

To be clear, some rights cannot be sold this way—film, television, merchandise, and so on. But some could.

It's an idea that, once more authors start dying, will probably pop up in some form.

LEARNING COVER DESIGN: DETERMINING MY "TRIGGER"

Learning cover design is still on my radar. It's not a high priority, but it's not a low priority either.

I thought it would be helpful if I developed a "trigger" that would prompt me to start doing my own covers. In other words, what event has to happen for me to make this switch?

As I wrote in previous volumes, I believe we're headed for a cover designer shortage. The cost of covers and wait time goes up every few years and you don't get any more for your money. As the cost goes up, new designers charge more too. This isn't sustainable and I need to protect myself against this risk. Otherwise, it'll make the costs of book production too high.

I'll use simple, simple money to illustrate the exercise I did to help me develop my trigger.

If I were to design my own covers, it would take me at least 100 hours to learn Photoshop and cover design techniques to the point where I would feel somewhat comfortable doing it. After a few covers, I estimate that designing a cover would take me approximately five hours (and that's being conservative).

I value my time, so let's say that it's worth $50 an hour (my time is worth more than that, but I'm using simple math).

100 hours x $50 = $5000 just to learn the craft of cover design.

5 hours x $50 = $200 to do my own cover (plus design materials like fonts and stock images, so we'll move the number up to $250).

This means that it will cost me $250 to design a book cover.

What could I be doing instead of designing a cover? Well, I could be writing words. If my daily minimum is 2000 words a day, then we can quantify this even further.

Each book cover would cost me $250, 5 hours, and *at least* 2000 words of writing. If I write 10 books per year, then that's $2500 per year, 50 hours, and 20,000 words. I would lose approximately half a novel per year.

The reverse is also true: every cover I buy from a designer *saves* me $250, five hours, and *allows* me to write 2000 more words than I would have if I didn't hire the designer. Annually, hiring a designer saves me $2500, 50 hours, and allows me to write 20,000 more words.

Is that worth the cost?

The last time I checked, the average *good* cover design costs between $400 and $600 right now.

Cost-wise, using the numbers in this chapter, I'd save money, but I'd lose time and words. I'm not ready to do that yet, and, holistically, the cost of hiring a designer is still cheaper than doing it myself.

But in a few years, when average designers raise their rates again to, say $500 to $750…then I'll *have* to make the switch, designing my own covers and hiring someone only when absolutely needed. I don't like it, but I don't see any way around it.

That means I need to start learning the art of cover design in 2021 and 2022. I need to get over the learning curve so that I can be ready when the time comes. This change could be just around the corner. I hope I'm fast enough to beat it, because if I am, it will become a competitive advantage.

That said, I hope I'm wrong in predictive cover designer shortage and rate increases, but I probably won't be.

WRITING APP DATABASE

When I wrote *The Writing App Handbook*, I had an idea to create a database of writing apps that I could promote alongside the book. The concept was that users could use the database to find the perfect writing app in just a few clicks. The database would contain all the major writing apps on the market, organized by operating system, price, and features.

I sketched out what I thought the database should look like and contracted with a developer. After a short phone call, she told me she could do it and gave me a price. It was an easy job for her.

Several weeks later, The Writing App Database was born! It's a free tool that lets you search, filter, and sort by:

- Writing App Name
- Operating System
- Price and Payment Type (Flat Fee, Subscription, Free)

It also catalogs which apps have the following features:

- Dark Mode
- Splitscreen Mode
- Writing in Multiple Tabs/Windows
- E-book Formatting
- Paperback Formatting
- Autosave
- Automatic Backup

- Dark Mode
- Simultaneous Collaboration
- Outlining Support
- Distraction-Free Mode

You can also download your results to PDF and Excel, as well as in a printer-friendly format.

Of course, I also included the cover for *The Writing App Handbook* and a link to buy the book! I will also promote the database in my writing books where it makes sense.

I designed the database to be a proof of concept. If people use it and like it, I'll make updates to it. If not, it's quite good and helpful in its current form.

I have no idea how this database will be received, but it was a fun experiment that taught me a lot about WordPress and app development, which was worth the expense. This was a very cheap lesson, all things considered.

PERFECTIT AND THE CHICAGO MANUAL OF STYLE: AN AUTOMATION DREAM TEAM

Earlier this year, I tested and reviewed the proofreading app PerfectIt. I've discussed the app in previous volumes, so I won't rehash my love for it here. In short, I believe it is a secret weapon, and many editors agree with me, but most authors don't. I'll keep talking about it...

Well, this year, the PerfectIt team further validated my hunch about PerfectIt. They announced a partnership with *The Chicago Manual of Style* (CMOS). PerfectIt will check your work against the CMOS and flag errors for you. Even better, it will show you what error you potentially made, why it is an error, and it will link to the section of the CMOS so you can go and learn for yourself. Wow.

Now, I don't believe that you should follow a style guide completely. I don't agree with everything the CMOS says, and neither should you. However, consider that:

- The CMOS does pose valid points that can help make your work stronger, particularly with formatting, correct spelling of words, proper hyphenation, and so on.
- Your editor is probably adhering to the CMOS, so whether you do or not, it matters.
- The less you adhere to basic CMOS rules, the more edits you will probably receive.

Essentially, PerfectIt with CMOS integration automates the review of the manual. It pretty much ensures that you never have to read the manual to figure out what your work might need. Most authors don't read the CMOS anyway (myself included), so the fact that an app exists that helps you find additional edits is a godsend. Any edit that PerfectIt finds is one that your editor won't!

This integration is a wonderful example of automation. By simply enabling the CMOS integration, I instantly decreased the number of edits present in my work.

BECOME THE WRITER OF
THE FUTURE

PROTECTING YOUR IDENTITY ONLINE

I read a disturbing news article about a high-ranking Catholic priest who was outed by shady methods.

Apparently, this priest had been living a gay lifestyle. He visited gay bars and used the gay dating app, Grindr.

How did anyone know this? A Catholic news organization somehow got access to Grindr location data. It's not uncommon for corporations to give their customer data to third-party vendors for some purpose—data analysis, sales, performing a service, and so on. The Catholic news organization got a package of location data and mined it to discover the priest's travels. Even though the data was anonymized, they were still able to match it to a unique ID for his phone.

I share this article not because it has anything to do with homosexuality (I don't care about anyone's sexual orientation). I share the article because it is terrifying, and it illustrates how we operate under the illusion of privacy.

If someone can do this to a Catholic priest, they can do it to you.

To relate this to writing, I think about all the apps and services writers use daily—on their computers, in the cloud, and on their phones.

I watched an interview with John Grisham where he mentioned that he has two computers—one for his writing (that is not connected to the Internet) and one for regular consumption. He was terrified of being hacked, so he kept his work on a secure computer. Imagine if a big-name author like him were hacked. It would be devastating.

There's also the issue of revenge, or other malicious intentions. I've said for a while that it's just a matter of time before indie authors start getting hacked or hit with cyber and ransom attacks with regularity.

That article was a chilling reminder for me to review my data security practices.

THE PROBLEM WITH BEING PROLIFIC

I stumbled upon an opinion piece from 2015 about prolificacy that got me thinking.

The article is written by a literary fiction writer, who, at the time, had a debut book in the works and to date has only published that one book, aside from content in reputable literary magazines.

The article is a direct reply to an opinion piece that Stephen King wrote in the *New York Times* in support of prolific authors. I won't discuss King's opinion, but only the reply.

The article in question made the following arguments:

- Prolific authors have a big body of work and therefore more entry points, but maybe it's better that some authors' works are lost to time or unpublished rather than having to deal with the problem of reading through a prolific writer's bibliography.
- When readers like an author's work, they want to devour everything that writer has written, and prolific writers just make it too hard for poor readers (so therefore they shouldn't be prolific).

I'll end with a quote from the final paragraph: "It's true that telling Oates, et al., not to write so much might deprive us of great works, but the net effect is the same either way. Each new book is, for me anyway, another lost in the flood."

The article smacks of snobbery and the typical vapid attacks that critics make against prolific writers. These critics are usually people who have little to no writing experience or credentials.

The arguments in the article are idiotic at best. I won't hold the writer to the article because he may have evolved his opinions since then (or not). But I appreciate the opinion because the writer *does* (accidentally) make a valid point in the article, and that valid point is what the heart of the article should have been, but we'll get to that in a minute.

First, let's address the point of "Prolific authors have a big body of work and therefore more entry points, but maybe it's better that some authors' works are lost to time or unpublished rather than having to deal with the problem of reading through a prolific writer's bibliography..."

It's hard to put into words how arrogant and condescending this argument is. To tell a writer *not* to write, not to pursue their dreams, and not to practice their craft by publishing more books is offensive and writer malpractice in my opinion. Just because *you* don't want to wade through a bunch of books doesn't mean that other readers will care. And the least obscure books in a writer's catalog may be life-changing for someone. You have no idea how your work will impact people. Withhold your work from the world, and the universe will withhold rewarding you for it.

When you die, are people going to say "Thank you, fellow author, for NOT publishing that book you wrote many years ago. The world is so much better for it."? No, they're going to be grateful for the work you published, and your death will probably give you a sales bump...

To the second argument of "When readers like an author's work, they want to devour everything that writer has written, and prolific writers just make it too hard for poor readers..."

It just makes me want to give writers like this a box of tissues. So *what* you have to wade through a bunch of books to find what you want to read? Have you never been to a library or browsed an online bookstore? Come on.

That brings me to the valid (and astute) point the writer made in the article, that, if he had made more forcefully, would have contributed meaningfully to the prolificacy conversation. That point is that prolific writers have published so much work that their portfolio causes analysis paralysis for their readers, and these authors aren't doing anything about it. Therefore, they're missing out on readers and readers are missing out on books they would love.

That's the heart of the issue, not whether an author should or should not be prolific. Most authors will not be as prolific as Stephen King, or, say Barbara Cartland, and that's okay. But if they choose to be, then they have a professional obligation to wield their prolificacy responsibly. That's the conversation we should be having.

Stephen King has published 63 novels at the time of this writing. Many readers have read all 63. But sure, there are readers who browsed King's portfolio, couldn't decide where to start, and bought a book by someone else instead. Stephen King doesn't need the money and probably doesn't care because he has legions of readers who serve as a recommendation engine for him, but it's a legitimate point.

A quick browse of Stephen King's website reveals no easy way to determine which of his books to start with for new readers. Instead, the work is in alphabetical order, including his short stories. Very overwhelming.

(Again, if I were going to reply to Stephen King's article, and I knew he would read it, I would call him out for this. Way more productive than "No, you're wrong because prolificacy is wrong." Oh well. Missed opportunity.)

Let's take the next step up to Dean Koontz, who, at the time of this writing, has over 100 novels. Dean does attempt to solve this problem by:

- organizing his books by stand-alones and series
- offering a collector's page that contains details for completionists

He also offers a database that you can sort by title and date, which again, is probably overwhelming to a newcomer. But Dean does a much better job of trying to solve this problem.

Let's step it up even further to Barbara Cartland, one of the most prolific authors in the English language, who wrote over 700 books. Whoever manages Barbara's estate understands the problem at hand. No one (and I mean no one) is going to read an alphabetical or chronological list of her books and decide what to write. Instead, the book contains a sortable database where readers can sort books by the locations they take place in, the time period, and genre (Barbara wrote romance). The tool is stunningly easy to use. It's funny how out of all the authors I looked at, *only* the super-prolific one got it right.

Therefore, you can learn how to solve this problem NOW when you're not prolific so you can scale it.

At the beginning of my career, I knew I was going to be prolific, so I tried to think about how to make the browsing experience easy for new readers. I set out to "get the right book to the right reader at the right time." I created a tool called Book Wizard, which is a questionnaire that serves up a Book 1 in a series based on a 2-question survey. The tool worked very well, but it's time for an upgrade. I have considerably more books under my belt and I need to remain cognizant of it because every book I read increases the chance of analysis paralysis for my readers.

Here's how I can tackle that problem:

- Hyper-consistent cover design so that my portfolio has a unified look.

- Creating a filterable database like the one Barbara Cartland's estate built.
- Determining helpful ways to "tag" all my books so readers can exclude the books they don't want to read. Helping them exclude books is more important than anything.
- Including a "series reading order" when possible.
- Including a "Greatest Hits" page for easy choices as well as a dedicated experience for completionists.

Whether I have 30 novels or 300, these methods will help me scale the browsing experience. This method will also help me incorporate short stories, media interviews, and other short-form content too.

Book Wizard was a great start, but I am ready to take it to the next level when I publish my next website.

To bring this home, making the point that prolific authors need to do more for their readers is a legitimate one. This article took me 30 minutes to write, and it took me five minutes to brainstorm potential solutions to the problem of prolificacy, which is what the author of this unfortunate opinion piece should have done instead of trying to gatekeep. Trying to discourage writers from being prolific to save readers time is cynical, arrogant, and does neither writers nor readers any good.

SKINTERFACES

I read a great newsletter by The Future Today Institute about the future of smart fabrics that can interface with and influence the human body.

Got writer's block? Put on a special sweater to improve your mood.

It's an interesting technology that companies are already experimenting with. Google launched its Jacquard product and other tech companies are experimenting with this.

Privacy and security concerns aside, you can't help but be intrigued by the prospect of biotechnology for improving writing.

In Volume 2 of this series, I wrote: "The second area is writing assistance. AI has the potential to help us become better versions of ourselves. I don't need AI software that gives me generic spelling and grammar recommendations. I *do* need software that can look at all of the mistakes I've made in my past writing and help me avoid making them again. That would save me editing costs and help me create cleaner books. AI models need a lot of data, so this isn't likely possible until someone finds a way to generate better models that require less data.

Further out, imagine integration with biohacking technology. What if my writing app could track my vitals during writing sessions and tell me when it's time to stop writing because I'm too tired? Or maybe it could sense when I'm distracted and gently redirect me to another function in my writing business instead where my attention would be more productive, like marketing? If

I ignored it and wrote anyway, the app could mark those sections with a recommendation for my editor to pay more attention to them and why. It would know my error rate and compare that to my vitals over time. In a sense, your writing app could assume a function similar to a nurse. Your editor would become more like a (true) book doctor, treating the most problematic areas of the manuscript. In the future, if the book has been run through developmental editing software and more sophisticated grammar and spellchecker software based on prior mistakes, an editor's approach will have to be different and more holistic."

The way the technology is evolving, I don't believe my statements were wrong.

I can already determine my past mistakes through my editing workflow. Imagine being able to hook that up to biological information. Technically, I could do that today if I wanted, using a smart watch to monitor my heartbeat, sleep, and light levels. It's not a big leap to integrate these monitors into clothing, or into data and analytics that one can use.

This is an area I'm keeping an eye on, if for nothing else than for a great entrepreneurial opportunity. ("Buy the Writer's Block Bracelet today!")

I believe it's not out of the realm that writers of the future twenty, thirty, or even fifty years from now will treat biotechnology the same way we treat Scrivener today—as an indispensable part of their workflow, and a source of data to help them manage through the mental part of writing. This is because writers face inconsistency. Some writing days are better than others and we don't always know why.

If you told someone (and proved) that you can help them optimize when and how to write by recommending the best times and days to write, based on science, they would line up to buy your product.

"Author X functions on six hours of sleep. On the days she got seven or more hours of sleep, her writing contained X percent fewer errors and X percent fewer suggestions from her editor."

"Author X is a morning person, but we discovered that they actually did their best writing at night because..."

Oh, man. That's a whole new level of technology, and it's already here in its nascent form.

ON BEACH FLAGS AND DEATH

I read a fantastic book this summer called *The Five Invitations* by Frank Ostaseski. It's about learning how to become comfortable with death so that we can live better. I heard Frank give an interview on "The Unmistakable Creative" Podcast with Srini Rao and loved it so much that I bought his book. It did not disappoint.

The main idea of Ostaseski's book is that we can become more comfortable with death in our lives if we cultivate five mindsets. Frank ran a cutting-edge hospice center for many years and helped many families and patients come to terms with death. The stories he tells in the book are gripping, heartbreaking, and inspiring.

While I was reading this book (which I bought purely out of curiosity), my grandfather passed away. I remember making a long drive to the small town in Iowa where we buried him, and I listened to the audiobook as I drove through rolling cornfields and gravel roads. It took me a while to process what Frank wrote in the book.

Shortly after that, we took a family vacation to Orlando, Florida. We spent a day in West Palm Beach, and we visited the city Municipal Beach.

I'm not really a beach person. I've only been to a beach a handful of times in my life. When I was walking on the beach, I noticed the beach flags on the lifeguard tower. I don't know why, but I was fascinated with them. I kept staring at them so much that my wife even asked me, "What are you staring at?"

I researched beach flags and how they are used. And then I

realized why I was so interested in them.

At one point, Frank talks in the book about recognizing your emotions and how they can well up inside you. The key is to understand them, acknowledge them, and reflect upon them. That helped me understand the grieving process better.

But it also helped me understand something about writing that I hadn't been able to articulate until I wrote my book *The Pocket Guide to Pantsing*.

That advice, combined with the beach flags, inspired me to write about recognizing the effects of your emotions while writing.

I'll post the passage from the book here.

Emotional undercurrents are another phenomenon while pantsing that no one told me about when I started.

In addition to story visibility, you need to keep in touch with your feelings while you're writing.

Before you write me off as a typical millennial, consider a few things.

Our feelings interfere with our writing more than we like to acknowledge. Anything that happens in your personal life will affect your writing.

However, here's what I wish someone would have told me when I wrote my first book into the dark: feelings are like the weather. If you don't like them, just wait a little while.

Writing can be an emotional rollercoaster if you're uninitiated. Many types of feelings can manifest themselves in your writing sessions:

- happiness
- euphoria
- excitedness
- contentment

- "flow"
- self-doubt
- anger
- fear/anxiety
- exasperation
- sadness
- and more

Feelings are fleeting. You may experience self-doubt in a morning writing session, but later that night, you may slip into flow and write an amazing scene. The key is to understand yourself, acknowledge the feelings, and wait them out if necessary.

Recently, I went to West Palm Beach, Florida with my family. We spent a day at the beach. As we walked along the shore, the moody waves of the Atlantic Ocean rushed across our feet and beach flags flapped in the wind on a lifeguard tower.

Beach flags are interesting. They tell you how the ocean is feeling.

- Green flags mean safe waters.
- Yellow flags mean choppier currents and to swim with caution.
- Red flags mean unsafe conditions, such as rip-tides and tall waves.

Is the ocean always calm? No. It changes. If you don't like it, just come back tomorrow.

Your soul is a beach, and there are emotional undercurrents. There are rip-tides too—they always take you by surprise and they're pretty awful.

It's normal to experience many feelings as you write. No feeling is out of bounds. But feelings are also fleeting. They never stay for long. This is true of both good and bad feelings. Emotional undercurrents are ever-changing.

———

It's interesting how ideas coalesce and come together. I would have never known that a book about death and a family vacation would lead me to think about writing in this way. It goes to show you that consuming media (of any kind) is always beneficial for your writing because it fills your creative well. Sometimes, things spring out of that well that you don't expect.

My readers have consistently said that the chapter in *The Pocket Guide to Pantsing* on emotional undercurrents is one of the most impactful in the book.

NOTES FROM AN "EFFECTIVE COMMUNICATION" COURSE

I took a course on executive communication and wrote down some advice that I found helpful in both my day job and in my writing life. I'm capturing my thoughts here for the future.

Think ahead in space and time. Most people can't see beyond the present (i.e., today). Others are stuck in the past. Effective executives (and authorpreneurs) must think ahead in space and time. This allows them to see things that others may miss. To do this, it's important to:

- study others in your industry
- read industry reports
- expand your perspective
- ask "what if" questions
- surround yourself with other strategic thinkers

Act decisively and courageously. Hard decisions come with uncertainty and risk, and an effective executive (and authorpreneur) must learn to be comfortable with these types of decisions. You won't always be right, but people will respect you if you act decisively and courageously.

How to act decisively and courageously:

- Make clear, justified choices
- Collect diverse inputs

- Challenge your assumptions

There were other lessons in the course that I found helpful, but these resonated the most with me.

LESSONS LEARNED IN ESTATE PLANNING

Estate planning has been on my mind a lot lately. It started when I did my taxes this year and realized I was over my head. Then I read about Michael Crichton and how he messed up his estate and excluded his pregnant wife and son because he didn't update his will. Then my grandfather passed away, and he did such an amazing job with his estate plans that it inspired me to take action.

My grandfather died with everything in place: a clear will, life insurance, medical directives, his gravestone and plot picked out, and every other detail you could think of buttoned up. In a way, he taught me how to die. He really took care of the people that he loved and he ensured that his death would not be a burden for the family. I respected the hell out of it.

If I died right now, I'd be leaving a mess. My goal is to die like he did. I don't know how long I'll live, but I can at least make sure my death is as organized as my writing life is.

Here are some lessons I've learned in estate planning.

I read *Estate Planning for Authors* by M.L. Buchman. It was a good primer on the topic that taught me good information and where to look next. The book contains a template letter that I can adapt for my heirs.

I learned that Iowa is a very good place to live and die as an author. There are two taxes my heirs will have to worry about after I die. The first is the estate tax. The federal estate tax kicks in after your estate is valued at over 5.25 million dollars. Then there's a state estate tax on top of that. Iowa does not have an estate tax. This means that I will pay no federal death tax if my estate is worth less than 5.25 million dollars.

There's also the inheritance tax, which is assessed when property is passed from one person to another. In Iowa, the tax does not apply if property is passed to a spouse or child. Also, Iowa's inheritance tax is 15 percent. Well, rather, it was 15 percent until the Iowa legislature phased it out earlier this year. I'm generally not a fan of the legislators here in Iowa, but that's a decision I can get behind!

A local law firm sums up the law: "With the passage of the new bill, if one were to pass away in 2021, the inheritance tax imposed on the inheritor would be reduced by 20 percent from the original rates. If one were to die in 2022, the inheritance tax imposed on the inheritor would be reduced by 40 percent from the original rates. If one were to die in 2023, the tax would be reduced by 60 percent from the original rates. If one were to die in 2024, the tax would be reduced by 80 percent from the original rates. And, lastly, if one were to die in 2025, the inheritance tax imposed on the inheritor would be reduced by 100 percent from the original rates, thereby eliminating the tax entirely."

This means that, assuming I live past 2025, the only estate tax I have to worry about is the federal estate tax...if my estate is worth 5.25 million at the time of my death. That's incredible.

Bankruptcy is bad. Copyrights are intellectual property, and in a bankruptcy, a court can take *any* property to pay creditors. So many authors never think of their work as intellectual property and as something that has intrinsic value, but I never made that mistake. However, this means that when I die, my copyrights will be assessed and valued by a court to determine how much tax is owed (if the federal estate tax applies). This also means that in a bankruptcy, a court will do the same thing. If you file for bankruptcy, you can LOSE your copyright. (And no, you can't

transfer it to an LLC or corporation to "avoid" the court.)
What is my IP worth? Well, that's a difficult question.

I took a course with Dean Wesley Smith this quarter on Estate Planning. In it, he talks about some ways that courts evaluate intellectual property. There are many methods and there is no standardized way of doing it. You would have to pay a law firm a lot of money to determine this number, but it can be done. At least I know about it now. If I ever sign a film contract or find breathtaking success, I need to have my IP professionally valued.

Failing to plan can and will bankrupt your heirs. I read many stories of celebrities who died and, when a court valued their IP, assessed more in taxes than the estate had in cash. And then they had to file bankruptcy and lost the IP...All of this sounds silly when you only have one or two books, but the longer you do this and the more books you publish, the more real this threat becomes. Other people might laugh at me for pursuing proper estate planning, but *I'm* not going to put my family in jeopardy if I can help it. For the people who laugh at me, I feel bad for their heirs.

I re-recognized the need to be vigilant and diligent in an online world. Whenever I open accounts or purchase subscriptions, I need to be more careful and leave better documentation. I also need to track my passwords better. I do a pretty good job of this currently, but I have room for improvement.

IP management is a lucrative field. In prior volumes of the series, I talked about an intellectual property service that perpetuates the distribution and licensing of your work after you die. As I walk down the path of learning proper estate management, I'm convinced that this idea is more important than ever, and possibly the biggest need that self-published writers will have in twenty to thirty years. I'm also convinced that this is an extremely dangerous business model that can, in the wrong hands, be a tremendous force for evil. In the right hands, it could be a billion-dollar company.

Anyway, that's what I've learned about estate management so far, and I've got a lot more to learn.

LESSONS LEARNED FROM BOOKS PUBLISHED IN 2021

2021 will be my most productive year ever. In fact, I published more books this year than in other years combined.

Every book teaches me something, and I want to capture those lessons while they are fresh in my head.

Here are the lessons I learned from the books I published this year.

Indie Author Confidential Volumes 4-7. This series is easy to write and a wonderful way to bolster my word counts every year. If I do nothing else in a year, this series nets me four books per year, and around 100,000 words. In 10 years, I will have created 40 volumes. In 50 years, it will have generated 2000 volumes. If every volume is 25,000 words on average, that's 1.25 million words over my lifetime, which is completely unprecedented for a series of letters/essays by an author. This series alone could be bigger than other authors' entire discographies. The *Indie Author Confidential* series continues to be a masterclass in prolificacy for me.

Authors, Steal This Book. I repurposed the "Ideas You Can Steal" sections into a book that became a lead magnet for my nonfiction, increasing my sales.

The Self-Publishing Advice Compendium. I unpublished my book, *250+ Writing Tips Vol. 1*, and instead, I combined Volumes 1 and 2 into a single collection, rebranded it, and made it part of my flagship Author Level Up series. I initially launched the *250+*

Writing Tips brand as a separate series, but I decided not to continue it. Sometimes you change your mind and that's okay.

Dead Rat Walking (The Chicago Rat Shifter, Book 1). This book was a microcosm of lessons. I wrote almost all of this book while dictating on an exercise bike. It also helped me rebuild my dictation muscles. I also built my editing engine with this novel, laying the groundwork to dramatically decrease the number of errors in my work. I also experimented with fact-checkers with this book, which helped me drive higher-quality stories. Craft-wise, this novel was a testing ground for a lot of micro craft techniques, especially in the first few chapters. I adopted a thriller format for urban fantasy: first-person POV, short chapters, shifting POVs, cliffhangers. But I also kept the character-driven parts of urban fantasy. This was also the first time I wrote a brother and sister as protagonists in a story.

Rat City (The Chicago Rat Shifter, Book 2). This was one of the most challenging novels I've written to date. It was a long, intricate, fast-paced novel that kept me in the dark. I had no idea what would happen until the very end, and even the ending surprised me. Fast-paced yet extremely character-driven, it also covers weird emotional ground. It gets very dark very quickly. But it solidifies that this series is a practice ground for me. I continued to experiment with many craft techniques I've seen mega-bestsellers authors use. Near the end of the book, I switched from the third-person to first-person POV for one chapter, just to see what would happen.

Cold Hard Magic (The Good Necromancer, Book 2. I started this book in 2019, and I didn't pick it up until 2021. It taught me that no matter how long you walk away from a book, you can always return.

Spirit Chaser (The Good Necromancer, Book 3). This was the only book I wrote all year where there was no writer's block. I wrote it straight through with no problems. It's also the first book this year I wrote with a 2000-word per day daily minimum. I don't think that's a coincidence. I only missed one day of writing due to personal circumstances. I still finished the novel early and I never fell too far behind. I also experimented with different types of villains. This novel was definitely showier and flashier (action-wise) than the first two in the series.

The Indie Author Strategy Guide. The book was the perfect opportunity for me to revisit my own author strategy. It prompted me to draft my 2022 goals early.

The Writing App Handbook. I learned in-depth knowledge about all the major writing apps on the market, and also how to partner with a developer to create a WordPress database tool.

The Pocket Guide to Pantsing. This book taught me so much. It helped me articulate many things about pantsing and writing into the dark that I knew intrinsically but had never explained before. It was also a helpful exercise in teaching people how to do something from beginning to end.

How to Dictate a Book. This was a lesson in how to write a book in a thoroughly saturated niche. Everyone has written books on dictation, but no one wrote a book with a free accompanying course. That was fun.

The Author Editing Problem. This was the most advanced book I've ever written, with lots of numbers and data analysis, which I know most authors will not be interested in. I tried my best to warn people upfront that this book is likely not for them. I also filmed a free accompanying course teaching people how to use Microsoft Word macros.

Anyway, those were some of the many lessons my books taught me this year.

SUCCESSES AND FAILURES IN 2021

2021 was an amazing year. Compared to 2020, things "felt" as back to normal as they could be despite being in the middle of the COVID-19 pandemic.

2020 was about survival and about finding ways to stay focused on my writing. My "Beast Mode" challenge helped with that. 2020 was my best year ever productivity and sales-wise.

2021 was about building on that success, and in almost all respects, I parlayed my success in 2020 this year.

In this chapter, I'll talk about my successes and failures this year.

SUCCESSES

Productivity. I wrote a record number of books and words this year. I did this by doing what I've been doing all along—hyper-focus, commitment to learning, keeping my writing fun, writing on my phone, dictating my stories, and taking care of myself.

"Beast Mode." I wrote 10 books for my Beast Mode challenge this year.

Picking up after a long time. My book *Cold Hard Magic* was on the shelf for 18 months, and I picked it up and finished it this year. That's a success.

Streamlining. I stopped doing a lot of things this year. I stopped teaching insurance classes, podcasting, and finished law school, and ceasing these activities gave me a lot of time back in my day.

Implementing a daily minimum word count. Streamlining my life allowed me to start abiding by a daily minimum word count. It has worked wonders for my productivity. My goals are 2000 words per day Monday through Saturday and 1000 words on Sunday. I usually write well over the minimums every day.

New teaching styles. I experimented with a white-boarding teaching style in some of my public speaking events this year, and it went very well.

Publication in *Writer's Digest*. I pitched an article to *Writer's Digest* on writer's block and it was accepted. This was my first time appearing in a print magazine. It went well enough that I got a second article accepted in *Writer's Digest*, and it will be appearing in January/February 2022.

Speaking engagements. I did a *lot* of speaking engagements this year, and except for one, they all went very well. I now have prepping for speaking engagements down to a science. Speaking at virtual events now only has a minor impact on my productivity. I did nine speaking engagements this year and still managed to write 14 books, so I'd say I've got balancing the two figured out. Some things that helped me were saying yes only to events that fit into my wheelhouse. I'm less likely to speak on odd topics now than I was in the past unless they really interest me.

Editing success. I've talked enough about reducing the number of edits my editor finds with automation enough that I won't go into it any further here.

Estate planning. My estate planning is far from perfect, but I consider it a major success that I started thinking about it this year. I took the first few steps toward cementing my legacy for decades after my death while also providing for my family, and that's something to be proud of.

New video setup. I invested in new studio camera equipment this year, which paid off in an evolution of my YouTube video style.

Eye contact on conference calls. I discovered a way to make eye contact on conference calls, which is a big deal for me since I am on conference calls a lot.

Story Bundle. I was invited to join an exclusive Story Bundle for National Novel Writing Month (NaNoWriMo) this year, which was a fun marketing opportunity, and it paid very well.

Dictation revival. I started dictating again this year, and I leveled up my dictation skills by finally using transcription. I even invented a new method to dictate cleanly and accurately ("The Pikachu Method"). This method exploded my word counts in the fourth quarter, and it should give me a nice bump in 2021.

I created my first hardcover book. It took forever, but I am now able to unlock this format, which should help increase my sales over the long term.

Permafree. I experimented with a permafree nonfiction book that improved my sales.

Backing up my work. I invested in new hardware to back up my work this year.

FAILURES

Video consistency. My YouTube channel was one of my casualties this year. While I haven't stopped making videos, I have stopped making *edited* videos right now. Finishing law school and starting a new job threw off my publication schedule.

Video content quality. While my video quality has improved, my YouTube content quality has not. It's a missed opportunity for me to get back up-to-speed with YouTube best practices.

Taxes. I had a win with my taxes and a major loss. I didn't hire the right accountant and I had to redo their work. I covered this in previous volumes of the series. I ended up okay, but it was a sobering lesson learned.

Email management. I completely lost control of my email inbox this year. I still haven't figured out a way to solve the problem.

One public speaking engagement didn't go well. I think it was just a bad audience fit. My message didn't land at all, and the participants were downright hostile. I probably should have seen it coming, but you live and you learn.

Email newsletters. I didn't send out regular newsletters this year to my audience, and that was a missed opportunity for sales.

Too many priorities. My 2021 strategy had five pillars. It was too much to keep track of. I'll discuss this further in my 2022 strategic priorities.

Unorganized. I'm more organized than most, but I still have significant opportunities. I need to reorganize all my files, clean up my platform, and make some updates to improve my author professionalism. There's always room to be better.

Losing weight. I lost a few pounds this year, but I have a long way to go. I suppose this could also be viewed as a success!

Those are my successes and failures for 2021. Here's to a good 2022.

Q4 PROGRESS REPORT

It's time to provide an update on the progress I've made toward my goals in 2021.

I've shared a detailed mind map about this at www.authorlevelup.com/2021strategy.

I accomplished a lot this year, but I did not hit all of my goals. That's mainly because I set so many of them. I very much viewed this year as a transition year into a smoother strategy. I also did some course-correcting mid-year. Next year, I will set fewer goals and hopefully will achieve all of them.

MY STRATEGY

My mission is to educate and entertain my audience in the genres I write, and to remain nimble in an ever-changing industry.

I will achieve my mission through five strategic priorities:

- Become a world-class content creator
- Become a world-class marketer
- Become a technology-driven writer
- Become a data-driven writer
- Become the writer of the future

WORLD-CLASS CONTENT CREATOR

Goal: 64 books published by 12/31/2021. I'm currently at 65 books for the year with the potential to write at least one or two more before the year ends, so I exceeded my production goal.

Develop a way to ensure consistency across my platform. I started this in Q4, but I won't finish it this year. I course-corrected mid-year because I realized that I need to do a lot of cleanup on my platform before I start standardizing things. For example, I need to refresh some covers, book descriptions, website pages, and so on. This will be a key priority for me in 2022.

WORLD-CLASS MARKETER

Grow my Amazon Ad imprint. Completed.

Improve my copywriting skills. Completed.

Reduce my tax liability. Successfully failed (and completed). See Volume 5 for more information.

BECOME A TECHNOLOGY-DRIVEN WRITER

Develop an automated way to enforce consistency. Completed.

Redesign my Book Wizard tool on Michael La Ronn.com and Author Level Up.com. Not started, but I'm glad I waited because the Barbara Cartland Database gave me some great ideas on how to manage my books on my website. I think I can do it for cheaper than I originally estimated.

Implement a flexible book database that houses all the metadata for my books. I started this work but did not finish it. This ties in to the cleanup I need to do on my platform and this work will be rolled into that.

Automate my bookkeeping. Successfully completed.

BECOME A DATA-DRIVEN WRITER

Make minor enhancements to my sales database. Completed.

Invest in learning the basics of Python, Webhooks, and Application Programming Interfaces (APIs). Completed.

BECOME THE WRITER OF THE FUTURE

Read 50 books. Completed.

Implement direct print and audiobook sales on my website. Did not accomplish.

Complete my law degree. Completed.

Complete 12 WMG workshops to improve my writing craft. Completed.

BRINGING IT ALL TOGETHER

All told, I did a great job sticking to and executing on my goals this year, and my author business is better for it.

On the way to becoming a world-class content creator, I produced a copious number of books that will forever be a part of my legacy. I now have 65 books published to my name and over 2.5 million words published. I also experimented with multimedia content to help readers enjoy my books better. I also experimented with new teaching methods that will make my public speaking better.

I've laid the groundwork for a way to standardize all of my content so that everything is consistent and I can keep better track of it. Prolificacy breeds all sorts of problems, but I'm well-positioned to deal with it better than most.

On my way to becoming a world-class marketer, I made a killing with Amazon Ads and cut my copywriting time in half with my Sales Builder tool. I also reduced my tax burden, ensuring that I keep more money in my bank account.

On my way to becoming a technology-driven writer, I explored ways to "get the right book to the right reader at the right time" (that I discussed in this book). I'm on my way to developing a database that houses all the important metadata for my books that will become both a database and the engine for creating the 2.0 version of my websites so that I no longer have to "create" book pages myself. Book page management is the biggest time suck in maintaining an author website, and this year, I think I came up with an idea to solve that. I also automated my bookkeeping by creating a process that automatically archives and tags all my expenses.

On my way to becoming a data-driven writer, I learned the basics of the Python programming language and application programming interfaces (APIs). These will be critical skills in the coming age of AI.

On my journey to becoming the writer of the future, I read over 50 books of fiction and nonfiction, instilling in me endless interesting ideas that will emerge creatively someday in the future.

I also learned a lot about many different random topics, which will help me become a better writer because they expanded my awareness of the world.

I completed my law degree, which made me a more business-savvy writer.

I completed 12 workshops by Dean Wesley Smith and Kristine Kathryn Rusch at WMG Publishing, and their craft workshops have immeasurably improved my craft.

I completed a "virtual" mentorship with Michael Crichton, a mentor who taught me some important craft and business lessons that I am now using in my writing business and will carry with me.

I also streamlined my responsibilities, giving up teaching insurance classes and podcasting so I could devote more time to writing books. As you can see from my productivity this year, both of those things resulted in a banner year. I saw results approximately six months after ceasing those activities.

If you'd like to see the goals I set for 2021 on a mind map, visit www.authorlevelup.com/2021strategy

In the next chapter, I'll cover my 2022 strategy.

MY 2022 STRATEGIC PRIORITIES

If 2020 was about survival and staying focused and 2021 was about building on success, 2022 is about creating stability and a new normal.

In 2022, I'll reap the full benefits of being done with law school, podcasting, and insurance classes. I'll have a lot more time to focus and streamline my operations so that I'm moving faster in the direction I want to go.

As such, I evaluated my goals for 2021 and need to make some changes.

First, five pillars is too many. They worked very well for me in 2020 because they helped me stay focused, but I don't need five strategic priorities anymore. I'm reducing my focus down to two. This is a radical shift, but it's needed.

Moving forward, my strategy will be as outlined in this chapter.

My mission is to educate and entertain my audience in the genres I write, and to be the author that readers think of when they're looking for a new book to read.

I will achieve my mission through two strategic priorities:

- To become a world-class content creator
- To become a technology and data-driven writer

WORLD-CLASS CONTENT CREATOR

To achieve my goal of becoming a world-class content creator, I will focus on the following tactical priorities:

- Demonstrate a commitment to learning the craft of storytelling and teaching
- Demonstrate a commitment to outstanding quality AND quantity
- Examples of day-to-day activities that will help me carry out my tactical priorities include:
- Keep learning through online courses and workshops taught by professional writers who are further down the path I want to write
- Reading
- Developing mentorships
- Finding new ways to increase my daily word counts
- Mastering different writing methods
- Documenting my process of becoming a successful writer in the *Indie Author Confidential* series
- Cleaning up my platform to ensure a consistent quality reader experience

BECOME A TECHNOLOGY AND DATA-DRIVEN WRITER

To achieve my goal of becoming a technology and data-driven writer, I will focus on the following tactical priorities:

- Use technology to make the business more efficient
- Use data to get insights

Examples of day-to-day activities that will help me carry out my tactical priorities include:

- Developing a tax plan
- Developing an estate plan assisted with technology
- Learning how to design my own covers
- Hiring a personal assistant for small tasks where it makes sense
- Developing a metadata database for my work
- Improving my readers' experience on my website
- Implementing direct sales for my fiction

You'll notice that "become the writer of the future" is not an explicit category. It's still a priority, but here's how I see it: if I become a world-class content creator and a technology and data-driven writer, I'll *become* the writer of the future.

As I move into 2022, I'll adjust the structure of *Indie Author Confidential*:

- World-Class Content Creator
- Technology and Data-Driven Writer
- Looking Forward

The "Looking Forward" section will function much like "Become the Writer of the Future," with me opining on miscellaneous items that don't fit into the other two categories but that I'm paying attention to.

Future volumes of *Indie Author Confidential* may be a little shorter, but that serves my goals.

I'm excited for 2022. You never know what a new year will bring, but I've put my author business in a great position and I'll be able to start the year strong.

CONTENT CREATED WHILE WRITING THIS BOOK

Books

The Writing App Handbook

M.L. Ronn covers the most important features of writing apps on the market, and what to look for when you are shopping for a writing app. It also comes with a free writing app database you can use to help you find the perfect match.

Buy at www.authorlevelup.com/handbook.

Access The Writing App Database at www.authorlevelup.com/writingapps.

The Self-Publishing Advice Compendium

(This book contains 250+ Self-Publishing Tips Volumes 1 and 2, but has been rebranded). In this self-publishing advice guide, M.L. Ronn covers 500+ writing, publishing, and marketing tips to help you perform at your very best.

Buy at www.authorlevelup.com/compendium.

The Indie Author Strategy Guide

Learn how to craft a winning strategy for your author business by developing a mission and vision statement, sound strategic priorities, and key tactics.

Buy at www.authorlevelup.com/strategy.

The Pocket Guide to Pantsing

Discover how to write a novel without an outline and feel amazing doing it. Building on the concepts that Dean Wesley Smith teaches in his groundbreaking book *Writing into the Dark*, M.L. goes deep, deep, deep into the rabbit hole to give you strategies and tactics on how to write a great novel without an outline every time.

Buy at www.authorlevelup.com/pantsing.

How to Dictate a Book

M.L. Ronn covers his process of dictation and breaks it down in this short and easy-to-understand volume. It also comes with a complimentary 90-minute video course to help you see dictation in action.

Buy at www.authorlevelup.com/dictationbook.

Podcast/Video Appearances

"Bringing a Creative Endeavor to an End" with Michael La Ronn. The Indy Author Podcast with Matty Dalrymple.

In this interview, Michael discusses how and why he decided to end his two podcasts, "The Writer's Journey" and "Writing Tip of the Day."

"Emerging Tech for the Indie Writer" with Michael La Ronn. The Indy Author Podcast with Matty Dalrymple.

In this interview, Michael discusses emerging technology he's watching for his writing business.

"Questions for Black Authortubers." Zarina Macha's YouTube channel.

In this montage interview, Michael talks about his experience being a black authortuber, and what it's like to write books and make YouTube videos as a black creative.

"How to Write Nonfiction." Self-Publishing Advice Conference October 2021.

In this interview, Michael turns the tables and interviews fellow nonfiction writer and friend Dale L. Roberts about how to write nonfiction and how to craft a compelling message. (This video is behind a free registration and I do not know how long it will be available).

MEET M.L. RONN

Science fiction and fantasy on the wild side!

M.L. Ronn (Michael La Ronn) is the author of many science fiction and fantasy novels including *The Good Necromancer*, *Android X*, and *The Last Dragon Lord* series.

In 2012, a life-threatening illness made him realize that storytelling was his #1 passion. He's devoted his life to writing ever since, making up whatever story makes him fall out of his chair laughing the hardest. Every day.

Learn more about Michael
www.authorlevelup.com (for writers)
www.michaellaronn.com (fiction)

www.ingramcontent.com/pod-product-compliance
Lightning Source LLC
Chambersburg PA
CBHW022041020426
42335CB00012B/492